HORSESHOES ★ AND
HAND GRENADES

Tales from the Other Mötley Crüe Frontman
and Journeys through a Life In and Out of Rock and Roll

HORSESHOES AND HAND GRENADES

JOHN CORABI

with PAUL MILES

RARE BIRD
LOS ANGELES, CALIF.

RARE BIRD
THIS IS A GENUINE RARE BIRD BOOK

Rare Bird Books
6044 North Figueroa Street
Los Angeles, California 90042
rarebirdbooks.com

FIRST TRADE PAPERBACK EDITION
SPRING 2026

For more information, address:
Rare Bird Books Subsidiary Rights Department
6044 North Figueroa Street
Los Angeles, California 90042

Artwork by Adam "The Kid" Wakitsch

Set in Dante
Printed in the United States

10 9 8 7 6 5 4 3 2 1

Library of Congress Cataloging-in-Publication Data

Names: Corabi, John, author. | Miles, Paul, 1969- author.
Title: Horseshoes and hand grenades / by John Corabi and Paul Miles.
Description: Los Angeles : Rare Bird Books, 2022.
Identifiers: LCCN 2021052563 | ISBN: 9781644282564 (hardcover)
ISBN: 9781644285480 (paperback)
Subjects: LCSH: Corabi, John. | Mötley Crüe (Musical group)
Rock musicians—United States—Biography.
Classification: LCC ML420.C65716 A3 2022 | DDC 782.42166092 [B]—dc23

LC record available at https://lccn.loc.gov/2021052563

DEDICATED TO:

The remembrance of my parents;
the endearment of my wife, kids, and grandkids;
the loyalty of my fans.

perseverance
/ˌpər-sə-ˈvir-ən(t)s/
noun

Continued effort to do or achieve something despite difficulties or delay in achieving success.

"Let me tell you something you already know: the world ain't all sunshine and rainbows. It's a very mean and nasty place, and I don't care how tough you are, it will beat you to your knees and keep you there permanently if you let it. You, me, or nobody is gonna hit as hard as life. But it ain't about how hard you hit, it's about how hard you can get hit, and keep moving forward. How much you can take and keep moving forward. That's how winning is done!"

Sylvester Stallone in *Rocky Balboa*, 2006

CONTENTS

Introduction

A Memo from Paul Miles

When I first came across the internet here in Australia way back in 1995, the first thing I did was search for information on my favorite band: Mötley Crüe. When I couldn't find much on them, I decided to create my own website dedicated to the band, with a focus on their crazy, checkered history. At that time, John Corabi was their singer and rhythm guitarist.

I launched my *Chronological Crue* history website on the day Vince Neil publicly returned to Mötley on the American Music Awards in January 1997. As I watched it on TV from my lounge in Australia, Corabi watched it on TV from his lounge, too, having declined an invitation to attend in person.

Since little about Corabi's life was known by rock fans at that point, I wanted to interview him to learn some more, which I first did in 1998, via an email exchange, while he was in Union.

We didn't meet in person until the Eric Singer Project toured Australia in 2006 and brought Corabi to Melbourne. It was great to finally hear THAT voice in person, and for a laugh, I gave him a souvenir gift of a genuine, fluffy kangaroo scrotum with balls.

The promoter asked me to drive the band to Melbourne's airport the following morning. As my hired van left St. Kilda, we soon passed the windows of a women's gym where some Aussie ladies were seen working out, and Corabi instantly informed us all that when he dies, his wish is to be reincarnated as a towel in that gym. It didn't take long to realize he was a fun guy to be on the road with.

It wasn't just in Australia that we would catch-up, though. We hung out after he supported Cinderella in New York City, and I photographed his solo performance in Hollywood at the Whisky a Go Go in 2014. Needless to say we spent the rest of that night farther down the Sunset Strip at the infamous Rainbow Bar and Grill.

Mötley Crüe's autobiography *The Dirt* exposed the band's sordid stories to many more people across the world, but while Corabi told a few tales of his time in Mötley in that bestseller, his life's story has largely remained a mystery. And I always felt he deserved more spotlight to be shone on him.

So, when a 2019 Australian Tour was announced, where Corabi would play the entire 1994 Mötley Crüe self-titled album from top to bottom, I organized with the promoter to join the tour party for all four shows in four cities in four days.

Critically, this allowed me to spend more time around Corabi, to further understand his day-to-day character, and to make the pitch that it was time for us to actually bring this autobiography to fruition. When the promoter dropped us back at the hotel after dinner on the night before the first show, the jet-lagged Corabi and I stood outside yakking on a Sydney street. His sweet, pancake-scented vape smoke wafted over me during the next hour, as we began to hash out a plan.

Following that tour, I got to know "Crab" more over the course of our countless hours on the phone together—usually me in Melbourne with a cup of tea on a Saturday morning, and him in Nashville with a cocktail in hand on a Friday evening—as he opened up and recounted all these entertaining stories you're about to read.

Through the experience, we have become firm friends: he calls me buddy and I call him mate, but that's just one of the American and Australian differences we joke about from our opposite sides of the world, 10,000 miles away.

Prologue
An Epiphany

Have you ever had one of those deeply profound moments that just changes your view on your life?

Mine was on Christmas Day, 1996. It was like how I imagine Isaac Newton felt when he realized that a falling apple and the orbiting moon are both pulled by the same force—except my scenario was more akin to a rockstar orbiting the world and falling from favor. Gravity can be a bitch.

I was sitting on a couch with my son, his head in my lap while watching a Disney movie. That's suddenly when this moment of great realization hit me. I had experienced all the highs of joining one of the world's biggest rock bands in the years prior and enjoyed all the fruits that went along with it. When you've climbed so high, though, the downward spiral can be brutal in all sorts of ways. You see, Mötley Crüe did a 180-degree turn and cut all ties with me; my fiancée had dumped me; my mom had lost her battle with cancer; I had spent the last of my money covering her medical bills; and I was stressing about where the next body blow was going to hit me from. Having experienced so much recent loss, I was naturally feeling like a loser.

With four simple words, though, my perspective totally shifted. It was four words I had heard before, so they weren't new to me…it was just the right fucking words at the right fucking time that brought about my epiphany.

As my nine-year-old son lay in my lap on my first wife's couch that Christmas Day, he thanked me for coming and hanging out, and simply said to me, "I love you, Dad."

It turned my world around. I had been in such a panic with anxiety raging in my head, but it instantly dawned on me to stop worrying about all that shit because I was actually doing what mattered the most.

It didn't matter that I was no longer jamming with the singers from AC/DC and Aerosmith. It didn't matter that I would no longer get an invite to party with Queen. It didn't matter that I would no longer find myself hanging with and playing on a stage with Robert Plant. It didn't matter that I'd no longer get to drive around in a US military tank, or the finest European sports cars, and get thank-you blowjobs after concerts.

In the coming pages, you'll read that all these things were certainly fun for me, but my epiphany focused me on the importance of taking care of my family and spending time with them. That's not an easy fucking feat though when playing rock-and-roll is your chosen career…or destiny.

Truth is Stranger Than Fiction

Friends, family, and former band members might remember aspects of these occurrences differently than me. This is my side of the stories of my life, as I now recall to you to the best of my ability. It is my honest perspective in all instances. I live by the truth, and just like the song you may or may not have heard, I'll die by the truth. 'Til death do us part.

PART I

THE BEGINNING: PHILADELPHIA, PENNSYLVANIA

1
Father, Mother, Son

I was born in Philadelphia, Pennsylvania, on Sunday, April 26, 1959. Yeah, that's right: the fifties. I'm categorized as a Baby Boomer, which essentially means once the explosion of bombs during World War II ended, people happily started fucking more, and there was soon a worldwide explosion of babies instead.

After a healthy pregnancy, my mom was in labor for more than seventeen hours before I was born late that Sabbath night of April 26 (at 11:06 p.m., to be precise). Delivered by Dr. Capucio, all eight-and-a-half pounds of me came into the world screaming (see what I did there?) in the Albert Einstein Medical Center Southern Division, a hospital in South Philadelphia's Italian district, where the fast-food Philly Cheesesteak was also born.

My Italian dad and Irish mom were married at the time. My twenty-two-year-old dad had married my eighteen-year-old mom during the last week of April 1957, and I was their first-born two years later, so anticipation was high, and it was a big event for the family, of course. As in Italian family tradition, my dad simply named me John Nicholas Corabi in tribute to his dad, and I was christened a few days later in the Roman Catholic Annunciation of Our Lord Church. I don't have any memories of my grandpop at all, because he died April 5, 1961, just weeks before my second birthday. My dad told me, though, that out of all his grandkids, I was the only one my grandpop came to see in the hospital.

My dad's parents were old school, hardworking first- and second-generation immigrants from the Calabria area of southern Italy. As I recall being told, my grandfather came to the United States with his cousin in the early 1900s. He served overseas in the US military during World War I and was honorably discharged in 1919 at Fort Dix, New Jersey. After the war, he came back to Philadelphia and became a masonry worker.

He soon met my grandmother and they began dating, and then realized they were from the same southern region of Italy. They were soon married (I was born on their anniversary), had children, and began their journey searching for the American Dream. It was difficult, but I guess their former life was pretty tough in their hometown of Catanzaro, on the sole of the Italian boot when you look at the country on a map.

They say Catanzaro is known for its three V's: 1) Saint Vitalian, the patron saint; 2) Vento, which means wind in Italian, due to the strong breezes blowing in from the Ionian Sea; and 3) Velvet, since it's been an important silk center since Byzantine times. And the Italian seafood dishes aren't bad either.

The original spelling of my grandparents' last name wasn't Corabi though. According to my dad, it was actually Corapi. When their ship came into America, it arrived in the port of Philadelphia instead of New York City's Ellis Island. My grandfather didn't understand English, so he copied what his cousin wrote on the immigration forms. They apparently made a mistake writing their surname and misspelled it with a B instead of the P. I'm kind of glad, though, as I'm sure by this time in my life, I would have lost count of the number of times people would have fucking called me Crappy instead of Crabby. I'd much rather have people thinking I'm miserable than thinking I'm a big pile of shit.

My parents lived in a second-floor apartment during my first year alive, which was right around the corner from my dad's parents'. They ended up having four kids: me in '59, my sister Anna in '61, my sister Janet in '63, and my brother Nicholas was born in '65.

While it was convenient living so close to my grandparents, apparently it was trying at times. My dad said my grandmom adored me and used to call me Giovanni, the Italian equivalent of John. But after having raised five kids of her own, my grandmother had plenty of parenting suggestions, which weren't always wanted or appreciated by my first-time mom. One day my mother put her foot down and told her mother-in-law to butt out, as she would be doing things her own way.

My dad told me that one night I was really suffering with colic as a little baby. I was crying and screaming intensely as my parents paced and tried to figure out what to do for me. An elderly Italian woman living in the apartment downstairs heard all the commotion, so she called her friend—my grandmother—to let her know what was going on and to see if there was anything she could do to help.

My grandmother soon knocked on our door holding a bottle of olive oil and a stick of fresh parsley. When my dad opened the door, she went directly to my mom and took me from her arms, without saying a word. She set me down on the kitchen table, quickly removed my diaper, and coated my little asshole with olive oil. She then took her stick of Italian parsley and gently shoved it up my ass.[1] After a few minutes of lying there skewered, with parsley protruding from my ass, I suddenly let out the loudest, longest, most beastly fart ever, and my crying stopped. I guess that was the strong wind blowing in—vento!

My grandmom then simply put my diaper back on, handed me over to my startled-but-relieved parents, then curtly said, "He had gas," and left.

I'm not sure what happened with the parsley from there, but the incident helped my mom to appreciate and embrace some of my grandmother's old-fashioned Italian parenting tips and remedies.

After living in their apartment for a year, my parents bought a two-story house in North Philadelphia in 1960 for $8,500 via a Veteran's home loan. I was raised through my childhood in that Philly row house at 4812 North Franklin Street. When we first moved there, it was kind of a middle class, predominantly Jewish neighborhood in a city of two million people. Several years later, as with many inner-city neighborhoods in the US, as soon as more minority people started moving in, all the white people started to panic and say, "Oh, we're out—there goes the neighborhood!" The whites started moving to new spacious housing in the suburbs.

These days, that neighborhood is barely recognizable. Beirut would be like a resort complex compared to where I grew up. The house has been demolished leaving just a vacant lot, but you can see with online mapping sites that the location is now a very dilapidated, run-down, ghetto neighborhood.

The house may be gone, but I still have vivid memories of that three-bedroom home. My brother and I slept in one room upstairs once he was old enough to sleep in his own bed, and my sisters slept in another. I remember it had gray carpet over hardwood floors and ornate doorways and stairs throughout. Our front door had a carved symbol of a *mezuzah*. I never knew what it was until I had a couple of Jewish friends come over to play. Every time they walked through the doorway, they'd kiss their

1 Don't try this at home, kids!

hand and try to touch the *mezuzah*. They eventually told me it was a Jewish blessing for the house.

The front of the house had a giant bay window bookended by two sets of those old sixties-styled slat-glass louver windows, which were also in the front door. I used to just sit on the enclosed patio with its two green wicker chairs and wicker rocking couch, pulling toys from a huge toy box and playing for countless hours daily.

I also had a hobbyhorse on springs, so I'd put on a little white cowboy hat, strap on my holster, slide my toy cap gun in, and adjust my mask like an outlaw. I never really wanted to be the Lone Ranger, though, because I always thought Tonto was much cooler and more badass. Unfortunately, they didn't sell his outfit, but I had hours of fun doing such typical kids' shit.

I remember Franklin Street being a friendly neighborhood. Like, if one of your neighbors ran out of sugar, they wouldn't hesitate to come over and borrow a cup full. Everybody helped everybody, and everybody knew everybody. Kids played stickball, hopscotch, and dodgeball in the streets.

Our family had four kids and our friends and neighbors, the Miller family, lived across the street. They had three kids and their daughter, Lori, was a bit of a tomboy, so she played baseball with all my friends and me. Their mom, Marilyn, would come over and pop in to check on us at times when my mom was going to be home late from work.

There was another girl, Margaret Lacy, who lived across the street and three doors down. If ever my mom and dad wanted to go out for an evening and see Frank Sinatra sing or a movie, she would be our babysitter. It seemed all very community-oriented, very *Wonder Years*-like.

We had a glass fishbowl on top of a radiator cover, in front of another giant bay window in our living room. One day when I was three or four years old, I decided to try and pet our goldfish. The problem was it would always swim away from my hand in the water. So I went and got a pencil.

I tried to not hurt the fish as I attempted to just pin it down with the pencil, so I could stroke it. Unfortunately, I left the goldfish with a gaping hole in its side. If the wound didn't kill it, it probably died from lead poisoning.

I panicked when it then floated to the surface, gaping-hole-side up. My dad came home from work and saw the fish. He said, "Johnny, what did you do to the fish?"

"Nothing," I said, "I didn't do anything." He kept grilling me.

My parents always told me that my tongue would turn black whenever I was lying. I kept denying any involvement, so my dad asked, "Are you lying?"

Again, I said, "No, I'm not lying. I didn't do anything to the fish."

That's when he said the dreaded words, "Okay, well, stick your tongue out then."

I had no option but to open my mouth and put my tongue out, the smallest amount I could get away with. Of course, I couldn't see the color of my own tongue, but my dad said, "Oh, it's as black as black can be! What did you do to that fish?"

I showed him how I tried to grab the goldfish and finally fessed up about the pencil. He said, "Why, what were you thinking? Why did you do that?"

Apparently, according to my parents, I stood there, put my hands on my hips, and looked into his eyes and matter-of-factly said, "Well, Dad, I have to tell you: I don't think any of us are perfect."

He said, "Go to your room," and the minute I got to the top of the steps and shut the door, he and my mom started pissing themselves laughing. He said to my mom, "You've got to be kidding. Did our little boy just say that to me right now?"

Little moments like this apparently caused my parents to think I was somewhat intellectually bright.

We had a black and white TV that had three channels on it: channel three, six, and ten. Then one day we upgraded and got a UHF TV that doubled our viewing capacity with channel seventeen, twenty-nine, and forty-eight. That was a big thing in my world back then.

I remember waiting for Saturday afternoons to come around so I could put the TV on one of those channels, sit down in front of it, and watch the boxing. I was into watching sports as a kid, and I was big into boxing—I loved all those old-school boxers like Sonny Liston and Joe Frazier. I remember being on the edge of the couch watching Muhammad Ali fighting Earnie Shavers.

I also watched old-school wrestling, too, with guys like Andre the Giant, Bruno Sammartino, and Professor Toru Tanaka. It was a crazy, entertaining boyhood thing to watch and get into. I loved that whole era.

The next logical step was to try such fighting sports for myself. When I had a buddy over one day, we decided we were going to box, but we only had one set of boxing gloves that I got as a gift for Christmas. Like a dumbass, I shared the fucking boxing gloves, and gave him the right-hand glove. I kept the left-hand glove; I'm right-handed—not a smart move on my part!

So, we were standing in my backyard, and we started boxing each other. It was so stupid: we were each holding one hand behind our back, the one that didn't have the glove on. We started punching the shit out of each other with the gloves, but he was just whooping my ass with his right glove, because he was right-handed, too. He was punching me in the face, and as much as I punched back with my left, there was just no power in it.

I started backing off, trying to avoid all his punches. I kept backing up the four wooden steps to our backdoor, and at the moment I reached the top step, he fucking connected. I flew off the top step and landed onto a section of wrought iron fence, which split my head open. My mom came running out, and we were off to the hospital at like ten o'clock in the morning. I got five stitches just under my eyebrow, right above my eye. So much for floating like a butterfly, 'cause the stiches stung like a bee.

When we got home from the hospital, my sisters were playing in the yard with friends. As I approached my younger sister, she had just found an old-school razorblade and picked it up. I quickly went to grab it off her, scared that she might cut herself. Right when I reached for it, she snapped the single blade in half down the middle and it sliced my fucking left thumb wide open. I went right back to the same hospital, to the same doctor, on the same day, and got five more stitches in my thumb.

I wasn't really accident-prone or a clumsy kid, though. I was just somehow often in the wrong place at the wrong time. I guess, in hindsight, I've always had a knack for being in the wrong place at the wrong fucking time.

I remember falling off a back doorstep another time when I was returning a dinner plate to my next-door neighbor. My mother asked me to return the plate, and I obliged, so I left our backyard, crossed the alley behind our house, and entered the neighbors' yard. As I climbed to the top step and knocked on the door, it opened out toward me, so I moved to my right to get out of the way. My dumb ass didn't realize there was no more step under my foot. I fell about five feet while still holding the plate and somehow managed to jam the fork deep into the side of my stomach on the landing. I can still hear my mother and the neighbor screaming in shock as I stood up with an eating utensil sticking straight out of me. As much as it fucking hurt, I pulled it out, and I had four holes in the side of my stomach. It was another trip to the hospital to get it cleaned out.

Another incident was when I got a job as a "hugster," selling fruit and vegetables door-to-door on a truck with an older guy from New Jersey; I was probably about eight or nine years old. I asked if I could work with him selling his produce, and he happily obliged me after speaking to my mother. He assured her I'd be fine, and he'd bring me home after each day's work. Off I went selling corn, tomatoes, and peaches from the back of a flatbed truck for about ten bucks a day. He would drive up and down streets in different neighborhoods, ringing his bell, and my job was to load wooden baskets with samples of all the products and go door-to-door asking the women if they needed any fresh produce.

One day, we got to a street and he stopped and started ringing. I started getting my basket filled and moved to the end of the truck to jump off, and just as I jumped off the truck, he hit the gas pedal, which launched me off the truck. I somehow managed to land on my feet, but the force of my landing caused me to hit the ground so hard that I slammed my face into my knees, which promptly split my lip wide open. I started bleeding all over myself, and I remember to this day the look on the guy's face when he saw my wound. I thought he was going to pass out.

Luckily, a woman that had come out of her house to buy some peaches saw what happened and came to my rescue. She cleaned out my wound and gave me a butterfly Band-Aid, and I went back to work for the day, which was, needless to say, my last as a hugster. When I returned home, Mom took me to the hospital again for seven more stitches in my lip. To this day, I still have a nice little scar on my top lip from that ordeal, buried deep beneath my facial hair.

After sharing these stories with you, I realize I may have been a bit clumsy, too.

As I got older, I wanted to participate in sports more but was smart enough now to steer clear of the fighting ones. I became quite athletic and found I was actually a bit coordinated. I was pretty fast as a kid—the complete antithesis of now—so I tried some track and field at school and the YMCA. I did a lot of swimming, and we were always running around playing tag and dodgeball and all those typical kid games.

I'd go to the park with friends and play baseball quite a bit. I was a big baseball fan and loved our home team, the Philadelphia Phillies. I enjoyed batting, but loved fielding in the outfield more where I could run, catch, and get the ball in quickly to base.

There was a public park near our place, just a few blocks west of our house called Hunting Park, and they had a public swimming pool. My mother would take us there sometimes during the summer. I remember there were "white days" and "Black days" for the pool: there would be times I'd ask, "Why can't I go swimming today?"

"Well, it's Black day," I'd be told. Us kids would swim on the white days, and we saw all these Black kids just staring at the fence, and vice versa, wanting to swim in the ninety-degree summer weather.

Everybody associates that kind of segregated racial behavior with America's south, but it was definitely prevalent in Philadelphia through the sixties as well. And to think they call Philly "The City of Brotherly Love."

One of my friends was a cool little Jewish kid named Michael Lippman who lived on Eighth Street, directly behind our house. Every chance I got, I would walk out my backdoor, through our back gate, across the little alley, and then go through his gate and in his back door. Our yards essentially backed onto one another.

We'd hang out all the time, often eating and watching TV at each other's houses, and he had an old bicycle. As much as I would pester my parents for one, they just couldn't afford to buy me a bike, so I used to love a ride on his. I would take it for a spin around the block: I would go up his street to Rockland, make a right, go one block to Franklin, turn right down Franklin, past my front door to Louden Street, make a right, and go to Eighth, turn right again, and come back to his house. Then I'd get off and pass the bike back to him and sit on the curb and wait for him to lap the block. We would take turns doing that for hours, and I think his dad was sitting outside watching us one day.

At Christmas, they bought Michael a brand-new Schwinn Stingray bike, and amazingly, his dad bought one for me, too! I couldn't believe it. They wheeled the bike over and gave it to my parents and said they wanted to give it to me.

So, Michael and I would just go out and fucking tear it up on our cool Stingray bikes, with high handlebars, long banana seats, and sissy bars on the back. We'd build ramps and jumps with bricks and pieces of plywood. We sometimes attached clothespins and baseball cards around the forks of the bike so they would rub against the spokes of the tires for a motorcycle sound as well. Life was good.

The Stingray gave me more freedom and the power to explore a bit more of my city. Back then it was nothing for me and a bunch of my friends to get on our bikes and go and play baseball somewhere, or ride for miles to go swimming in Tacony Creek and throw rocks at each other from the creek's edge, or shoot BB guns at each other—lots of stupid pranks and dumb shit like that. I was definitely into baseball, football, pranks, and riding bikes.

One day when I was maybe ten or eleven years old, we rode our bikes to the creek and one of my other buddies pulled out a little yellow envelope that had fucking weed in it. He had "borrowed" a pinch from his older brother. I had never smoked marijuana before. For that matter, I don't think I'd smoked anything at that point, but he also had a little one-hit pipe and we put some weed in there, and we passed it around for shits and giggles.

We were fucking blown out, man. I was fucking wasted. I sat there completely paranoid and said repeatedly, "Oh my God, did I say that eight times? I just said that eight times. Did I say that, wait, oh fuck his eyes are red, are my eyes red? Yeah. Oh fuck!"

I was just freaking out with my buddies the whole time. I was young, and it was crazy that first time I "smoked the sky!"

My dad Nicholas was a classic, old-school Italian American. He was just this nuts-and-bolts Roman Catholic guy who stood maybe 5' 9" or 5' 10". And like me, in his youth he was skinny and could eat whatever, whenever, and as much as he wanted. As he got older, though, he was a bit heavier and a little paunchier than me, although we have a similar build. Now that I'm in my non-athletic stage of life, I recently told my wife that I should go on a fucking diet because I look exactly like my dad…except for the hair.

Younger, he totally looked like he could have been an extra in *Goodfellas* or *The Godfather*, or any of those Italian-American mob crime films—he and all my uncles, actually. When he wasn't wearing a suit and tie for work, he was in a leather jacket, a T-shirt, Vitalis-soaked pompadour, and his always-present gold crucifix necklace, as he smoked his Chesterfield non-filter cigarettes.

His view on life was basically that you go to school, you study, you get out of school, you get a job, you work hard, you pay your taxes, you save money. That was his thing. He taught me honesty, but typical of males, and even more so back in those times, he was not a hugger; he was not a big affection guy. He was usually mellow, but a sleeping badass.

As quiet as he was, he would get to a point where he would just fucking explode with a crazy temper. There were times when I'd be thinking, "Who the fuck are you, and what did you do with my dad?"

He rarely cursed, and I never heard him drop the f-bomb. He never said it in front of us ever! I'm definitely different than him in that fucking department.

My dad honorably served in the United States Army from May 1954 through May 1957. We found out after he died when we came across some items at his place, like a marksman / sniper certificate and a marksmanship badge from when he was at a base in Georgia State.

My dad never talked about the military at all, so I'm not sure if he went to war zones and was a sniper. I know he was stationed in Germany for a while because I remember him telling me that while he was in that country, he took a trip to Italy to visit some cousins. Aside from that, he never said a word about his time or service in the military. I've actually tried talking with other people that were snipers in the army, but it seems none of them ever really want to talk about it.

My dad played with my friends and me occasionally, as he was never really around much when I was a kid, because he was always working. At one point, he worked three jobs at once. There was a large men's clothing retailer in Philadelphia called Bond's Stores, best known for selling two-pant suits, and he was the accountant and bookkeeper in their store. He was also the night manager at a couple of Wawa convenience stores, which are a chain like 7-Eleven all over the Philadelphia, New Jersey, Delaware area. Plus, he had a medical debt collection agency. When people went to the hospital and didn't pay their bills, he called and harassed them to get the money.

I loved throwing a football as a kid; it was a little bit of a passion for me. But I never threw one around with my dad much, due to his schedule. However, there was a flipside when I was a kid: football players didn't earn the money they do today. Back then, even if they did get a contract with the Philadelphia Eagles, most of the players also had full-time jobs to make ends meet. So, as a perk to signing, our NFL team had a deal with Bond Stores. When players needed a new suit that was mandatory attire for road trips and other events, they always came into my dad's work to purchase their dress attire.

Famous Eagles football players like Chuck Bednarik, Tom Brookshier, Norm Snead, and Pete Retzlaff came into Bond's and got fitted out for say, a new navy-blue suit with a vest, shirts, and ties. My dad kept records of their purchases, and sometimes players came back in to make layaway payments and pick up their new threads. I got to meet quite a lot of these guys when I was a kid, which was fun.

I've always followed the Philadelphia Eagles, because of these experiences with Dad, and it's so unfortunate to me that he never got to see them win their only Super Bowl early in 2018. Later in the book, I'll tell you about my family's tragic circumstances leading into this game that made it such a bittersweet time for me.

When my mom Janette (maiden name Hayes) was eighteen, she met my dad and very quickly married him. She was slightly taller than him and did some modeling when she was young. She had piercing blue eyes, but in some ways she was also a bit rough around the edges. Even though she was the kind of pretty woman who looked great on your arm walking into a party, if you looked at her the wrong way, she'd knock your teeth out. She was a feisty Irish woman who did not take any shit from anybody, including my dad.

She worked as a telephone operator for the Bell Telephone Company. For all you young smartphone junkies, this was before exchanges were automated; operators connected telephone calls on manual switchboards. Someone would call and say, "Hey, Operator, give me a line," and she would insert a pair of phone plugs into the appropriate jacks to connect the telephone call. It was the sixties, mind you.

Once she married my dad, though, she started popping out kids every couple of years, so she stayed home and was a mom and housewife instead.

I say my mom was Irish, but actually, she and her mother were born in and around Philadelphia. My grandfather was born in Cincinnati, Ohio. It was two generations back that was from Ireland, but there was still strong Irish blood running through her. Maybe that's why I've loved a pint or five of Guinness and the very occasional Jameson at times over the years. Mom used to joke when I got older that, "God invented whiskey to keep the Irish from ruling the world."

My mom was the third-eldest child in the Hayes family; she was in the middle of the pack. Jack was the eldest child, and then Mary Anne was her older sister. Her younger sisters were Peggy, Kathleen, and Betty.

There were still relatives living back overseas, though. I remember coming home from school one day and walking into our backyard from the alley behind our Franklin Street house. There was a young blonde lady sitting in my yard. At that point, I was about ten and getting quite mouthy, so I said, "Who the fuck are you and why are you in my fucking yard?"

Then this strange accent came out of her mouth when she responded with, "Hello, lad, you must be Johnny. I'm your cousin, Patricia!"

Basically, she was a cousin from Ireland via England. My family is very extended: I've got cousins in Ireland, I've got cousins in England, but I've also got cousins in Argentina, as well as Italy, of course. All over the world, it seems.

When I wasn't hanging out with my buddies and playing, I went to school. From kindergarten through seventh grade, I went to a place called Incarnation of Our Lord School, which was only a mile or so away from our house, at Fifth and Lindley Avenue.

It was a Catholic school, so some of the teachers there were nuns, but there were also lay teachers. I had the biggest crush on my second-grade teacher, Miss Kirby. God, she was hot! I would intentionally do shit wrong so she made me sit in front of the class, right in front of her for the rest of the day. She wore short skirts most days, and sat behind a desk with no front to it, so do the math. My little hormones were beginning to blossom. (Little did I know that decades later I would record a version of one of my favorite Van Halen songs "Hot for Teacher.")

As I started getting older, though, I found myself doing shit wrong for other reasons. On the one hand, it was awesome going to a Catholic school because I can certainly say I got a good education, but on the other hand it was fucking conformity at its finest. I fucking hated it, and I was constantly fighting it. I remember my mom having to come to the school whenever I got in trouble.

A big part of the conformity was I had to wear a uniform of gray or blue pants, a white shirt, a blue tie, and a blue jacket. And I had to have a certain school bag, and I had to have a pencil case, and I had to have my ruler, my protractor, and my eraser; the fucking list went on.

"I don't want to fucking wear this monkey suit," I would say. "I want a fucking Nehru jacket like Paul McCartney wears on the fucking *Sgt. Pepper's* record. Fuck off, I don't fucking want to wear this tie."

I was starting to get such thoughts in my head about the way I dressed, much to the dismay of my dad and school, and to a degree, I think my discovery of The Beatles was totally behind that.

You see, there was a girl named Arlene who lived behind us and who was around the same age as me, perhaps a little bit older. Her bedroom was up on the second story of their home, and I could see her window from my yard. I always had a bit of a crush on her.

Arlene had a transistor radio that sat on her windowsill. One day when I was around eight or nine, I heard a song coming from it, and I saw her sitting in the open window. I yelled up to Arlene, "What is that?"

She said, "It's The Beatles, dummy."

I asked, "Really?" and she told me it was the song "Help." It sounded awesome to me.

My mom liked The Beatles to some degree as well, but she liked the mellower stuff like "And I Love Her" and "Michelle." However, I didn't realize that the song "Help" I heard from Arlene was the same band that did "Michelle." I hadn't put two and two together yet. That didn't come until I saw them on TV, probably a year later.

I remember seeing a show on our black-and-white TV one day that was a repeat or replay special compilation of The Beatles performing at different times on *The Ed Sullivan Show*. It was Ed Sullivan introducing them for their first time in America saying, "Ladies and gentlemen, The Beatles" and they played "All My Loving" and then "She Loves You." It continued with "I Saw Her Standing There" and finished with the last song they played, "I Want to Hold Your Hand."

Then after these *Ed Sullivan Show* video clips, they played another one where they started getting a little psychedelic; they played "Ticket to Ride." I said to Mom, "Oh, wait, is that the same band? Look at them there!"

Still to this day, I vividly remember how freaked out I was when I heard it. They then played another video, and it was Paul McCartney at a piano with all the other guys sitting around, plus an audience, and they did "Hey Jude." It was like the beginning, the middle, and the end of The Beatles that I saw in one hit, and it all clicked. I was like, "Wow, this is fucking awesome! Holy shit!"

Then, on occasional Sundays after church, we would pack into a bus—my parents, siblings, and yours truly—and head down to my cousin Andrew's house (my aunt Theresa and Uncle George's son on my dad's side.) They had a record player downstairs, and Andrew had the 7" single for the song "Hello, Goodbye."

I swear to God, we'd get to their house for dinner and Andrew and I would go downstairs into the basement to listen to music. And if we played that song once, we played it a thousand fucking times to the point where I memorized the vocal pattern at the end of the song.

I didn't know if it was Paul, George, Ringo, or John singing at the time, but the vocal pattern at the end of that song caught my ear, where the song repeats "*hella, hello*." (Feel free to YouTube it now and listen along.) I still chuckle to myself whenever I hear it, as it takes me right back to sitting down there with Andrew. That's the power of music. Fucking brilliant.

I have to say I've always been very inquisitive about things, and I struggle at times with things that make absolutely no sense to me, even to this day. I also remember getting in trouble at my Catholic school for asking a very simple, sensible question…or so I thought.

If you're familiar with the Catholic religion, we're taught at the start of *The Bible* that God made the world in six days, then rested on the seventh—the Sabbath. He created Adam, who became lonely, so God took one of his fucking ribs out and created Eve. Then he told them, "Don't eat the fruit in the Garden of Eden. This is forbidden," before a fucking talking serpent somehow seduced them into eating the fruit and they got knowledge.

That's your beginning of human life in the Book of Genesis. Adam was the first man (molded out of clay by God, mind you) and Eve was the first woman. They started procreating and had two boys, Cain and Abel. After Cain murdered Abel, *The Bible* says Adam and Eve had sex with demons until they reunited after 130 years and had another son, Seth. They're the only children the first couple had, three boys.

So, my question to a school nun was, "Where did we really come from? If we came from Adam and Eve and they only had sons, where did we come from?" Now mind you, I didn't KNOW about sex at this point, but I KNEW it took a man and a woman to have babies.

They also tell you in The Ten Commandments that murder, adultery, and all these other things are outlawed. Incest wasn't specified as one, but I think that comes under the category of adultery in this scenario anyway.

If Adam and Eve are the father and mother of all, and they had three boys, the bloodline stops, unless one of them starts fucking their mom. I still think that's a legitimate question. I didn't get an answer, but I sure got suspended for it. That just made me question things even more.

Once I saw The Beatles on TV, it wasn't long before Mom and Dad bought me my very first guitar—a twenty-five dollar Sears and Roebuck Silvertone acoustic guitar, which was a Christmas gift. I have no idea what possessed my parents to get it though, as I don't even really remember saying to them that I wanted a guitar, but I'm glad they did.

I started playing it, and I fucking hated it. I didn't know any chords or anything, so I tortured my parents with it because I would go into my room and stand in front of my full-length closet door mirror and just strum the fuck out of it. I realized that if I touched the strings with my other hand, it would mute the sound, so I'd just move my fingers around above the strings like I was playing, but without really touching them.

I would stand there doing that and at the top of my lungs, I would "sing" "Hound Dog," "Johnny B. Goode," "She Loves You," "Hey Jude," whatever. My dad would jokingly say to my mom, "Oh my God, I'm going to kill him, take you to the bedroom, fuck you, and make another kid so we can start all over again. This is brutal!" The language here may have been colored a bit, but you get the point.

They finally decided to have me take guitar lessons at my Catholic school, where I was first taught how to play the guitar by a nun named "Sister Charles Fucking Bronson"—just a mean, terrorizing, old bitch! The best part was, she didn't even play guitar. She played piano, but she was teaching me to play the fucking guitar!

I had to buy a Mel Bay instructional guitar book and bring it to my lessons. We sat there together, and she looked at the photos in the book and had me copy them. She'd say, "Sit up straighter," and she'd smack me with a pointer or a ruler on the back. "Hold your arm like this. Hold the pick like that. You're not holding the pick right. It's not like the photo."

And I'd be like, "Okay, Goddammit."

"No, like this!" she'd insist.

So, I was like, "Fuck it, and oh by the way, you're teaching me 'Kumbaya My Lord'? I don't want to learn that, Motherfucker! I want to learn how to play 'Hey Jude.' I want to learn how to play fucking 'Hello, Goodbye'! Oh, and by the way, if you hit me one more time with that pointer, I'm going to shove it up your penguin-looking ass!"

I just said fuck this and lost interest. I started going out and playing ball, riding my bike more, and my guitar sat in the corner collecting dust for a while...until my friend, Lori Miller, the girl across the street that I'd hung out with, got a guitar and all of a sudden her mom was telling mine, "Oh God, you should see how good Lori's getting on the guitar."

After my mom popped over there, she came back saying, "Oh my God, Lori is so good on the guitar."

"What do you mean, she's got a guitar?"

"Yeah, and she's taking lessons and oh my gosh, she's so good."

I couldn't help but run across the street to Lori's and ask to see her guitar. We sat down, and Lori started playing shit like "Blowing in the

Wind" by Bob Dylan and "Scarborough Fair" by Simon and Garfunkel. I just sat there, thinking, "You bitch!" I was pissed. How the fuck did she get that good that quick?

Well, her mom told my mom, "We're getting her lessons at a music store about a mile away from our houses. It's called Zapf's Music, and her instructor's name is Jim Newett."

It was expensive, probably five bucks a week or something. It was a struggle for my mom to come up with that kind of money, but to her credit, my mom was like, "All right, if you want to go there and take lessons, you need to promise me to practice." I swore on a stack of Bibles I would commit, and *boom*, she put me in there!

My mom took me to Zapf's, and I walked in the first day and took up position in the chair, the same stiff upright way that I learned from the nun. First thing Mr. Newett did before I tried to play anything was to ask if I was comfortable.

When I told him not really, he said, "All right, hold on then, scrap everything, stand up. If you were sitting at home by yourself playing the guitar, how would you sit and hold it?" I just grabbed the guitar, sat down and kind of hunched over a little bit. He then told me to hold the pick however it felt comfortable.

Now, to this day, I've got a little bit of an odd technique with my picking. If you look at how some people hold a guitar pick, they flat pick up and down on the strings. I don't use the flat face of the pick; I use the edges of it. I actually turn the pick almost sideways. I've always done it that way, from that moment.

So, once he made sure I was comfortable enough with my pick, he started showing me the basics—quarter notes, half notes, whole notes, and chords, like a D chord and A chord, a G chord. Next, he said, "Who's your favorite band?"

When I instantly said it was The Beatles, he asked if I knew the song "Hey Jude."

"I love 'Hey Jude'!" I said.

He took the chords and transposed it, so it was in an easy key for me to learn.

To help me remember songs, he would then write say a D, and underneath it he'd mark line, line, line, line, and then a new measure. If it was still D, it was line, line, line, line again, then move to say D7, line, line, G...whatever. Each line was a symbol, i.e., one down, one up, one down, one up for strumming.

He just basically broke it down to its simplest form to teach me, and we just took it from the bare bones. I swear to God, in about three months, I was playing "Hey Jude" and all these other great songs. I would be at parties, sitting in my aunt's house with all my cousins, aunts, and uncles around me, and my mom would be yelling out, "Play us a song, Johnny!" My family was the first audience I performed in front of.

Mr. Newett inspired me, and it was honestly out of sheer jealousy and fuck you-ism that I learned. I was like, "No fucking way that Lori Miller got a guitar after me and is better than me? Fuck that!" I was off to the races at that point, so I guess Lori inspired me, too.

Eventually, both our families ended up moving out of Franklin Street and I lost touch with the Millers. I wish I could reconnect with Lori and just say hi, and thanks.

I was about ten years old when we heard there was going to be some sort of world premiere of a new Beatles song on TV. It was at the end of their career, they were breaking up, and it was said, "This is it: this is the last video you're ever going to see from this band."

Mom and I were on the couch together, and they started playing "Let It Be." I remember watching the video and being filled with overwhelming sadness.

When George went into his guitar solo, he never looked up; he was just staring down at his guitar. It was a very somber moment, and I remember looking at my mom, and she was teary-eyed. She just kept saying, "Look up, George, look up!" It was like she just wanted him to look up to the camera, to see his face one last time. And then the song ended and that was it. We were both thinking that was it, we're never going to hear that band again. They're done; it's over! We were both moved to tears. We were both just so sad that The Beatles were breaking up. I could feel the heaviness of the sadness, and I was like, "What, why, how is this happening?"

Isn't it amazing how you can hear a song and something happens in your brain that takes you right back to that very moment you heard it? It's weird, but beautiful. You remember her face when you hear that tune. Maybe you were going through a divorce, or maybe somebody passed away, or you were getting laid in the back of a car, whatever it was. But it gets so intense that you can practically smell that person's cologne, or you can smell the sex in the back of that car. It's just so fucking intense; music is so powerful!

I've been on stage in recent years with The Dead Daisies singing "Let It Be" in front of thousands of people. It's such a beautiful song, the story behind it, the whole thing, and every time we played it, I would be taken right back to that somber moment on the couch, crying with my mother. To me, that was not only the end of The Beatles, it was like the end of innocence.

America was in a really dark place with the Kennedy assassination toward the end of 1963. I was only four, but I totally remember sitting in my living room watching TV coverage of it with Walter Cronkite. I remember seeing my mom crying, my neighbors crying, and the newspaper headlines. I vividly remember days later, them escorting Lee Harvey Oswald out, and he was shot and murdered by Jack Ruby while being transported from the jail in Dallas, and I saw the whole fucking thing on live TV and was mesmerized by it.

The Beatles came along just at the right moment when America needed something fun-loving, something light, and my generation all kind of grew up with them. They were these happy-go-lucky kids from Liverpool playing this cool little bubblegum pop music. And then they started growing up, and experimenting with drugs, music, and fashion, and we took that journey with them from *Rubber Soul* to *Revolver*, from *Sgt. Pepper's*, *Magical Mystery Tour*, and *The Beatles* white album, to *Let It Be* and *Abbey Road*. We just grew with them and then they got to a point where they couldn't do it anymore. It was over; it was the end of their happiness, glory, and innocence. And right around that time, it was the end of mine as well.

2
Broken Hearts, Broken Dreams

My mom and dad were not getting along. As much as my dad was a mellow badass, he had that hot temper, which we were seeing way too often. That feisty Irish blood in my mom made her equally hot-tempered, so it was just volatile. There was violent arguing every evening and us kids would just freak out. My brother and sisters would look to me for what to do when all hell broke loose, since I was the oldest. But at that age, I didn't have a fucking clue what was going on.

My parents both accused each other of cheating, and it all blew up. Oddly enough, it was Father's Day when I was ten years old when my dad moved out. Life changed for all of us, and their ugly divorce soon followed. They say life's not always fair, so we just had to build resilience and learn how to persevere. But, at ages ten, eight, six, and four, it's easier said than done. Listening to our parents constantly complain to us about each other, or tell us shitty things to sway our view of the other parent was tiring to say the least, and, in hindsight, really fucked.

Mom could no longer afford to be a stay-at-home mom, so she got a night job working at a place called Fleer's. Fleer Chewing Gum Company was the first in the world to manufacture bubblegum, and they were best known for their brand of pink-colored bubblegum called Dubble Bubble. Mom worked in their warehouse, packaging thousands of boxes of gum up.

After about a year at Fleer, she got a better paying daytime job instead, from like six in the morning till four, at a place called Progress Lighting, which specialized in residential lights. After World War II, they grew to become the world's largest manufacturer of home lighting fixtures, churning out over thirty thousand items a day in the mid-fifties. My mom worked in their Kensington factory on Erie Avenue for almost thirty years, basically until she died.

Like my dad, she also had that strong work ethic. To give you an example, it would get fucking cold and it would snow. Back then, there sure were long, cold winters in Philadelphia. My mom drove to and from work in a used Ford Falcon she purchased, but if ever she couldn't drive the car there because it wasn't running, which was quite often, or if there was too much snow, she still went to work. There were a couple of times I recall where she actually got up and trudged on foot through the snow over that four-mile walk to be there on time. Brutal. She never missed any time (except when she had to meet with my fucking school principal.) She seriously had to be having brain surgery if she were to have a day off from work.

I was probably in fifth grade when my parents divorced, so school became more trying for me. While the Catholic school was providing a good education, on top of the uniform and conformity struggles I was having, I was starting to see things differently and question them more; I thought the priests, nuns, and rules were being very hypocritical about shit. It was like I was being taught that God wants you to love your neighbor, embrace your neighbor, forgive your neighbor, but only if they follow these rules, or else they'll burn in Hell…blah, blah, blah.

It sure was tough for my mom, too. It was toward the end of the sixties and my Roman Catholic parents were divorced—my dad was out, my mom had to get a job. She was struggling to keep it together financially with four fucking kids. I think my dad's alimony or child support payments were like twenty bucks a week per kid—next to nothing!

To go to that school, you had to pay an annual tuition fee of say two hundred dollars for the first kid, and then it dropped down slightly per kid after that; you got the "bulk discount." The church that the school was connected to also sent home a box that had fifty-two envelopes in it. On the envelopes, it said, "Donations," and then in parentheses it said, "Twenty percent of your annual income."

Every Sunday Mass at 9:00 a.m., you would have to write your name and address on the front of the envelope and put the money inside before dropping your envelope in a collection basket. So back then, if my mom was making 150 or 200 bucks a week, she was expected to put like ten more (give or take a few) bucks in their little envelopes each time. They collected the envelopes and applied it to their records. It wasn't long before they were thinking this Corabi family wasn't putting their envelopes in the baskets.

Now on top of the tuition and the church envelopes, every Wednesday in school they also had another envelope where you had to put $1.25 per kid. So that's four kids and another five bucks per week.

Mom was struggling, and she couldn't fucking pay. We were already somewhat shunned because my parents did the dastardly, unholy act and got a divorce—a big a no-no in the Catholic religion in the sixties—and now she's wasn't paying her share. I remember us getting suspended because my mom fell behind on payments and couldn't afford to pay it all. They literally pulled me and all my siblings out of class and sent us home! It was like, you're not welcome here until you fucking pay your tuition. At that point with everything going on, I started lashing out saying, "Fuck you, fuck off, and fuck you, too!"

Mom went into school, and she sat across from the principal and pastor, and she said, "Listen, I've got four kids, and I know you guys don't want to hear this, but look, I'll give you what I can, but I can't pay you all this." My mom worked out some sort of a deal with them, for them to let us back into the school, but it was like dealing with loan sharks, and I know some of those people that are more forgiving!

I'd no sooner gone back to school when a nun started telling me, "Hey, your hair is touching your collar. You need to get a haircut." I was like, "Okay, whatever." I just brushed her off. She warned me a couple times, and as I left on a Friday, the nun said, "When you come back in here Monday, I want to see that hair cut or you're going to the principal's office."

I said okay, just so I could start my weekend. I never relayed the message to my mom, and I didn't get a haircut. Fuck that. The Beatles had long hair, right?

When I got into my homeroom class on Monday, the nun came up and made me turn around. She looked at my collar, and said, "I told you to get a haircut!" There wasn't much I could say, since I clearly hadn't.

She then handed me a piece of bubblegum, told me to go back to my seat and chew it. I was perplexed at this point, thinking I didn't get my haircut and you just gave me a piece of gum? I unwrapped the Dubble Bubble gum, wondering if my mom had packaged this one while working there, and started to enjoy the familiar flavor as I chewed it.

After about ten minutes, the nun walked up to my seat in the class, put her hand in front of my mouth, and said, "Spit out the gum!" Once it was in her hand, she took her other hand and grabbed my ear, almost ripping it off the side of my fucking head—it literally bled in the crease where my ear connects to my head. She then took her hand with the bubblegum in it and slapped it palm down on the top of my head and just rubbed the pink gum into my hair!

For the whole day, I had this bad Rod Stewart, Tweety bird thing going on with a big, sticky wad of gum in my hair. I tried to get it out during lunch break but couldn't. I tried again once I got home after school but couldn't. My mom walked in from work and said, "What the hell happened to your hair?"

I told her the story, and she went ballistic! She walked into school early with me the next day and knocked on the classroom door. I can't remember the name of the nun, but she answered the door, and Mom asked, "Are you Sister Clint Eastwood?"

She had no sooner said, "Yes, I am, Mrs. Corabi," and my mom punched her right in the face!

We then went to the principal's office, and they suspended me for two weeks. However, my mom told the principal, "I don't give a shit; I'll keep him home. You send his homework home with one of the kids from his homeroom class that lives across the street from us. But, you know what? This was completely unnecessary. You can do whatever you want; suspend him. I'm just telling you this right now: if you, or anybody else, embarrasses my son, does what that nun did to him again, or lays a finger on him again, I'm going to come back here, and I'm going to kick all of your asses!"

I didn't care that I got suspended. At that point, I was certainly getting out of control. My dad wasn't around. My mom was getting up and going to work at six o'clock in the morning, so me and my brother and sisters were left to our own devices all day long, much to the usual dismay of our mother.

I was beginning to goof off and cut class a lot. I'd wake up and be like fuck it, I'm not going to school today. It would take weeks for my mom to figure that one out, and then even when she did figure it out, what could she do? It's not like she would take more time off work to go to school and meet with my principal again and again. She couldn't afford to not go to work.

I was beginning to hate the Catholic religion and all that it stood for; I thought it was all a crock of shit. Their story/pitch was basically God takes care of those who believe. God takes care of those in need. That God gave us his only son Jesus, who gave his life for us. Jesus fed all these followers with three loaves of bread and all this fish, and never JUDGED anyone for their sins; yet you're going to fucking send us home because we can't afford to pay you? Fuck you! You're going to send me home because I have hair touching my collar? Fuck you! Jesus clearly has long hair in the photo, people! What the fuck?

It all turned me into this pissy, spiteful kid with a mouthy, fuck-off attitude. I was just angry with everybody, including my dad who split from us that Father's Day. After my parents got divorced, my dad took us four kids to the Philadelphia Zoo one Sunday as he had visitation on the weekends, and this lady Carol came with us. Since Dad was pretty cautious about bringing people into our lives, I knew he must have been somewhat serious about her. That got confirmed when they started dating, and he married her soon after that.

On one corner of my street, there was a drycleaner, and directly across from that, on my side of Franklin Street, about five doors down from my house, there was a little candy store called Harry's. He sold newspapers, candy, cigarettes, and he had a pinball machine in there. He also had an old school ice cream soda fountain counter.

Harry was a little, older Jewish guy, and a great neighborhood character, but every now and then the cops would come and arrest him. Apparently, on the side, he was a bookie, taking bets on horseraces or whatever. But I didn't care; I liked Harry.

I was around ten years old in 1969 and really starting to get into music more, not just The Beatles. I started noticing there was always a crowd of older kids, probably between sixteen to nineteen years old, who would hang out on Harry's corner. There were the older Getner brothers and sisters, a guy named Crazy Jake, another named Bulgarian Louie, and a few others.

These teenagers had all grown their hair and were wearing fringe vests and low hip-hugger, bell-bottom jeans. The girls wore embroidered halter-tops with flowers in their hair, feathers, and most of them never wore shoes. They just hung out there, smoked their pot right out in public, and always seemed to be having a carefree time. I don't know why, but I was drawn to them, like oh my God, they're so fucking cool. They're just cool.

My dad thought they were a bunch of hippies and drug addicts, and would freak out about me hanging and talking to them.

Aside from my previous teacher, Miss Kirby, the first crush I can remember having was one of these hippie girls named Mindy. She was Crazy Jake's girlfriend and a few years older than me but I was beyond infatuated. She had long straight hair, a petite body, and the sweetest face. I had the biggest crush on Mindy and if she even remotely said hi to me, I would lose my breath and turn into a blathering idiot. We never did anything like kiss or even hold hands, as much as I wanted to. I was too petrified and quite a bit younger.

There was one older guy who they used to call Birdman. He was this tall, lanky cat with really long, dark brown, almost-black hair, and a bit of a moustache and beard, and always wore hip-hugger jeans with a tan suede vest and no shirt. I don't know how old he was, or if he had a car or lived nearby, but he must have, because he would go get his hollow-body F-hole acoustic guitar from somewhere upon request, and he would sit down on the corner step and play shit like Bob Dylan, The Beatles, and whatever was on the radio. All the girls would gather around him and request songs and sing along with him. Back then it was a lot of Vietnam protest shit, too, like Creedence Clearwater Revival. I would often sit down on the corner curb and just watch him and listen, thinking all the girls love this guy. He was cooler than shit, a rock star, the coolest guy ever!

One day I went down to Harry's and put a quarter—probably stolen from my mom's purse—in a pinball machine. You got five games for a quarter back then, so I was standing there in front of this pinball machine, playing it, when Birdman walked in the front door just to my left. He said to me, "Wassup, little man?" as he walked in, to which I responded with, "Hey, Bird!" Birdman walked around behind me and along the L-shaped soda fountain and sat in the last seat in the corner, somewhat tucked away behind a Tastykake's display where you couldn't really see him or what he was doing.

At one point while I was playing the pinball, I turned around to say something to him, when my glance saw him holding onto a long rubber band. He was tying off to shoot up. I didn't say anything and just turned back around. I didn't know exactly what was happening but I felt uncomfortable and knew it didn't look good.

A couple of minutes later, I heard a thud. I turned around and saw Bird on the floor, foaming at the mouth. Harry was marching toward me yelling and screaming. He started kicking me out, saying, "Get out, get out, get out! You need to get out of here!"

I stood outside the candy store thinking, "What the fuck is going on here? What happened to Birdman?" Harry called the cops and an ambulance came, too. After about thirty minutes, they wheeled out this big black bag on a stretcher, zipped-up. It then dawned on me that, fuck, Birdman died.

I didn't realize it until later but witnessing that incident as a young boy had a very strong impact on me. Over the years, there have been a lot of people who have looked at me and said, "Okay dude, so you're shitting me, right? You were in Mötley Crüe, and you NEVER did heroin? Cocaine? You never did meth? You never…"

I always reply, "Fuck, no. No, I never did that." Sure, I've smoked weed and popped a few pills, but I've never snorted or injected shit into my body. Birdman overdosing stuck with me forever. To watch somebody drop dead right in front of you when you're ten or so, it was not good.

I began smoking with the kids at Harry's. By eleven or twelve, I was smoking Marlboro Red cigarettes regularly, which also meant I was stealing regularly and doing whatever I had to do to get money for cigarettes. It wasn't unusual to go into my mom's refrigerator and steal a beer out of the fucking case when she was out. I'd steal an occasional beer or raid the whiskey decanters my mom had, and at that age, I'd fucking drink a beer and be so blown out, like, fuck, I'm so drunk! At eleven or twelve, it doesn't take that much.

My mom started dating a Puerto Rican guy from work named Tony Gonzalez. I fucking hated him from the get-go. They started hanging out a little bit, and then a little more often. Then soon enough, I felt like this guy was living at our house because he was there all the time. I was resentful, angry, and feeling like, who the fuck are you? This piece of shit also had a bit of a Napoleon complex since he was short, way shorter than my mom.

We were having dinner at the table one night and my brother Nicky did something that this guy didn't approve of. He yelled at my brother, who started crying, and this guy just lightly slapped my brother on the back of the head. I knew that was a bad move on his part, right away. I looked at Tony, and he told my brother to get away from the table, but he cursed; he said, "Get the fuck away from the table!" I looked at him again like wait, did you just say fuck in front of my brother and sisters? I was furious!

My brother ran upstairs into the bathroom next to our bedroom. I then left the table in a huff and followed him up the stairs and went into the bathroom. I sat on the tub, calming my little brother so he would stop crying. I told him, "Don't worry about it, Nick. You know what? I'm telling Dad. I'm going to go and tell Dad tomorrow!"

Well, asshole Tony followed me up the steps and he was standing right outside our bathroom door. When I opened the door, he was standing right there, and he goes, "Oh, you're going to tell your dad?"

I said, "Yeah, I am," and with that, he grabbed me by my neck, and threw me against the wall. I was probably eighty fucking pounds (if that) soaking wet at that age.

I could feel a rage well up in me, and I let it rip with, "Fuck you, you don't live here! I don't like you. I never liked you; I didn't like you the minute I met you. You have no right to talk to my brother or my sisters or anybody in this house that way. You're not our father! You don't rule the roost. Fuck off. Fuck you. I fucking hate you!" And I just started swinging at him. I didn't give a shit. That was when he threw me down the stairs.

My mom freaked out; I could see the panic in her face as I got up after tumbling down the fifteen or so steps to the staircase landing. She told me to go back up to my room and from there I could hear her giving him some shit, saying, "You don't touch my fucking kids."

Later that night, she came up to our bedroom and apologized, saying she was so sorry. I wasn't fazed, whatever. I didn't give a shit. I had a mission.

I got up the next day and got dressed for school. When we left the house, my brother and sisters went one way and I went the opposite way, to my dad's. I walked into my dad's house at nine o'clock in the morning and told his wife Carol what happened. I hung out there all day long, and when my dad got home from work, he sat and listened to me tell him what happened.

When I told him that this guy slapped Nicky in the back of the head, and said fuck in front of us, I could see my dad's blood pressure rising. I knew it wasn't going to be good. Dad asked if anything else happened, and when I told him that I got into a fistfight with the guy and he threw me down our flight of steps, he said, "Get in the car!"

The whole way home, I said things like, "Dad, I don't want to go. I don't want to go. Can't I just live with you?"

"No, you cannot live with me. You're going home."

We pulled up and walked to the door. My mother answered, and Tony was standing behind her like a little bitch when she opened the front door. Dad looked at my mom and said, "I don't give a shit what you do with your life. I know you're going to date; you're going to do whatever you want to do—that's fine. But I'm telling you, and I'm telling your flunky boyfriend back there: if any of your guy friends touch my kids, or curse in front of my kids, or act inappropriately in front of my kids, I'm going to come back here and there's going to be hell to pay!"

Dad then turned around, walked down the front steps and drove off in the car. Mom was mad at me, but I didn't give a fuck. It had gotten to the point where I fucking hated my mother, too, and it was because of that asshole Tony.

With Mom working long days from six in the morning until around four every day, us kids had to be self-sufficient. She'd already be out of the house by the time we got up, so we made breakfast and got ourselves ready for school, before walking there, no matter what the weather.

Mom always made sure we had food in the house. It was quick food, like mac and cheese, SpaghettiOs, and Mrs. Paul's frozen fish sticks. We'd have a treat night where mom would go out and get us pizzas on Friday or Saturday, and we would have an ice cream cone, donuts, or something like that on the weekends.

She did what she could, but us kids were left to our own devices a lot; I was eleven or twelve at this point. Being home alone so much, Mom was pleased when a family member or friend could just swing by and check on us kids from time to time.

Mom's brother, John Hayes Jr.—or Jack, as he was known—was a fireman for as long as I could remember and was stationed only about five blocks from our house. If you walked to the corner of our street and took a right, he was just along Louden Street at the Philadelphia Fire Department Squad 72 Headquarters.

On occasion, my uncle Jack would swing by in his white Volkswagen bus, and then he started coming by a little more often. One day, he arranged with my mom that while she was busy working, he would pick us four kids up and take us to the park for the afternoon, along with a couple of our cousins, since my mom's sister Kathleen had moved in just two doors down from us with her new husband Carlos.

He drove us all in his VW bus to Pennypack Park, which was a twenty-minute drive, seven miles northeast of our house along Roosevelt Boulevard. It was a huge park with a creek, playgrounds, hiking trails, and it was teaming with wildlife—it wasn't unusual to be walking there and see deer, and lots of other wild animals.

When we got to the park, Uncle Jack said, "Okay, let's hike! We're going to explore. Johnny, you take all the kids that way, and I'm going to take Anna this way."

Naïve and not thinking, "This was odd," I was like, "Oh, okay, whatever." We split up; he went to the left with my sister, I went to the right with the other kids, and we walked along a hiking trail.

After we had walked a couple of miles, over what seemed like an hour or so, we were on a path running along the side of the creek underneath a giant bridge where Roosevelt Boulevard passed overhead. That's when a park patrol car stopped us, and a super nice cop asked us what we were doing. I told him, "Oh, we're just hiking. Our uncle brought us to the park for the day."

He immediately asked, "Well, where's your uncle?"

I said, "Oh, he's hiking in a different direction." The cops told us to get in their squad car, so we all piled in.

They asked me where my uncle would be, but I didn't know what entrance we came in and where he parked the VW. I said, "Well, we just walked straight down this path, so it's got to be that way."

The cop drove back and pulled up at the VW bus in the parking area, and we sat there, but there was no sign of Uncle Jack or my sister, so we waited.

When my uncle eventually came out of the woods, this cop laid into him with, "What the fuck are you doing? Goddamn it, you can't leave these kids like that!" He said that just last week a patient from the nearby Byberry psychiatric hospital escaped and did a swan dive off the overpass bridge into six inches of water, thinking he was Johnny Weissmuller of Tarzan fame or some shit.

The cop laid into my uncle verbally, but I couldn't hear the whole conversation. My uncle just kind of backtracked, and we soon left.

He took us for ice cream on the way home and said, "Okay, kids. Listen: let's not freak your moms and everybody out. I'll take you guys out for ice cream, but don't say anything about the police." We just kind of kept our mouths shut.

Maybe a month or two later, I was upstairs in my bedroom, playing guitar. I thought I had heard my uncle come in the house, but he didn't know I was there. I started to walk down the steps toward the landing, where the stairs then turned and had three more steps that ran off to the right.

I didn't see anything as I was coming down the steps, but I heard my sister and I thought I heard my uncle. When I was about halfway down the stairs, I leaned out over the banister railing and looked into the kitchen to my right.

I saw my younger sister kneeling, doing something to my uncle Jack. I pulled my head back in, and I was like, "Uh, I don't know what I just saw, but it didn't look right." My brain tried to process it but there was vagueness to it. I sat on the steps for a second, and yelled to my sister as I was coming down the stairs, and I could tell my uncle was putting himself back together. Something was really wrong here, and I didn't know what to make of it, so I stewed on it for some time.

Eventually, I somehow approached the subject with my sister and talked with her about it. She told me he would come into our home, and she would do things with him, and he would give her like twenty-five cents, fifty cents, or a dollar. He gave her money in exchange for pain. It helped me understand what was happening, but I sat on it again, not knowing what the fuck to do. So, what does a kid trying to make sense of a dark family secret do?

REBEL, and get even angrier, of course!

It was around this time I had another blow up with my mom, which led to me running away. I was just becoming a teenager, or close to it, and my grades were slipping. I was hanging out with edgy people who were friends of mine, like the Getner brothers, the Elliott brothers, and a guy named Poye. I was starting to get into huffing, which is taking paint thinner and putting it on a rag in a brown paper bag. You then put the bag over your mouth and nose and breathe in deeply, causing a quick five-minute high that goes as quickly as it comes, so rinse and repeat. Stupidity at its finest! I was doing really dumb shit!

Another morning, Pat Getner and I stole a case of Frank's root beer and orange soda (a local brand in Philadelphia) from their bottling plant on our way to school. We sat by the railroad tracks and drank almost the entire batch—forty-eight bottles of soda. I was so sick, and I had such a sugar high. We were going to be late to school, so we said fuck it and just didn't go. I ended up getting busted for cutting class. The thought of all that soda still fucking makes me feel sick.

There is a huge automotive chain in America that will remain nameless, as I don't know how the statute of limitations works, and they sold windshield wiper blades, oil for cars, and all this other shit. They also sold and kept bicycles, as well as these little gas-powered minibikes, in their store window. Mom was usually exhausted after work and would fall asleep around 7:00 p.m., so I would sneak out of the house, and my friends and I would have a couple of beers and go to the store a mile or so from my house at nine or ten o'clock at night, after everything was closed and traffic had died down.

We'd throw cinder blocks or bricks through the windows and just grab all the Stingray bikes and minibikes; we would split with them and chop them up. We would saw the front forks off one of the bicycles, take the front tire off, attach the forks to another bike and drill a hole, put a little screw and a bolt through the forks, and then throw the tire back on. Ta-dah! We now had a chopper!

We would file all the serial numbers off everything. We'd spray-paint the minibikes a different color and ride them for a couple of days, then just throw them in the high grass on the side of the train tracks. Then it was off for another pillage session, often rotating stores throughout the city.

One day, I was walking along with the Elliott brothers when one of them said, "Oh, this house is abandoned." (The house was on Ninth Street, on the same block as the Elliot's.) "The people moved out, but they left everything in it." I was a gullible dumbass and bought that story—hook, line, and sinker.

We broke a window, reached in, unlocked the door (which should've been my first clue), and walked right in. I sat in the living room and said, "Fuck, who would move out and not take the TVs, radios, and stereo, and this fucking couch?"

The guys grabbed shit and walked out. I picked up the fucking TV that was way heavier than I thought it would be. As I struggled out the front door with the thing in broad daylight, somebody came up behind me and threw me to the floor.

It was the owner of the house, screaming at me, "What the fuck are you doing?" I was freaking out and told him I thought the house was abandoned. He asked me who was with me, but I wasn't going to tell him anything, so I said I was by myself.

He called bullshit on me, and then said his next call would be to the cops or my dad. I was hoping for the cops, knowing my dad would fucking kill me! He ended up calling my mom at work, and she unfortunately couldn't leave work so she called my dad, who showed up at this fucking house, beyond pissed, and apologized to the guy, promising to pay any damages and find out who was with me. I put the TV back and the guy let me go, but my dad whipped my fucking ass all the way home. It still hurts to sit sometimes.

By this point, my mom was suspicious of my every move and tired. My aunt Kathleen was fed up with me as well, as she and/or her husband were usually chasing me around the neighborhood and bringing me home to the dismay of my mom. I was coming home high. Mom could smell beer on my breath. I was smoking cigarettes; I was going to school late, and I was failing subjects. I was just rebelling against anything and everything, and I think it was just a culmination of my parents' divorce, the people I was hanging with, and perhaps to some degree, the weight of the Uncle Jack thing I was carrying around. Evil was still creepin'.

3
The Shoemaker

After my housebreaking incident, Mom was at her wits' end, unable to handle me. She felt she couldn't raise me on her own and that I needed a male influence. She arranged for me to move in and live with my dad and his wife Carol, which is what I wanted—or so I thought, anyway.

I also moved to a different Catholic school in Dad's neighborhood called Ascension of Our Lord School, where I was in eighth grade. I'm sure my parents hoped this would have a positive impact on me. My sisters and brother would come and visit on weekends. I don't think Carol was mentally or emotionally prepared, even just on weekends, to have the four-kid family that came with my dad, so there started to be some tension during their visits almost immediately.

After I had been living with Dad and Carol for almost a year, my siblings came to visit one weekend. Out of curiosity, I talked with Anna again. I asked her if the stuff was still happening with Uncle Jack, and she said it was. I decided I was going to tell Dad, but she didn't want me to, like she was afraid she was the one who was going to get into trouble. I told her not to worry.

That Sunday night while my dad was taking my brother and sisters back home to my mom's, I sat down at the kitchen table with Carol. I told her that I knew something that my dad was going to be really, really angry about. When she asked me what it was, I told her what I saw and what my sister told me. She said I absolutely needed to tell my dad right away!

Once he came back home, Carol made my dad sit down at the table, where he poured a cup of coffee and lit a cigarette. I then proceeded to tell him what I saw and what Anna had told me. Needless to say, my dad was beyond fucking furious. He was absolutely beet fucking red.

He called my mom, who got my sister and asked her about it while my dad was on the phone. Anna started crying and said that it had been going on for a year or two now.

The next morning, my dad drove my sister to the Sex Crimes Unit of the police department, where she went through an agonizing all-day process of reliving and recounting everything that happened in detail to a bunch of police officers—total strangers. The process was made even longer because Uncle Jack was a uniformed city employee, which invoked more rigorous protocols that had to be followed. To this day, I don't know how she put up with all that. They arrested my uncle Jack at home that night. The monster was out of the closet and in a cell.

My mom's father was also named John Hayes, except he didn't go by the nickname of Jack. He was a chief petty officer in the navy, so he worked down at the Philadelphia Navy Yard where the Schuylkill River meets the Delaware River. He passed away of a heart attack in '65 or '66 and in time, my uncle Jack had moved home with my grandmother, so she was no longer living there alone.

The house was a three-story row home at 9 E. Silver Street in the Kensington/Fishtown District of Philly, just three and a half miles south of Mom's place on Franklin Street. There had been a big fire in the house when I was about four. My grandparents and younger aunts had to climb out of an upper-story window and swing to another window next door to save themselves. They could have easily died in the blaze, as my grandmother passed out from smoke inhalation.

The house was eventually repaired but the neighborhood was old, made of brick with cobblestone streets and a lot of deserted warehouses and textile mills around. Silver Street was narrow, so while there was some street parking, there were about six garages on both sides, and at both ends of the street, which the residents used.

As well as being a fireman, Uncle Jack was also an amateur photographer. When the cops arrested him, they went through all his shit, including one of these garages he used. They went through all his camera equipment, and they found boxes of Polaroid photos. I'm not talking shoeboxes; I'm talking multiple moving boxes, full of them. There were hundreds of old Polaroids of my young brother and sisters, and six or seven other kids in that neighborhood that he had been fucking around with. My siblings weren't his only victims.

Things were fucked at that point, but things got even weirder in the family: my mom's side of the family became very divided as some of them helped Jack with his legal fees. I also remember my mom being devastated when one of her sisters, sarcastically said, "Well, you know, Anna's always been a bit of a flirt."

It was like, wait; you're justifying STATUATORY RAPE by a forty-year-old man of a fucking ten-year-old girl because she was a flirt? FUCK YOU! You can choose your friends, but not your family. It was certainly a tense time.

I was living with my dad, and he petitioned the court to take all four kids. He eventually got custody of all of us, so we were all together again. It was a parental role reversal with Mom and Dad.

It wasn't long before something happened with our old house on Franklin Street, where my mom wasn't able to make payments, state taxes, etc., probably due to her divorce's legal fees to some degree, so she rented our house to a lady named Helen, who originally lived across the street and had recently gone through a divorce. Helen moved out of her house and into ours, and then my mom moved into Silver Street with my grandmother to save money and keep my grandmother company, but she never unpacked a box.

After being convicted in court for his charges of statutory rape and sexual assault of a bunch of neighborhood children, Uncle Jack went to prison. I thought he'd be locked away for the rest of his life, but while in prison for a couple of months, other inmates harassed him and threatened him. Of course, inmates target pedophiles because it's probably considered to be the most heinous of crimes. So, what did the fucking authorities do? They RELEASED HIM! They let him out of fucking prison!

He was to report to a probation officer for ten years, who had set him up in a one-bedroom apartment. But because he initially couldn't get a job and afford the room, the city provided him welfare, which in turn entitled him to a medical card and other benefits.

One of my relatives helped him get a job as a janitor...in a...wait for it...Catholic elementary school after his stint in fucking prison for child molestation! This is the beauty of the Catholic archdiocese. If you've read any news in the last twenty years, you've probably noticed more than once how fucked they are with this sort of shit.

To say my dad was pissed about this would be an understatement. And at one point, my uncle John (on my dad's side) and my father, had to be removed from the trial for threatening to kill Jack. I just despised that "human being," too. It ripped my heart out to know he was living somewhere amongst us. I would rather see him dead on a floor or in an unmarked grave. I despised him so much because our lives were ruined.

I say ruined because on Sundays, Dad would drive us kids the ten minutes from his place to go see my mom and my grandmother. It was not pleasant at Silver St. I would look at my mom and know she was mentally and physically defeated by it all. My grandmother had lost her husband, and then her son got convicted for molesting her grandkids, so she had now become a raging alcoholic. She was probably drinking a handle of gin a day, which is like sixty fluid ounces.

The house made *Sanford and Son*'s home look like a fucking palace. We would walk in through her front door and have to follow a slim path through all the boxes, piles of clothing, and just shit everywhere. There was a little space where you could see the TV and change the channel, and there were thin walkways left to walk upstairs or right to the kitchen. It was a hoarder's house, and it was in shambles. It was fucking horrible, but there wasn't much sunshine living at my dad's during the week either.

Music became an escape for me. I started getting into it more and more and getting into the bands and music that grabbed my attention.

I had already played in a few bands that played school talent contests at my old school, Incarnation, and actually brought home the gold at one of them! That was a great night; my dad was at that show, and he was shocked when he saw me start playing and singing. I was only meant to play guitar that night but as the curtains opened, our singer Mary got stage fright and froze, so I stepped up to the microphone and sang "House of the Rising Sun" and "(I'm Not Your) Steppin' Stone." Dad was so impressed with my achievement that he actually took me out for pizza after, and in later years said that was the moment he realized I had real musical talent.

He also became a bit more supportive and bought me another guitar from a friend of Carol's named MaryAnn. It was a used Sears Silvertone electric guitar—a Strat-shaped cherry burst with a mirrored pick guard, and a small Fender amp—he paid a hundred bucks for it in weekly installments of five dollars, and I was off to the races.

I desperately wanted to play in a cool band and had made several attempts at doing so to no avail at that point. But I accidently found this band called Street People, and they rehearsed right around the corner from my dad's house. I used to sit outside and listen to them play all these great songs that were on the radio, and I thought they were amazing! I would walk our dog past their house every day just so I could hear them practice in the basement.

One day, I met the guitar player, and he sat down and chatted with me a while. His name was Jimmy Kaznicky, and when I told him I could play, he grabbed a guitar and let me play him a few things. I played him "Travelin' Band" by Creedence and "House of the Rising Sun" by The Animals, and he basically offered me a gig playing with the band on the spot. I was much younger than them, and he thought it would be a cool little novelty thing having a pint-sized guitarist/singer. Needless to say, my hiring didn't go over too well with some of the other guys, but I did get to do a couple of mall openings in front of large audiences, and I made a little money, which really made me want to play music even more!

That is, until my dad made me quit.

My dad's wife Carol realized that I was smoking when she caught me stealing one of her cigarettes, so she would let me smoke cigarettes in the house until my dad got home. She even gave me cigarettes of hers occasionally without me asking. As much as I thought that was cool on the one hand, it was odd on another, and I just couldn't figure her out. Some days she had a volatile temper and was just fucking mean, and at other times, she was as cool as could be—very hot and cold.

One day my dad and I were coming back from the store, and I heard some commotion coming from our front window. I ran up to the house ahead of Dad, and I saw Carol smacking my sister Anna with a vacuum cleaner pipe. I obviously saw her do it, and I complained to my dad about it, but Carol denied it. Again, I said, "I just saw you doing it. There's four of us sitting here saying you did it." She still flat-out denied it and unfortunately my dad sided with her—I was crushed he didn't stick up for us.

We were living at Dad's for the better part of a year and during this time I was experiencing his temper, and Carol's, go off the charts frequently. I remember I was being grounded for something as a punishment, so I wasn't permitted to go do a gig with Jimmy and the guys, which was devastating and wound-up costing me the gig, but I was allowed to leave the house to go to the store and get him a newspaper. The store was out of papers when I got there, but they were expecting a delivery, so I waited and read some magazines in the meantime. After perhaps half an hour, a new bundle came in, so I bought one for Dad and took it home. When I walked in, my dad was like, "Where the hell were you?"

I said, "I was at the store..." and before I could even finish answering, he took a swing at me. I put my hand up to block him, and he broke two of my fingers.

Dad was angry all the time. Not only was he pissed that they let Uncle Jack out of prison, it was now costing him a lot of money. Every Tuesday or Wednesday, all four of us kids had to go to a therapy session and talk with a psychologist. This was costing about eighty to a hundred bucks a week, which back in the seventies was a lot of money for Mom and Dad to be spending. But what really goaded the shit out of my dad was the fact that, as a parolee, Uncle Jack got his therapy free from the state!

Also, during this time, Carol was pregnant. She was unwell through her pregnancy and spent the best part of seven months mainly in bed. She had a bell at her bedside, and I would be doing things for her constantly. I fucking hated every minute of it.

My daily routine consisted of making myself breakfast, walking the dog, making Carol breakfast, and taking it up to her in bed. I would wash the breakfast dishes, walk myself to school, come home again during lunch break, make the two of us lunch, walk the dog, and then go back to school for the afternoon session, and then come home immediately after. I also had chores to do, like cleaning up the yard after the dog, let alone bringing her whatever she wanted when she rang that fucking bell. I was fucking twelve or thirteen years old and felt like her personal fucking slave.

Carol had a miscarriage and spent quite a few more months bedridden, depressed with yours truly at her beck and call. It all got to a point where I had had enough and said fuck this, again. I was doing time in yet another broken home. Before my brother and sisters moved in, things were relatively okay living at Dad's, but everything had changed now; it was a different dichotomy. Everybody was fighting, bickering, and arguing in that house.

I said, "I'm going back. I'm telling Mom I don't want to be here anymore. I'm fucking done with this shit."

The next day, I cut school and took off to Silver Street and told my mom everything. I was frustrated and angry and wanted to come back and live with her again. So she called my dad that night and said, "The kids are coming back with me. I'm coming to pick them up tomorrow."

I had to ride with my mom to go pick up my brother and sisters the next day. I remember being petrified; I was so afraid of my dad that I was sitting on the back floor of the car, clutching a baseball bat, ready to start swinging like Dick Allen of the Phillies if he or Carol fucking started anything. It's so sad in hindsight, but we were all just so bitter and fucking ANGRY!

Us four kids all moved into my grandmother's house, and my mom still hadn't unpacked her things. Our possessions just added to the chaos in this junkyard while Mom worked her ass off every day, only to get home, light up a Newport cigarette, and draw on it with that defeated look on her face.

Living in the same house where my uncle Jack had lived for so long was difficult for me, so I can only imagine how much tougher it was for Anna and my other two siblings to move in there, but there was no other option.

Now that I was living with my grandmother, I got to see firsthand just how much she was drinking. She was making us dinner one night, and we could see her wobbling and hear her slurring her words, talking funny to us. We knew she was drunk; Grandma was totally fucked; she was trashed. By this point, she was frail, with sores on her arms and legs because she had severely dry skin and scratched at herself constantly. Most of her teeth were gone, her hair was unwashed, and she wore an old "house dress" every day. She was chain-smoking so many cigarettes down to the filter, that her first two fingers on her hands had burns, and were stained yellow from the tobacco. She was a mess!

While dishing our food out, she slammed the bowl down, doubled-over, and quickly grabbed the sink and her stomach. That's when she literally shit herself, right in front of all four of us kids, who were already sitting at the dinner table. I was like, "Ugh, what are we having for dinner? Beef stew? No thanks; I'll pass." My mom quickly came into the kitchen and yelled at her mother and took her upstairs for a quick clean-up and sent her to bed. Needless to say, that was a pizza night in the Corabi household.

Her drinking continued to escalate from a handle of gin, if that's even possible. She was a raging alcoholic, plain and simple—drunk, basically every minute of the day, and dehydrated. A couple of days before my fifteenth birthday, she took the trash out, slipped, fell, and broke her hip. She went into the hospital, but never made it out; she died April 25, 1974. So, then it was just Mom and us kids living there, trying to make the old 1920s-era house a fucking home.

I was still so angry with my dad; I just didn't even talk with him. I was pissed at him for not believing us about Carol's attack on my sister.

I hated him. I hated Carol. And I just didn't care if I saw or spoke to either of them. I was like, "Fuck you!"

Dad would come and pick up my brother and sisters from my mom's on the weekend. He would park at the end of Silver Street, and they would walk down to get in his car. He'd stand at the end of the street, and he'd wave to me, and I would flip him off, mumbling, "Fuck you; I don't even want to talk to you!" And I didn't for a very long time.

Once I got settled into the house with my mom, I met a guy named Ricky Stevenson, who lived directly around the corner from us on Sterner Street. He was probably four years older than me, perhaps nineteen. He had joined the Marines at eighteen but said fuck it and left, so he was AWOL and basically hiding out from everybody…but he sure could fucking play guitar great. After hanging a bit with Ricky, and sharing a love of Grand Funk Railroad, Led Zeppelin, and Bowie, we decided to try and put a band together, but we needed a drummer, so I called up an old pal.

Enter: Bobby Clark, who I knew from my old neighborhood where my dad lived. We went to Ascension school together and had discussed doing something musically in the past, but it never materialized. I thought Bobby was perfect for what Ricky and I wanted to do, so we started hanging out and planning.

Problem was, we didn't have a place to rehearse. My basement was packed with boxes of bullshit with little room to spare, and Ricky lived in his mom's basement, so that was out of the question. Bobby lived with his grandparents, and they weren't even remotely interested in having a bunch of noisy, mouthy assholes hanging around their place.

My aunt Peggy (my mother's sister) and Uncle Bob came to the rescue and told us we could practice in their basement. Now we were set! A bonus of living on Silver Street was I didn't have to travel to get to my aunt's basement for rehearsal; it was right across the street from us.

I had taken my Sears Silvertone guitar that I previously got for Christmas and I traded it in at a pawnshop along with a boost from some savings bonds that my dad cashed in and gave to my mom to help. With the money, I bought a green Gibson type ES-335 bass and an old Sunn amp. I switched to playing bass and vocals for the band that we also christened Street People after the now defunct band I had previously been in.

We first learned how to play songs together like "Smokin' in the Boys Room" by Brownsville Station (oddly enough), "Black Dog" by Led Zeppelin, "We're an American Band" by Grand Funk, and the panty-removing ballad "My Love" by Paul McCartney—all the good shit that was happening in the seventies. I was trying harder to do the music thing. The music was there, but we were just hellions, and clueless.

You see, I had this incredible knack of finding these little hoodlums to hang with. First it was the Getners and the Elliots back in my Franklin Street neighborhood, where there were like two girls and five boys in both families.

Now in my new Silver Street neighborhood, I was hanging out with another Irish clan of misfits named Chris Dugan, Mickey Dugan, and Franny Dugan, Johnny Harbison, as well as the misfits in my band.

I used to hang out at Ricky's with the crew watching *Don Kirshner's Rock Concert*, *The Midnight Special*, and the *California Jam* and all that shit on Friday and Saturday nights. We'd stay up all night and then once dawn was breaking, we'd go out and raid everybody's home deliveries of milk, chocolate milk, orange juice, donuts, and eggs that were left on their front doorsteps at 6:00 a.m. We would then go back to one of their houses and make scrambled eggs for breakfast with our loot.

It was a tough area, with a lot of segregated, racial tension. Much like the Southie area of Boston or Hell's Kitchen in Manhattan, it was staunch, Irish Catholic. Not long after I moved in with Mom, a Puerto Rican family moved into the neighborhood, much to the dismay of many of the residents. One day their house was fire-bombed because the Irish-Catholic neighbors didn't want Puerto Ricans "ruining" the neighborhood, and the fire fucking killed them all—a husband, a wife, and their two little kids.

Other teens would come into our turf from other neighborhoods, and the little hoodlums I hung with would get pissed. One summertime afternoon, there was supposed to be a gang coming, so we got ready for a rumored showdown.

Since I was small, probably 5'5" and maybe ninety pounds max, they positioned me sitting on top of a garage with a soda case of about ten bottles full of gasoline, with rags in the top. They said, "Hey, Mouse (my nickname at the time), go up on the garage here, take these fucking Molotov's, and if they come down our street, just light 'em up, and start bombing the shit out of them."

I sat on top of a garage with all these Molotov cocktails, smoking a cigarette like a dumbass, while waiting for these guys to come down the street. Directly across the street from our house was a family called the Brennans. They were close family friends, and my mom's older sister Mary Ann had married Jerry Brennan (one of the five Brennan brothers), so we all just referred to them as aunts and uncles. Aunt Millie saw me up on the garage roof, and she yelled out, "Get off that goddamn garage, you little fucking hooligan. I'm going to call the police and your mother, Goddammit."

The cops ended up coming and found the Molotov cocktails. I told them, "Nope, they weren't mine. I just went up there and I found them. They were there. Somebody put them there; they're not mine." I denied it, but still got into a ton of trouble with my mom. Apparently Millie told my mother, but someone else called the police.

Along with the Dugans, I also hung out with these other neighbors that lived on the adjoining street behind our house, James "Jimmy" Kallinger and Joey Kallinger. They were wise-asses, but they were just off—something about them was wrong. They were extremely weird kids, but as you do when you're young, you adapt and learn to hang out with the other kids near you.

Joey was about my age, and Jimmy was younger. They had another brother Michael, but I rarely saw him out on the street.

If I walked through the backyard of our East Silver Street house and out the back gate, I would be on East Sterner Street. Turning right, there was the rear of our neighbor's, Dan Hughes, house and then some garages. If I crossed to the other side of Sterner, the Kallinger's shoe shop was on the south corner of North Front Street, and it was above this shop that the Kallinger brothers and sisters lived with their parents—just one hundred and fifty feet from my place.

Jimmy and Joey's dad was named Joseph, and he was also a bit weird. Let me rephrase: he was VERY weird. He was mental, at times a raving lunatic who didn't make sense to most of the folks in the neighborhood, and we tortured him for it. Like, if you were standing in front of his shoe shop, just standing there talking or leaning against the fire hydrant, he would come out screaming with an old camera, and he would take a picture of you, then run back in his shop, freaking out and cursing at the top of his lungs!

He'd do all this weird shit constantly, like mumble to himself, walk around in the dead of winter with no shoes or jacket on, and just yell and freak out and scream at all the kids in the neighborhood. So, Crazy Joe became a bit of sport to me.

I would go across the street with one of the Dugans or Johnny Harbison, and we'd climb up the billboard directly across from his shop on Front Street. We'd then throw shit like oranges or rotten fruit at the window of his shoe shop. This would freak him out of course, so he'd come out and take pictures of us. We'd laugh, moon him, and flip him off from up there, yelling out, "Fuck you, you fucking weirdo!" Stupid, crazy shit.

Sometimes we'd see one of his daughters, Mary Jo, on the street. She was super quiet and never said a word, even if you said hi to her. She never spoke or would even acknowledge you. One time we asked Jimmy and Joey about her, and they said, "Oh, fuck, our dad, man, he's crazy. My sister got her period, so he tied her up with a cord and put a hot spatula on her bare leg at knifepoint. He freaked out because she got her period, and therefore she's not pure." It was things like this that made us realize he was nuts.

My next-door neighbors had two giant Great Dane dogs. One day I asked the daughters Ruthie and Debbie if I could fill up a bag with their dogs' shit—of course they had no problem with me doing this stinking chore for them. Once it was full, Johnny Harbison and I doused the full bag of shit with lighter fluid. We carried it to the Kallinger's, dropped it in front of their door, lit it on fire, knocked on the door, and then ran into my yard, shutting the door behind us.

We peeked through the tiniest of holes to see the reaction, completely out of sight by the time the shop door opened underneath the big WHILE U WAIT sign that hung overhead. This was torture for old man Kallinger. He came out to see a flaming bag, which set him off, "Fuck you! Who's the motherfucker that left this?"

He stomped on the bag to put the flames out and then got dog shit all over his shoes. As a shoemaker, he loved clean shoes, so this set him off even more, but he never knew who the fuck was doing it. We never broke his windows, or did anything too crazy, but these were the sorts of games that we'd tease the fucking weirdo with. Of course, as we allowed his sons Jimmy and Joey to hang out with us, we never told them that we were the ones torturing their dad.

At fifteen, I was a bit younger, and certainly smaller, than some of the other guys. One day during that summer of '74, Mickey Dugan came up to me and said that Joey Kallinger had been in his house and stole his mother's food stamps—she was going to get some groceries with her welfare assistance, but they were gone.

Somehow Mickey got them back from Joey, but he wanted to make a point with him. Mickey said, "Hey, Mouse, I want you to fucking kick Joey's ass, just whip his ass. He stole my mom's food stamps."

Since Mickey was older, he would get in more serious trouble if he got caught whipping Joey's ass. So I agreed to do it.

Joey came around the corner and onto my street. I walked up to him, and I fucking punched him right in the face and started whipping his ass. Just like the old boxing matches that I used to watch on our black-and-white TV as a youngster, I was dancing around him, waiting for him to get to his feet. He tried to get up and fight me, but he wasn't the most coordinated kid.

In my hood, none of the neighbors would even think about breaking up a good fistfight. They would literally sit out on their front steps with a forty and watch it for a while until it got too bad or too vicious. Maybe somebody would then break it up. It was like fucking Friday night boxing with people making wagers. "I think the Corabi kid is going to kick his ass."

I rolled my fucking sleeves up and still wanted more of this kid. "Come on, you motherfucker." I punched him again.

He got up and managed to get a couple of good shots but in my mind he was easily behind on points. We were beating the shit out of each other, and I fucking hit him again. He went down, and I kicked him a few times while he was on the ground. I stopped for a second and when I leaned over him, he said he was done and was going to go home.

As he got up, I yelled at him, "Don't come back. Stay the fuck off Silver Street. You're not wanted here." Then as he walked away, I finished with, "If I fucking see you on this street again, I'll kill you!"

Later that summer, I was at home when I heard a solid knock on the door, and then heard my mom scream, "What? Johnny, get down here!" I was up in my bedroom listening to some records, and I just had my jeans on, so I threw on a shirt and went downstairs.

There were two cops in our doorway, and one said, "Are you John Corabi?" I said I was, so they said, "Can you come with us please?" They marched me out handcuffed and put me in the back of their police car.

My mom then got in, too, and they drove us both directly to the police station. We sat in a jail room where they questioned me for what seemed like forever. "Do you know Joey Kallinger?"

"Yep."

"Did you recently have a fight with him?"

"Yeah, I did."

"Neighbors said that you said that you would kill him. Did you say that to him?"

"I don't know; I don't remember. Why?"

They kept silent.

Thinking that Joey or his parents complained about the fight, I said, "Look, if you want to know about this fight that I had with him, it was because he stole my friend's mother's food stamps when he came in her house. We then got into a fistfight over it."

They said, "Well, why didn't your friend do something?"

"Well, my friend is older, and he didn't want to get into trouble because he's eighteen and Joey's more my age. So, you know, I took care of business for him, and I fought the kid."

Then the cop said, "Did you kill him?"

I said, "Excuse me, what did you just ask me again?"

They repeated, "Did you kill him?"

I said, "Uh, no, of course not! He walked home."

They then reached into a folder and pulled out a photo and slide it across the desk in front of me. My mother went fucking white. I looked at the photo and saw it was an extremely dead-looking Joey Kallinger. It freaked me out because he was all bruised up, and I almost threw up—it was not good.

You see, construction workers were breaking ground for a huge new mall in Center City, Philadelphia, called The Gallery at Market East. Underneath a pile of rocks, they found Joey's body, under all this rubble at the demolition site. He had been reported missing after apparently running away. They found his body, and the coroner couldn't determine the cause of death. Earlier that year, Joey had been released from a juvenile reformatory after he was evaluated as being seriously disturbed.

The cops had cased our neighborhood, asking people questions. "Hey, do you know this kid?"

Someone was like, "Oh, yeah, that's the Kallinger boy. Haven't seen him for a little while, maybe a month or so. Last time he was on the street, one of the kids from here got in a big fistfight with him, beat the shit out of him. You know, I think I heard him say when he left, 'I'm going to kill you.'"

It was a weird feeling that overcame me when the cop slid the photo of dead Joey Kallinger in front of me. I was just sitting there thinking, "Holy fuck, are you kidding me right now? Can my life get any worse?"

I kept telling the cops that I didn't know anything about what happened to him.

Hours went by like years. It felt like I was in there forever. They also did a lot of talking with my mom. I remember they asked her, "You're not taking any trips anytime in the near future, are you?"

Mom said no and asked, "Do we need a lawyer?"

The cop said, "Not yet," and they begrudgingly let me go home.

I pulled my head in a bit after that. I assured Mom that I had nothing to do with it, but it just added to her load, and she was already fucking defeated.

But I couldn't help thinking that I'm sure it wouldn't be the first time that cops have pinned a crime on someone. [Cue Bob Dylan's song "Hurricane."] It'd be just my luck that I'd be sent to Holmesburg Prison for this and Uncle Jack was allowed to go fucking free.

Before I moved back in with my mom at Silver Street, I told my parents that I didn't want to go to Catholic school anymore. I had a pretty good argument saying a) you can't afford it, and b) I fucking hate their rules, so I ain't going!

So I enrolled at Stetson Junior High School for ninth grade instead, my first time in the public-school system in Philadelphia. It was a very integrated school, with a mix of Black, white, and Hispanic kids. Being white, I was in the minority there, and it definitely took some adjusting.

I immediately noticed it was a pretty rough school, and when I got into class, I realized I was so much more advanced in my work than the other kids, having come from the Catholic education system. For example, my math at Stetson was like: Billy has nine apples, Mary takes three. How many apples does Billy have left? Are you fucking kidding me? I learned that in second grade! Tell me what two plus two is. No, it's not five! I checked-out mentally and started cutting school again.

Mom would already be at work when I left the house in the morning for school, so instead I would walk down our street and around the corner to Ricky Stevenson's house. We'd sit there at his place sucking down the hooch while listening to fucking Grand Funk Railroad, Deep Purple, David Bowie, Led Zeppelin, Ten Years After, and all the good shit. We'd talk about what we were going to play at rehearsal later that night with our drummer, Bobby. Plus, I was smitten with Ricky's younger sister Donna.

The coolest thing I remember about Stetson was when I went to my homeroom teacher and said I wanted my band to play one of the school assemblies they had twice a month. The teacher pulled it off, and they let us play an assembly.

We were so fucking excited to do this gig and rehearsed like we were doing Woodstock. It was a giant theater-like assembly hall. They gave us about forty minutes to make our statement, so we played "Smokin' in the Boys Room," "Smoke on the Water," and "We're an American Band." We then did extended versions of "Soul Sacrifice" by Santana for the Puerto

Ricans, thinking they would dig that, and finished with a rough hard rock version of "Sex Machine" by James Brown for the Black kids.

Previously, I was completely invisible at Stetson, but I swear to God, even though I was one of the few white kids in this school, as soon as I did that show, all these Puerto Rican and Black girls became really friendly with me. I started to see what kind of reaction playing music had on girls. They said, "Oh, your show was so great, you guys are awesome!"

Everybody started to say, "Oh, fuck, Corabi's cool." I'd sit in the schoolyard at lunchtime and didn't have to worry about getting fucking hassled anymore. After I played that concert, Black kids talked and smoked weed with me. The Hispanic kids came over, too, and it was great.

It helped bridge my fear of these other types of people that, where I came from, you just didn't hang out with. And where they came from, they didn't hang out with people like me either. However, in the schoolyard at that point, after that one concert, it was like the United Nations. It was awesome!

I had the biggest crush on a Puerto Rican girl named Zoraida Cologne, and we kind of dated a few times. She was super cute, as was her friend Gladys.

Zoraida came up to my neighborhood, and I went down to hers, but both neighborhoods were so segregated back then. It was like she was taking her life in her own hands coming into my Irish, Catholic neighborhood; Puerto Ricans were not welcomed! She got hassled a couple of times coming to my house while walking or taking the bus.

I was white, short, and skinny, and had started to grow my hair out really long, like Roger Daltrey or Robert Plant, so when I walked in her neighborhood, I was just asking to get my ass kicked by the Puerto Ricans as well, and I wasn't about to let that happen, so outside of the schoolyard, it was a relationship that was very *West Side Story* and doomed from the beginning.

The next winter in the middle of January '75, there were reporters in our neighborhood—it was big news! The cops arrested old man Kallinger, along with his sons Jimmy and Michael, from their home behind ours. They linked Kallinger to a crime spree from a bloodstained shirt and one of his sons was an accomplice. Since they looked alike, they weren't sure which one it was initially, but they soon let Jimmy go—turned out it was fifteen-year-old Michael.

It was a father and son tag team: they went around and cased homes, watching and waiting for husbands to leave to go to work. They waited a little bit, pretended to be salesmen and went in, tied the wife up, stole money, stole jewelry, stole whatever. Once the wife was tied up, Kallinger senior would have his son fuck the woman!

This little crime spree went across the states of Philadelphia, Maryland, and New Jersey. At the last crime scene, the father got blood on the shirt he was wearing when he slit the throat of a young nurse and killed her because she wouldn't chew off another hostage's penis, and then he threw the shirt away in a nearby park as they fled. Police found the shirt.

There was a laundromat and drycleaners on Somerset Street at the corner of Front Street, literally one block around the corner from our place on Silver Street. It had been there forever; my mom used to get dresses and shit cleaned there when she was a kid. Amazingly, I think it's still there today.

When they did the dry cleaning of shirts or pants, they printed the first three letters of your last name on the inside collar or waistband so they wouldn't lose anybody's shit. If it were my shirt, they would print COR. The bloodstained shirt that Joseph Kallinger ditched had KAL on the inside of the collar, and somehow the police tracked things back to that drycleaners.

They went in there and asked about the shirt. The guy there said, "Oh, yeah, that's one of Mr. Kallinger's shirts, the shoemaker that's literally across the street, and down half a block."

That led them into Kallinger's shoe shop where they then arrested them on kidnapping, rape, and murder charges.

Articles included his picture and immediately some of the construction workers that were working on the mall where they found Joey Kallinger's body were like, "Oh, wait a minute, I know this guy. That's the weirdo who used to come down at fucking seven or eight o'clock in the morning while we were breaking ground for the mall. He would just sit there and talk with us workers and say, 'That's a pretty deep hole. You guys are digging the foundation, huh? Do you ever find any bodies or anything in there?'"

They just thought he was off at the time, but they told the cops about it, and they dug into it more.

Soon we read more news articles in the paper. Kallinger took out a $45,000 life insurance policy on his sons and then drowned his own fucking son Joey before putting him under that rubble. The insurance company refused to pay out on his claim, suspecting some sort of bullshit was going on, and they pieced it together with the police.

It was at this point that I knew I was off the hook for the dead Kallinger boy; it clearly wasn't me who killed Joey. It was a huge relief.

It also turned out that during the summer of '74, while I was torturing the Kensington cobbler Joseph Kallinger with fucking oranges and flaming bags of dog shit, he tortured a ten-year-old Puerto Rican kid from our neighborhood, then severed his genitals and murdered him.

Kallinger's kids testified at his murder trial that he had a fucking torture chamber in their shoe shop basement, where he would punish them whenever an itch in his hand told him they had misbehaved.

Mary Jo testified that he beat her about five times a week after midnight from the age of ten to thirteen. She said that only one of the kids would be taken down to the chamber at a time, and that he came after the kids with a gun when they ran away. She also testified that he once tied Joey to a refrigerator and beat him with a hammer every hour on the hour. What a fucking psycho!

"The Shoemaker" was found guilty of three murders and sentenced to life in prison, where he slashed an inmate's throat and spent years in solitary confinement on suicide watch. He died in prison in 1996 from a heart seizure.[2]

Like most serial killers, Kallinger had a fucked-up childhood and was severely abused by his adoptive parents. He was also sexually assaulted by a group of neighborhood boys when he was nine, so it was no wonder he fucking freaked out when we did shit to him.

That was my close call with a fucking serial killer. My career in music could've easily been over before it fucking began!

---

2 You can read more about Kallinger in Flora Rheta Schreiber's biography on him titled *The Shoemaker: The Anatomy of a Psychotic* (Simon & Schuster, 1983).

4

Let Me Go, Rock 'n' Roll

Philadelphia radio didn't play a lot of new music. They just seemed to play old Stones, songs from The Beatles, and some Philly soul, but not all the cool, new rock that was happening at the time. I heard the fresh shit from other friends; that's how discovering new music worked back then when you couldn't fucking YouTube or Google something, or have a device tell you an artist you might like—it was a real person instead. It was word of mouth from a buddy.

I remember this guy Steve Slaven who lived in my dad's neighborhood. He was the one that first turned me on to Bowie. He also turned me on to Alice Cooper, and eventually to Jethro Tull's *Aqualung* record. The few records I had were basically purchased because of suggestions from friends. At this point, I think I owned the first live Grand Funk record. I also had their *We're an American Band* album. I had Deep Purple's *Machine Head*. I had the Jimmy Hendrix *Are You Experienced?* album. I had only one Led Zeppelin record—*IV*, with "Stairway to Heaven" on it.

If I wasn't picking up new music from friends, it would be from a jukebox wherever I was hanging out. Sometimes it would be standard songs like an oldie from Chubby Checker, who grew up locally in South Philadelphia, or a rock-and-roll number like Three Dog Night's "Mama Told Me Not to Come," or "American Woman" by The Guess Who. If I heard it and liked it, I bought it!

Once, I walked into a store when someone was playing some new rock song on a jukebox, and I asked, "Who's this?"

"Oh, it's Creedence Clearwater Revival."

"Oh, fuck, this is great!" I was blown away. I had heard some of their stuff from Birdman but didn't realize it was Creedence. I was sold!

It was their song "Travelin' Band," which was actually one of the songs we did in my bands that played mall openings, beer parties, and prom dances. And so, it was just all word of mouth. A buddy would go, "Check out this record I got. It's by this band called Mountain," and you'd hear and fall in love with "Mississippi Queen" or "Nantucket Sleighride."

In my neighborhoods, it was next to impossible to come across stores or newsstands that sold *Hit Parader*, *Creem*, or *Rolling Stone* magazines, so I only knew what bands looked like from their album packaging and cover art.

One of my friends bought the Kiss *Alive!* record and when I saw it, I was like, "Holy shit! Look at these guys on the cover. Fuck, what are these guys about?" Then we just sat and listened to the whole double album. I soon went and got my own copy of it. I didn't even know they had put out three records before that one.

I lost my guitarist Ricky Stevenson somewhere along the way; I think he got arrested for being AWOL from the Marines and got himself into trouble. He had become extremely difficult and volatile to work with around that time, so I didn't care much anyway. I kept jamming with our drummer Bobby Clarke, and we tried to put a new band together.

One day I was sitting with Bobby as we tried out a guitarist named Tom. As we sat outside Tom's house, I picked up one of Bobby's drumsticks and was tapping it as we chatted, just fiddling, before I leaned back against a brick wall and tilted my head up. As I looked toward the sky, I noticed that higher up the wall there was one brick jutting out from the rest of them all, by about three inches. It must have presented as some sort of challenge to me, because I suddenly decided to leap up and tap the front of that brick.

Unfortunately, as I extended my left hand upward, I misjudged my motion, and the plastic tip of the drumstick that my hand was also holding, hit underneath the brick that jutted out. From the force of my body's upward spring for maximum height, the fucking drumstick impaled my palm—it went right fucking through my hand!

Crashing to the ground, I looked at the drumstick going into my palm and turned my hand to also see it coming out the other side. The sight made me light-headed, but I put my hand out toward Bobby—who pulled out the drumstick, doing even more damage to all the surrounding muscles and tendons. That's when I passed out.

I got taken to hospital where they extracted fragments of wood from my wound and cleaned it out. They wanted to stitch it (as much as I refused) and my hand remained bandaged for a good deal of time afterward. Even after I no longer needed the dressing, it hurt to even attempt to play guitar for quite a while. At least I got to joke with friends by telling them, "My initials are JC, and now I've got a hole through one of my palms, so I must be the messiah."

That injury is the reason why to this day, I'm unable to play guitar for a really long time, as my ring finger and pinkie on my fretting hand can lock-up from fatigue. It also prevents me from doing Eddie Van Halen-style hammer-ons properly, as I have to do them with my index and middle fingers instead, if ever I need to play them.

Another day as we walked down the street, Bobby told me about this kid named Chris Pisano who played great fucking guitar. He lived on Cornwall Street, right around the corner from Bobby in my dad's neighborhood, so we decided to visit his place. I'd never met him before and had no idea who he was.

As Bobby and I walked up to his house, this guy with long black hair was sitting on his step with a guitar. Bobby introduced me to Chris, and we started bullshitting. Then he started playing and, holy fuck, the guy was leaps and bounds ahead of anyone else I'd seen play; he was amazing on guitar. He was literally playing the solo in "Stairway to Heaven" note-for-note; crazy shit like "Highway Star" note-for-note. It was pretty impressive for a fifteen- or sixteen-year-old, about the same age as me.

He said he had a band, and they were rehearsing that night at his house, so I was welcome to come back later, which I did. Chris was on guitar, he had a singer named Noni Diaz, I think the drummer was Joe Cherico, and the bass player's name was Richie Wisniewski. They started playing, and I was blown away. They played Deep Purple, Jethro Tull, and all this other great stuff, nailing it note-for-note, or at least that's what it sounded like to my ear at the time.

I thought they were fucking great so I just kind of hung around them. Bobby and I kept trying to put something together, but each guitar player would be a fucking space cadet, or we'd get into an argument about whatever and things would fall apart.

Finally, after about a year of watching Chris play, Noni (the singer) bailed because his girlfriend Dori was having a baby, so I wound up hanging and jamming with Chris a lot more. He was actually the one that turned me on to the Kiss *Alive!* record. He also turned me on to Aerosmith *Get Your Wings*—life-changing stuff.

One day, the oldest Dugan boy, Micky, and a few of his friends from the Fishtown area came over to me and said, "Hey, Mouse, take these shopping carts up to the salvage place and see how much money you can get for this copper tubing."

They had about six carts of it, and the salvage place was only like two blocks away. I went up with one cart, and said, "Hey, guys, I got some copper tubing here. Can you tell me how much?"

They were like, "Yeah, bring it all up and we'll price it by the pound." I left the first cart with them, walked back to get the next one, and kept doing that. When I finally pushed the last cart up there, there were all these cops just sitting there, waiting for me.

The cops started asking me where I got it. I immediately knew something was wrong but I wouldn't rat anybody out, so I said, "I found it. There were just a bunch of shopping carts sitting there down at Front and Lehigh Avenue. There were like six of them, you know, carts. They were just sitting there." Obviously, I was a nervous blathering idiot again, trying to explain my way out of a stupid situation.

The cops asked, "Nobody gave you these?"

"No, they were just sitting in the street, and I just saw them; they were just sitting there. I sat there with them for like an hour, and nobody showed up. So I brought them here."

The police took me to jail. My friends saw me get arrested, so they bailed and left me hanging. At the station, they told me that somebody (my friends) went into an empty house, shut the water off, ripped the walls out of the house, then ripped all the copper tubing out of the place, cut it up, and stuck it in those fucking shopping carts. Me, being a dumbass, I went to go cash it in for them.

I kept telling the police that I didn't steal it, I just found that shit. I got charged with breaking and entering, and vandalism and theft. I got fingerprinted and then had to go to court. My mother was incredibly pissed at the whole ordeal, because it was another day of missed work thanks to yours truly, and she refused to help, due to my stupidity, hoping it would scare me.

I couldn't afford a lawyer, so I had a public defender. The judge looked at me, and he said, "So, is this the story you're sticking with?"

I said, "There's nothing to stick with, your Honor. The carts were honestly just sitting in the street. I sat there and watched them for like an hour. Nobody came and claimed them, so I took them up to the salvage place for cash."

The judge then turned to the cops, and he said, "Do you have anybody that saw this boy go into that house and rip the copper tubing out?"

They said, "No, but he showed up with the pipes."

The judge said, "Yeah, but that's not what I asked you. Do you know for a fact that he was in the house and took the pipes?"

When they said no, the judge dismissed the charges against me. Thank fucking God!

My mom didn't know what to do with me. She was talking to Aunt Millie about my latest incident, on top of all the others—you'll recall Aunt Millie was the one who busted me on the garage roof with the Molotov's—so she suggested having a chat with her brother next time he came around, who I called Uncle Gene Brennan. Mom filled him in on the situation, and he said, "Let me talk with him."

Uncle Gene always drove a brand-new Cadillac. He even had a phone in his car—in the seventies! The day after my grandmother passed away from her hip issues and complications from drinking, Uncle Gene drove down our street and motioned for me to come over to his car. We exchanged the normal pleasantries, and he expressed his condolences about Grandmom's death. After a nice, long dissertation about "growing up" and "getting your shit together," Uncle Gene asked me if I wanted a job. He said he needed someone to clean up his office a couple of times a week after school and do odd jobs. So I started working part-time for him a couple of days a week. It was funny though: I don't think Uncle Gene or a couple of his employees totally trusted me. He would intentionally leave money around. Nothing crazy: fifteen or twenty bucks here and there. He wanted to see if I could be trusted, so he would leave it in odd places to see if it would still be there the next day. I never took the bait—never touched a penny!

One woman, Rita Kinney, who I knew from Silver Street, actually freaked out when I walked into Gene's place the first day. She ran into his office yelling, "Do you know who that is? That's that little son of a bitch Corabi! You can't hire him. He'll rob you blind!" And oddly enough I proved myself to Rita, too, and she turned out to be like a surrogate mom and one of the nicest ladies I'd ever met.

My job in the beginning consisted of going through his office to clean and polish all the desks, take the trash outside to the dumpster, vacuum the floors, and clean the windows—just basic shit.

Since Uncle Gene paid me for the work, I started having money to buy more records and go to concerts. If he was available, Uncle Gene would come pick me and Chris Pisano up and drive us to these shows. We didn't mind because we always loved a ride in his Cadillac.

He took us down to see my first concert ever. It was Bachman-Turner Overdrive headlining the Convention Hall in Philadelphia. The band right before them was called Wet Willie, who had a hit "Keep On Smiling," and the first act to play was some guy who I eventually figured out much later was Bob Seger & the Silver Bullet Band.

I then saw Queen at a place called the Tower Theater early in 1976. It was just after they started their *A Night at The Opera* US Tour. The show opened with a short, taped intro of the best bit of their new song "Bohemian Rhapsody" before they appeared on stage for "Ogre Battle."

The third concert I saw was a few months later when Kiss came to town on the *Alive!* Tour. It was at the same place I saw BTO, the Civic Centre complex. Fuck, it was fun; it was sick! We were all like holy fuck, these fucking guys are insane!

They were so fucking loud. The lights, the smoke, the smoking guitar, the whole bit. They opened with "Deuce" and ended with "Let Me Go, Rock 'n' Roll." And that's really how I felt about life at that moment: stop fucking holding me back and let me go rock-and-roll all night and party every day.

Shortly after that, I was more of a Kiss fan than Chris. He got me into them from that *Alive!* record, but he was in and out of Kiss really quickly. I bought all their albums when they came out: *Destroyer*, and *Rock and Roll Over* after that, *Love Gun*, and then I had Ace's solo record.

Chris was always a little bit more musically advanced than I was, and he started listening to shit like that Kansas song "Carry on Wayward Son," the band Yes, stuff like John McLaughlin and the Mahavishnu Orchestra—stuff he felt was more credible, like Zeppelin and Aerosmith's *Toys in the Attic*. He would play me shit, and I'd be like oh yeah, this is great...but I still like Kiss, too!

Chris and I put his old band back together, and we would just jam stuff like Cheap Trick, Zeppelin, Rainbow, Aerosmith...whatever was happening around that time. We tried to get into the club scene, even though we weren't old enough to play a lot of the places. At this point, we were jamming almost nightly in Chris's mom's basement, and everybody was starting to dig a lot of the music we were playing, so we were getting cheesy little gigs at the neighborhood VFW posts and stuff like that. We had bigger plans of getting into the huge cover circuit in the clubs around Philadelphia, New Jersey, New York, and Delaware, though.

Uncle Gene really helped us out by buying us our own PA, and he rented an old theater in Kensington for us to rehearse in sometimes. We thought we were King Shit at this point. I don't even remember if we had a band name, although King Shit in hindsight would have been a good one.

I remember finally doing one gig in a club, when they had an open mic night of sorts. It was basically a deal where you played for free, and if you got a decent reaction from the crowd, they would bring you back for a proper paying gig—a "prove it to me" gig. Uncle Gene took us to the club, and Chris's big brother, Bob, helped us with our sound. Since we were all underage, we weren't allowed in the club until we walked on stage. It probably made it feel like more of a grand entrance for us before we played our covers of the aforementioned Cheap Trick, Aerosmith, Zeppelin, and other great rock shit of the time. Unfortunately, Bob got shitfaced waiting for the gig to begin, and we went down in a hail of feedback and excessive volume, so we were never invited back again.

At this point, I had done my time and graduated from Stetson Junior High School and was going to Frankford High School…well, some of the time. I didn't even want to go to school anymore. I just wanted to be a rock star.

I got in trouble several times at that school for truancy. I think I only went there for two of the nine months. I was out of school all the time, and I was complaining to my mom, "I don't want to go to school. I fucking hate it. I already have a part-time job."

It got so bad that Uncle Gene would have to pick me up from my house, drive me to school, and watch me walk in. I thought I was slick and started walking in the front door, and out the back, but my counselor Mr. Bell called my mother again to report I was still truant.

That's when Uncle Gene drove me to school and had an ex-football player friend Ray Barrett stand guard at the back door to make sure I wasn't splitting from classes. That worked, but only briefly.

I was constantly busting my mom's balls about wanting to quit school, but she wasn't having it. I just wanted to work and be a "rock star."

My hair was getting longer, and I had this long, straight, nondescript, head of hair going on, down past my shoulders, but I wanted something cool, something rock star-ish! So, I walked into an old ladies' hair salon around the corner from my house with two photos: one each of Roger Daltrey and Robert Plant. I handed them to the perplexed, sixty-plus-year-old woman, and said, "I want this kind of hair," so she gave me the worst, smelliest, perm ever—I thought it looked great!

I was now rocking my new hairdo and skin-tight rock T-shirts and a faded, girl's denim jacket to school with some kind of crazy turquoise rings and jewelry. I had a guitar with me all the time, even in school. I sat out in the yard during lunch break, and sometimes when I should've been in class, and played guitar. I was stoned probably seventy-five percent of the time, too! I just didn't give a fuck about school at all. It was a waste of my time as I saw it, and I was totally ready to quit.

One morning that I actually went to school, I walked into my tenth-grade homeroom class and saw that somebody had used magic markers to draw all these band logos on the white walls. They did the Zeppelin logo on the wall. They did the Aerosmith "A" with wings; they did the logo that the band Yes had back in the seventies. They wrote Wishbone Ash, Black Oak Arkansas, and more.

I sat down at my desk and our homeroom teacher walked in soon after me. He looked at the class, looked at the wall, and calmly said, "Mr. Corabi, go to the principal's office." I was suspended, no questions asked, on the spot. They just assumed that I wrote all that shit on the wall, which to my grave, I swear to God I didn't do.

I got into trouble with my mom and Uncle Gene for being suspended and decided on a whim to run away. Maybe that Aerosmith logo with wings was a sign that I needed to fly away and be free to do what I wanted. I knew Aerosmith was from Boston, so I decided that's where I would go. What's more, I thought I'd just go and hang out with Aerosmith up there, convinced that they'd replace their guitarist Brad Whitford with me since I was so awesome and cool-looking with my perm. So I packed a little bag, grabbed my guitar in its case, climbed out my window, and headed to the train station, where I bought a one-way ticket for my six-hour trip to Boston.

After traveling all day, the train pulled into Boston South Station, and I thought I'd then just bump into someone who would tell me where Aerosmith lived, but that didn't eventuate as I wandered the city streets late into the evening. As much as I was constantly looking, I didn't run into Steven Tyler or Joe Perry either (and it didn't even dawn on me that they may have been away on their *Toys in the Attic* Tour.) I crashed on a park bench and some guys soon tried to steal my guitar from me, so I moved to a little nook in an alley to sleep for the rest of the night.

The next morning, with no idea how I would actually find Aerosmith in this unfamiliar city of more than three million people, my teenage brain realized I had chewed off more than I had bargained for. I decided to head back home, but I didn't have enough money to buy a train ticket all the way back to Philly again, only a quarter of the way there. I ended up hitchhiking the rest of the way down through Yonkers and the Bronx.

On the way back in between rides, I got chased by a bunch of kids before I decided to sleep on the side of the freeway, inconspicuous in some long grass. So nervous about someone stealing my guitar, I took my belt off and relooped it back through the loops in my jeans and through the carry handle of my guitar case—I didn't realize they could have just opened the case and taken the guitar anyway.

When my last hitched ride finally dropped me home, I got out of the car to see my mom crying. She hugged me before kicking the shit out of me. I found myself in more trouble than when I had left, and I never did get to join Aerosmith!

Funnily enough, years later while still in Philadelphia, as I was riding on public transportation to go to work, I ran into this guy Bill Cowie that was in that homeroom class with me. Bill finally fessed up to drawing all those band logos on the homeroom walls. He said he watched the whole thing go down and never said a word. He was a stoner guy, so he pulled out a peace offering, and we smoked a joint together on the fucking subway and laughed about it.

Another day I was in math class and there was a girl in the class that I had a big crush on named Robin. She came into class that day wearing a pair of hip-hugger jeans and a tube-top that she was filling out quite nicely. I don't exactly know what started it, but Robin dropped a pencil or something, and she bent down to pick it up off the floor. When she stood up, my grumpy, arrogant, piece-of-shit math teacher Mr. Sterm fucking humiliated her about the way she was dressed. He called her a slut, which stunned the entire classroom, and I wasn't having it.

I said, "Fuck off. Why don't you leave her alone?"

He said, "Excuse me?"

I said, "You fucking heard every word I said. What the fuck? She's dressed just fine."

He came over and grabbed me by my shirt, and he fucking dragged me to Mr. Bell, the disciplinarian's office. Robin followed suit.

I was suspended for a week for that one. Sitting there, though, I said to the principal and the teacher, "You can suspend me all you want, but I'm telling you right now, if her mother finds out, and she will, that he called her a fucking slut in front of all the people in class, you're going to have a problem. I'm telling you that right now."

The principal looked at Robin and asked, "Did he call you a slut?" She said yes, so he fucking reprimanded the teacher as well but still suspended me because I was ready to kick that prick's ass, even though I was all of maybe five foot five.

They must have gotten tired of me causing trouble on the days that I was there, because it wasn't long after that they said they had decided they were transferring me out of the school. They explained, "We found that you don't even live in this school zone's district. You live in the Kensington District of Philadelphia, so now you're going to go to Edison High School."

Edison was basically an all-black school. Eighty percent African American, ten percent Caucasian, ten percent Latino, and one hundred percent in a neighborhood I didn't dare walk through. The year before, as rumor or urban legend would have it, students hung a white kid from a flagpole. So, I said, "I ain't going there, that's a fucking death-wish. I ain't going, you can kiss my ass."

I told my mom, "They just helped me make the decision: I quit school. Sign the fucking papers, I quit."

She always said, "If you don't go to school, you have to have a job."

I already had a part-time job, so I talked to Uncle Gene, and asked, "Hey, if I quit school can I work full-time for you?" He talked with my mom, sorted it out, and they agreed, so I went to work with my uncle full-time.

When they talked, my mom also actually told him that she couldn't handle me, and I was driving her crazy. I was still getting into trouble, coming home late at night, and just being a total fuck-up when I wasn't rehearsing with my band, and she was sick of cops coming to the house. My uncle said he'd take me in, so I went and lived with Uncle Gene. He was a parental figure in my life and in later years he said I became like a son to him. He tried to instill respect in me, not only for my family, but also for myself. He told me it's just as easy to be a good guy as it is to be a bad guy, as he took me under his wing more and tried to get me on a better path in life.

Living with my uncle, I had no bills to pay, and now that I was working full-time at sixteen years of age, I was making three hundred bucks a week. I was putting all the money in the bank to buy a car.

I looked at cars with my uncle and there was a Chevy Nova Super Sport that I wanted. It was 4,300 bucks. It was also much cheaper than the Corvette,

Camaro, and Datsun 260Z that I initially had my eyes on. My uncle made a deal with me. He said, "I'll tell you what: you put half down, I'll give you the other half. We'll put it in the company name, so you get a better insurance rate on it; it'll be listed as a company car, but it's your car."

I basically saved up every fucking penny I had and came up with like two thousand down and financed the rest on my own, with Uncle Gene as a cosigner. I had wheels!

While I was saving for my car, though, I had to learn how to drive, and Uncle Gene taught me. He was a fucking psycho about it, though. He took me to a Kmart department store in Bucks County, when it was closed, so there were no cars in the big parking lot. I sat behind the wheel of his beautiful Cadillac, and I started slowly driving around the lot. Everything had to be so precise and perfect with Uncle Gene; he was like the husband in the movie *Sleeping with the Enemy*. He was so fucking anal and obsessively controlling about everything.

As I was driving, I literally took my hand off the wheel for a second. Instead of calmly reminding me to keep my hands on the wheel, he'd scream at me, "Get your fucking hands on the wheel!"

Everything with him was on eleven, just screaming, yelling, and temper tantrums. After a while, I pulled the car over and just told him to go fuck himself. "Fuck it, I'll just take public transportation. I don't need to drive this bad."

It was brutal having him try to teach me how to drive. He constantly yelled and cursed, having a freak-out over every little thing he thought I was doing wrong. Once I finally passed my test, got my license, and had the money, though, I bought the Nova. My Chevy was a three-door hatchback in some weird seventies green color with tan interior—the whole shebang. It had air conditioning, power steering, an eight-cylinder engine, and was faster than shit, which almost got me killed on several occasions. My last bout of racing stupidity came when I tried to illegally pass a car on a two-lane country road. I was flying, and the car in front of me was holding me up. So, I gunned it and entered the other lane, right at a curve, and a hill. A car I couldn't see was coming the other way, which caused me to swerve back into my lane, and right off the side of the road. I came to a complete stop narrowly missing a huge tree, and it was right then and there, that I lit a cigarette, wiped my ass, and realized my racing days were over. The guy that I passed politely honked, and flipped me the bird. Slow and steady wins the race they say.

The Nova also had an eight-track player, and I had everything from John Denver to Aerosmith, Zeppelin, and Queen. I had music for every passenger and occasion. If Uncle Gene was in the car, I'd put on John Denver, Frank Sinatra, and sometimes Queen, who I turned Uncle Gene on to. If my bandmate Chris was in the car, it was a Kansas, Yes, Jeff Beck, or the Billy Cobham *Spectrum* album. Just driving by myself, I was listening to Aerosmith *Get Your Wings*, Kiss *Alive!*, and Black Sabbath's *Masters of Reality*. I really had a little bit of everything.

When I wasn't working, I was rehearsing most of the time with Chris, either at his house or at the theater we rented for rehearsals. Like mine, his parents also divorced years earlier, and his family was living "hand-to-mouth" as well. Chris had three older sisters—Dee, Mona, and Valerie—an older brother Bob, and a younger brother Orlando.

His sister Valerie was a year or so older than him (so two years older than me at eighteen), and already married and pregnant with her first child when I met her. Her husband Bobby Luther was a drummer in the neighborhood, who I also knew and admired, but he was also a really bad drug addict. They split up a couple of times prior to her baby being born, who she also named Valerie—Valerie Luther—but I have always called her Little Val. Right after she was born, her husband just went on some sort of a fucking meth binge, so she split with him for good and moved in with her mom for a while.

I never really paid her any attention, but one day we were rehearsing at Chris's place and Val came down the basement steps. It was the first time I'd seen her after she had the baby. She was wearing the tightest, shortest pair of shorts with sandal wedge shoes, and an off-the-shoulder, brownish-reddish glitter top.

Her mom was watching the baby, and she was going out with her girlfriends to a club to see a band. I can still see her in my mind walking down those steps and then out the door. I was like, "Holy shit, she's fucking hot!" She was this kind of glammy, Studio 54, hippy chick, but I let it go, as I thought I didn't stand a snowball's chance in Hell with her, much to the delight of her brother Chris, who obviously noticed my interest in his sister.

I was there most days hanging out and goofing off with Chris and didn't think Val had any interest in me, but I still got a little tingly every time she walked into the room. I think about a year had passed before Val and I actually started really chatting. She started watching us rehearse, which was happening three or four times a week. I was singing my ass off and playing guitar. I was making more money from working hard, and now had another brand-new 1978 Monte Carlo to show for it, so things started to change. There was a couple of times where I bought a little stuffed animal or some other gift for Little Val, for no other reason than to just see the kid smile. Suddenly, Val started taking notice of me.

The more I talked with her, my crush on her got a little stronger. It seemed to me she was way more advanced about things than me, with clothing, makeup, music, and just life in general. I think she told one of her friends that she thought I was really cute, too.

We started flirting with each other, and then one day while I was sitting on the front steps at Chris's house, Val came out and sat down behind me on the next step up with her legs on either side of me. She was wearing denim shorts, and I was just sitting there leaning back with my elbows on her knees. I turned around to face her as we were talking about something, when one of our mutual friends Helen said, "Just do it. Just fucking kiss him." So we kissed for the first time.

Due to all the trouble I had gotten into up to this point in my life, my uncle was really tough with me. He would be adamant with me about following the rules, and bark at me constantly, "Be home by midnight. Be home by one. Be home by 12:30." He was super strict, but in hindsight, I know that living with him and working with him was a positive influence that was badly needed in my life. He sure kept me on a tight leash, though.

The first time I saw Black Sabbath in concert, Uncle Gene drove me and picked me up. Afterward, he said, "Jesus Christ, you smell like weed!"

I replied, "Ya think?"

Pissing with laughter, we stared at the doors of The Spectrum for about ten minutes as fans emerged from the billows of smoke pouring out of the venue after the show. And in all probability, I had been smoking sweet leaf, so we made a deal: if I was going to a rock concert, I was never allowed to drive. He would drive me there, then come and pick me up at the precise time it was to end. Or I would take public transportation. Better safe than sorry, they say.

I talked to Uncle Gene and told him that I really liked Chris's sister Valerie. He invited her to the house for dinner and thought she was a sweetheart. I started dating Val, and it wasn't long before we went over to Gram Brennan's house for dinner and cards. I wasn't sure how this was going to end, as I had previously brought a few girls there that I had dated, and every one of those visits ended in a disaster. Somebody would make a snide or inappropriate comment that would abruptly end the evening, and usually the relationship, so I was on eggshells. We brought her daughter, Little Val, with us and to my surprise everybody fell in love with Little Val and thought my new girlfriend was a sweet girl.

A few months later, I took Val to my dad's side of the family for my grandmother's seventieth birthday. Unfortunately, being a divorced woman with a kid is a fucking no-no with old school, hardcore Italian Roman Catholics.

I didn't hear it, but while Val was ordering a glass of wine at the bar, she overheard one of my uncles or cousins say, "Puttana." She then started telling me that she wanted to go; she wanted to go home, now!

As I was driving her home, she told me, "Your uncle called me a whore."

I was fucking livid. "Motherfucker! Are you fucking kidding me?" What the fuck is wrong with my family? [Cue the Whitesnake song "Here I Go Again."]

After dropping Val off, I immediately went back to the party. I walked back into the room where my dad was sitting with all my aunts and uncles. I said, "Get a good look at my face: you will never fucking see this face again. You insulted my girlfriend; you embarrassed me. The next time you see me, she'll be my wife."

I then fucking walked out and didn't talk to any of them at all for a couple of years. I was done with everybody's judgmental bullshit.

Valerie finally got her own little second-story apartment in a brick row home on G Street, right around the corner from where she was living with her mom. One day she asked, "What's with your uncle, why is he so strict with you?"

I opened up to her about some of my days huffing, smoking weed, drinking, and getting into trouble with the law. She said, "I'd really love it if you could stay over sometime."

I called Uncle Gene and told him I wanted to stay over at Val's and there wasn't going to be any drugs or anything like that. He said, "Okay. Just keep your fucking nose clean."

Val and I went out for dinner and then went back to her house. We made arrangements for Little Val to stay at Val's mother's house, so we were finally alone. No friends, kids, brothers, or bandmates to bug us. Next thing you know, we had smoked the biggest joint, and some opium, and we took a half a Quaalude each.

We started listening to Led Zeppelin's *The Song Remains the Same* on a red velvet bedspread she laid out on the floor in front of the stereo. A bunch of candles were burning, as well as some incense. We started taking our clothes off and making out, and it didn't take long before we were actually going at it. We had both waited for way too fucking long for this to happen, and the anticipation was almost painful! We literally fucked through side one and three of the records, and then stopped for a second, so Val could turn them over, and we continued fucking through sides two and four. It was "Rock and Roll," "Celebration Day," "The Song Remains the Same," "The Rain Song," "No Quarter," and "Stairway to Heaven." Then flipped for "Dazed and Confused," "Moby Dick," and "Whole Lotta Love." I think we fucked the first time for almost two hours!

I finally had my first real sexual experience with Val. I remember thinking, "Oh, that's what this thing between my legs is for." I had been so close with other girls, but for one reason or another never quite closed the deal. I remember Val getting the most devilish look on her face when I told her it was my first time. She was stunned but turned on even more! I was all-in (and now all the way in, per se), totally smitten, and it didn't take long before I was convinced that I was going to marry her. From that point, we became inseparable…until I joined Mötley fücking Crüe.

5
Nobody's Fault

A lot of the friends that I had hung out with either died or went to jail. A kid, Poye, that I used to hang out with on Franklin Street wrapped his car around a pole or a tree when he was in his teens. He was drinking, driving, and speeding.

I had two other older friends who got high on something and tried to rob a sporting goods store. The owner caught them in the act, and they beat him to death with baseball bats. They're in prison for life, and unfortunately the motivation behind the entire incident was to get some cash for dope. So many lives were wasted that day.

For most of us, though, we just went in completely different directions, or chose different paths, which I was fine with, especially as I got older and really started figuring things out. It was strange sometimes going back and visiting my mother and seeing a lot of the guys still doing the same shit and still getting into scrapes with the law. They always treated me great, but I felt like a lot of their lives had been wasted because of choices THEY made.

It's weird to describe my childhood now in hindsight. It started playing with GI Joe's on my front lawn, swimming, playing ball, and riding bikes with friends—just an average life. Then I discovered the hippie movement and wanted to be like everybody else on the street corner. I tried some drugs and got troublesome while growing my hair out and trying to play my music. But I grew up and out of all the negative shit and watched as friends dropped like flies.

I now see that Led Zeppelin had the biggest musical influence on me in the seventies. They are one of my all-time favorite bands. Robert Plant was a fucking God; everybody in that whole band was on some other higher level musically. Back then, too, there was a mystique and mysticism about Zeppelin that I loved.

I now had their *Led Zeppelin*, *Led Zeppelin II*, *III*, and *IV*, *Houses of the Holy*, and *Physical Graffiti* records. One of my biggest regrets, though, is that I never got to see them play live. They played The Spectrum and JFK stadium in Philly multiple times between '69 and '75, but every time the fucking tickets went on sale, I was either too young to go, unable to get out of school in time, or tickets for their entire tour would sell-out in a matter of minutes. Twice, later in Zep's career, I was finally able to get tickets, but they canceled both tours, due to the death of Robert Plant's son Karac, and then the death of John Bonham during rehearsals for the *In Through The Out Door* Tour.

In the summer of '85, the three remaining members played *Live Aid* in Philadelphia. Even though their drummer John Bonham had died nearly five years earlier, it was the hot news in Philadelphia that Jimmy Page, Robert Plant, and John Paul Jones were in town rehearsing, with a then-unknown drummer, and they were going to play. The 100,000 tickets sold out in a matter of fucking hours, and I had missed my last chance to see them again.

A lot of people have asked me over the years who my singing influences were. The two singers that I got into most at that stage of my life were Robert Plant and Steven Tyler, to the point where I would literally sit and listen to them, and I could mimic them. Like uncannily, every little nuance and crack and scream and whatever. Chris and I were playing "Nobody's Fault" by Led Zeppelin, and we were also doing "Nobody's Fault" by Aerosmith.

Val had a huge record collection and turned me onto a lot of great music I had never heard before—bands like Nazareth, Humble Pie, the Sweet, Detective, and Starz. I knew of David Bowie from the *Ziggy Stardust* record and used to wear his T-shirt to school, but I didn't know any of his other records. She started turning me on to deeper shit like *Hunky Dory*, *The Man Who Sold the World*, *Aladdin Sane*, and *Diamond Dogs*.

She saw Bowie at The Tower Theater live back in the day, and Alice Cooper. Again, I knew of Alice Cooper's album *School's Out*, but Val said, "Oh my God! Have you ever heard 'Cold Ethyl'?" She played me his other shit like *Billion Dollar Babies* and *Welcome to My Nightmare*, and it was awesome.

Val found me skin-tight shirts with a lace-up front and bell sleeves, like Steven Tyler and Ronnie James Dio wore. She got me my first pair of tie-up-front jeans, too. She'd say things like, "Let's put some eyeliner on you when you go play, and put some black nail polish on you, like how Freddie Mercury does on his left hand."

To some degree, she was a muse for me at the time. She was like what Angela Bowie was to David Bowie. She was like Kate Hudson in the movie *Almost Famous*—just like her free-spirited character Penny Lane. She actually came up with pet rock star names for the both of us as well: she was "Sparkle Plenty," and I was going to become famous as "Ian Hayes."

The names came about from her affinity of glitter clothing and make-up, and mine came from a combination of a few things. My uncle had an old Irish cleaning lady named Mary McCarthy for the longest time, who came to the house to clean and cook for us. For some apparent reason she never once called me John; she always referred to me as Ian. Val stayed with me one night and in the morning, I introduced her to Mary. When she heard Mary call me Ian, she immediately thought that should be my moniker on stage. So the plan was for me to change my name to Ian, and as for my last name, take my mother's maiden name of Hayes. We both thought it had a cooler British rock star ring to it. "Ladies and gentlemen: Ian Hayes!"

I was learning a lot from Val, and we both had huge aspirations of Zeppelin-esque rock royalty! And she would eventually introduce me to a few of my future bandmates as well, when the time came for me to call it quits with the band I had with her brother Chris.

I already told you about my drug experience with Birdman when I was younger, but there were a few other things that also kind of soured me with some drugs, or made me leery, I should say. This is one of those incidents that freaked me out quite a bit.

Valerie had a really cool, hip uncle named Donnie who lived in New York City, where he and his roommate John were starting a business as artisans with stained glass. We went to their place a few times for weekends to shop for stage clothing, hang out with them, listen to music, smoke weed, and just take in a little of The Big Apple. Donnie called us one night and told us that as they were working on a new piece and rushing to get it finished on time, John went out and bought some cocaine, unbeknownst to Donny. Once back at their place, he kept going into the bathroom and snorting lines of the blow.

Donnie told us he was working when he heard a thud on the floor, so he tried to go into the bathroom, but the door was locked. After eventually managing to kick it in, he saw John was lying on the floor—he had done so much cocaine over a day or two that his heart exploded, and he fucking dropped dead. It immediately took me back to Birdman, and I wondered if his heart had exploded, too. I realized later that heroin and cocaine have very different effects on you, but I definitely didn't like the outcome of either.

I wasn't a saint though, I did experiment with drugs a little bit: I tried acid a couple of times, and I didn't really care for it. I had a couple of little hits of opium with Val, and it was okay. There were a few times at parties, where I took a hit off a joint being passed that had some opium in it. I just sat back and listened to music and that was that. I never wanted to get into a habitual, everyday kind of bullshit thing with drugs. I was always paranoid about all drugs, even though I tried a few. And after what Val went through with her ex, she was extremely cautious as well.

To me, there's a huge difference between smoking weed and snorting and shooting shit into your body. I never did any of that shit, since I was afraid of it. I always felt like I'd be the guy who would try it that ONE time and my heart would fucking explode. Maybe I'm a bit neurotic but I just never got into the whole drug scene. I have always associated drugs with assholes, dependency, and death.

Weed is different, though. It always relaxes me, but even with that I never did large quantities. It was always only a joint shared here and there, or a couple of hits off a joint to chill after a show, while watching a movie. There were times when I would sit down with say Tommy Lee and take a couple of hits off a joint and have a cocktail, then we would write a song together, like "Babykills." I do still smoke weed occasionally, but only if I'm tense and want to go to sleep, or I might smoke a joint at a party or barbecue with a couple of buddies.

When I started working full-time for Uncle Gene, I was not only cleaning the office, but I would go get people their lunch, and do other menial, bullshit stuff. The longer I was there, the more reliable I became, so he promoted me to help him with his bowling tournament business.

Now, let me give you a little backstory on how he got started in business. Uncle Gene was one of those guys who could sell ice to an Eskimo. He had the uncanny knack of being able to size people up and tell them exactly what they wanted to hear, with every word of his pitch spoken perfectly. Basically, he was a guy that would tell you how great you looked, tell you a joke, offer you a cigar, sit down and smoke it with you, and convince you that you were blowing a great business opportunity if you didn't write him that huge check right now! He always said, "A great businessman always plays with the other guys' money."

When he was younger, he used to work at a bowling alley, and he had this genius idea for a bowling tournament like nobody had ever seen before. He approached a local brewing company in Philadelphia called Schmidt's Beer. Even though he only had a very basic outline of his concept, he walked into Schmidt's and pitched them the idea. He said, "I'm going to put a national bowling tournament together with you; it's going to be the biggest in the United States. There'll be a team tournament with five people on each team, and a doubles tournament with two people on each team." The enrollment fee for a five-member team to bowl in his tournament was one hundred dollars total, or twenty bucks per person—good money in the 1970s. The doubles tournament was a forty-dollar enrollment fee, again twenty per person.

When the people at Schmidt's asked what prizes the winners would receive, off-the-cuff he blurted out, "Five brand-new Cadillacs for first place, and second place gets five brand-new Chevy Impalas." Even though he just literally threw it out there, they were like holy shit!

He also piqued their interest in his concept because if you watch any bowling on TV or tried bowling yourself, you know there is obviously some skill involved, but for the most part, bowling is throwing a ball down an alley, knocking over some pins, then going back and drinking your ice-cold beer before your next throw. So they realized this was a ton of great advertising! Schmidt's literally wrote him a check that week for a quarter of a million dollars.

He went out and bought a Cadillac for himself with a phone in it. You see, from the time I was a kid, he always told me, "If you want people to think you're serious and you want people to think that you're successful, then you need to dress like a millionaire and need to show up in style. If they see you pull up in a badass suit in a brand-new Cadillac, they'll think you're doing something right and everybody's going to be drawn to you." This was something that was restated to me by my dear friend Fred Coury from Cinderella years later.

So, that's what he did. He went out with that check and bought a brand-new Cadillac, and had a phone put in it back in the days when the fucking battery took up half the trunk. Then he went to Willow Grove Park Bowling Lanes, which had 116 lanes and was then the largest bowling alley in the world, from the time it was built in 1961 as part of the larger Willow Grove Amusement Park, located right outside of Philadelphia.

Uncle Gene met with the Hankin brothers, the two multimillionaires who owned it. He told them, "You have the biggest bowling alley in the world. I want to put on the biggest fucking bowling tournament in your bowling alley." They gave him the green light.

Then he went to General Motors and said, "I'm going to advertise and give you press all over the United States in every major magazine you can think of. I'm giving away five of your brand-new Cadillacs in my bowling tournament."

He went to Chevrolet and made the same pitch for five brand-new Impalas. Both car manufacturers gave him the green light and the cars at cost, and loaded them with every option you can think of.

He put this whole massive tournament together and advertised it in every fucking bowling magazine you can think of. He was off to the races and then charged the hundred bucks per team, per entry, to participate in the tournament over ten weekends. Teams came from all over the United States, and in most cases would enter the tournament multiple times each weekend. We had five matches on Saturdays and three on Sundays. Whichever team had the highest score tally after ten weeks was the winner, five brand-new Cadillacs for them. Second-highest team score got the Chevy Impalas, then third prize was like $25,000, fourth prize $12,500, fifth prize $6,250, and so on all the way down to the point where like the last hundred people got their hundred dollars back.

He did a similar thing with the doubles tournament, where first place was two Chevy Impalas, and then all cash prizes after that. Even though he paid out a lot, he made a fucking fortune on it!

He promoted me from cleaning trashcans to a job where I was helping to print his own press releases and newsletters. Every person who signed up to join his tournament had their address, phone number, all their information added to a mailing list. He had bought printing machines and was doing everything himself.

He had a then state-of-the-art machine that took his newsletters, put them into one end of the machine, and they would get folded. Then on the other end of the machine, we would put in a stack of empty envelopes, and the folded newsletters would get stuffed into the envelopes. We had another machine with plates stacked into one side of the machine. I would just slide the envelopes in, hit a pedal on the floor, and it would print an address and then move them to a mail cart. I did all of his mailing shit for him for like three or four years, until his bowling venture eventually got a little funky and went south.

As a late teen there, I went from making like three hundred bucks a week to making double that. When I wasn't rehearsing or playing in my band, I also worked a few weekends with him down at the bowling alley. Since I'd never had that sort of money before, I was enjoying buying some things I wanted, but was always stashing what I didn't need to spend in the bank as savings.

The band I had with Val's brother Chris was definitely well rehearsed, but all of the practice was getting us nowhere fast. We were rehearsing three or four times each week at either Chris's mom's house or the theater Gene rented for us—he was acting as our manager. At this point, we added my cousin Mark (a keyboard player) to the mix because bands like Queen, Styx, Foreigner, The Cars, and Journey were beginning to dominate radio, so we thought by adding keyboards it would make us more appealing to the booking agents. After all, we just wanted to play in all the big cover clubs in the area and appealing to the guys that book those clubs was our first hurdle. I was starting to go to a lot of clubs at this point in New Jersey to scout what all the other working bands were doing to get gigs. Plus, on Friday and Saturday evenings, it was a bit of a date night for Val and me. The clubs in New Jersey had a younger age restriction (eighteen) than Pennsylvania, so a lot of kids went there to watch bands and party with friends.

One summer, Val and her two girlfriends Helen and Patrice rented a house for the entire summer season in Wildwood, New Jersey, and we all spent every night there in the clubs, checking out the bands that had residencies. Val and I would drive down on Fridays and stay until Monday mornings, then go right home to work. It was only ninety minutes from Philly, so it wasn't a big deal. I really noticed that all the bands played a bit of everything because the club owners wanted people dancing. The more they danced, the more they drank! Simple theory, really.

I would go home and talk to Chris and say, "We need to play 'Just What I Needed' by The Cars, or 'My Sharona' by The Knack," and Chris wasn't having any of it. He thought that stuff was boring and trite. So, we started really arguing about everything. I just wanted to play in the clubs and make a living, and Chris wanted to do some Frank Zappa or Billy Cobham shit. I dug that stuff, too, but it wasn't something that people would dance to.

Then we got into a massive argument about playing "Honky Tonk Women." At this point, we weren't seeing eye-to-eye on anything. So Chris stormed out, I stormed out, and we decided to knock our band called Toyz on the head.

Val took me a few times to see a band called Money and during one of their breaks, introduced me to the bass player Dan Duffy. Money was one of the bigger bands on the circuit, but Danny was getting tired of the routine and wanted to branch out a bit on his own. It took him a little while, but he eventually left and started another band. I was still working with Uncle Gene, but had no musical outlet at this point other than nights out to see a band. This went on for months. I enjoyed not having the commitments of rehearsals with the guys after having done so for so long with no real payoff.

Val, Little Val, and I went up to a place in the Pocono Mountains with my family called Lily Lake for a couple of long weekend getaways. The family had been going to the lake for years in the summers, and at one point, Uncle Gene and his siblings had lived in the area before moving to Philly.

I remember one trip up there in particular, Uncle Gene suggested that if Val and I wanted to go out, he would watch Little Val, so the two of us got in my car and went to a drive-in theater to see *Dawn of the Dead*. During the movie, Val pulled out some weed and a pipe she had stashed down the front of her shorts, and we got baked in my car…and I mean BAKED! We got so high, that we probably spent the entire night running back and forth to the popcorn stand and missed most of the flick. When the movie was over, I started my car, put it in drive, and ripped the speaker right out of the pole next to my car.

We were pissing ourselves laughing on the way back to the cabin, when suddenly we drove around a curve on the two-lane road and I almost plowed into a massive bull that got out of his barbed wire pen. I had seen this beast in the past. Sometimes he would actually aggressively run along the fence line chasing cars, so by no means did I think I could get out and shoo him back into his pen. I sat there beeping, trying to get him off the road and out of our way, but he wasn't budging. We sat there for about forty minutes trying to figure out what to do before the farmer finally came out to assist. The owner said we could've just driven around him, but this thing was massive and took up most of the two lanes. I told the guy I would've slept there all night before I took that chance! He put him on a chain, and walked him right back to his pen, and Val and I drove off, with a hilarious story to tell Uncle Gene the next day.

On another trip up to Lily Lake, Val and I found out there was a huge concert happening at a place called Pocono Downs Racetrack in Wilkes-Barre. Pennsylvania Jam was an all-day event that August '79 with Blackfoot, Edgar Winter, Mahogany Rush, Henry Paul Band, the Scorpions, and Ted Nugent headlining. So we made arrangements with my family to watch Little Val, and we hopped in the car and took off to find the concert and hopefully purchase tickets.

Unfortunately, I didn't really know my way around the area, so we got sidetracked a couple of times, and with the concert traffic, it took us forever to get there. By the time we did get there, tickets were completely sold-out. So Val and I cruised around the venue and found a spot to park on the grass by the side of the road overlooking the track. We could see the stage from the hill, but it was about a half-mile away, negating any real view, so we just sat and listened to each band. There must have been 40,000 people there that day.

When Ted was finished, we got back in the car and started driving back to Lily Lake. We inched along because the traffic had let out, when I heard this beeping coming from behind me on my right. I looked in the mirror and a cop was escorting a couple of limos, so I moved over a bit to let them pass on the shoulder of the road. We watched the cop drive by, then the first limo, and when the second limo went by us, the back window rolled down. The car came to a halt and Uncle Ted Nugent stuck his head out the window, with a towel wrapped around it, and gave me and Val the thumbs-up sign. We freaked out!

We pulled out of the line, and got behind Ted's convoy, and followed them to a Holiday Inn hotel/motel. We sat in the parking lot for a bit, looking around for any of the band members, when a guy stepped out of the room, and we both immediately thought it was the Nuge!

I put my car in drive and burned across the parking lot, to say hello, but in my excitement, my foot slipped off the brake when I tried to stop, and I almost jumped the curb. In a panic, the guy jumped back, and I started yelling, "Sorry, sorry, sorry!"

Stepping up to my car, the longhaired gentleman took off his glasses, and I realized it was not Ted! So, like an idiot, I said, "Who are you?"

He replied, "Rickey Medlocke."

I did that blathering thing again because I was excited and confused (and I almost ran this guy over), so again, I put my foot in my mouth and said, "What band are you in?"

Being as polite as ever, he simply said, "Blackfoot." (He was the Southern rock band's front man, as their singer and guitarist.)

Then my mouth forgot to communicate with my brain, which left me blurting out a bunch of wrong shit about the band. I couldn't remember the name of their song radio was playing ("Highway Song"), I thought they were from New Jersey (but they're from Florida), and after thinking he was Ted, and after he TOLD me his name, I forgot it when he left and I called him Robert! I had a perfect average in stupidity, and felt as awkward as Chris Farley when he interviews Paul McCartney (see for yourself on YouTube). I said to Val, "Let's get out of here before I do anything idiotic again!"

Years later, I met Rickey again when I was in Ratt and he was playing in Lynyrd Skynyrd. Our bands did a show together, and I told him the story. We both had a nice chuckle at my expense.

Dan Duffy had finally put his band together, and they were playing under the moniker of Lover. We went to see them a few times, and in a round-a-bout sort of way became friends with his drummer Ray. Val's friend Patrice went with us to see them, and Ray took a liking to her, so they all came back to our apartment to party after a show one night. As it turned out, Ray had been at the club the one night Chris and I did that horrific, open mic thing, but he was impressed with my vocals and guitar playing. We chatted a bit about music, and I hung out with him a few more times, until him and Patrice got tired of each other.

About a month or so later, I got a phone call from Ray saying they had made some changes in the band, and he wanted me to come to a rehearsal to jam with them. I learned a few of the cover songs they did, and I went down totally prepared. The band was now Dan on bass, Ray on drums, a guy named Barry Debenedetta on guitar, and a singer named Tommy who had a great voice for stuff like Journey, Styx, The Babys, and Foreigner. They wanted me to play guitar, sing some backing vocals, and possibly sing a few lead vocals to give Tommy breaks.

They were usually doing four sets a night, five nights a week. I was up for anything! I just wanted to play music for a living. As it turned out, I got the gig, and we started doing a lot of shows and building a bit of a following.

One night, Lover was playing at a huge club in Pennsauken, New Jersey, called The Penalty Box. We finished our set and took a thirty-minute break, and when I walked out of the dressing room to go to the bar, a guy came up to me and said, "Hey, kid, tell Dan, Rick's here."

I said, "Yeah, sure," and went back into the dressing room, and relayed the message. Dan rushed out to the bar, and sat down and started chatting with this guy but was really discreet about it.

Right before we went back on, Dan said to me, "Before you go home tonight, I need to talk to you." I went back onstage, but the rest of the evening I kept thinking I was getting canned, or I did something stupid that Dan wasn't happy about. After the show, we packed up our personal belongings, and everybody split to go home, and I walked Dan to his car and lit a cigarette.

He proceeded to tell me that the guy Rick was Rick Caldwell, who had been in a huge local band called Squeeze, and another really popular band called Gangster. Apparently, Rick spoke to Dan about putting a new band together. He already had commitments from an agent named Freddy Baker and a manager named Larry Mazer. He wanted to do some covers, but he also had a bunch of recorded original songs that he wanted to drop into the sets throughout the night. He wanted Dan on bass, but after seeing our band, he decided he wanted me on lead vocals. Dan asked if I was interested, because he had already said yes and committed to Rick. I said, "FUCK YES," and couldn't wait to go home and tell Val, as she was a huge fan of both of Rick's previous bands.

After making a few phone calls, they recruited Anthony Riccobono on drums, who was also in Money with Dan, and was a monster drummer, but also an amazing singer as well. Then they found a guy named Brian McMahon, who was insane on the guitar. Next, Dan had the unfortunate job of calling Ray, Tommy, and Barry, and telling them we were leaving Lover.

Once that ugly detail was taken care of, we started rehearsing tunes. We all wanted to make good money, so our agent Freddy said we should do a tribute set to one of our favorite artists. That was the big thing then to make really good cash. After much deliberation, we narrowed it down to our two favorite bands, Led Zeppelin and Aerosmith, but could not decide on which band should be our specialty. We all just said fuck it and did them both. So, on Fridays and Saturdays, our new band Fragile would end with an entire set of Zeppelin one night, then the following night we would do a closing set of Aerosmith, and alternate accordingly. It went over great! We were doing Van Halen, Bad Company, Rainbow, Black Sabbath, and the best part was everybody sang, so the backing vocals were always stellar. Rick started bringing these great originals to the table, which we threw into the set, and were being received quite well.

At this point in my life, I was happier than a pig in shit. I was making really good money doing what I loved, and I was in a great band doing it. But I still wanted more.

The longer I was with Valerie, the more seriously I thought about marrying her. She wanted to takes things slower than me, though, since she had already been married. I was working a ton with the band, and Val would always come on the weekends to watch me play, and we truly had a blast, for the most part, riding high in that whole scene. We had been dating/living together for about two years at this point, and I was still turned on by her and thought I had the hottest girl in the room when she got dressed up for my shows.

I got to the point of really wanting to get her an engagement ring. I mentioned it to Uncle Gene, who said he had bought a diamond ring for a girl that he was going to marry, but they split up before he asked her, so he had this engagement ring just sitting around in his drawer. He said he would sell it to me and give me a really good price.

I proposed to Val and gave her the ring that I bought from Uncle Gene. Later, though, Val and I found on a fluke while having it cleaned that it wasn't even a real diamond; it was just a cubic zirconia. So, I ended up buying her another real engagement ring to wear.

Planning the wedding really frustrated the fuck out of me. My family was absolutely a pain in the ass as I tried to schedule it. I tried to pin Uncle Gene down with, "Hey, can you make it on this weekend?"

"Oh, well, I've got something going on then."

And then I tried to pin my dad down, whom I had long since reconciled with, and he was the same. A few other family members and friends were noncommittal, too, and it drove me fucking crazy! Finally, I just remember being pissed, and I just blew up and told everybody, "I don't give a fuck if any of you guys come or not. I'm getting married, and I'm tired of fucking trying to work my schedule around your schedule. This is the day I'm getting married. If you show up, great. If you don't, that's fine too, but this is what I'm doing."

We didn't have a grandiose wedding. We had a few family members there to see me say, "I do" in my tuxedo while Val wore a wedding gown that she made herself. We got married at a courthouse Justice of the Peace outside of Philadelphia on May 16, 1981—no Catholic church for us. That was because the church was also such a pain in my ass with their rules, regulations, and costs for every little thing that I again blew up at the rectory after the priest told us he couldn't marry us until I got a real job. I stood up and told him to fuck off and shove his church up his ass, much to Val's dismay. I then stormed out of the room and smoked a cigarette, while she apologized to the priest for about ten minutes.

We did have two wedding receptions though: one that day at Val's mom's house that my mom came to, and another that my dad and his wife Carol wanted to have at their house, which my mom was not invited

to. Some of my cousins, aunts, and uncles also came, since by then, I had already kind of kissed and made up with them to some degree. But I did say, "The next time you see my face, she'll be my wife!"

Val and I planned to have a weeklong honeymoon in our favorite coastal stomping grounds—Wildwood, New Jersey. After hanging out at our second reception and having some food with everybody, we thanked them for coming, then took Little Val to Val's mom's place to babysit her while we went on our honeymoon.

Uncle Gene lent me his Cadillac, so Val and I cruised toward Wildwood, where I had made a reservation at a nice boutique hotel overlooking the beach.

We drove through Atlantic City and were taking in all these seaside resort towns and beach communities along the way as we were driving down the Garden State Parkway. Val's brother Bob was a tow truck driver, and as we drove along the highway, I saw an empty fucking tow truck on the side of the road and I said to Val, "Hey, is that your brother Bob's tow truck?" Then a little bit farther along, we spotted her brother Chris, my former guitarist, and best man for my wedding.

Always trying to be as rock-and-roll as possible, Chris was walking down the side of the dark road in a pair of skin-tight, white satin pants, a pair of knee-high red platform Kiss boots, a red sparkling girl's blouse, and a scarf. He had chopped-up black hair on top with the rest of it flowing halfway down his back.

He was just walking down the side of the highway, ninety miles from home, so I pulled over and said, "What the fuck? What the fuck are you doing?"

He said they decided to come down to Wildwood, too, since we were going, but fucking Bob's tow truck had run out of fuel, so Bob had gone to try and get gas. I was pissed with him, but we picked Chris up and took the first exit, where we soon found Val's oldest brother Bob with a full five-gallon can of gas. So now I had both dumbasses in the back of my uncle's Cadillac, and Bob was spilling the gas all over the back rug. Since we were almost in Wildwood, I told them I was going to check-in to our hotel first, and then take them back to get the tow truck.

We finally got into town and found the hotel, but reception said they had no room available for us. I flipped out and argued with them, telling them that we had reservations and were supposed to have a room. They said, "Well, we thought you weren't coming till tomorrow."

I said, "No, I fucking told whoever I talked to on the phone, we were going to be a late check-in TODAY."

"Well, we don't have a room for you until tomorrow, but we can give you one of these other rooms we have in another building."

So, I said, "Fine, give me the fucking room!"

It was basically a small bedroom with no windows, and if you had to take a piss in the middle of the night, you had to leave the room and walk down to the end of the hallway and use the community bathroom. I had to settle for the bullshit accommodation, as I really had no other option. My honeymoon did not get off to a good start.

After pulling our luggage into this alternate shithole, we got back in the Cadillac that now stunk of fucking gas and drove them back to Bob's tow truck. When we pulled into the spot where he left it, though, it was gone! Thinking it had most likely been towed, we got a phone number from a nearby sign on the roadside to find out if that was the case, since it was frowned upon to park there. We went to a gas station to make the call, and Bob started coming apart.

While we stood in the gas station waiting for someone to get off the payphone, a tow truck driver came in with another car. He pulled into the gas station, hit a lever, and the car he was towing just dropped, hard. Bob started yelling at him, "You better not have fucking dropped my truck like that!"

The driver freaked out at Bob's aggressive behavior and locked himself in the gas station, which riled Bob even more. Bob was outside with a huge wrench in his hand, yelling at this guy, "If you fucking dropped my truck like that, I'm gonna fucking split your head open!" And as fast as anything, about ten New Jersey state troopers showed up.

I stood next to Val and her brother Chris watching the cops pull up, when Chris told me that he had a little baggie tucked in his boot with some weed and about five Quaaludes in it. *You've got to be kidding me*, I thought.

They handcuffed Bob because he was off his rocker at this point, and they put him in a squad car. They pulled Chris aside and started talking to him, looking him up and down, thinking, "It's not Halloween for five months, why the fuck are you wearing these white pants, these red boots, and a fucking sparkle shirt? Why do you have eyeliner on? Why are you at a gas station dressed like this?"

Then the cop came over to Val and I and asked me, "So how do you guys fit into this?"

I said, "Well, those two morons are her brothers. We just got married, and we just left Philadelphia to go on our honeymoon."

The cop looked at me and said, "Please tell me that you did not bring her brothers on your honeymoon with you."

I said, "Nope, not intentionally, we just found them on the roadside along the way."

The cop pissed himself laughing.

They were going to arrest Bob for threatening the tow truck driver, but I talked the cop out of it, saying, "Look, buddy, can you just let him slide? The brothers are going to go home back to Philly. They're not staying here with us."

The cop diffused the situation and got it all smoothed over. He let Bob out of the squad car so he could get his tow truck back, put some gas in it from the can, then get to a gas station to fill up for the ride home.

But I was still pissed at them. I said to them, "Why the fuck would you guys come down to Wildwood? It's our fucking honeymoon! What would make you think that it would be okay for you guys to show up at our hotel room tonight?" Dumbasses.

The romantic honeymoon was a lost cause, but as usual, I persevered. The next morning, we had breakfast and moved our stuff into the room that we were originally supposed to have. It was a nice room overlooking the beach with a great view of the water.

This enticed Val and I to put our bathing suits on and go down to the beach. We were lying on the sand on a blanket and started making out. Val turned to lay on her stomach to tan her back, and I slid my hand under her into her bathing suit bottom, and started touching her and saying that I couldn't wait to get to the room, as we hadn't consummated our marriage the night before (no thanks to her brothers). Somehow that little bit of sandy foreplay gave Val the worst bladder infection. We spent evening number two in an emergency room drinking cranberry juice, and had a celibate honeymoon the rest of the week. Just my luck!

And then to top it all off, during our honeymoon week away, I wanted to go into the Atlantic Ocean for a swim. I had a fleeting thought that my new wedding ring may come off in the water as I swam, so I took it off and set it on the blanket. When I got out of the water after swimming, my wedding band was gone. It obviously fell into the sand somehow—and it was gone, forever.

So, the entire time I was married to Val, I never wore a wedding band. If anyone reading this happens to find a wedding band on the beach in Wildwood, New Jersey…burn it, it's cursed!

6
Fragile

After the disastrous honeymoon, I went back to work with my band, Fragile. Things were good for a while but there started to be a shift in musical styles, and radio was fully committed to bands that were being labeled as new wave. Everybody started cutting their hair, wearing suit jackets and skinny ties, and the audience reflected that as well. We started to become a bit overlooked for bands that were playing this new stuff that everybody wanted to hear and dance to. There were a few clubs that we still had a great draw in—one was called Bogey's in Bellmawr, New Jersey.

Bogey's was a dive on Route 130. A lady named Rog, who was always super cool and treated us great, ran it. We played there quite often, and always had pretty great turnouts. Some of the guys had been complaining to Rog during a soundcheck about where the industry was headed, and how hard it was getting to play the music we loved: classic rock. So, during one of our breaks that night, Rog came downstairs into the dressing room and said the owner Don Bogey wanted to speak with Dan and Ricky.

Don basically offered us some financial assistance for advertising and said he would help us get better gigs. They had heard a few of Rick's original songs in our sets as well and thought we just needed a little help. Don guaranteed to book us at least once a month there, got us some better promo shots, and pressured our agent Freddy to keep us busy.

Around this time, Brian was becoming a bit fed up with the schedule and some of the members more than casual drug intake, and gave us notice that he was leaving. So Rick called his buddy Don Denson, the lead guitarist of his old band Gangster. We took a bit of time off and worked Don into the fold, and we got right back to work.

One of our first gigs was at a place in Wayne, Pennsylvania, called Central Park. Rick had made arrangements for his manager Larry Mazer to come and see us there. The plan was to let Larry hear us doing a few of the original songs and have him try to get us some regional opening slots for national acts. After our three sets that night, we sat down on the stage, feeling pretty good about ourselves, to chat with Larry and hear his assessment of the band, but he clearly wasn't impressed.

Rick asked him why, and he basically looked at me, and said, "Hey, don't take this the wrong way, but I don't think your singer has got what it takes." I was stunned, then fucking livid! I sat there as Rick tried to defend what we were doing, but Larry wasn't having any of it and wanted no part of it at all. So we packed up and went home with our tails between our legs. We didn't quit immediately, but the business and some issues with drugs took its toll on all of us, and things just deteriorated from there quickly. Fragile came to an end, but as it turned out, it was only the Mark 1 version of the band.

It wasn't long after the band broke up that I started getting calls to join other bands. Tom Keifer, the lead guitarist in a band called Diamonds, rang me one day and asked if I'd fill-in for his singer who was in hospital with appendicitis. I said I would, as I just wanted to get back out and play. Tom gave me a list of songs they were doing, so I learned as many as I could in a few days.

I met the band at a club called Bullwinkles, where we planned on rehearsing during the soundcheck. Everybody played great, and we put a few sets together for that week's shows, and then we left to get showered and ready for the gig. When I got back, though, everybody was wearing lipstick, and bright-colored clothing, very reminiscent to the New York Dolls, or a tougher version of Poison. We got through the week with no hitches, and on the last night, as we were packing up, Tom asked me to join. I really dug the band musically, but was definitely not comfortable dressing the way they did, so I said, "Thank you for the offer, but I've got something going on that I'm digging."

Somebody saw me with Tom's band though and told a guitarist named Ron E. Kayfield that he should check me out. Ron had also been in a few big bands in the area, and there were rumors that he'd played in a later version of the Dolls in New York. Quite a few people had warned me about working with Ronnie, but I ignored it all, as I thought this was a person with connections. I met Ron and his wife Marcia, heard a few originals he had, and I was stoked about what I was hearing.

Ron wanted to do something a bit different. He wanted to do a Zeppelin tribute, but in a really grand fashion. The idea was to rent theaters and show their movie *The Song Remains the Same*, and then perform live after that. He wanted to build a following that way, then start eventually recording original material. It seemed like a good idea on paper, and he had an investor on the hook that used to be involved with an early version of Beatlemania, so I thought we had a winning team.

We recruited a buddy named Adam Ferraioli from a local band Thrust to play drums, and on bass we had Billy Childs, who eventually wound-up being a founding member of Britny Fox. We decided to reuse the name Fragile, and we did a couple of disastrous shows at The Waverly Theatre and a handful of clubs, but the entire thing ended as fast as it started due to the internal arguments because of egos, money (or the lack thereof), and…you guessed it: drug use again! Fragile (Mark 2) bit the bullet.

Around this time, I was starting to panic a little because my bank account had emptied quite a bit, and I had a family to take care of. I hadn't really made the money I thought I would in the last version of Fragile, and Uncle Gene had closed the bowling tournaments and bought a restaurant. Problem was, he didn't have all the money he needed for it, so he borrowed about fifteen grand from me and Val. He kindly reminded me of "all he had done for me," to my dismay, and as much as I didn't want to give him the money, I felt obliged to. Uncle Gene also went and got a job at a place called Stan Harris Vending to keep himself afloat.

I had traded my Monte Carlo in for a newer car, and it wound-up being a lemon, so I returned it to the dealership. I went out and bought a 1974 Chevy Malibu that had low mileage and drove it into the ground.

I ran into a guitarist at a club one night named Reggie Wu, and in conversation I told him I was looking for a day gig. Reggie told me to go down to the Hertz car rental counter at the airport and ask for a guy named Ed. He told me Ed was a super-cool, older Black gentleman, and he would more than likely give me a job—and he did.

Ed was exactly how Reggie described, and gave me a lot of freedom to take time off for gigs when I needed; he only asked for me to give him plenty of notice. So I immediately went to work the next day, shuttling cars from all of the Hertz outlets throughout the city, and on occasion driving cars back from Newark, JFK, and LaGuardia airports.

In the meantime, looking for new members to put a band together with, I eventually met with Frank Scimeca and Jimmy Marchiano, two guys from a local band called Kashmir. Frank played bass and Jimmy played guitar, and I tried to get this amazing young drummer Richie DeCarlo to play, but he was still in school, so he declined. I then tried to get Adam Ferraioli from my last band to play, and for the life of me don't remember why he declined, but he suggested Johnny Dee[3], who was drumming in a band called Blind Driver. Johnny accepted, and we were off. This lineup was again called Fragile (Mark 3), and I believed it would be a case of third time lucky, or so I thought.

I was putting in as many hours as I could with Hertz to try and rebuild my funds and rehearsing underneath a tavern in Northeast Philadelphia three or four nights a week. I also tried my hand at writing original music, because I realized if I wanted to "make it," I was going to have to commit to the cause.

Val went to cosmetology school and graduated, then worked in a salon at a five-star hotel in Philly's Center City. Things financially were starting to look up for us. After a few months of rehearsals and writing, we did another audition night at a club called The Galaxy in Somerdale, New Jersey. We had a decent draw, and actually had a great first gig. The owner, Bill Haigh, really dug the band and had us come in almost biweekly, like a shared residency, with a new band Tom Keifer put together during 1982 called Cinderella.

In Philly, there were two radio stations that played rock: WYSP and WMMR. Around that time they were both playing the safe stuff, like The Beatles, Zeppelin, Stones, Fleetwood Mac, etc., and if they did play anything new, it was all the new wave shit that was happening. The local original bands that were getting radio attention were playing music in that genre. Bands like Robert Hazard and The Heroes, Beru Revue, and especially The Hooters, were all kicking ass. For those who aren't familiar with those bands, Robert Hazard actually wrote "Girls Just Wanna Have Fun" that Cyndi Lauper recorded, and The Hooters followed suit and wrote "Time After Time," which Cyndi had another huge hit with.

There was a huge number of bands that were into rock, but no outlets for any help from radio, and not a lot of venues for us to play our original music. There was one band though that continued playing all over the East Coast, but even they would fall victim to a lack of radio support (and eventually drug use). We all looked up to them. The Dead End Kids had been playing all the clubs as far back as I can remember, and were just so fucking out of control. They wrote and played originals, but

---

3 Johnny would eventually become a member of Pete Way's band Waysted, Britny Fox, and Doro…and my son's godfather.

they also did a few cool covers that I always thought were originals. That's how I first heard The Sensational Alex Harvey Band's "Midnight Moses," which I recorded a version of with The Dead Daisies in 2015.

They were incredibly theatrical and doing shit that nobody else was doing anywhere. The two guitarists dyed their hair jet black, like Mötley Crüe before Mötley Crüe. They were early Mötley meets Alice Cooper meets Bowie, and they were badass. Some credit them as the first to swing their guitars around their bodies by the straps as they played live. I know Cinderella was known for doing the guitar-spinning thing, but the Dead End Kids were doing that in the seventies, long before I ever saw anyone else do it! They had pyro; they had smoke, and they would turn their backs to the audience for the intro of an original and insert special contact lenses so when they turned around on stage and opened their eyes, their eyeballs were pure white with no pupils—crazy shit like that, which bands like Marilyn Manson popularized two decades later. They played all up and down the East Coast and built a large following.

Fragile did a show at The Galaxy one Saturday night, and everybody had heard that Dead End Kids were supposed to have a huge showcase in the North Jersey / New York area for all these record labels that night. We'd just finished our set when I saw their guitar player Kelley James walk into the club, so I went over to him and said, "Hey, dude, how did your showcase go?"

I could tell he was fucking out of his gourd on something. He had typewriter jaw, just going back and forth as he got a basic reply out, "Ah, it's tomorrow, man."

I thought that was really odd, but said, "Okay, good luck tomorrow!"

I later found out that all those guys were so fucked up that they missed their own showcase; they no-showed on all these record labels in New York. They went on the wrong day because they were all just so fucking blown out and disorganized. It really was a pity because they were the fucking greatest and could've been (in my opinion) one of the biggest rock bands ever! They were very influential to all of us in the South Jersey / Philadelphia bands—very reminiscent of how the New York Dolls were to a lot of people.

One night in 1984, a guy came and saw me play at The Galaxy in New Jersey and told me about a great band up in New York City called Cathedral. I had never heard of the band before. The band's leader was guitarist Mark Cunningham, who replaced Danny Johnson in Rick

Derringer's band Derringer. Rick is best known for his hit song "Rock and Roll, Hoochie Koo," and I was a Rick Derringer fan growing up. This guy said I should come up to New York City where he'll introduce me to Cathedral and their managers.

Cathedral was being managed by Steve Leber and David Krebs who were also handling Aerosmith, Ted Nugent, Humble Pie, AC/DC, and all these huge bands at the time, which naturally piqued my interest. So, I went to New York City and met with Mark and his manager Paul O'Neill over a steak dinner. I eventually met the rest of the band at our first rehearsal: bassist Dennis Feldman, drummer Mike Gandi, and singer Tommy Farese. They had just recently finished a small ten-city tour with Aerosmith and made a couple of lineup changes.

Mark was interested in me singing for them but when I heard Tommy's voice, I said to Mark, "Why do you want to get rid of this guy? He has an amazing voice! Why don't you keep him? I can play rhythm guitar, and we can do an old Deep Purple thing stylistically, where Tommy can do the lower register David Coverdale parts, and I'll do the higher Glenn Hughes shit." I joined, and we began rehearsing, putting songs together, and getting ready for a possible second run with Aerosmith.

Before long, one of the other bands that Leber-Krebs was managing was Heaven, an Australian band that had relocated to Hollywood. They recorded their album *Where Angels Fear to Tread* at Cherokee Studios right next to Mötley Crüe when they were recording *Shout at the Devil*.

Heaven then toured America supporting Mötley on the *Shout* tour. They had guitarist Mick Cocks from Rose Tattoo and bassist Mark Evans from AC/DC in their lineup, but after those two went back to Australia, they ended up stealing Mark and Dennis from Cathedral. That was essentially the end of Cathedral; it just stopped existing. So I went back to Philadelphia with my tail between my legs and continued playing with Fragile.

Cathedral's drummer Mike Gandia was left high and dry, and he would often call me. One winter's day in early '85, Mike called and said, "Hey, dude, I don't know if you'd be into it or not, but there's a band out of LA that's looking for a new singer. I got it on the down-low, and I think you'd be great for it."

I asked him how he heard about it, and he said, "I'm friends with this band's manager. He's a New York guy named Doug Thaler. Just give me some photos, a cassette tape, and type out a resume or something with your contact info, and I can literally hand it to him."

I gave Mike a tape of a few rough originals I had along with a few photos. I never heard anything back about it and completely forgot about it for many years.

Johnny Dee went out to California for a week's vacation with a couple of buddies, and he came back raving about how awesome it was over there. He said there were heaps of rock clubs where everybody was doing originals. He told us how there was all these people in Hollywood walking around the Sunset Strip and the clubs with hair up to the sky and girls walking around in lingerie and fishnet stockings. He told us about this amazing band he saw called Ratt and said it was just pretty much original music everywhere!

We all started saving money and making plans to relocate. Bassist Frank got his cash together first and made the move to California sight-unseen with his wife Sharon and their young son Ian. They got an apartment on Ivar Avenue in Hollywood, right around the corner from the landmark Capitol Records Building.

In conjunction with our fourth wedding anniversary, Val and I decided to go out to California on a reconnaissance vacation for ten days or so to confirm if what Johnny said was true. Holy fuck, he was right! There was Gazzarri's, the Troubadour, the Country Club, Madame Wong's West, the Coconut Teaszer, The Roxy, Whisky A Go Go, the Rainbow Bar & Grill—just all these great fucking places. We stayed at Frank and Sharon's apartment and had a great time getting a taste of it all.

After our amazing vacation, I immediately went to work and started seriously planning a permanent move out to California. When I wasn't playing a gig, I used to go watch Cinderella play because I thought they were great. I liked their tune "Night Songs" and loved the riff in "Once Around the Ride." I was friends with all of the guys and liked what they were doing. They were full-blown: Tom Keifer was always a great player and vocalist accented with his over-the-top image, Eric Brittingham had his blond palm tree hair—all their clothes were tattered, with fishnets, rags, and scarves. They were fucking awesome, and I could see they had some pretty fucking cool shit going on.

However, they were having some lineup issues, and I wasn't sure they were going to get a record deal, primarily because we were in no-man's-land: Philadelphia. I was getting ready to go to LA, where the rock industry was turbo-charged, and they had no plans to move from Philly and just keep playing the same venues Empire Rock Club and The Galaxy over and over again.

As it turned out, Jon Bon Jovi was in Philly doing some recording at The Warehouse studio with his producer Lance Quinn and engineer Obie O'Brien; I believe it was for their *7800° Fahrenheit* album. One night, Obie took Jon to the Empire Rock Club. Jon walked in, saw Cinderella play, and thought they were fucking awesome. Through his A&R guy Derek Shulman, he walked them into Mercury/Polygram Records, which led to them getting a record deal, and then took them on the next Bon Jovi tour with him, in the opening slot for their huge *Slippery When Wet* tour.

But I digress…

As I said earlier, following the demise of Uncle Gene's bowling tournaments, he ended up working for this big vending company in Philadelphia called Stan Harris Vending. I became friends with one of his work buddies, Bobby, who was the mechanic for all their vans and other equipment.

I sold my Chevy Malibu and bought a big old red Philadelphia Fire Department ambulance, and Bobby helped me convert this ambulance into a cheap motel on wheels that we could travel cross-country in.

We sanded it down and painted it inconspicuous white (with a cool black stripe through the center), then ripped a lot of the guts out of it and built a bed and a bench-seat inside. When I started its motor, I could turn a switch and some sort of generator would kick in since it was an ambulance. That gave us electrical power running on 110 volts, so we had a lamp and TV setup in there, too. It had an air-conditioner in the front and another in the back.

It took a bit of time for us to work, save, and get the van ready for the trip, but we eventually had a date and made all the necessary arrangements to hit the road. We hitched a U-Haul trailer up to the back of the ambulance to cart our belongings. We didn't have a lot of stuff since we sold off a lot of shit, but everything we owned was packed in there. By late summer of '85, we were ready to set-off on our epic relocation, driving across America in my ambulance. It was east-meets-west for me, my wife Val, Little Val, our feisty red Siberian husky named Star, and an actor friend of ours named Jay Paseka.

I had the trans-American route all figured out: we would leave Philadelphia on Interstate 76 and travel west to Interstate 70 through cities like Columbus, Ohio, then Indianapolis, Indiana, and once we reached St. Louis, Missouri, we would cut down Route 44, which is called the Will Rogers Turnpike.

That would basically bring us out onto Route 40 a little past Tulsa, Oklahoma. We would take Route 40 all the way from Oklahoma through Amarillo, Texas, then Albuquerque, New Mexico, and Arizona.

Lastly, we would go south on Interstate 15 to Interstate 10 West, then across into Los Angeles, before taking the US-101 freeway right into fucking Hollywood, baby!

Val didn't drive, so we had our actor friend Jay join us on the journey, since his family lived in San Diego and he wanted to visit. We thought it would be good to have him help with the driving when I was too tired.

I love Jay to death, but he was fucking torture as a road-tripper. He would do things like sit in the back of the ambulance with a flashlight constantly under his face and say spooky shit, just scaring the shit out of nine-year-old Little Val.

Somewhere after Albuquerque, we pulled into a roadside café in Bumfuck, New Mexico. It was probably about one o'clock in the morning, so we all went in to get some coffee and shit to nibble on. As soon as we walked in, all these redneck truckers laid eyes on me, checking out my long hair, looking all 5'9" of me up and down. As I was getting shit to go, the lyrics of Bob Seger's "Turn the Page" ran through my head. When I was paying for our shit at the register, I could hear one of them saying, "Faggot…Faggot…Faggot," and I was getting fucking pissed. Val could see me bubbling and told me not to say anything and just get out of there. As we walked out, I flipped them off, before the door swung closed behind me.

We got back in the ambulance and started driving again, when suddenly we heard this fucking clanging. Our muffler fell off and was dragging, shooting sparks out from underneath the van, so I pulled over onto the shoulder of the road.

All the rednecks from the café must have gotten in their trucks to follow us, and on their CBs or something, because next thing I knew there was soon a flurry of trucks playing fucking chicken with us, while we were pulled over on the roadside.

I was under the vehicle trying to fix the scalding hot muffler, using T-shirts to hold the muffler up in place, while connecting it again using an old chain dog leash of Star's to tie around it and lock it in there.

Each truck that came along saw us on the side of the road and just drifted into the shoulder, coming extremely close. It looked like they were just going to plow right into the fucking ambulance, before they'd pull back onto the road at the last minute and lean on the horn. The ambulance was swaying. Val was freaking out, Little Val was freaking out, and I was under the van freaking out. They were playing chicken and fucking with us the whole time, but I managed to fix the muffler to get us going again.

I drove a while longer until the coffee buzz wore off and I just couldn't drive anymore. I decided to take a nap and let Jay take a turn driving, especially since I had driven almost the whole way so far. I fell asleep in the back of the ambulance and was out like a light.

Next thing I remember, I woke up because the van was literally rocking back and forth and bumping over potholes. I got up and said to Jay, "What the fuck is going on? Where the fuck are we?"

As he was driving, Jay looked at our paper map, and noticed that heading west soon after Flagstaff, Arizona, once we got to Kingman, the I-40 freeway takes a turn south before going west again and then back upward north. The reason it detours like this is because it goes around a fucking mountain, unbeknownst to Jay. He instead sees that there's a straight and shorter-looking route along Oatman Road.

I woke up when we were literally a quarter of the way through this supposed shortcut that Jay decided to take all by himself, which ended up being the longcut because we couldn't drive faster than five or ten miles an hour along this fucking dirt service road that wound through the mountain. When I looked down out of out my window, I was looking down a fucking ravine. I was so pissed, yelling at Jay, "Why the fuck would you get off the freeway? Why?"

We literally bounced and cut our way up over this Arizona mountain on a skinny fucking fire service road. If another car had come the other way, we would've been fucked because we couldn't back up with a trailer full of our only possessions. We couldn't turn around; we had to keep going straight.

Jay was an actor, but I wasn't—I was fucking angry, for real! He laughed it all off as an adventure, which elevated my blood pressure further. The whole cross-country trip was a nightmare, and I couldn't wait for it to be over and finally get to our new lives in Hollywood.

PART II

THE MIDDLE:
LOS ANGELES, CALIFORNIA

7
Angora

When we finally arrived in Hollywood, we again stayed with Frank and Sharon for about a week while we sorted our own place to rent. We wound up getting apartment number one in the front of the same building as them on Ivar Avenue. Our guitarist Jimmy moved out to California next. He got a temporary gig in Santa Barbara playing with a band called Sibling Rivalry. He played gigs with them and made some money before eventually moving to Hollywood, too.

Johnny Dee was going to move out, but I could tell he was the most unlikely to. Back in Philly, Johnny had introduced me to a guy from New Jersey named Dave Sabo—or "Snake," as he was nicknamed. He was a guitarist looking to put a band together. I told him to keep in touch, but I really wasn't interested in singing with him since I was committed to moving to LA. Johnny seemed interested in playing with Snake though, but Snake apparently didn't hear from him for some time.

Johnny had been playing with a band called World War III, but then formed a new band in Philadelphia called Britny Fox, which was started by "Dizzy" Dean Davidson, an old drummer of mine from Philly, after he hooked-up with a guitarist Michael Kelly Smith, who had left Cinderella. Dean was now writing and fronting this new band.

We started looking around in LA for another drummer, to no avail, until Jimmy and Frank said they knew a guy in Philly named Robert Iezzi. I had met him before but never heard him play.

We called him and worked all the moving details out. Robert and his girlfriend Gina were able to move out to California and amazingly all four band members lived in the same complex on Ivar Avenue: it was me and Val in apartment one, Frank and Sharon in apartment three, Jimmy and Lynn in like apartment ten, and Robert and Gina had apartment six—all in the same fucking building.

In Philadelphia, as I mentioned before, I worked at Hertz car rental during the day and mainly played shows on the weekend, and I told you I had an old boss Ed who was super cool with accommodating my rock-and-roll schedule.

When I came back from the LA vacation and started making plans to move to California, I told Ed about it and asked if he could transfer me to work at Hertz in Los Angeles instead. Ed said, "Yeah, sure, no worries. I'll see what I can do to transfer you." He put the transfer papers in and told me I was good to go.

I drove across the country thinking that I had a job at the other end, and I then spent basically all my money to rent the apartment. I drove down to the Hertz Los Angeles location and told them that I had arrived and wanted to tee-up and figure out what day I could start work.

The manager stared at me and said, "I ain't hiring."

I explained, "Well, I've got paperwork here that says I'm being transferred."

He coldly said, "Yeah, well, I don't care what your paperwork says, I ain't hiring."

Yours truly was out of work for a while. I was freaking out inside and had to collect unemployment for a few weeks. The band, in the meantime, started looking for a rehearsal room to begin banging out some music to play live and record. We did a little investigating into where we could play, and some friends of ours from Philadelphia named Jerry Best, Pete Preston, and Doug Aldrich told us to try Gazzarri's. They had started a band in LA called Mansfield (a couple of years before our move) that garnered some attention, but now Doug and Jerry had a new band called Lion that was playing regularly with a record deal on Scotti Brothers Records. So they were incredibly helpful with the do's and don'ts of the LA scene.

We went to Gazzarri's as advised and spoke to the in-house promoter, Michael Fell, who was more than happy to book our band there. But much to our dismay he told us we needed to sell one hundred tickets at ten dollars a pop and give him the money on the day of the show. We were dumbfounded! We have to pay to play? What is this?

Maybe yours truly should've done a little more homework before the move, but as they say, "If something is too good to believe, it probably is." Onward and upward, kids!

Knowing we also needed a killer new band name, for two or three shows at Gazzarri's, we changed our name from Fragile to Raggady Ann, but it wasn't right. Somebody suggested Angora. We thought it had a pretty tough sound to the word, so we looked it up in the dictionary and saw it was essentially a longhaired fluffy animal—it was the complete opposite. But we all had long, curly hair, and even without teasing or hairspray it was naturally fluffy. We couldn't find that cool fucking band name, so we just ran with it. Fragile became Angora.

After a year or so of still trying to get settled in LA, we knew we needed a few things to get a record deal and make it big. We started looking for a manager, writing more songs, and building our growing fan base, while recording more of our newer songs, which would also help us secure bigger live shows. With the help of a friend Donna Cardellino, we went into Rock Steady studios at 7000 Santa Monica Boulevard and recorded with Rob Cavallo, who in his own right has become a very popular producer after doing so many albums with Green Day, Goo Goo Dolls, Linkin Park, and winning a few Grammy Awards along the way.

We recorded "Shake, Shake," plus "Jailbait" and one other song. A couple of years later, "Shake, Shake" got released by Los Angeles radio station KNAC on their album *Son of Pure Rock* that promoted new, unsigned LA acts. We had submitted it for a contest they were running where the top band would win a record deal and all this other shit. Angora came second, but we ended up on their album, and it was the first time my vocals were released on a vinyl record.

Rob Cavallo really loved and believed in the band, so he took our demo songs to Ted Templeman at Warner Bros. Records to try and get us a deal. Ted had persuaded that label to sign Van Halen, and he produced their first six albums. He was then producing David Lee Roth's solo music, since Van Halen had split up.

Ted passed on us, though, preferring to work with a new band he signed called BulletBoys, and the record label lost interest in us. However, we caught the attention of Pete Angelus during a show at the Troubadour. Pete was a very creative music industry guy who had worked with Van Halen all through the eighties, doing everything from writing and directing their classic video clips; designing their merch, lights and stage shows; plus art direction of their album covers. He was now managing the solo career of David Lee Roth.

Pete talked to Roth's solo band guitarist Steve Vai, who was not only a guitar virtuoso, but also had a recording studio called The Mothership in his own home in the Hollywood Hills. We were excited to record three more new songs with Vai producing—"Hey Operator," "Are You Waiting?" and "Making Love"—however, we didn't make a good first impression.

On the way to his home studio the first day of recording, we stopped and got a bunch of McDonald's food. Our now manager Donna Cardellino had told us that Vai was a hardcore vegetarian, so we left the burgers in the vehicle while we took all our gear into his house.

After we loaded everything in, we sat outside eating the burgers, but we left his front door open. Next thing we heard, "Who's eating meat? Get that shit away from my fucking door!"

He was up the stairs and around a corner in the control room of the studio and could totally smell the meat we were eating outside. "Oh, shit—sorry, Steve." But he was super cool; he was incredibly great to work with during that recording session.

In typical record label fashion, as soon as Cinderella got signed and became Bon Jovi's label mates, there came a wave of other signings in the Philadelphia scene over a short period. Britny Fox got signed, then Tangier got signed, and Reggie Wu's band Heaven's Edge got signed. And I had been in bands with some of the members of all three.

Tom Keifer came out to the Record Plant in Los Angeles for the mixing of his first Cinderella album. He called and invited me over to the studio on Sycamore Avenue, where he was mixing it with Andy Johns, so I went with Val and heard a couple of the tracks. "Fuck, it sounds great," I told him. And it still does.

He was staying at the big old round Holiday Inn on Hollywood Boulevard at Highland Avenue, so once he finished at the studio, we headed back to the hotel where we had drinks on the roof—the whole rooftop was a glass-enclosed round bar—and we had a great night talking about rock. Six months after that album *Night Songs* came out, it had gone double platinum, selling millions of copies. I chuckle about it now because it's like nothing happened in the Philly scene until I fucking left. It figures: I leave to find the golden ticket in LA, and suddenly there was this huge fucking explosion of signings in my hometown of Philadelphia—hilarious! Nice timing, Corabi.

After the letdown by Hertz, it took me a while to get a job, but the first one I got in LA was doing telemarketing. There was no hourly rate; I was only to be paid commission for any sales I made. I sat in an office with Frank and Robert all day long, trying to sell fucking inflatable boats. I was literally answering calls for seven or eight hours a day and there were days where I made only thirty or forty fucking bucks. It was brutal.

One day my phone rang, and it was Val. She said, "How are you doing, Dad?"

I'd been sweating all morning because she told me she hadn't gotten her period, so she was going to the doctors. As excited as I was that we might be having a kid, it freaked me out. Now it was a reality!

Here I was selling fucking inflatable rafts that you wouldn't even put your dog on in a pool. Once I actually saw the product and how cheap and flimsy it was, and knowing how much I was charging people for them, I struggled selling them even more. I tried selling this dodgy photocopier toner, too. I knew it was all a fucking scam. I was the worst liar on the planet, and I just couldn't bring myself to cheat people out of their hard-earned money. I couldn't do it.

They ended up transferring me to the shipping department so I wouldn't have to sell, but that was a crock of shit, too. My wife was pregnant, and we were going to have a baby, so I was extremely nervous. I was really worried about how I was going to pay for all this shit. Somehow, I had to find a way to make it work or find another way of making money. As it turned out, I quit just in the nick of time. Shortly after I left, the FBI raided the office where we worked and the owner was arrested, convicted, and jailed for mail fraud.

Donna, Angora's manager, was investing quite a bit of money into the band and trying to get us signed. Rachel Matthews, an A&R rep, loved the band and was interested in signing us to Capitol Records, but they ended up signing another band instead. It was like we were always at the right spot, but always at the wrong time, which is pretty typical of my life.

Donna also made a call to Gene Simmons from Kiss, and we heard he was really interested in working with the band. Everybody knew Gene discovered Van Halen, and at one point, there was talk that Paul Stanley was going to produce the first record for Guns N' Roses; those guys had their hands in all these different bands like Slaughter and Vinnie Vincent Invasion. There we were, ready, and thinking we could be the next big thing.

Our manager set up a meeting with Gene at SIR rehearsal studios to play a few songs for him. We were in this huge room of SIR, where there was a basketball court. It was surreal to think that after paying money to see Kiss all those years ago on the *Alive!* Tour, Gene was now coming to see ME play.

He walked in and the God of Thunder was wearing a sweatshirt with sweatpants, and he just disarmed everybody and started shooting fucking hoops with us. Even without his demon makeup on, he had a very intimidating presence.

When we played for him, I started singing, and he soon stopped us to give us some songwriting pointers. He said, "If you're going to write a song, you need to be more direct lyrically: it doesn't need to be *they*—it needs to be *you, me, I.*"

The things he said made sense. I don't know if I've totally stuck to what he told me over the years, but he gave me some good pointers. He also wasn't a fan of our band name Angora. He said, "I fucking hate it. It's stupid, it's fluffy, why do you want to use that name? It's a fucking sweater."

He said he wanted to change our name to 8-Ball. Thinking he was referring to drugs, I said to him, "What the fuck does that mean?"

He replied, "You're four guys, therefore you have eight balls."

When he left that day, he said, "If you have anything on your mind, feel free to call me."

I built up the nerve to call him one day to ask him a question. He answered, so I said, "Hey, Gene—John Corabi, how are you? How's the family?"

He just totally cut me off, and said in his deep, stoic voice, "Mr. Corabi, time is money. You're wasting my time, so you're costing me money. What do you want?" He had no time for chitchat, but I respected him. He was always larger than life.

We met with Gene a couple more times before he invited us to lunch one day to discuss a deal that he was going to offer us on his Simmons Records label. Excitedly, we met him at a deli he liked near his house in Bel Air. Over lunch, he told us all the shit that he was going to do for us.

At the end of the lunch, the waitress brought the check over and gave it to Gene, who put it down on the table and slid it across to my manager. As she went to pick it up to pay, I reached over and slid it back to Gene. He smirked, looked right into my eyes, and said, "You know, I'm offering you a record deal."

I said, "I know you are, but where I come from, if you invite someone to lunch, you pay."

From that moment on, Gene started telling me, "You're going to be a rock star." I think he enjoyed the fact that I wasn't a pushover.

While I was certainly intimidated by him, there were some things that I disagreed with him on. Like, even though I had been married for six or seven years, he told me that I needed to have my wife sign a prenuptial. I pushed back, saying, "No, I'm not going to do that. I didn't have her sign one then, why would I ever make her sign one now?"

"You're stupid then; you're a fool," he said.

"Well, that's your world, Gene. In my world, I don't have to worry about 'gold-diggers!' Not yet, anyway."

We bickered a little bit, but I think he respected the fact that I was willing to argue with him a bit and stand my ground on things that I believed in.

Gene also didn't trust Donna, our manager. We had a few conversations where he was like, "Why the fuck would I give you a couple hundred thousand dollars to do a record? I don't trust her. I don't think she's capable of managing her way out of a paper bag, let alone managing your career."

So, the probability of a record deal from him just fizzled out and went away because he didn't trust her and didn't like her. And unfortunately for Donna and us, he wasn't the first or last to say it. He was very observant. Quiet, but very opinionated, when he had an opinion. He didn't sugarcoat anything, he would just say, "Nope, you're wrong."

Gene's always been super cool with me and supportive, always telling me I was going to be a rock star. Years later when I did The Scream record, I ran into him, and he said, "Mr. Corabi, Gene Simmons said it, you're going to be a rock star." And then when I got the Mötley gig, he walked over to me one night and said, "What did I tell you, Mr. Corabi?"

He's always been in my corner, always been very nice, and always had great advice for me. I don't know if he still feels the same as he did then, because I've made a career out of shooting myself in the foot with a grenade launcher, but he was always very supportive.

It was great to be living in Hollywood during that whole Sunset Strip era. I met Guns N' Roses while they were playing clubs before they were signed and hung out with them on occasion.

A lady named Jonni Teagarden had been interested in working with Angora in a management capacity, but we already had a manager. Jonni lived in a house in the Hollywood Hills on Laurel Canyon and would always have parties and barbecues. I remember going over there a few Sundays and Duff, Izzy, and Slash were usually there, and Axl would pop by once in a while. They were the hottest band on the strip back then and getting very popular.

Poison was a really big band in LA then as well. They were originally from my home state of Pennsylvania, about a hundred miles from Philly, and made the move west a couple of years before us. They were selling out every club they were playing, and I ran into them a few times at clubs while passing out flyers to promote shows.

Racer X was also one of the big bands then. Great White was just starting to pop back up after a dip, and they were writing songs for what became their *Once Bitten* album. Jetboy was getting big, and Faster Pussycat was popular, too. Hurricane was a band that was getting a lot of attention at the time as well. After touring with Stryper, they became label mates on Enigma Records, where Poison also landed.

Once Poison got signed, Guns N' Roses got signed. Then it was odd walking down the Sunset Strip because you'd see a wide variety of pretty-looking guys like Tuff, and tough-looking guys like LA Guns, and the up-and-comers like us would be like, "Oh God, do I put lipstick on, or do I wear a vest and some leather gloves?" People were fucking scratching their heads trying to figure out what was popular and what to do to be successful.

I'll admit Angora went through a stage of trying to figure out what niche we fit into, but fuck it, we just said, "We are what we are." We weren't comfortable walking around in fucking nail-polish, leotards, and long Jon Bon Jovi leopard jackets. We stopped dying our hair, and we stopped being anything we were not. We just put on our ripped jeans again, T-shirts, and black leather vests. We went out there, and we were just Angora—advertised as pure 100 percent rock 'n' roll from Philadelphia—a bunch of East Coast Italian guys, led by yours fucking truly.

If you lined us four guys up and looked at us from behind, you couldn't tell us apart. We all had the exact same dark brown hair and the same build. Once my wife even walked up behind Jimmy, grabbed a handful of his ass and balls, and put her arms around him. I looked over and said, "What the fuck are you doing?"

She was horrified and screamed, "Oh God, I thought it was you!"

And Frank took full advantage of the fact that we all looked a lot alike. On several occasions I went out with Val and a girl would come over to me and be uncomfortably friendly, and try to talk to me. Obviously I was with my wife, so I'd be polite and say hello, then walk away, leaving the girl dumbfounded. But a couple of times, different girls made a scene, and started screaming, "You didn't tell me you were married! I would've never fucked you if I knew that!"

Val would look at me suspiciously, like what the fuck was that all about? And I was as dumbfounded as most of the girls, until Frank told me later that he would go out on occasion with some chick and tell her he was the lead singer of Angora. Thanks, buddy!

One of the first gigs Angora played was opening for Uriah Heep, and then we did a few shows opening for Racer X, who were huge at the time. If Poison was selling out the Country Club in Reseda two nights in a row—so was Racer X. I believe they were the band that I went to go see play live more than any other.

I'm not normally into that technical neo-classical music; I'm not into that at all, but they were just so great! So fucking talented. It wasn't like watching Yngwie Malmsteen, where there's one guy who's a shredder, it was the whole fucking band. Their guitarist Paul Gilbert was doing these crazy guitar riffs and two-handed tapping and all this other shit. The other guitarist Bruce Bouillet would match him note-for-note doing synchronized guitar harmonies, and then John Alderete on bass would rip just as fast as the guitar players. It was amazing, like what the fuck am I seeing right now? The singer Jeff Martin was like listening to Rob Halford, and then you had Scott Travis, this beast on double bass drums. They were a fucking machine, and I didn't realize it then, but a few of those guys would have a huge impact on my life, and my career.

After opening for a few bands, it didn't take Angora that long to reach the point where we were doing our own shows and making some money. Things were working quickly for us, but we did have issues in the beginning with some of the clubs because we were way too loud. When we played live, the soundmen wouldn't even mic the guitars, just the drums and my vocals. They never mic'd the amps because we were just fucking louder than shit. Every fucking gig we did, we never put the bass and guitar through the PA, just drums and vocals. If the guitar needed more volume, Jimmy turned around and turned it up a little louder, perhaps to eleven. It was a very unorthodox way of doing shit, but it worked for us.

Bassist Robbie Crane said to me years later when we were in Ratt together, "Goddamn it, dude. I fucking remember going to see you guys.

You had all this gear on stage. Nothing was mic'd, but the fucking mix was perfect."

I think I played acoustic guitar on a couple of songs, but for the most part I just fronted Angora and sang. I wrote music on my guitar at home on my own, but I didn't play guitar live much.

Angora's songwriting was definitely a bit primitive. I'm not real proud of song titles like "Making Love;" "Jailbait;" and "Shake, Shake." It was immature, and it was childish, but it was loud fun. The band looked good and played well, so it didn't take very long for us to build up a little bit of a reputation and a bit of an audience.

Once I quit working at the telemarketing place, I wound up getting a job working with a buddy, Chuck, doing electrical contracting work with him, building new homes. He would read the blueprints and say, "Okay, I need you to run wire from here to here, to here, to here, to here, then to that circuit box over there." I would do it, and then he would check my work. I did that for a little while, but it wasn't steady work. Finally, I got a decent job through my friend Ingryd, driving around town for a company called Ad Delivery, which was basically a courier service delivering movie contracts, films, and scripts for the film industry. Another friend of ours, Nate, had a car that he was going to give to Valerie. Since she didn't drive, I sold our ambulance to a fucking pastor, and put a little money into this little old Japanese car to fix it up so I could run around town in it.

I would have to go to Universal or Paramount or whatever movie studio, pick up copies of movies, contracts, or scripts, and drop them off at the homes of actors like Glenn Ford, Jimmy Stewart, and Bob Hope. A lot of these guys had little movie theaters in their houses, so I delivered movies to them all the time. Mike, the owner of the company, was totally cool, and the job worked well for me while I was trying to make it in the music industry.

Angora kept getting industry interest; we had Rob Cavallo, Pete Angelus, Steve Vai, and Gene Simmons all involved along the way, but we still couldn't break through and land a record deal to take us to the next level, which frustrated me.

I got a call from Dave Sabo, who said, "Hey, I want to send you a demo of some songs because my band Skid Row is auditioning singers." Snake told me all about their situation, saying, "Yeah, Jon Bon Jovi is working with us. He loves the band. We'll do a production deal with him."

Snake was friends with Jon as teenagers, and he was even in Bon Jovi for a moment before Richie Sambora joined, and he had some sort of pact with Jon that if one of them made it, they would help the other out. I listened to the songs and two of them stood out to me most: "18 & Life" and "Youth Gone Wild." Since they were just recorded on a four-track, they obviously weren't as produced as they eventually were on their debut record, but I listened to their demo and even in their raw form, I thought, "Man, this stuff is pretty fucking good."

I also got asked to audition for Quiet Riot when Kevin DuBrow got fired. Apparently the band members had grown tired of Kevin's public criticisms of other bands and his ego and left him after their last show in Hawaii. Eric Singer spoke to Frankie Banali and told him that they should check me out. Eric was one of the first people I met when I moved to LA—he had replaced Bill Ward as drummer of Black Sabbath, as well as having toured with Lita Ford. Valerie got a job working at a hair salon called Joey's Hair Fantasy at 8857 Sunset Boulevard, and that's where I met Eric when he came in for a cut one day. Other dudes like Quiet Riot drummer Frankie Banali, Billy Sheehan, and Dana Strum from Slaughter all used to get their hair cut there.

As much as my mind entertained these other opportunities, I couldn't leave Angora because I felt that I was the reason why they all up and moved cross-country from Philadelphia. I started the band back in Philly, and I was the one who was so adamant about going to LA. That caused Frank to move out before me, then Jimmy after me, then Robert as well, so I wholeheartedly felt responsible for them packing up their lives and moving.

It wasn't just the band members, though, their partners had also uprooted to come out on my whim—everybody was from Philly, and left family and friends behind. I just couldn't fucking bring myself to leave the band for another opportunity; I couldn't leave and fucking do that to them. It wasn't the right thing to do!

My mom came out to visit us in Hollywood during July of 1987, as Val got ready to have the baby. She wanted to be there for the birth, too, and provide some support.

Val didn't gain a lot of weight during her pregnancy, perhaps only twenty-five or thirty pounds. It was funny, because she would go out with me to my shows, and put on a little mini skirt and heels, and unless you saw her from a side view, she didn't look pregnant at all.

When she went into labor and started having contractions, I freaked! We had the suitcase packed at the door in advance, but Val decided to take a shower and lie across the bed to put her makeup on. I was thinking, "What the fuck are you doing? Let's go, we've gotta go! We better not have this kid in the fucking car!" My mother was laughing her ass off at me, but we eventually got Val in the car and to the hospital for the big event.

There were some complications during labor, which we were all tense about. It seems every time she had a contraction, her stomach tightened up, and they worried as it caused the baby's heart rate to go down to almost half before it came back up again. Val was in labor for at least seven or eight hours, and they were afraid that the heart rate situation would affect the baby's breathing and introduce the possibility of some sort of a mental or physical disability in our baby. Val was freaking nervous with the situation, which was also contributing to the baby not coming.

On a side note, to any of you thinking of having a baby in the future, I have to say the birthing classes that couples take are a total crock of shit! I spent eight weeks eating cookies and drinking juice and getting advice on how to comfort my wife. "Tell them how proud of them you are," the lady said. "Tell them how beautiful they are," I was told. "Help them with their breathing techniques and rub their bellies when they're having contractions," they said.

I followed this advice to the letter, and you know what it got me? Val looking at me in a sweaty daze and telling me in some crazy, guttural, Satanic voice to, "Leave me the fuck alone so I can concentrate!"

So I left the room as advised and smoked a few cigarettes with my mother. After we talked about the different scenarios with the hospital staff, it was decided it was best for her and the baby to have a C-section. They gave her an epidural injection into her lower back and started to prepare to cut her open for the caesarean. While they were getting ready, I walked back out of the room to give my mom this update, since she was in the waiting room.

I was out of the birthing room for no more than two minutes when the nurse came running out, telling me, "She's dilating, she's having the baby right now!"

I threw the hospital jacket and cap back on and ran back just in time to watch our baby boy make his appearance and come out. Holy shit, wow!

Watching my wife give birth on July 23, 1987, shifted my entire viewpoint and gave me a whole new respect for Val and women in general. Childbirth truly is a miracle. Twenty-eight-year-old me got a bit emotional at that point.

We named our baby boy Ian Karac Corabi—choosing Ian after my old nickname and Deep Purple's singer Ian Gillan, and Karac was the name of Robert Plant's son who tragically died from a stomach virus at age five, while Robert was touring America with Led Zeppelin back in '77. (He wrote their song "All My Love" in Karac's honor.) I was still clearly obsessed with the singers that I loved.

After the nurses cleaned him up, Val held baby Ian for a little while, then I held him for a bit before they put him in a small humicrib. I couldn't fucking believe we had made this beautiful little baby boy, until he started screaming and turned on his side, and his little ass erupted, shitting all over the window of the crib. At that point, I was filled with a sense of pride, and I walked out of the room saying, "That's my boy!"

Val was exhausted and wanted to go to sleep, so my mom and I went outside, smoked a cigarette in the hospital parking lot, and then drove to the Rainbow.

Mom and I had some drinks and pizza, and I sat there in the Rainbow thinking, "Fuck, I just had a kid today!" I couldn't believe it. I saw C. C. Deville from Poison, Robin McAuley from Michael Schenker Group (who knew Val and I from the hair salon), and Ted Nugent. They all sat with us and my mother told them about our big day, so they all bought us celebratory drinks as I whooped it up a little bit that night. I went back to the hospital the next day to see Val and Ian, and then I brought them home a day or two later.

Angora rehearsed at an old warehouse called Fernando Rehearsal Studios, down in East LA. On the first October morning of 1987, the 5.9 magnitude Whittier Narrows earthquake struck and did quite a lot of damage to our rehearsal room. The whole front wall of the building separated from the structure and the building was condemned; it was fucked. There was no way we were leaving our gear in there, though, so we had to sign all these waivers before being allowed to go in and pull our gear out. Every time a train or truck passed the building it would shake, and the entire face of the building would sway back and forth.

We kept playing gigs, trying to get signed, and another year zipped by. But right before Christmas in '88, we had strong interest from a guy at EMI Records who loved Angora and wanted to sign us to the label. He offered us a deal, and we had a letter of intent from them but ran out of time to finalize and sign the agreement before a break for the holidays.

I went back to Philadelphia over the festive season to visit my folks, where all my family got to meet seventeen-month-old Ian for the first time, and I told them I was looking forward to finally signing my deal and recording my debut album come January.

Once I got back to Hollywood, though, we were informed that right before the holidays, EMI laid off a bunch of people and our champion at the label was one of the first to go. There went our fucking record deal! I was crushed.

But honestly, as time had gone by, I noticed the guys in my band were being a little irresponsible, and I felt Angora was starting to fall apart. We had always put money in together equally for our rehearsal room, which I think was five hundred bucks a month, so everybody usually paid $125 each.

Now, when the rent would be due, I would have my $125, Frank would give me his $125, but there were more times than not that Jimmy and Robert didn't have it, so I had to cover their share. I really started to get pissed about it because they didn't have the money for rent, but they always seemed to have money for weed. And to boot, Frank and I were the only two members who had families, so to me that wasn't fair at all, and I was at the end of my rope.

We had worked with some great producers and industry people, but just couldn't land a fucking record deal. The pieces of the puzzle were just not fitting together. Rob Cavallo tried to get us on Warner Brothers. Steve Vai produced songs with us. Gene Simmons liked us but not our manager, thinking she was going to be a complete pushover and not be taken seriously. David Lee Roth's manager Pete Angeles had said to me, "I love your vibe, but I'm not real crazy about the guys you're playing with, and I'm not real crazy about your manager."

Allen Kovac was the head of a management company called The Left Bank Organization, whose artist list included Lita Ford, Richard Marx, Vixen, LA Guns, and Shark Island. He came to see us perform, along with three or four of his staff including a younger manager named John Greenberg, who initially started with Kovac as an intern.

They showed some interest in Angora, too, but said to me, "We'll sign you, but we're not going to sign the rest of the guys. We don't feel like they're up to par."

Greenberg gave me his business card and said to keep in touch.

I filed all these opinions and viewpoints in the back of my head.

Hollywood was glorious but also a devious adult playground at that point in time, and we were all wide-eyed about being there—in the beginning.

One night, I was walking to the 7-Eleven around the corner from my house to get milk for the kids' breakfast, and I happen to see this really pimped out Cadillac El Dorado parked on Yucca Street by this funky little bar. As I walked past the car, a Black guy got out of the car with a white fur hat and matching fur coat. We made eye contact for a second, and he looked a little "off." He looked familiar to me, but he was really jittery, and talking to himself, and kept getting in and out of the car, just acting weird, like he was looking for something. I watched him for a second or two, trying to figure out where I'd seen him before, and kept walking to the store.

I grabbed some cigarettes and food, then paid and headed back to my apartment. On my return home, I passed the car again, and the guy was now sitting in the driver's seat, sucking on a glass pipe, smoking crack. Again, he looked right at me and smiled. But now he wasn't wearing his big furry hat, and it immediately clicked who this guy was. I was staring at Sly Stone, one of my childhood heroes, all sweaty and out of his head smoking crack alone on a seedy, dark street in "Hollyweird."

Another time in almost the same fashion, I walked to the same 7-Eleven with a neighbor friend from the apartment building. As we were walking into the store, a bum was lying on the ground, and he asked us for change. So as we left, I gave the bum a couple of bucks and started walking home. My buddy turned to me and said, "You don't know who that was do you?"

I said, "No, should I?"

He then asked me if I liked Three Dog Night. I said, "I fucking love that band! Yes!"

He said, "Well that was Chuck Negron, one of the singers, that you just gave money to." I couldn't believe it. I went back and looked at him again, for a second from across the parking lot, and it was him! His hair was dirty and matted; he obviously hadn't bathed in ages, but he had the moustache and the unforgettable face that sang "Joy To The World," "One," and "Pieces Of April."

It was so sad to me; I felt horrible. I kept thinking, "How does someone go from the heights of massive rock stardom, like those two guys had, to literally becoming a bum begging for change?" It was just another reminder why I never wanted to get involved with any of that shit.

I met Chuck again later in my career, and told him the story, and he told me some horror stories about his addictions. After thirty-one trips to rehab, he finally got his shit together, found his faith, and continues to tour to this day. I highly recommend his book *Three Dog Nightmare*. I bought it, read it, and couldn't believe what he went through. It truly was a legendary fall from grace. Little did I know, I was about to experience Angora's demise, and a friend's fall from grace for the same reasons.

Lynn Hillesheim was the girlfriend of our guitarist Jimmy, and she was also a photographer, so naturally we had her shoot some Angora promo photos for us. Lynn came to me one day and said, "Jimmy's really bad with drugs; he's smoking crack. He took our rent money and spent it, and he took some of my cameras and pawned them for cash." I soon realized Jimmy had also taken a couple of my Marshall heads and some cabinets that I had lent him, and he pawned them, too.

I knew Jimmy and Frank had always smoked weed and were kind of dabbling with other drugs, but I didn't realize they were getting so carried away smoking crack. I could now see they were both somewhat gaunt, starting to lose weight, and starting to lose all interest in anything else. I was all about going out and doing shows and having some cocktails and partying, but not to this extent where people are losing control of their lives and not taking things seriously. The priorities just weren't right to me. Angora had indeed fallen apart.

Frank was a mess and was trying to get his shit together, but I had reached the point where I thought, fuck this, I don't need this anymore. I told them, "This is bullshit. I didn't come here to babysit. I didn't come here to just party. I want to be a fucking rock star, so I'm done. I'm quitting, I'm out," and I fucking left.

According to Lynn, Jimmy's mom had sent him some money a few times, thinking she was helping him pay rent or helping him out of a financial jam. I was pissed but concerned for my friend, so I picked up the phone, and I called Jimmy's mom and said, "Hey, Mrs. Marchiano, listen, I don't know if you know this or not, but your son is a fucking drug addict. You're sending him money, and he's not using it for what he's telling you; he's buying drugs with it."

Jimmy's brother Joey got on the phone with me, and I told him he was fucking smoking crack. He flew out to LA within days and took Jimmy immediately back to Philadelphia. I felt horrible that I had "ratted" Jimmy out, but in hindsight, I feel that we all saved his life to some degree, and he eventually got his shit together and is doing quite well.

Hate was growing fast in their hazy cloud of crack. (How true those words ring in my ears!) If they were choosing to be crackheads instead of rock stars, then I no longer felt obligated and responsible for them moving from Philly. I was done with Angora. It was time for me to change course and find another way forward.

8
Let It Scream

John Greenberg soon called me in the summer of 1989 asking, "Hey, man, what are you doing?"

I said, "Well, I'm actually looking for something new because I left my band."

He told me that Paul Gilbert had left Racer X to play guitar in a new band called Mr. Big with David Lee Roth's bassist Billy Sheehan. Furthermore, the singer of Racer X, Jeff Martin, had switched to playing drums for Badlands, led by Ozzy Osbourne's former guitarist Jake E. Lee and former Black Sabbath singer Ray Gillen, who I'd met a few years earlier when I was in my brief stint with the New York band Cathedral.

The remaining three Racer X guys—guitarist Bruce Bouillet, bassist John Alderete, and drummer Scott Travis—had started a new band with a singer Jamie Brown from a band called Roxanne. I went and saw them play, and Greenberg called me the next day and said, "Listen, between you, me, and the fence post, I love the band, but every person from record labels that has heard them so far has basically said they didn't think the singer was right for the band in some form. So, do you want to audition?"

I said, "Abso-fucking-lutely!"

I first spoke with John and Bruce on the phone, and then met them at a rehearsal place in the San Fernando Valley. We jammed on Bowie's "Moonage Daydream," which Racer X had covered, followed by a couple of new Racer X songs. That felt cool, so we started working on some more new originals.

They played me a riff that I took home and further developed, as we put together our first song called "Hard Times." We wrote another two songs through rehearsals and recorded the three songs as a demo at a studio. We would also jam on Van Halen covers a lot and slip off the tracks a bit, so rehearsals felt a bit disorganized; it was not totally focused, but we were working on shit nonetheless.

Racer X had been popular in San Francisco, so we booked a mid-October gig up in Northern California at The Stone in San Francisco. We even played that weekend under the name Racer X. After our last gig, we left the Bay Area about three in the morning on a Sunday. Scott Travis and I were in a car with his drum tech, who rolled a big fat joint and passed it around.

As we drove over the four-and-a-half-mile-long Bay Bridge, Scott took a long toke on the joint and as he exhaled the smoke, he said, "Man, bridges fucking freak me out. I have a little anxiety when I go over bridges. Brother, could you imagine if this bridge fucking collapsed?"

We got back to Los Angeles, and I began another working week with Ad Delivery. On Tuesday afternoon, I swung by home and picked Valerie up, so we could go out as soon as I finished my last drop-off for the day.

Val stayed in the car while I ran into my last delivery, and when I got back in the car, she asked, "Hey, is the San Francisco-Oakland Bay Bridge a big bridge?"

I said, "Yeah, it's huge! It's massive, why?"

With a somewhat worried look on her face, she replied, "They said on the radio that they just had a 6.9 magnitude earthquake in San Francisco and it collapsed."

As we listened to the radio, more news came in. There was panic at the 1989 World Series game between the San Francisco Giants and the Oakland A's; they lost TV reception across the nation before game three. And they said a whole fifty-foot section of the south-westbound upper deck had completely collapsed onto the north-eastbound freeway lanes below.

I just fucking drove over that bridge two days ago. All I could think about was seeing Scott in a cloud of smoke, talking about that bridge collapsing. Scott fucking Nostradamus Travis! Who knew!

One day at rehearsals, Scott told us he got a phone call to audition for Judas Priest, since their drummer Dave Holland was no longer in the band. We were all really bummed that he might be leaving but really happy for him. They flew Scott over to London for a week, during which he jammed with Rob Halford and the other guys. Before he headed back to LA, they told him, "Yeah, you're the right guy for us. You've got the gig!"

He then recorded the *Painkiller* album with them, which begins with a little showcase of his powerful double-kick drumming style, before any other instruments join in on the title track. More than thirty years later, Scott Travis is still the drummer in Judas Priest.

As pleased as we were for Scott, it meant we needed to find a new drummer. We tried everyone we knew, and even put an ad in the fucking paper to audition all these different cats that came and tried out—it seemed to take forever.

We tried the drummer from Salty Dog, Khurt Maier. We tried Anthony Focx, who at that point was best known as the drummer in Alice Cooper's video for his hit song "Poison." We wanted Jimmy D'Anda from the BulletBoys, since he was a cousin of our bass player Alderete, but that wasn't to be either.

Greenberg said to us that he knew a guy, Walt Woodward III, who was the drummer in Shark Island, but Shark Island were done and dusted. We sent Walt a few tracks and invited him to audition. He wasn't technically the greatest drummer on the planet by Racer X standards, but he sure had great feel and great chops, and fit perfectly with what we were doing. So, as the new decade began, he became our drummer.

At this point, Greenberg came down to rehearsals and heard the three or four songs we had written. He said the right vibe was there, so he wanted to showcase us to some labels.

One of these first songs was called "Man in the Moon," which Bruce and John had started writing with Jamie Brown prior to my joining the band. I thought the song was really cool but felt there was something lacking with it. We pulled it back a little bit and slowed it down and gave it a little more swing. Another track was "I Don't Care," which Scott had helped to write before he left for Judas Priest.

The showcase was to be for Hollywood Records, a new label created by The Walt Disney Company. The label's President was Peter Paterno, who had been Racer X's attorney for years, and they had just bought the North American distribution rights to Queen's entire catalog for fucking ten million dollars. The label's A&R Rep was Rachel Matthews, who had been very interested in Angora when she worked at Capitol Records.

Even though we had great connections there, Greenberg did what all good managers do: he picked up the phone to other record labels to start what industry insiders call a "bidding war," and told them, "I've got this all-new band. They're great. I'm getting a lot of interest from labels. They're doing a private showcase for Hollywood Records, so I'm wondering if you would like to check them out, too, before they get signed?"

He called Capitol, then he called Warner Brothers, then Atlantic, and then EMI, and Polygram, and more. Even though our lineup had never done a gig together before, we performed our four songs during two showcases per day over four or five days, and by the end of that week, three or four labels had set a deal on the table for us.

We discussed the various merits of each deal with Greenberg, and his new partner Tim Heyne, and decided to go with Hollywood Records. We thought they were going to be hungry since they were a new label, and they would have deep pockets because Disney owned them. Plus, we already had established relationships with Peter Paterno and Rachel Matthews.

I finally signed my first record deal, and at that point they just told us to go and write songs!

The Queen Mary is a huge ocean liner that primarily sailed on the North Atlantic Ocean from 1936 to 1967, when it docked in the port of Long Beach, California, and retired with a permanent mooring there ever since. It was converted into an ornate floating hotel with restaurants and a museum.

It was the perfect location for Hollywood Records to throw a massive party as their recently signed Queen released their new studio album *Innuendo*. It was the most decadent fucking party I think I've ever been to. And I've been to my share of parties, mind you!

Everybody who was anybody in the music industry was there, walking in on the red carpet. They flew press in from all over the world. All the members of The Scream weren't asked if we wanted to go, we were told we HAD to go! The four of us got all dressed up and joined in the festivities.

They had a whole room with seafood buffets for guests—all the lobsters, shrimp, oysters, and scallops you could eat. Then they had the beef room, and the pork room, and the chicken room, and the fucking dessert room!

As we ate and ordered drinks from the open bar alongside the guys from Metallica, Lisa Marie Presley, Steve Vai, Weird Al Yankovic, Steve Jones from the Sex Pistols, Jim Kerr from Simple Minds, Billy Sheehan, and Cheap Trick, all of a sudden, word boomed out that Queen was arriving on the ship.

The crowd parted like the Red Sea. As I stood two-deep back, behind the people lining the red carpet, I watched their drummer Roger Taylor walk through, followed by guitarist Brian May, who glanced at me as he walked past in his red jacket, then stopped and came back. He took a longer look at me and waved hello. I looked around to either side and then pointed to myself, and he gave me a thumbs-up, before he reached in, shook my hand, then turned and kept walking.

I had no idea what the fuck that was about, since I'd never met him before. I was freaking out, since I was a huge Queen fan. Did somebody tell him about us? Maybe there was some talk of The Scream at the label? I didn't know, but I was sure happy I got to shake his fucking hand!

Freddie Mercury was seriously ill back home in London at the time and was unable to attend, so they had an animatronic robot in one of the rooms that played Queen music while the robot did all Freddie's signature stage moves.

We watched them do a Q&A with the press, followed by a photo session. They had a fire-eater, a juggler, a pirate with a real monkey, and more on-board entertainment.

Toward the end of the party, everybody was invited up on the Queen Mary's top deck. They absolutely blasted a few Queen songs through a massive fucking PA and put on an over-the-top fireworks display from a barge out in the harbor for the finale song "Bohemian Rhapsody," which lit up the Saturday night Long Beach sky.

The party for 2,000 people apparently cost about $200,000 and was as much a launch event for Hollywood Records as it was for Queen's album. We were now signed to this label and feeling we were going to be the next Led Zeppelin, so parties like this would be a regular occurrence for us.

John Alderete and Bruce Bouillet split after the fireworks display, but Walt and I hung out at the bar to have another free cocktail or five. As we continued quenching our thirst amongst the thinning crowd, Brian May and Roger Taylor came into the bar.

Walt was Mr. Social Butterfly and led the way walking over to them and said, "Brian, Roger, great fucking party! I'm Walt from The Scream, and we're label-mates now. This is John, our singer."

I got talking with Brian and asked why he shook my hand on arrival. He said, "Oh, I thought you were somebody else that I had met," and we laughed about it.

We chatted for quite a while until they called last drinks and closed the bar on us. That's when Brian said, "Hey, do you guys want to get another cocktail or something from somewhere?"

Roger said, "I've got some booze in my room," so we went down into the fucking hotel part of the ship and into his cabin room, where we sat and talked about The Scream, Queen, just all kinds of shit. Roger and Walt kept leaving the room, so I talked with Brian mostly and enjoyed his stories.

I could tell Roger was a bit more outgoing and ready to party, while Brian was super fucking cool, down to earth, and sweet as pie. I kept pinching myself thinking, "Oh my God, I'm fucking hanging out with Brian May and Roger Taylor, drinking cognac and everything else out of their minibar." As much as I love Freddie, Brian and Roger were just as fucking cool to me. The whole event was awesome and super surreal.

Crazy party aside, my routine was getting up every day at six or seven o'clock in the morning. I still worked driving for Ad Delivery all day long, before going home to eat some dinner, see Val and the kids, and grab a quick shower.

John Alderete would then come by and pick me up, and we'd get a coffee on our way to a seven o'clock start at our rehearsal room in Van Nuys. Bruce had a little four-track recorder that we used to record everything good we came up with.

We worked on writing songs until about 10:00 or 11:00 p.m., and if we had written anything decent, I'd then sit at my kitchen table and try to write lyrics until one or two o'clock in the morning. Rinse and repeat. We rehearsed and wrote five nights a week for the better part of a year. We even rehearsed two Saturdays a month from ten in the morning until one or two the next morning. It was grueling, man.

As we wrote and demoed songs, we gave them to Rachel and Greenberg, and they'd tell us, "Yeah, that one is great. That one, I'm not so sure about. That one's awesome." We just kept chipping away the stone.

One of the first songs we all wrote together was "Catch Me If You Can," and it had a Van Halen vibe to it. Personally, as much as I dug Van Halen and saw them live a few times, and I love David Lee Roth, I wasn't familiar with all of their songs. Stylistically, I was more about Humble Pie, Grand Funk Railroad, Led Zeppelin, Aerosmith, and The Beatles.

I think John and Bruce naturally adapted to my vocal stylings and based their playing on what I was all about. While we were writing a song called "Outlaw" that I worked up the riff for, I said to Bruce, "This would be sleazier than shit if there was a fucking slide guitar on it." Bruce had never really played much slide guitar.

We started turning him onto Aerosmith's Joe Perry slide, ZZ Top's Billy Gibbons slide work, and that of Mick Taylor in the Stones. Bruce bought some old blues records and locked himself away for about a week and figured it out. I swear to God, when he came out of the room in a matter of a week, he was playing slide guitar like he fucking invented it! The dynamic was very cool.

I would write a song, and it would be very basic, like a riff verse, chorus, riff verse, and chorus. I would say, "I don't know what to do for the solo, or a cool ending."

That's where John and Bruce would come in, they would take my simple thing and add things to it that made it cooler. Especially John, who would say, "No, don't do that. Let's go to the left instead of the right."

All these great ideas came together, and I thought it sounded killer. Their music in Racer X had been very different and quite technical. Some of their songwriting and style started to wear off on me, and I think my style and sound started to wear off on them, too. We were all starting to think about songs a little differently, and it just worked.

Rachel Matthews wanted us to do a show for a bunch of people at the label, at a club called Sash in North Hollywood. Even the label head Peter came to see us along with all their marketing staff.

A Canadian singer Sass Jordan was also there, with her manager Lisa, so I got to meet her and briefly chatted. We did a set of our new original material, along with a couple of covers at the end.

We couldn't think of a name for the band to save our lives. We were called Black Cloud for a minute and passed through Virgin Voodoo and Rhythm Riot, too, before we came up with SOS, which was Saints or Sinners.

When we were done playing the gig, Rachel came over to us and said, "That was the worst fucking gig I've ever seen in my life." She said, "Everybody is walking out of here, thinking why the fuck did we sign these guys?" We were mortified.

To Greenberg's credit, he went to the label the next day and explained, "These guys have been locked away writing in a room for almost a fucking year. You can't expect them to stand on stage and perform one show and just crush it or knock it out of the ballpark."

We doubled down in rehearsal, knowing we had to reprove ourselves again. A month or so later, we threw our gear in a van and did a southwestern run in eight to ten cities like Phoenix, Tucson, Albuquerque, Dallas, and Austin, before we turned around and came back home.

All the label heads flew out this time to see one of the shows in Austin, Texas, and we fucking destroyed them. And when I say destroyed, I mean, we fucking nailed every fucking person in that club to a fucking wall! We were not taking "no" for an answer. There was no way we were losing that fucking record deal. We were so pissed they doubted us and walked on stage on fire! They were like holy fuck! That's the band we signed, that's what we want! And as the story goes, we absolutely redeemed ourselves—thank God!

The label then started talking to us about producers and sent three or four different guys down, but none of them felt right, so they asked us, "Who do you guys want to work with? Give us a list."

John and Bruce had Ted Templeman on their list, for example, who had produced Van Halen, The Doobie Brothers, and more recently the BulletBoys. But across the board, there was only one name that we all had on our list, and he was at the very top of my list: Eddie Kramer.

Eddie had worked with the Rolling Stones and The Beatles (as engineer on their song "All You Need is Love") and then worked with Jimi Hendrix to create his classic albums, including *Are You Experienced?* and *Electric Ladyland*. If that wasn't enough, he then engineered four fucking Led Zeppelin albums!

But wait, that's not all: he then produced Kiss *Alive!*, *Rock and Roll Over*, *Love Gun*, *Alive II*, and Ace Frehley's solo album. He also mixed Humble Pie's double live album, and engineered Bowie's *Young Americans* album, among so many more. All he was missing from my life's soundtrack was fucking Aerosmith.

The label said, "All right, we'll send the tape to Eddie Kramer. Let's just take a shot and see what he says."

Eddie had an office in New York but lived upstate. The label told us that when he got the envelope, he opened it up and popped the cassette in his car's deck for the drive home. After hearing "Man in the Moon" and "I Don't Care," he stopped his car and lost his shit. They said he ran over to a phone booth and called the label saying he wanted to see us as soon as possible.

They flew Eddie out to LA, and we did a showcase for him, where he just fell in love with the band. His ponytail was flopping around, as he was headbanging away while we played. Two songs in, we all looked at each other and smiled—we knew he was the guy we needed to produce our record.

We then told him we had a faster Van Halen-esque song that a lot of people hated called "Catch Me if You Can." We played it for him as he began headbanging again. "This is fucking awesome. You know what? Every record needs one of these songs! It's great," he said.

Eddie made us feel awesome; he made us feel good. He was excited.

The label started making arrangements to have Eddie Kramer produce our fucking record for us!

Our A&R Rep. Rachel Matthews knew Duff McKagan from Guns N' Roses. Duff was a Seattle guy, and Rachel had tried to sign grunge pioneers Mother Love Bone and was very much tied into that whole Seattle circuit. The label was looking for angles to market our brand-new band, so she wanted Duff to be involved as a coproducer, thinking that it may help sway some of GN'R's huge fanbase to check us out.

Duff helped us greatly with some demos and was to coproduce the record with Eddie Kramer. However, that was in the days when Duff was drinking copious amounts of vodka a day from breakfast on, and he was pretty messy. Freshly divorced, he was also doing pain pills as he needed shoulder surgery. He partied and drank hard in his Laurel Canyon house or in the LA clubs every night, and he was a bit of a mess.

We were nervous about it all and didn't want the arrangement to continue. We let Duff go to have his surgery and go do his thing, and we gave him thanks in the record. Duff has since described that period as one of the darkest of his life.

We did preproduction for the record at a place called Leeds Rehearsal in North Hollywood. Eddie was working with us to break all the songs down to their barest form. At one point, we were working on Walt's bass drum pattern, and how to sync that with what Alderete was playing on bass.

As we were doing this, two guys came in and sat in the back of the room wearing overalls with their hair pulled back in a ponytail under baseball caps. They would briefly talk to Eddie then leave, as Eddie refocused on hashing things out with us.

After this happened a few times, Eddie then said to us, "Oh, hey guys, I'm sorry, let me introduce you to some friends of mine. This is Steve and Peter." We looked at them for a second and then flipped out, as we put two and two together. Holy fuck, it was Steve Marriott and Peter Frampton from Humble Pie.

They were working in the adjacent building on the other side of the complex's driveway. Steve and Peter were over in that recording studio working on new material with the intention of putting Humble Pie back together in its original form. They had a couple of new songs down in "The Bigger They Come" and "I Won't Let You Down." Once Eddie was done with our record, he was going to record their reunion record next.

One day I was out in the lobby, by the studio's coffee machine, and Steve walked in to get a coffee. I didn't want to be too fanboyish, but I approached Steve and said, "I've always been such a fucking fan of your voice, especially on songs like 'C'mon Everybody,' 'Hot 'n' Nasty,' and 'Black Coffee.'"

He said he thought that was cool, and offered up some advice in his English accent. "I really dig your material, too. There's melody there, and your chords follow the melody. Just remember when you're writing, if you can write a song and play it stripped-down and entertain people with just an acoustic guitar, then you've done your job as a songwriter. Don't forget it!"

In recent years, I've been touring solo with just my acoustic guitar and my voice on stage, doing exactly what Steve said.

Before we finished our chat that day, I said to him, "Hey, man, I would love if you would perhaps play harmonica, guitar, or sing with me on our record."

Without hesitation, he said, "Oh, yeah, mate. Absolutely, I'd love to. I'm going to London and when I get back, I will absolutely do whatever you guys want me to do on it. I'll do it for sure."

I told Eddie and the fucking guys, "Oh my God, this is going to be killer: Steve Marriott said he would sing on the fucking record with me!"

We started recording some of the drums for the album at Ocean Way Recording before we moved on to Conway Studios. We finished the record at American Studios in Calabasas and that's where we were when we got the call: Steve Marriott had died. We were all devastated. Especially Eddie, who was not just going to produce their record, but he was great mates with the guys. We took a couple of days off so Eddie could wrap his head around it all and grieve.

Apparently, Steve flew home to England from LA with his wife Toni Poulton, who said that during the flight he drank heavily, was in a foul mood, and they argued. They then went out to dinner with a friend at one of Steve's favorite restaurants, where he drank more and continued to argue with his wife into the night before eventually getting a taxi to his house by himself. Someone driving by at dawn saw the roof of his place ablaze and called the fire department.

It's believed the most probable cause of the fire was that soon after he got home drunk, jet-lagged, and exhausted, he lit a cigarette while in bed and passed out in a deep sleep. Investigators recorded it as an accidental death by smoke inhalation on that Saturday morning of April 20, 1991.

We recorded all the guitar tracks a couple of times at American Studios, but Bruce wasn't completely happy with the sound, and neither was Eddie Kramer. Bruce had a great tone but didn't like how it sounded on tape, so he redid them, which caused some friction. There was a push and pull, and everybody was tense.

Eddie played us the shit he recorded with Led Zeppelin like "The Wanton Song" and "Trampled Under Foot," and we listened as he highlighted things, keen to get similar guitar sounds. Bruce was of the school where he had some old Marshall Plexi amps, and he ran it through an attenuator to get his sound, more like Eddie Van Halen.

Eddie sat us down one night and said, "Listen, unless you get rid of that attenuator and you get rid of this pedal and that pedal, you're never going to have that Zeppelin sound you're all looking for. Just forget it."

Eddie shared more knowledge with us, "Listen, man, Led Zeppelin worked because they each had a specific place in the grand scheme of equalization, their EQ. The way John Bonham tuned his drums, he was the middle of the EQ spectrum. Jimmy Page would take his Marshall and open it up volume wise, so it would be cranking, but he would roll his bass down really low or off. That made his guitar very bright and listening to it alone, it was almost annoyingly bright. Then John Paul Jones would roll off a lot of the treble on his bass sound."

It sounded horrible listening to him explain their tones individually, but when you put the three of them together, Jimmy Page had the top, John Bonham had the middle, and John Paul Jones was moving all of the air underneath. And it fucking worked!

He said, "Your tones are so fucking huge, you're not going to get that sound."

It got to the point where Bruce started insulting Eddie.

Eddie simply said in response, "Well fuck you then, I don't want to work with you." Alderete, Walt, and I were stunned and panicked, thinking, "This is it; we're blowing this royally before we even get off the ground." Greenberg spoke to Eddie and Bruce, and came up with a working schedule or arrangement, if you will, so we could continue moving forward.

With Eddie and Bruce being out of sync, we had to bring in Garth Richardson to work with Bruce, while Walt, John, and I continued working with Eddie. Even though there was this tension, I had such a great fucking time recording the album over those five weeks.

Alderete was the one who was always getting into new music coming out. He listened to a lot of Tupac, and he was listening to the Red Hot Chili Peppers, particularly their *Blood Sugar Sex Magik* record, which we all enjoyed. You can hear that influence in his funk-infused bass lines during "Tell Me Why."

While work progressed on the album, Greenberg ran a copyright search on the band's name Saints or Sinners, and coincidently found that one of my old guitar players Ron E. Kayfield from Philadelphia actually owned the name. How fucking weird is that?

Greenberg called him and said, "Hey, Ron, we're called Saints or Sinners, and we really like this name. We're working on a record and want to know if you will sell us this name?"

When he said he wanted twenty-five grand for the fucking name, Greenberg told him to go fuck himself. He said, "I'll call this band Hamster Balls before I pay you twenty-five fucking grand for it. It's not going to happen!"

We still liked the initials SOS, so we thought we'd call the band Sons of Silence instead. I was at Tattoo Mania one day, and I told my buddy, tattoo artist Gill "The Drill" Montie, about the name. He immediately said, "Dude, you absolutely cannot call your band Sons of Silence. That's the name of a fucking motorcycle gang out in the Midwest, and they're the meanest fucking biker gang ever! If the Hell's Angels want to do a hit on somebody, that's who THEY call. They will not ask you to change the name, they'll just kill you all."

Good to know, Gill, good to know.

Sons of Silence—out!

Sitting around one day, Walt said, "How about The Scream?" We had literally come up with hundreds of potential band names, and all the good ones were taken. The Scream? It was so fucking obvious, surely somebody already had the name. Greenberg ran the copyright search and surprisingly, it was available. We became The Scream.

Once we had finished the record, we sat with the label's art department to come up with the album title and cover art. We all felt it had to make some sort of a statement. We had always liked The Beatles' *Let It Be*, and the Rolling Stones' *Let It Bleed*, so we called our album *Let It Scream*. We then had a skull and flames logo designed for it, and we were all set to go.

9
I Believe in Me

We shot a video for "Man in the Moon" in Los Angeles before the record came out. It was a two-day shoot where the first day was all outdoors, which included the video's opening scenes by a white church with Walt perched way up in its tower, banging a tambourine.

The location was a place off the San Pedro Freeway route I-110 in LA where there were a few old historic Victorian homes picked up from around the city and transported to the area. My young son Ian joined us on set that day, and even made a little cameo at the very start of the video, pushing a big lawnmower across the grass.

After a full-day's shooting from dawn to 10:00 or 11:00 p.m., we arrived at dawn again on the second day to shoot live performance footage in a video staging rehearsal room in LA's Silver Lake neighborhood.

The producer brought in a little PA system that you'd see at a wedding reception—two little speakers on poles, basically. While he played the song through it, we performed, lip syncing to the track, but with the noise from Walt's drums and cymbals, we couldn't hear the song properly, so they had to go and get a much bigger PA system. That delayed the process for several hours, so we sat around bored, which lead to Walt sending out for some beer, whiskey, vodka, and some other goodies for us to kill the time… And we did. By the time the PA actually arrived, we were all pretty fucked up, but we had a job to finish, so we got back to work.

Toward the end of the song, there's a scream that I do, and the producer wanted me to put my head back and look up at the camera that was filming me from above and panning out. Next thing I knew, everyone was standing around me on the ground, trying to give me fucking orange juice. I had passed out for some fucking reason, maybe the drinking or perhaps it was low blood sugar level.

We shot until midnight, and I was exhausted but happy with the way my first video clip turned out.

We worked on promotions with a fan club company called American Noise that also worked with the BulletBoys and the Black Crowes. We held a listening party for the album on the Disney lot in Burbank for some radio people and our friends, and the label then sent Bruce and I out in a tour bus with Greenberg on a huge radio promotional tour.

Eddie Kramer also came to a bunch of the dates, which was cool. We hit three or four radio stations a day across America over the course of a five-week period. The fan club often invited fans to come and meet Bruce and I at the hotels we were staying at for a meet and greet in our ancient but awesome tour bus.

I remember going to radio station WNEW in New York City for an interview that turned out to be quite disastrous…almost. Bruce and I arrived in town the night before and decided to hit a watering hole. After a bit of a search, we found a late-night bar that was apparently co-owned by the Hell's Angels, called The Scrap Bar. We bellied up to the bar around ten that night and stayed there until almost five the following morning, at which point the management of the club politely asked us to go home. We cabbed it back to the hotel and slept for about two hours, when our label rep called our rooms and told us we had a huge interview with a big radio station in town at 9:00 a.m. Still very intoxicated, we showered and got ready to go.

The station sent a limo for us, but the air conditioning wasn't working, and it was extremely hot in the back of the car. Between the booze, the lack of sleep, and the heat, we were both feeling a bit woozy. When we arrived at the station, we were told to wait for the program director—a guy named Ian who was in charge of adding new music to their playlist. When Ian entered the lobby, I stood up to shake his hand and my nose started gushing blood and wouldn't stop. Eddie Kramer rushed me to a bathroom, and I stuffed my nose with toilet paper to stop the bleeding.

After a few minutes, I came back, and we were escorted into the control room for the interview. Feeling a bit embarrassed, I apologized. Ian then asked if we wanted some coffee or water, and Bruce, Eddie, and I all said, "Coffee would be great, thank you." We started doing the prerecorded interview, when Ian's assistant walked into the room with the coffee. As soon as I smelled the aroma of the coffee, I started to violently throw-up all over the console, and the room. Eddie rushed me out again, back to the bathroom, and upon our return, I was asked to leave. I never thought I'd ever have a song played on any station in New York City, but after some smooth damage control by our label rep and management, they added us to their playlist.

The band members, myself included, were starting to become tired and quite volatile with each other at times. We all had worked tirelessly for a year, and it was starting to show. For example, soon after we got back from the radio promo tour, John and Bruce saw Skid Row play at the Whisky a Go Go in LA. The next time I saw the guys at rehearsals they were saying something like, "Holy shit. We need to be more like Skid Row." They wanted us to dress and present ourselves more like Skid Row.

I just sat there drinking a quart of beer in a brown bag, getting pissed off at their insistence that we needed to be more like Skid Row, when I finally had enough and said, "Well I'm not Sebastian Bach, guys, and we're not Skid fucking Row!"

Bruce made a derogatory comment back to me, something along the lines of, "That's because Sebastian Bach would eat you alive!"

Without hesitation, I threw my bottle of beer at him and said, "I'll fucking kill you right now, motherfucker. Fuck you!" The other guys had to separate us.

Walt was the kind of guy who just wanted to go and have a beer and fucking hang out and have fun. He was just like John Belushi's character Bluto from *Animal House*. I wanted to have fun, too, but I was always more concerned about the show and the bigger picture of the band. The fucking problem with all of us was we were fine when we were sober, but we were getting exactly like that joke phrase: For instant assholes, just add alcohol.

The record label pushed "Outlaw" as a teaser track, and then went to radio with "Man in the Moon." One of our managers Tim was absolutely convinced that we were leading off with the wrong song, mainly because the track was too long at 5:40. He said, "If you guys get ten radio stations playing this fucking track, I'll be shocked."

The first Tuesday's radio report came in and showed thirty-five radio stations across the US had added the song to their playlists. After six weeks it had grown to almost two hundred radio stations playing our song, which far exceeded all expectations.

This was done without any MTV exposure to this point. While we kept submitting the video to MTV, they would only add a few new videos to their roster each week from the hundreds they must have been receiving from labels.

One week we heard that we were definitely going to be added to MTV. We got all excited about making our MTV debut, only to see that we had been bumped again, this time by The Simpsons and their video for that stupid song "Do the Bartman." They blew us off for a fucking yellow TV cartoon kid fucking rapping on a song cowritten and coproduced by Michael Jackson. What the fuck? Eat my fucking shorts, you little yellow prick!

It took a while, but we finally got the video on MTV. By the time they added the song, it actually gave the single a little more life, since it was starting to die down on radio.

We hit the road opening for the BulletBoys behind their *Freakshow* album, who were very supportive of us. They also had a band Blackeyed Susan on the tour that played before them. They were a new band on the scene from Philadelphia, formed by "Dizzy" Dean Davidson after he had a big falling out with Britny Fox and brought in Cinderella's keyboardist Rick Critini to play guitar with him.

My Angora guitarist Jimmy actually ended up replacing Rick in Blackeyed Susan, and I had earlier turned down Britny Fox's offer for me to replace Dean and join them as their singer—it's funny how the world works!

About a week or so into the tour, Blackeyed Susan left to go home, so it was then just The Scream and the BulletBoys for the rest of the six- to eight-week run.

Our poor fucking tour manager was a guy named Quake, and we all drove him crazy.

We were in Buffalo, New York, when BulletBoys drummer Jimmy D'Anda turned up preshow with a baggy. He said, "It's my birthday, fuckers," as he reached into the little plastic bag and gave me, Bruce, and John some of his mushrooms.

We were tripping our balls off when we hit the stage. We fucking crushed our set, and then the BulletBoys went on and tore it up, too. Back on the bus after the show, we were enjoying cocktails and drinking beers when Quake came to us and asked, "Where's Alderete?"

We said, "Fuck, we thought he was still in the club or something."

Quake went into the club, then came back, looking everywhere for him but he was nowhere to be found. We were freaking out, tripping out.

It got to two in the morning, three in the morning, and there was still no sign of Alderete. We had a five-hour drive to the next city and our bus driver Billy Hardaway had been sitting there for hours, ready to get going.

Finally, one of the guys from the club came over to the tour bus and said, "Hey, guys, your bass player is on the phone."

Quake ran into the club and started fucking yelling into the phone at Alderete, "Where the fuck are you?"

He goes, "Dude, I'm at fucking Niagara Falls, bro. I'm just tripping my balls off with these two chicks and having a great fucking time. Come and join us!"

Another time Greenberg lost a bet to Alderete, so he bought him a high-powered pellet gun that looked like a real handgun. Alderete was drunk on the tour bus one night in North Carolina and started shooting us all in the back of the head, the neck, the fucking ass, you name it. He then fucking shot the windshield of the bus and cracked the windshield and put a nice little divot in it. We had to fucking pay for that.

And then, after our show at a club in Raleigh, North Carolina, we were sitting on the bus drinking. Alderete was wasted and fucking hanging out of the bus door, yelling at people, waving his pellet gun around. There were cops everywhere in the parking lot keeping an eye on the night's proceedings, so we grabbed him by his hair and pulled him back into the fucking bus before he got fucking shot by a cop or something.

It was definitely four really green fools that had never been on tour before figuring it all out as we went. It was fun signing autographs for fans, the press, radio stations, and we appreciated all the attention we were getting. Who wouldn't? But the rush was that hour or so on stage each night, watching the audiences grow, and seeing the songs become recognizable to the point that everybody would sing all the words with us while we were on stage.

We no sooner got home from that tour then we turned around and went right back out again playing a lot of the same places with a band out of Texas called Dangerous Toys, who were also touring behind a sophomore album, *Hellacious Acres*.

During the middle of November, we headlined the first night of the Livestock 2 festival in Zephyrhills, Florida. Their local 98 Rock radio station created the three-day event as a fusion of the spirit of Live Aid and Woodstock festivals.

We had played a few small outdoor shows before and when we pulled onto the grounds, I watched them put some of the stage together in this empty field before I went and took a little nap that turned into a long sleep.

I smoked a cigarette, had a nip of whiskey, and did some vocal exercises once I woke up in the bus, then got dressed, fixed my hair, and got ready to take the stage. I opened the tour bus door to the sound of the PA cranking music, and walked up the backstage ramp, then took a quick peek out through a gap in the stage curtain. I couldn't believe what I fucking saw. While I slept, a massive fucking crowd had rolled in.

The festival organizers estimated that we played in front of about fifty thousand people that night. It was an incredible rush performing in front of a crowd that size. It remained the biggest audience of my career for decades.

After a short break, we went right back out and started headlining our own shows, having now built up a strong following in American rock clubs, particularly in the Southeast and the Midwest. We also played cities like New York, Boston, Baltimore, and New Haven quite regularly, as well as a memorable hometown show for me at the Chestnut Cabaret in Philadelphia that September of 1991.

My dad came to see the show at the Chestnut, which was at Thirty-Eighth and Ludlow Streets. After we finished our encore, I went over to him and said, "So, what did you think, Dad?"

He looked at me, and after a long, silent pause, he said, "You said the f-word quite a bit. It's not good to say that so much, but you know, it was okay."

As I said previously, as much as he had a badass side to him, I never heard him drop the f-bomb. He never said the word fuck, ever! How the fuck can someone not do that their whole fucking life?

Our record came out in Europe about a month after it was released in the US, so we were already on tour. After a show in Panama City, Florida, Walt and John got on the bus and went to New Orleans. Bruce and I got on a plane the following day from Panama City to Miami, then Miami to London.

We got off the plane and immediately started doing press for the record, which lasted all day. We announced that we would come back to play a one-off show at the iconic London Astoria on December 6. During the day, we found out that we were doing an unprepared acoustic performance at a club later that night.

We got back to The Columbia Hotel following the acoustic set and drank until five or six o'clock in the morning with some new British friends, then got back on a plane and flew from London to Dallas, connected to Shreveport, Louisiana, where we were picked up and literally driven straight to the venue for the night's show.

Our trip was insane but apparently not quite as crazy as John and Walt's. You see, they went on a day off to the bar Pat O'Brien's in New Orleans and drank hurricanes all day. They got completely shitfaced drunk, which was becoming the everyday norm for the band. Walt had to take a piss, so without hesitation, he pulled out his dick and relieved himself in front of a patio full of tourists in one of the outdoor fountains. Obviously, a ruckus ensued, and the guys were shown the exit door. We laughed about that for a week.

While we were on tour in America, we had a crew come out on the road with us for a few weeks and film shit. They edited all the backstage and performance footage into a video for the song "I Believe in Me." We all loved the live video and thought it was great.

When we gave it to the record label, one guy there said that it was boring and everybody was doing live videos like that. He pushed the point and the label filmed a different video for the song instead.

We ended up with a stupid fucking video of some chick covered in mud in a bathtub, who eventually grabs a gun and shoots a TV that we were performing on, all in a dark blue hue. It made no fucking sense to anyone in the band, and we felt it didn't correlate to our vibe or the lyrics.

At least the previous live video showed everybody in the band having fun backstage and doing our thing. A lot of my family members including my dad and Uncle Gene were even in some of the backstage footage from our Philly show. That one guy overrode us, and we ended up with this completely different chick-in-a-bathtub bullshit. We were pissed…beyond pissed.

When we got to London, I walked into the beautiful Astoria on Charing Cross Road and said, "Who's fucking genius idea was it for us to play here? This is a two-thousand-seat theater and we've never done one gig outside of America! Why the fuck would they put us in this big theater?"

John Greenberg just laughed and told me to relax. I said, "Just for the record then, I disapprove of us playing at this place. We've built so much momentum, I do not want to walk out on stage in front of a half-full or a quarter-full crowd."

After soundcheck, we went upstairs and did an interview with Vanessa Young from MTV, who married The Almighty front man Ricky Warwick that year (now of Black Star Riders). The European press were supportive and generally gave us great reviews. *Kerrang!* magazine named us their Breakout Artist of the Year and Best New Band. I can't remember if it was *Kerrang!* or one of the other UK magazines, but they touted The Scream as a cross between Led Zeppelin and Guns N' Roses. You couldn't get any bigger rock-and-roll plug at that point.

We headed back to our dressing room and while we were getting ready, somebody knocked on the door and said, "Oi, hey lads, there some guys that have come to see the show and want to say hi to ya."

When the door opened, in walked the fucking Ramones! We were like, "What the fuck? Holy shit, it's the fucking Ramones!" We couldn't believe Joey, Johnny, CJ, and Marky had come to see us play.

It came time to perform and when I walked on stage I looked out to the audience. I was shocked to see a completely over-sold-out crowd before me in the theater. We were on fire and had an awesome show that night and were so happy to be playing in London.

The night before our show, the record label people took us to a gig at the Kilburn National Ballroom to see a new band that everybody was talking about. They said we had to check these guys out because they were fucking awesome. It was packed in this London club and then this band took the stage—they were called Nirvana.

They had released their album *Nervermind* just seven weeks prior, and as they played their new single "Smells Like Teen Spirit," Alderete said to us, "These fucking guys are really good, but they're doing something really different than what we're all about." The fucking English were eating them up.

After their set, Walt said to me, "Dude, I can't go home until I have a fucking Newcastle Brown Ale and a whiskey in an English pub."

So, we went to the Marquee Club in the Soho District. We sat at the bar while a band called Tigertailz played, who were like the UK's version of Poison. All the love bomb babies were walking around in zebra spandex, big hair, big earrings, lipstick, the whole nine yards.

Walt and I sat there with the noise level pumping through the club and ordered a couple of whiskeys with our Newcastle Brown and Guinness. Then we had another one, then another one. We were pretty lit when a fucking dude came up to me and said in the thickest of accents, "Uh, hi mate, got a fag?"

Confused, I said, "Excuse me?" to which he said, "Oh, yeah, mate, got a fag?"

I still didn't understand what the fuck he said, so I asked him to, "Say that again, one more time, and speak slowly."

"Got a fag?"

Walt overheard part of it and he said, "What did he say to you?"

I said, "I don't know what he wants bro, but I think he's calling us faggots."

Before I knew it, Walt got up and pummeled this poor fucking guy. He just beat his fucking ass, at which point the bouncers came and started kicking our asses—it was action city.

The record label guys were laughing hysterically the next day, "Oh, no, man, fag means a cigarette here." Thanks for the fucking heads up, asshole!

All in all though, it was a very memorable, fun, crazy time in London with The Scream. We had a blast on my first trip playing over there; it was killer. Since it was just the one show, I looked forward to coming back on a full tour through Europe.

After our London jaunt, we hit the road back in the States and played more of our own shows right through to Christmas 1991. Come January after the festive season, we went right back out on the road again in America to keep playing more of our own shows for a few weeks.

During that run, a fan gave me a copy of a music magazine where Nikki Sixx of Mötley Crüe was the cover story. In the article, they asked him what new music he was listening to lately, and he talked about The Scream and how great he thought we were. We were all stoked, especially John and Bruce, as they were huge Mötley Crüe fans.

While Nikki thought we were great, not all was great in The Scream, though.

One day I was in the front lounge of our tour bus as we were driving to the next show. The record label wanted to release another single, and it was one that Bruce hated, "You Are All I Need." By this point, we had already done three videos for "Man in the Moon;" "I Believe in Me;" and "Father, Mother,

Son." Now the label felt we needed to do a video for the power ballad on the record. From the back of the bus, he said, "I fucking hate that song. I never liked that song." He pointed forward at me and said, "He fucking wrote that song. I'm not going to fucking do that song. And if we do a video for it, I QUIT!"

I took offense to it, got up, and started marching down the aisle toward him. On the way, I put my fist through the fucking glass on the microwave door, and started tearing the bus apart, shouting, "Fuck you, Bruce!"

The driver pulled over and our manager John Greenberg grabbed me and took me outside. I smoked a cigarette and calmed down. I knew Bruce wasn't happy in the band either, and I'm sure that after playing such technical music in Racer X for so long, what we were playing was probably boring for him.

It seemed like everybody was walking on eggshells around Bruce, nervous about what Bruce would say or what Bruce would do. I was tired of it all and seriously thinking about leaving the band. I know Walt had said it before. He and Bruce got into a few fistfights over time, and Walt was like, I don't need this shit, dude. Even Alderete, who was usually the happy-go-lucky mediator, was getting frustrated with everything, and none of us had any answers on how to lighten things up.

One of the things that made The Scream great was the tension, though. So many great bands had tension between its members, like Keith Richards and Mick Jagger, Steven Tyler and Joe Perry, and we certainly had a lot of that.

One day, Sass Jordan's manager and my friend Lisa Jansen called and said, "Hey, could you do this video for Sass? You don't need to play. I just need you to play some air guitar."

I recalled having met Sass at the ill-fated showcase The Scream played for the label people at Sash. I had some downtime, so I said, "Sure, but give me the song because even though I'm playing air guitar, I still want to learn the song because nothing irritates me more than seeing someone air guitar the wrong fucking notes."

Lisa gave me the song "Make You a Believer," and they also had Kelly Nickels from LA Guns join us on bass for the shoot. Sass was living with the drummer Eric Gloege, who was also her road manager.

Kelly, Sass, and I had a blast that day on the dusty set. The whole time we were doing the backing vocals, instead of singing "Ooo, I will make you a believer," we were just making shit up like, "Ooo, you're a golden retriever." We were pissing ourselves laughing the entire day.

That girl was sexy and could fucking sing her ass off, and I thought her fucking lyrics were genius, too. I remember having a little crush on Sass. I was kind of flirting with her, and Sass was flirty with me. The producer said at one point, "Oh, there's some weird chemistry between you two and I fucking love it," so they wound up doing all these extra shots of us with the cameras.

I still get emails from people asking if I was in Sass Jordan's band, but I only did that one video, and we've remained very good friends ever since.

It was around this time that my mom had a heart attack. And when she soon had a second one, the doctors gave her a full CT scan, probably looking for clogged arteries or valve issues. What they found though was that she had terminal stage four lung cancer.

I'll never forget when she called me and said, "The doctors here in Philadelphia told me it's in both my lungs and it's inoperable. They said to get my things in order, since I've only got maybe a year or two left." My mom smoked cigarettes her whole life.

After working so much at Progress Lighting, she had earned herself a nice pension and other benefits from her twenty-six years of service; Mom rarely missed a day of work in her life. She stopped working when diagnosed, but after a month or two, she started feeling better and getting bored.

She called her doctor and said, "I know I'm sick, and I've accepted it's terminal. My kids know, too, but I can't just sit here in my house and do nothing, waiting to die. I can't do that. I want to go back to work."

The doctor asked, "Well, how do you feel?"

"I feel good," she said, so he obliged by telling her, "Okay, well if you want to go back to work, just take it easy. Don't overdo it."

She got in her car the next morning and showed up at her workplace on Erie Avenue in Philly's Kensington neighborhood, only to see there was a chain on the Progress Lighting door and a notice that the company had gone bankrupt—they were permanently closed. They had a massive fucking factory, and just like that, they were gone, along with her fucking pension.

She was about fifty-five, and at the time, the retirement age was sixty-five. Social Security was available for the sick or disabled, but when she called and applied, they looked at her paperwork and said, "Well, no, you're not eligible now because you've been cleared to go back to work. You'll have to go get a job."

My mom said, "Who's going to hire a fifty-five-year-old woman with a fucking heart condition and terminal lung cancer. Who's going to do that?"

She investigated it all thoroughly and explored all angles but was ultimately unable to do anything about the situation. She was left alone in desperate times by her American policymakers who failed her. I decided I would have to take care of her financially.

The last video The Scream shot was for the song "Father, Mother, Son," as we never did get the chance to shoot the video for "You Are All I Need." Hollywood Records hired Sam Bayer to produce it, who had just done Nirvana's "Smells Like Teen Spirit" video and another for Ozzy.

We shot the video, and it all went well that day, although it was difficult singing the second verse, given my mom's terminal disease.

The producer mentioned to us that he was shooting a video for Richie Sambora the very next day, who had his first solo album out after splitting with Bon Jovi.

When I saw Sambora's video for "One Light Burning" on MTV, I was pissed. This producer used the exact same fucking set as our video. It had the same fucking textured wall, the same bullet-shaped window with ledge, all these candles, and all shot with the same angles and lighting as ours—just a different color to it, basically.

He was charging us something like a hundred grand for it. At best, I figured we should only give him half the money. I called Greenberg and said, "We're not fucking paying for that fucking video. The label picked that guy, so they can fucking pay him, not us!"

We were at a show in Arizona in early February. A fan had flown in from Canada just to see the show but was late getting there due to delays with her flight, and she unfortunately missed our entire performance.

I felt bad for her, so I invited her back to our hotel where we were going to have drinks for Walt's birthday. I said, "Come back, we're going to hang out, and you can have some cake and drinks with us." She appreciated the gesture.

Back at the hotel, Walt was already very drunk by the time he cut his birthday cake and we dished out slices. Walt then said something rude to this girl that I really took offense to, basically he said, "Who's dick are you sucking?"

I called him out on it and said, "Dude, seriously? That's not why she's here. She missed the show after traveling all fucking day to see us play. Don't be fucking rude!"

I was holding a piece of birthday cake on a plate, and Walt fucking slapped it out of my hand. He said, "Oh, you're going to pick up for this whore instead of me?"

I fucking punched him right in the face. We started beating the shit out of each other and trashed the hotel.

Walt was usually really cool, but once he started drinking, he would get to a point where you could see in his eyes, his whole demeanor changing, and he wouldn't think twice about a fucking thing. He didn't give a shit about what he said, and he didn't give a shit if it led to a fistfight, because he was built like a bull and more than capable of handling himself.

I used to kid him that he was our version of John Bonham, and as he was a massive Bonham fan, he proudly modeled himself to be just that! Everything I've read about John Bonham is the same, so far as he was a caring family man and a good dude, but when he would drink he was scary to be around, and he wouldn't think twice about fighting his own fucking shadow. Walt was always apologetic and horrified at his behavior after he sobered up, so I couldn't really stay mad at him.

10
Welcome to the Numb

I kept that music magazine the fan gave me and came across it again while unpacking the day I got back home to Los Angeles. It was the afternoon of February 12, and we still had more West Coast tour dates to play, including a show that night, plus we were booked to tour Europe with LA Guns and Love/Hate in a few weeks.

I phoned Mötley Crüe's management company and asked them to please pass on my thanks to Nikki Sixx for the plug in the magazine interview. She said thank you and asked me to leave my number, too.

In all honesty, I thought that if my call somehow led to me being able to write a song with Nikki and the guys for the next album by The Scream, or even for Mötley Crüe's next album, that would be awesome.

Minutes after leaving my message with their management company, I had just walked out my front door to head to soundcheck for that night's show when our home phone rang. I didn't want to be late because the show that Wednesday night was being recorded for a radio broadcast, plus we had to go to the radio station KNAC for an interview and acoustic performance.

Val answered the phone and ran outside to get me back in to take the call. Little did I know, but Mötley Crüe had split with their singer Vince Neil the day before and then met with management that very morning at Nikki's house where their manager called Vince to underline the point. With business out of the way, Tommy was now with Nikki in his car, which is where they were calling me from. Nikki said he got my message, so I thanked him again and said he just caught me as I was heading out for a show.

As we started chitchatting, I had another call come through from John Alderete, so I told him, "Hey, bro, I can't talk right now. I have Nikki Sixx and Tommy Lee on the other end of the phone. I think they want to come down and see us tonight."

When I switched lines to finish my conversation with Nikki, he then told me that Vince was out of the band and asked me to come down and audition for the vacant spot. He also made it clear not to say anything to anybody about it. He said they weren't going to put out anything in the press about Vince's departure.

I got off the phone and got in my car. I sat there for a moment freaking out, trying to process what the fuck just happened.

During soundcheck, all the guys in my band were asking me about the call. "Oh, dude, were they cool?"

I told them, "Yeah, they seemed cool. We didn't talk long, we just chitchatted for a bit, and I thanked them for the plug."

We did the soundcheck and then headed to the radio station KNAC. We sat ourselves down in the studio lined up with me on one end, then John, Bruce, and Walt on the other end. After playing a couple of songs acoustically, we did an interview on air with Long Paul.

We had a little break when they threw to a commercial, and a guy came running into the room, saying to Long Paul, "Dude, I've got a big announcement for you!"

He handed him a sheet of paper with some news that I guess had just come into the station over some sort of newswire. Long Paul took the paper and read it. He then said out loud, "Wow, Vince Neil is no longer in Mötley Crüe. Get ready, we're going back on air now."

He put his headphones back on, hit the On-Air button and told all his listeners that Vince Neil was out of Mötley, so they were looking for a new singer. I was totally expressionless, looking straight ahead at Long Paul. I could feel the other three guys lean forward on their chairs and turn and look at me. Fuck!

It was a very long ride from the radio station back to the Marquee, everybody was silent. Once we got backstage though, we sat there with Greenberg, and they asked me what was going on. I told them, "Nothing has happened at this point, but I'm going to be honest with you guys, they have asked me to come down on Monday. They want to jam with me, and you're not to say anything to anyone."

Surprisingly, the guys were all very supportive, saying things to me like, "Dude, you've got to do this. You need to do this. This is crazy, dude. If you get this gig, you're gonna be playing the fucking Forum! You'll be playing all the big places. This is huge. This is fucking huge. Man, you'll be able to take care of your family, too."

They knew I had some heavy medical bills because while we had just been out on tour, my son Ian spent two fucking weeks in Cedars-Sinai Hospital and was diagnosed with diabetes, as well as everything that was going on with my mother.

We put on a great show that night at the Marquee Club, which was transmitted out to radio listeners as a live broadcast. We ended our set with a cover of the Aerosmith classic "Lick and a Promise."

None of us realized that would be the last concert The Scream would ever play.

Philadelphia radio didn't seem to give a fuck about Mötley Crüe or their first record in '81. They started picking it up on their next album *Shout at the Devil* and played "Looks That Kill" after that video got airplay on MTV. I saw that song and their video for "Too Young to Fall in Love" on MTV at the time. I thought they were good and a cool band, but I was never into them. I was familiar with them, but I never considered myself a fan.

As much as The Scream was considered part of that whole hair metal scene, I didn't see what the big deal was with so much of that eighties material. I just didn't fucking get it. I grew up listening to music totally from the late-sixties and all the seventies, stuff like Grand Funk Railroad, Aerosmith, Kiss, Bowie, Humble Pie, Free, Bad Company, Deep Purple, and Led fucking Zeppelin. That's what I've always loved.

Therefore, I felt Kingdom Come was pretty good because of the Zeppelin-esque thing they had going on. I loved Tesla and the Black Crowes. Even Cinderella, as good as their first record was, I thought they got bluesier and better with their later records. With most of those eighties bands, though, I just didn't fucking get it.

After we got our record deal, The Scream was at a WEA convention with bands under the Warner Elektra Atlantic umbrella of labels and all their subsidiaries. We were there mingling with the likes of Mr. Big, Southgang, and the Electric Boys.

Suddenly this giant screen came down, and they premiered Mötley Crüe's video for "Primal Scream." We watched the video and all went holy fuck! I fucking loved that song the minute I heard it—killer riff. I said to my bandmates, "Holy shit, they're going to have another huge record again there." They were on fire.

I really only knew the songs they had on MTV and didn't know anything about the band or them individually, let alone own any of their albums. But I did know they were huge. When Mötley asked me to audition, I never thought I would actually get the gig. I wasn't well-versed with their catalogue of songs to walk into an audition with enough confidence that I knew their shit.

Without telling Nikki that I didn't know their songs, I tried to pin him down over the phone again that weekend before my audition. I asked, "What songs do you guys want to do on Monday?" I was hoping he would give me some sort of a set list so I could cram my preparation.

Instead, he just said, "Oh, I don't know, dude. We'll figure it out when you get there."

At that point, I was just praying they would want to play something I knew. It just made me think even more that there was no way I was going to fill their vacant spot, but if we could write a song that would be cool.

I walked into my audition in Burbank as the guys were jamming on Jimi Hendrix's "Angel." After introductions to the guys and their crew, they soon asked, "What do you want to play, dude?"

I thought "Helter Skelter" would be a good starting point, since I love The Beatles and they had recorded a cover of it many years ago, so that's where we began. After I hit and held the first strong note at the end of the first verse, Tommy stopped playing. I thought I did something wrong. I thought this audition wasn't going to last long. I waited for the thanks, but no thanks.

Tommy called to the sound guy and said, "Holy fuck, dude. Turn his mic down."

As Mick then asked me if I needed some water or soda, I could hear Tommy say to Nikki, "Fuck, dude. He's so much louder than Vince. He almost blew my fucking ear out."

They turned me down, and I said, "Let's do 'Jailhouse Rock.'"

We started playing that and got about halfway through the song when they all stopped again. They were all laughing. Tommy told the sound guy again, "Bring him down some more."

We then played most of "Smokin' in the Boys Room," which I used to cover back in Philly, before Nikki handed me some lyric sheets, and we jammed on bits of "Dr. Feelgood," "Don't Go Away Mad," "Shout at the Devil," and, I think, "Live Wire."

They kept laughing all the time and saying, "Holy fuck!"

The sound guy said, "I've got his volume on two." They told me that Vince doesn't push that hard when he sings, whereas I push really fucking hard when I'm singing. So, as they were making a big thing of this and laughing, I thought I wasn't fitting in, but then they asked, "Can you come back tomorrow?"

I headed home, where Val was chewing her fucking nails off. She greeted me at the door, asking how it went. "I guess it went okay, but they were really hard to read. They told me that my voice was super powerful, but we didn't finish any of the fucking songs—not one! So, I don't know. I don't think I'll get it, but they want me to come back again tomorrow."

I got very little fucking sleep that night.

I went back to Audible Sound the next day and this time the guys had their wives there. Mick's wife Emi Canyn had been one of Mötley Crüe's two female backing singers they dubbed the Nasty Habits. Nikki's wife Brandi Brandt was there—music fans probably knew her as the Elevator Operator in Aerosmith's video for "Love in an Elevator." Tommy's wife Heather Locklear was a high-profile actress on the TV series *Dynasty* and *T.J. Hooker*.

Their gorgeous wives weren't the only ones in the room. There was their manager, their lawyer, and accountant. I was introduced to everybody and chitchatted with the ladies for a bit before we got going.

We played the exact same songs as the day before. We got a little further into each of the songs this time, but we still never actually finished any of them—not a single one.

When the music ended, everybody got up and walked around a bit. The girls came over, and they said I was great. The manager came over and said, "Hey, it was nice to meet you."

The accountant said, "See ya, I'm out now, good to meet you."

And lastly, their lawyer came over to me, and he said, "Hey, here's the deal: It was really nice meeting you, but you were never here!" I looked at him, and he said again, "You were never here."

I didn't put two and two together, but basically since I was still in The Scream and signed to Hollywood Records under contract, they didn't want to risk any lawsuits by me auditioning, so it was a case of keep your mouth shut and don't tell anybody you were here.

Once the business guys left, Tommy stood up from his kit and said, "What are you guys going to do now, do you want to knock it on the head?" I looked at my watch, and it was only about two in the afternoon, so I suggested, "Why don't we jam?"

They asked me what I wanted to jam, so I said, "I don't know. Let's just jam some blues or something."

I honestly thought I wasn't getting the gig—not in a million years. My initial intention had been to call and say thank you for the magazine plug, and when they asked me to come down and audition, I thought there was no fucking way I would get this gig; I didn't know anything about this band. As I said, I was just hoping for an opportunity to possibly write a song with them for their next record, or for my next record, or both. Maybe this was my moment to seize that opportunity.

I chatted with Mick about the Les Paul he was holding and asked if I could check it out. He passed it over to me, and I put his guitar on. He showed me his rig and turned the fucking amp back on, so I just started playing some riffs. Tommy and Nikki stared at me and said, "Fuck, you can play!"

I told them, "Yeah, I started out as a guitar player, I then got into the singing thing, but yeah, I started as a guitarist."

I just started playing all this shit, so they quickly set up a rig for me and gave me one of Mick's other guitars to use. We started jamming on the blues song "Reefer Head Woman" and soon Mick and I just started trading solos back and forth. We then jammed on "Honky Tonk Women," just goofing off and having some fun.

I then showed them a riff I had. It was one that I came up with when I was in Angora and nothing came of it. I showed it to The Scream guys, and nothing came of it with them either. I started playing this opening riff with the Mötley guys, and they immediately jumped on it, and we worked up a song called "Hammered." We wrote seventy-five or eighty percent of "Hammered" together throughout that afternoon and evening.

Mick had a twelve-string Ovation acoustic guitar on a stand that he then played a sweet acoustic piece on. I started scatting, just phonetically saying anything that I thought fit with the melody of the tune. With his infectious energy, Tommy said, "Oh, dude, fuck, this is fucking insane."

That music eventually became a song called "Misunderstood."

Nikki said, "Hey, man, let me give you these lyrics that I have written. I want to see what else you come up with."

We noodled around with the song a bit more, and then I guess there must have been a look or nod or something between them that I didn't notice, because Tommy got up and left the room, Nikki slyly put his bass down and left the room, and Mick lit a cigarette and walked out, too. I was left there so I went to the bathroom for a piss and then started bullshitting with their tour manager Mike Amato, feeling pretty happy that we had already got most of this song "Hammered" down, and they loved the melody that I came up with for the acoustic piece.

I sat down on the couch and lit a cigarette. Tommy, Nikki, and Mick soon walked back in and sat right on the drum riser facing me. I took a long drag on my cigarette thinking that moment had now come where they will thank me and tell me it's just not going to work out. I exhaled the smoke.

Tommy took the lead and said, "Well, you know what dude, we went outside, and we talked and discussed a few things, and it doesn't take a rocket scientist to figure this out: welcome to the Crüe!"

I was taken aback and said, "Excuse me? Wait, what?"

He said again, "Welcome to the Crüe, dude. You're our new singer!"

I couldn't believe it. I said, "Holy shit! Are you fucking kidding me?"

Nikki said, "Nope, you're in. You cannot tell anybody anything though—nothing!"

I looked at him and said, "Can I tell my wife?"

They all started laughing and said, "Yeah, dude, of course you can tell your wife, just nobody else." Fuck, I couldn't believe it!

They had a phone in the room, so I picked it up and called Val. I said, "Hey, babe, it's me."

She said, "Well, what happened?"

I told her, "You're talking to the new lead singer of Mötley Crüe!"

She turned around to the guests at our apartment and yelled out, "He got it!" She ecstatically said, "Fuck yeah, we're celebrating when you get home!"

I told her I had some things to figure out, but I'd be home in a little while.

The Mötley guys were more than happy, and I think I was still in shock; it hadn't sunk in yet. We hung out a while longer before I got in my car and drove home. I walked into my Ivar Avenue apartment and Neil Zlozower was sitting there with his wife Denise and a few bottles of Dom Perignon on ice.

Neil Zlozower is a rock photographer who had worked a lot with Mötley over the years, including shooting the famous "blood session" with Nikki back in the *Shout at the Devil* days. Zloz already knew about my audition because I was told Nikki called him and asked, "Hey, do you know this guy John from The Scream?"

Neil said, "Yeah, dude, I fucking know John really well. His wife Val works for me doing hair and makeup for my shoots, and he's a great dude. He's really talented, and I love his band The Scream."

Neil did indeed love The Scream, so he told me that night that he was pissed that I was leaving them and joining Mötley because it was breaking up one of his favorite bands. But he put in a good word for me with Nikki, so he knew what was going on.

We had a great celebration that night. It was a surreal time, though, as I didn't grasp what was about to happen. And it was all so honestly unexpected. Literally, in the space of less than a week, my entire fucking world had changed. I was suddenly the singer of one the biggest fucking rock bands in the entire fucking world!

11
'Til Death Do Us Part

The band wanted to meet Val, so they said I should bring her up to the studio the next day. As I was driving to Burbank with Val along US 101, my car broke down—it just died. We waited on the side of the freeway for a AAA roadside assistance guy to come and get it started again. It was my first day of being in Mötley Crüe and I was a fucking hour late because of my piece of shit car.

When we got to Audible Sound, the guys gave Val a huge crystal vase with a couple of dozen red roses, along with a note that simply read "Welcome to the Family!"

That sure impressed me. I thought these guys have it all figured out: happy wife = happy life.

After a week or so of jamming and rehearsing with the guys, I said to Nikki, "Just so we're all on the same page, we're in writing-mode now, right?" After he confirmed with a nod, I said, "Well, I'm going to have to take six weeks or so off soon because I have a European tour with The Scream that I'm contractually obligated to do."

Nikki said, "No, fuck that. You're not going anywhere. No, you need to be here."

I had specifically been told not to tell anybody about me getting the Mötley gig because there were legal things that had to be worked through and sorted out. My dad called me a week in, though, and said, "Hey, I've got a question for you: what the hell is going on—did you leave The Scream?"

I asked him why he was asking me that, and he said, "Well, I've got a friend who works in the entertainment industry as a lawyer and he told me that you left The Scream and you joined a band called The Motley Crews."

So, I said, "Okay, here's the deal: I'm not supposed to say anything to anybody. There are legal things that we need to take care of, so nobody can know this. Yeah, I've left The Scream, and I'm joining Mötley Crüe."

He was pissed with me, and said, "Jesus Christ, I don't understand you. You work your whole goddamn life for music. You pack your family up, you move them across the country, you go to get a record deal, and then you got the record deal. You go on tour and then you leave the band to start all over again?"

I explained to him, "I'm not starting over. This band is huge. They're one of the biggest bands in the world right now. The last time you saw me play was at a seven-hundred-capacity nightclub in Philadelphia. Next time you see me, I'll be at the basketball arena or the ice hockey arena playing with Mötley Crüe. They're big, Dad. They're huge!"

After a long silence, a long pause, he simply asked, "Do they have benefits?"

A lot of people ask me where I got the nickname "Crabby," so here ya go: It all started with Mick Mars and this silly little trick with his lighter when he'd light a cigarette. He'd say, "Hey, Corabi, watch this." Then somehow it was like, "Hey, Corab," then "Hey, Crab." It just morphed from Corabi to Corab to Crab. Then everybody called me Crabby. "Where's Crabby?" "What did Crabby say?" "Let's get coffee, Crabby."

Not the greatest of fucking nicknames.

So, if you were one of the people wondering if I'm Mr. STD and need to have A200 dispensers in every room in my house—nope! And, no, it's not my disposition; it's just a play on my fucking last name!

Although the older I get, the more meaningful the name is, as I have become more like Clint Eastwood in *Gran Torino*: Crabby says, "Get off my lawn, punk."

As I quickly got on great with the Mötley guys, it was clear to me that we had very different upbringings and were used to living very different lifestyles. So even from the very beginning, there were a lot of little disconnects between us.

Mike Amato, the band's tour manager, was getting married and had already invited everybody to his wedding before I joined the band.

Graciously, he said that he was sending Val and I an invitation to join them on their special event off the LA coast at South Catalina Island's casino ballroom.

The day before the wedding trip, Tommy said, "Meet me at my house tomorrow, dude, nine a.m., and we'll go together."

Val and I arranged a babysitter to watch the kids for the weekend, and we drove over to Tommy's mansion.

Heather answered the door and once we got inside their hilltop home, Tommy said, "Cocktails!" and started making drinks.

As we sat drinking vodka cranberry at 9:30 a.m. with Tommy and Heather while taking in the panoramic views of the morning, I said, "So, out of curiosity, what time is the car coming to get us?" Whenever there was drinking involved, we always took limos, and let's face it, there was always drinking involved.

Tommy looked at me and smiled. "Don't worry about it, dude. I've got it; everything's taken care of. Ready for another cocktail?" he said.

Mick soon showed up with Emi and as we were all standing around drinking cocktails and chatting, I heard a noise that got louder and fucking louder.

I looked out the kitchen window and there was a fucking helicopter landing in the empty lot right next to Tommy's house—the big lot that he had bought so he could have more room to park his fucking cars. I said to Tommy, "What the fuck is that chopper doing?"

He said, "We're all flying to Catalina, dude."

I was wide-eyed, wondering how much this would fucking cost.

I'd never been in a helicopter before, so they let me sit in the front. We took off and buzzed Nikki's house before going up higher over the mountains. Mick instructed the pilot through the headset microphone to fly over his mountain top house, before we then flew a hundred feet above the beaches all the fucking way from Malibu to Santa Monica. The pilot then cut out over the North Pacific Ocean to Catalina. It was a pretty thrilling twenty-minute trip.

As the helicopter was landing, I looked down and saw two guys driving golf carts toward us. I could tell one was Mike Amato but couldn't figure out who the other guy was. We got out of the chopper, where Mike came over to greet everybody with a hug.

The other guy in a hat walked right over to Tommy and hugged him, then hugged Mick. They turned to me as I was thinking this guy looked so familiar and was trying to figure out where I'd fucking seen him before. Tommy said to me, "John, this is Brian."

I said hey to him but must've had a weird look on my face, because Mike clarified, "Brian…Brian Johnson from AC/DC."

"Oh, shit! Holy fuck, right!"

We got in the golf carts, and Brian drove us over to the hotel, where we checked in and proceeded to have the most drunken, debaucherous fucking weekend ever.

Brian and his wife Brenda asked if we wanted to go get some Mexican food at a place a couple of blocks away. Between Brian, Brenda, Tommy, Heather, Mick, Emi, Val, and I, I can't even begin to fathom how many fucking pitchers of margaritas we drank, but we were there the whole fucking day.

On the way back to the hotel that evening, we literally stumbled upon this little club. We went upstairs to the second floor where there were about eight people in the whole bar, and a band playing some bad covers. We ordered some more drinks.

It wasn't long before Brian said to Mick, "Let's jam!"

Mick got up from the table, walked over to the band, and dropped his black sweatpants to his ankles. He stood there in front of the band with his cock hanging out and asked with a deadpan face, "Can we use your gear?"

Tommy got on the kit, Mick took the guitar, I picked up the bass, and we started jamming some covers. I remember standing there on the little stage, three sheets to the wind with a cigarette in my mouth, as Mick then started the legendary opening riff of AC/DC's "Back in Black." As Brian started singing, I looked over at him saying to myself holy fuck, that's the fucking guy. That's the fucking voice!

But then it really hit me because I looked over and saw Mick Mars playing "Back in Black" with Brian. Then I turned around and looked at the drum kit and there was Tommy Lee spinning his fucking sticks playing "Back in Black."

It was a total somebody-fucking-pinch-me moment when it then really dawned on me that I was also playing "Back in Black" with Brian fucking Johnson of AC/DC and these guys.

I needed another margarita after that.

I had already been in Mötley for a couple of months and all the businesspeople were negotiating back and forth, trying to sort out the financial arrangements of me joining, given the various contractual obligations. As a bargaining chip in negotiations for me to leave The Scream, Hollywood Records came up with the grand idea of me recording another song with The Scream.

An old punk band called Rubber City Rebels from Akron, Ohio, wrote and released a song "Young and Dumb" back in 1979. I hated that fucking song then and still do today, but Hollywood Records had me record a cover of it with Garth Richardson producing for their *Encino Man Soundtrack*. In a strange twist, Vince Neil's first solo song "You're Invited (But Your Friend Can't Come)" was the first song on that soundtrack.

A lot of people who loved our album *Let It Scream* have said to me over the years that it sucks I left, but I don't see that we would have lasted that much longer anyway, to be honest. With the fights, the disagreements, the cursing at each other, and all the tension that was there, though, we had a fucking blast. Overall, being in The Scream was an awesome time for the most part.

Our bass player John Alderete goes by the name Juan Alderete these days. He played with The Mars Volta from 2003-2013 and has been Marilyn Manson's touring bassist since 2017, when he took over from Twiggy Ramirez. We call each other sometimes, and it's always great to catch-up.

A couple of weeks into 2020, though, Juan unfortunately had a very serious accident on his bicycle, when it suddenly flipped, and he hit the pavement. Even though he was wearing a helmet, as always, he suffered a traumatic brain injury that put him in a coma for some time. He has a long road ahead but has been making progress in his recovery and rehabilitation.

I'll tell you more about Walt later in the book. I saw Bruce fairly recently at an acoustic show I was doing in Las Vegas. He came down with his wife, and we did a few Scream songs together on stage, and it was great to hang and jam with him again.

I love all those guys like brothers and always will because we shared a lot of "firsts" together. The album I did with The Scream was reissued in the middle of 2018 by Rock Candy records as a special deluxe collector's edition with half a dozen bonus tracks recorded at our very last show together—a nice memento of a great period in my life.

In Mötley, we sometimes worked on songs five days a week and then had Bill Kennedy and Scott Humphrey come down to assist with our first demo. They did some Pro Tools editing, some keyboards, and other shit for us.

If I recall correctly, the first demo was the tracks "Hammered," "Misunderstood," "Hypnotized," and "Hell on High Heels," which is not the same song they released on their *New Tattoo* album eighteen years later.

This song used a bastardized riff of a song that I had written during my short time with Cathedral in New York City.

Tommy and Nikki weren't in a hurry to get the record done; they wanted to take their time. We worked and rehearsed in Audible Studio for two or three weeks, then everybody would tear everything down and set it up in a studio where we would record the demo songs over four or five days before mixing it.

Then the guys would take little mini-vacations to some exotic island. Mick was always content sitting at home watching *The Three Stooges* and playing video games. So I would sit home scratching my head, thinking, "Are you fucking kidding me? I used to rehearse with The Scream six days a week plus work a full-time job! This is nothing."

It used to irritate me, as I would get myself to a point where my voice was fucking nice and strong and I would get in the studio and knock it out of the park, but then we would take a month off, and I'd have to start over to get it back to full voice through rehearsing again.

They did say that part of the reason why they did that was they wanted to make sure that I didn't have any LSD...Lead Singer Disease. They didn't give a shit about what anybody wanted. They wanted to take their time to make sure they weren't stepping out of one situation with their singer and into another.

I've always had a different viewpoint on money to them, too. I couldn't believe how Tommy, Nikki, and Vince all went out after the *Dr. Feelgood* Tour and bought new Ferraris—Tommy bought a black Testarossa, Nikki bought a red one, and Vince bought a white one.

I didn't know shit about luxury cars and one day Tommy pulled up to the studio in a black sports car, and I said, "Holy shit, dude! Fuck, that car is badass. What is that?"

He said, "It's my Testarossa. Come on, jump in."

He took me for a ride in it and soon asked me if I wanted to drive. I gladly got behind the wheel and as I was enjoying the feel of it, I said, "If you don't mind me asking, what does something like this go for?"

I thought he was maybe going to say eighty grand or so, but I really didn't have a clue. When he said something like $260,000, I literally shut the engine off and got out of the car at an intersection and walked back around to the passenger's side door. I told Tommy, "If I can't afford to buy this car, I ain't fucking driving it one inch farther. I got it to this point unscathed; I don't want to drive it another fucking inch."

He sat there laughing his ass off at me.

They had been making money hand-over-fist for years, but my mentality (that I probably got from my dad) was if I won a hundred million in the lottery and could splurge, I might go out and maybe buy myself a seventies Corvette Stingray or a Shelby Cobra kit car with a 427 in it for fifty-five thousand, and then invest the rest of my money or just put it in the fucking bank. I'm more about putting money in the bank for your future and for your family, so they have a leg-up in life.

One day I was at Nikki's mansion, and we were in his home office. He pulled out a box and started going through it, looking for something. He was digging in and pulling out his *Theatre of Pain* tour pants, some headbands, wristbands, and all this other shit.

There was some mail down in the bottom of this box, and I spotted a familiar package. I reached in and pulled out a fucking envelope with my handwriting on it. Inside was the cassette tape, a few photos of me, and a resume from early in 1985 that I sent to my former drummer in Cathedral, Mike Gandia, who gave it to his manager friend, who was Mötley's manager, and gave it to Nikki fucking Sixx.

I said to Nikki, "Fuck, how weird is this? It seems I sent this to you guys for the *Theatre of Pain* sessions after Vince had crashed his car and was up on charges."

Nikki said, "Fuck, no way, dude. That's fucking trippy as fuck," as we sat looking at the photos.

I didn't know who the band was that I had passed on the package for, but here I was now in that very same band on the other side of the country so many years later. The world works in mysterious ways, they say.

We wrote a song called "'Til Death Do Us Part," and we thought it was such a great song title that it should also be the name of the album. After rehearsing it one night, Nikki had the idea of all four of us getting a band tattoo—the name of our new album we were writing.

Tattoo artist Greg James from Sunset Strip Tattoo would sometimes come by the studio, so I had met him a few times. We went to his studio, where one of the artists tattooed the album title around the top of Mick's left arm. Another guy did Tommy's above his ankle going around his leg.

Nikki and I got the exact same tattoo, a banner on the top outside thigh part of our left legs that reads "Til Death Do Us Part," done by Eric Blair. We had a fun night in the tattoo studio and at one point the guys were all laughing as I sang "Shout at the Devil" in a style as would be sung by Frank Sinatra.

When we finally started recording the album, Greg did an amazing drawing of a death tarot card that was to be the album cover. He said that everybody assumes the card means death or bad things are coming, but he explained that it's more about you leaving something bad behind, like a relationship, and reinventing yourself and starting over with more self-awareness. The meaning was perfect for us in so many ways, and his fucking elaborate artwork was insanely good.

Greg came up to Vancouver while we were recording, so we could get more tatt work done. He turned his hotel room into a tattoo studio and did a lot of work on Tommy and Nikki's left arm sleeves.

I told him that I loved the drawing he did to match the album title, so I wanted that tattooed on my upper right thigh. I told the guys that it wasn't like I would walk around with my pants off, and I never wore shorts, so nobody would see the album cover before our record came out.

So, now that I had tattooed the name of the record on one leg and the record cover art on my other leg, things changed, and I was pissed. "What the fuck do you mean we're changing the name of the album and cover? You can't do that now; I've got them tattooed on my fucking legs!"

It's like the old adage of never get a fucking person's name tattooed on you. Well, rule of thumb: that includes album names as well. (But I'm sure the more fanatical of you reading this will be showing me your *Horseshoes & Hand Grenades* tattoos before long!)

Prior to recording the album, I went to Nikki's house to write lyrics one day. We took a little break and stepped outside of his hotel-sized home for a little fresh air, and next to his house was a vacant lot with some big dirt mounds on it. Along with his Mercedes, his Suburban, and his red Ferrari Testarossa, his garage housed a couple of dirt bikes.

Nikki looked at me with a grin and said, "Come on, let's take the dirt bikes out." It was fun riding up and down the hills, fucking around on the dirt bikes for a while.

Putting them back in his garage, I also noticed he had a beautiful Harley-Davidson in there—a Heritage Softail painted in Seven-Up soda can green and white. I looked at the gorgeous bike and said to him, "Fuck, that bike is so badass!"

He asked, "Have you ever ridden a Harley before?" When I said I hadn't, he took it out of the garage and started it up. He took it for a spin down his street and back. It was fucking loud.

He got off the bike and said, "Here, Crab, take it for a fucking spin." I got on the bike and rode it like a fucking grandmother, doing about five miles per hour down the street, down the hill, around the stop sign, and back up to his house.

"Oh my God, dude. That was so fucking awesome!" I told him.

We kept working on lyrics until late, so I ended up staying overnight, though in a separate zip code of his massive fucking estate.

The next morning, Nikki said, "Hey, Crab. I've got some errands to do, but you can come with me."

His wife Brandi said, "Hey, where are you going?

He said, "We're going into the Valley, I need to go to the bank."

"Well, when you're down there, would you mind swinging by Barger Harley-Davidson for that part for my bike that I need, please?" Brandi had her own little pink and white Harley-Davidson Sportster 883.

We drove down into the Valley in Nikki's car and pulled up at the Harley dealership Barger's. While Nikki was talking with the guy at the counter, I wandered the showroom floor checking out the bikes. Lots of them were cool. Nikki was taking a while, so I sat on the one I thought looked the most fucking badass; it was a red Heritage Softail Classic with white-wall tires.

Nikki came over as I was getting off it, and as we headed for the door, he thanked the guy at the counter and said, "Don't forget to get that part for me then. I'll be back a bit later."

We went to the bank next and when we walked in, Nikki said, "Wait here, I'll be right back."

He wasn't long doing his business and as we got back in his car, he said, "Hey, are you hungry? Let's get some lunch." So, we got some lunch then headed back to Barger's to pick-up the part for Brandi on the way back to his place.

As we pulled into the dealership, we saw the red bike that I had been sitting on was now sitting outside with a fucking bow on it. Nikki said, "Dude, isn't that the bike you were just sitting on?"

I said, "Fuck yeah, look at that. Somebody bought it already. That fucking thing is badass."

We walked past the bike on the way into the store, and Nikki walked over to the counter. The guy gave him some papers, which he signed, then passed him something, which I presumed was Brandi's part, even though it looked quite small.

That's when Nikki turned to me and threw the part over to me. I caught it, and said, "What's this?"

He said, "The keys to your Harley. It's yours. Welcome to the Crüe!"

I said, "Are you fucking kidding me right now? That's my bike?"

"Yep, I talked to Tommy and Mick, and we're all chipping in, and we've just bought you the bike—welcome to the Crüe, dude."

I was freaking out. "Holy shit! Fuck. No fucking way! Thank you!" I said.

I got a helmet but had no license. I got on my brand-new Harley and literally crawled up the fucking freeway back to Nikki's house. When I arrived there, Val and my kids were standing outside, smiling and laughing as they watched me roll-up on my new Harley with the biggest shit-eating grin on my face.

It had all been a set-up with Brandi; she knew the whole thing was going down and drove down to our Hollywood apartment while we were out in the Valley, so she'd have time to bring Val and the kids back to their place. I was beaming from ear to ear. What a fucking insanely cool thing to do for someone. The hardest part of that day was having to leave the Harley at Nikki's house because I couldn't risk bringing it back to Hollywood. Everybody was afraid it was going to get ripped off.

Contrary to popular belief, nobody is more aware of how genuinely awesome those guys were to me when I joined the band. They all went well out of their way to accommodate and welcome me. I've always recognized and fucking appreciated that. To this day, I can't thank them enough for their generosity and making this kid feel like part of their family!

I wasn't supposed to tell anybody that I was in Mötley Crüe, yet I was showing up at the Rainbow and other places all over town with Nikki Sixx and Tommy Lee, some nights after closing until three, four, or five o'clock in the morning.

Val and I started having marital problems because I would get calls, "Hey, dude, what are you doing? We're going out."

I'd say, "Well, I'm getting ready to have dinner."

They'd say, "Well, I'm on my way, dude. I rented a limo. You're coming out with me!"

I would look at Val, cover the phone, and say, "They want me to go out again, fuck." I would've been more than content just staying at home with Val and the kids and watching TV, working on some lyrics or just doing whatever.

I invited Tommy down for dinner one night, and his stretch limo double-parked in front of my apartment the entire time. Val made some pasta and we sat and ate. She then sent our kids on a walk to the store and when they came back, Tommy and I were sitting in front of my apartment smoking a cigarette.

Not even ten minutes after the kids got home, it literally sounded like World War III outside with all this gunfire. Tommy jumped and said, "What the fuck is that? What's fucking going on?"

I shrugged it off and said, "I don't know, whatever. It's probably just the bar around the corner; there's shit going on down there all the time."

Calmed by my notion of the gun noise being a common occurrence around home, Tommy went back inside with me, and then we got in the stretch and went and hung out at The Viper Room for the rest of the night.

Unbeknownst to me, the next day Tommy told Nikki and Mick about it, saying "There was a fucking gun fight just fifty feet away from Crab's house last night! We've got to get him out of there. It's not safe for him and his kids."

They didn't say anything to me, though. I think they were going to have to talk to their people to see what could be done.

About two weeks after that, Val sent me to the store to get milk. She needed some milk for Ian's cereal the next morning after she checked his blood and gave him his insulin, and I wanted a pack of cigarettes.

So around midnight, I walked down our street using the "sidewalk" then turned the corner. There were three Mexican guys there and as I walked past them to the store, one of them asked, "Coca, Coca, Coca?" meaning do you want some cocaine?

I said, "No, no, I'm good, dude."

I came out of the store and lit one of my cigarettes from the fresh pack and started walking back home. I was looking down, humming and drumming to myself in my head whatever song we were to be playing at rehearsals the following afternoon. As I walked back past the Mexican guys, I suddenly saw stars. I was knocked-out for a moment, had fallen to my knees and dropped the fucking milk.

They hit me in the back of the head with something. I heard a crash and saw glass from a forty scattered everywhere. While I was groggy and trying to stand up, I turned and saw three guys coming at me. One of them reached into his pants and grabbed a screwdriver handle. As he pulled it up, that fucker kept coming out; it was one of those long-ass screwdrivers a mechanic would use. He swung that fucker around, and

I did my best to duck and weave. They pinned me against a wall, and one of them punched me. I had a crucifix on as some cheap costume jewelry, and he ripped it off my neck and ran off. They didn't even try and take my wallet.

I walked back in the fucking house and was just dazed. I didn't even realize from the shock and adrenaline of it all, but Val said, "What the fuck? You're bleeding!"

When I looked at my hand, I saw it was cut, and I had all these little screwdriver stab holes in my chest and the side of my stomach and my ribs. That's when I fucking lost my shit.

Neil Zlozower's photo studio was (and still is) on the corner of my street Ivar Avenue and Yucca Street. Right next to Neil's, there was a little Korean grocery store, and then there was a soul food place. Then there was the Yucca Street bar where Tommy and I had heard the shooting. It was a little Mexican kind of hangout bar, and right next to it were some rundown apartments where all these Mexicans lived.

I stood there with my two hundred-pound dogs and my fucking bat, like, let's do this! I was still thinking that motherfucker was going to come out with his fucking screwdriver; I was so out of my head, that it never crossed my mind about them possibly having a gun. But they would have to put a bullet in my head if they wanted to keep me down. Val was so pissed at me when I got home, and yelled at for me being a complete idiot and going back to fight.

I went to rehearsals the next day, and I had a black eye and a fucking lump on the back of my head with a little split in it. I told Tommy and Nikki and Mick what happened and showed them all the little fucking holes in me. They were like, "What the fuck? Fuck this bullshit."

Three days later, they told me to start looking for a house. I said, "I don't even know where to look," so they said to look up near where they lived.

There was a disconnect though because the Mötley guys just said, "Go and move home," but I told them, "I don't have that kind of money right now." All through The Scream, I had been living hand-to-mouth.

Knowing my old car was a piece of shit, too, they said, "Go buy another car, you're the new singer of Mötley Crüe."

I told them, "I can't walk into a fucking car dealership and just go, 'I'm the new lead singer of Mötley Crüe, I'll take that car right there, thanks!' They're still going to have to run my credit, and I'm still going to have to put money down that I don't really have." The whole fucking situation was a nightmare to figure out, especially since my credit score wasn't very good.

I found a house in Thousand Oaks that I liked. It was probably nineteen hundred a month, which was quite a lot back then, but it was a nice ranch-style home on a cul-de-sac, so I knew my kids could go out and play safely. There was a decent school close by and it had a pool, so my kids could swim. My kids' happiness was all I really gave a shit about.

I lived just two miles from Nikki and Tommy in their gated community with movie stars like Dan Haggerty from *The Life and Times of Grizzly Adams*. I lived probably fifteen miles from Mars' mountain.

As much as Val was like a muse to me in our early days and taught me a lot of the rock-and-roll style, and I married her because I surely was in love with her, we had some very difficult times in our marriage that got amplified when I finally got a record deal and went on the road with The Scream. I was not happy. Val was not happy. We persevered.

When I got the Mötley gig, I thought that having money, moving my family into a nicer home in a nicer neighborhood, and having a new car would change everything. It did for a minute, but those old issues started to rear their ugly head again.

We went out on another big night at the fucking Mondrian Hotel in Hollywood. Val and I were toast and ready to go home at the end of the night, so Frank, the assistant manager, called a car service for us. We went downstairs, and we were waiting, and waiting, and waiting for this fucking car to arrive. Val was tired, so she lay across my lap and closed her eyes. That's when a security guard came over and started giving me a fucking hard time about it.

I told him, "Hey, listen, I've got some friends partying up there, but we're just leaving; we're waiting for a car," but he was giving me shit that Val was passed out sleeping.

So I nudged her for a minute, and when she was upright and seemed somewhat awake, I said, "I'm going to go upstairs and get Frank to see where this car is and get him to come down and tell the security guard to fucking lighten up."

I left Val sitting there while I went back up to Nikki's hotel room and told Frank what was going on, who replied, "Let me call the limousine company."

I went back down to Val, but as I came down in one elevator, the fucking security guard woke her up again and put her in another elevator going back up, so when I got to the lobby, Val was gone.

I turned around and came right back up again. Val was in the room, wondering where the fuck I was. She didn't remember that I told her I was going up to get Frank and thought I had just left her in the lobby.

When I then walked in and saw Val, she saw some chick walking in right behind me, and to her it looked like we had walked in together, but I didn't even know the chick was walking behind me, let alone know her. Val walked over, didn't ask me anything, and fucking punched me in the face, which was basically how our relationship was by then.

I grabbed her, and we went downstairs again, where our car had finally arrived and took us home. At that point, though, I knew our marriage just wasn't going to work anymore. The jealousy and insecurity was out of control. In hindsight, as jealous and unreasonable as I thought she was being, I get it now. I realize how hard it must've been for her at that time of our lives as well.

12
Get a Grip

The Mötley lifestyle did not sit well with Val. It was the hours I was keeping and all the partying. She would hear rumblings, and it was really getting to her.

I told Val that I wasn't happy in our marriage and it was not going to work. As much as she already knew that, she was pissed, and we both said some things that we didn't mean—and we separated.

She didn't drive, and I didn't want her to be just stuck in the Thousand Oaks house, so I bought her a brand-new Honda Civic and told her to get some driving lessons. I was going to move out into an apartment somewhere, but Mick said, "Don't get an apartment. Fuck that, Crab. Save your money, dude. Come fucking stay on the mountain with me."

Mick lived in the middle of fucking nowhere, high up on top of what he called Mars Mountain—a two-thousand-foot-high peak in the rugged Santa Monica Mountains. To get there, you had to go along all these really tight, windy roads through the canyon before taking more windy roads and then even windier fucking roads. When you reached his gate, you punched in a code for the gate to open, allowing you to then go up his fucking driveway that was at least a quarter of a mile long.

When the incline finally leveled off, there was a guesthouse, before the driveway then took you farther up to Mick's main house.

Mick graciously let me live in his guesthouse. I packed my stuff in the back of my Bronco truck and moved into his single-bedroom, one-bathroom house with a kitchen and nice living room with a fireplace. Like the main house, it too had panoramic views. I had a carport, and Mick didn't mind me having my dog with me, too—I had recently bought an Alaskan Malamute named Cody while Val had our other dogs Star and Angus at her place.

Mick had an intercom system of sorts put in prior, where there was a direct line from his house to the guesthouse. I'd be sitting at home, and he'd go to the window and look to see if there were any lights on. My intercom phone would ring, and Mick would say, "What are you doing, you bastard?"

I would say, "I'm just fucking hanging out, dude, watching TV and playing some guitar."

"Get up here then. I've got a bottle of Grand Marnier cracked, so come up and pay the toll with the Mars man."

I would throw my shoes on and walk up to his house, where we would sit on his Italian leather L-shaped couch, pour a shot each, toast, and down the hatch with it. We'd sit there and play guitars together, but a lot of times I'd be sitting there noodling around on a guitar while he would be playing a video game on his massive TV screen, and we'd chat. I'd be working on a riff, and he'd say, "Hey, what's that riff you're playing?"

I'd say, "I don't know, I'm just jamming and came up with it."

He'd say, "That's a great riff, put that one down on tape."

One day when he summoned me to pay the toll, Mick had all these guitars laid out on his couch when I walked in.

He was noodling around with one, and then I grabbed a Telecaster and started playing it. I immediately started playing a riff and he said, "What is that?"

I said, "I don't know, dude. It's just a riff."

He said, "That's great. Record it on the little DAT machine."

Once I did that, he got up and took the guitar off me, walked around looking for a case, then set it by the front door. "Take that guitar, it's yours."

I said, "Nah, dude, it's fine."

He said, "No, no, no. I know this sounds weird, but I've got this fucking theory that if you buy a guitar and you don't bond with it right away, if it doesn't talk to you right away, then it's not meant to be." He continued, "I was playing that guitar and couldn't come up with anything. You played that guitar for five minutes and just got that great riff—that guitar is meant to be yours." So he gave me the guitar.

I sat back down and after another couple of shots, I grabbed a Strat and started playing it. In a moment, Mick said, "What's that riff?"

I said, "I don't know, dude. Why do you keep asking me that?"

He said, "Because it's a great fucking riff. Put it on tape."

Then he did the same thing: he took the Strat off me, put it in a case, closed it up and set it by his front door. "Keep those two guitars, they're yours."

We had already been working in Vancouver and were now recording in A&M Studios. The next day, we were working on the song "Livin' in the Know," and Bob Rock wanted me to play a clean, funky guitar part on it. I had all Les Paul guitars, so I took in the two guitars that Mick just gave me and thought I'd use one of them on that part for a different sound.

I had Mick's guitar tech Bobby O string them up for me. I set them in the guitar boat and Bob was looking at the Strat and asked me where I got it. I told him that Mick gave it to me last night, and Rockhead said, "Bring it here."

Bob flipped it over and started looking at the serial numbers. He thumbed through a book and found the serial number range in it. He said, "Dude, that is a 1954 non-tremolo Fender Stratocaster. That guitar's worth about twenty-five grand."

My frugal brain was shocked. Bob said, "Bring that Tele in, and I'll look that up, too."

He found that listed in the book as well and said, "It's an original 1951 Fender Telecaster, worth about ten grand."

So, in one evening, I was sitting up there fucking hanging out with Mick, just sitting there drinking Grand Marnier, jamming, watching his favorite *Three Stooges* videos, and playing video games, and I walked out with $35,000 worth of guitars that he gave me.

I used the guitars for the tracks, and then I gave them to Bobby and told him I couldn't take the guitars. When Bobby told Mick, "Crab gave the guitars back to you," Mick said to me, "I gave them to you!"

I told Mick, "No, Mick, it's fine. I can't accept them, they're worth too much money, bro."

He argued the point with me, so I wound up giving him the Strat back and I held onto the Tele. Years later, when Mötley let me go, the Tele never came back to me, so I don't know where it is these days. But to me, Mick Mars is one of the most genuine, normal, nice guys you could ever meet, and that's just one example.

One Christmas he loaded up my kids with five-grand worth of presents. I was like, "Fuck, dude. Like, seriously, you're making me look bad, stop!" But what a sweetheart, what a great dude. Mick is what he is, and he makes no bones about who he is, so he's truly one of the most genuine people I've ever met or had in my life.

We decided to go to Vancouver for six months or so to record with Bob Rock, then had him come down to LA to record the rest of it—we split it half and half.

I had heard of a couple of recording studios in Vancouver: Mushroom Studios, where Heart had recorded; and Little Mountain Sound Studios, where we were going to be recording. I was stoked like fuck to be recording at such a world-famous place.

Not only had Mötley Crüe recorded their biggest selling album *Dr. Feelgood* there, along with new tracks for their recent *Decade of Decadence* compilation, a heap of other big albums were recorded there, like AC/DC's *The Razor's Edge*, Bryan Adams' *Reckless*, and The Cult's *Sonic Temple*. Aerosmith recorded their huge comeback albums *Permanent Vacation* and *Pump* there, and Bon Jovi recorded *Slippery When Wet*, *New Jersey*, and *Keep the Faith* there, too—their three most commercially successful albums.

The day we arrived in Canada, we checked into a really nice hotel called the Pan Pacific Vancouver with scenic waterfront views out over the harbor and inlet. We got up the next day and drove fifteen minutes to the studio, where the crew guys were setting everything up in Studio A and getting ready for recording.

Tommy and Nikki said to me, "Hey, Crab, there's a local band recording in Studio B. We should go in and say hi. I think this band would get a kick out of meeting the new lead singer of Mötley Crüe."

So, I said, "Yeah, sure, let's go meet them."

I wasn't subtle about my entrance through the door of Studio B, and when I walked in, I saw a guy sitting in a chair in front of me with his back to me while playing guitar. When he heard me come in, he turned around and looked at me. My brain instantly triggered the thought that he looked exactly like Joe Perry from Aerosmith. Immediately, everything went into slow motion.

It seemed like an hour went by before my brain registered that it was indeed Joe fucking Perry. Unbeknownst to me, Aerosmith was in the late stages of recording their *Get a Grip* album with Bruce Fairbairn.

As I looked across the room, I saw Steven Tyler running at me, all hands and arms and feathers and bangle bracelets. He came running over and grabbed me, then put his arms around me and started hugging and shaking me—and gave me a fucking kiss on the cheek. In that familiar Steven Tyler voice, he said, "Hi, you're the one that's being shot out of the cannon, brother!"

I was just completely dumbfounded; I was in shock. I had no idea what to say. We sat there, and he talked to me for a minute, but I didn't say a word.

A few minutes later, Nikki took me back into our Studio A and said, "Dude, you have to remember now, Mötley Crüe is on the same level as Aerosmith. You can't act like a fucking fan. Don't be a fanboy, you have to be a fucking peer."

I spat back, "Fuck, that's easy for you to say! That's the dude that I fucking went and saw at the Philadelphia Spectrum like twenty times and idolized my whole life, since fucking *Toys in the Attic*. I ran away from home as a teen to go join Aerosmith. I sang a whole Aerosmith tribute set every weekend for fuck's sake! How the fuck do I shut that off?"

I held it together the best I could, but it was just crazy to me. Every day for a week or two, every time I would leave the room to smoke a cigarette, get a beer, get a soft drink, or smoke a joint, I would run into Steven. He would always say things like, "Hey, dude, how's it going? How's recording coming along? How are the songs turning out? You know, if you need anything, let me know." He was sweet as fucking pie.

Tommy and Nikki were used to being in one of the biggest rock bands in the world by then; they had had years of experience to adjust to fame and celebrity encounters as the band climbed to the top.

While The Scream had done quite well, I went from playing American clubs and one London theater, to sitting there hanging out with one of my idols as we recorded. I struggled to fucking process that and figure out how to treat him like a peer.

Steven wrote their hit "Dude (Looks Like a Lady)" about Mötley's last singer. Who knows if he was now having thoughts about writing a song about a silent cannonball?

About a week or two in, Steven said to Nikki, "Dude, like, seriously? What is wrong with your singer?"

Nikki asked, "What are you talking about?"

Steven jokingly said, "I've literally tried talking to Corabi every day for the last week or two. He just stands there with his mouth open and doesn't say anything. What's the deal? Is he high or is he stupid?"

Nikki smiled and said, "Both."

It wasn't just Aerosmith that I was hanging out with at the studio either. Bryan Adams lived up there, so he came by a few times. Mike Reno from Loverboy also came by the studio, since he was very good friends with Bob Rock, and he gave me some pointers vocally. Pretty much all of Loverboy's records were done there, and I grew up playing these guys' songs in cover bands.

The whole situation of meeting these people who I grew up watching on TV, or paid to see them play, was certainly odd to me. Now I had to process it and not act like a fan at all to be on the same level with them, which I didn't know how to do because I had never been in that position before.

Eventually, I got to the point where I could sit down with Steven Tyler and ask him things that I was always curious about, like, "Hey, the song title 'Bone to Bone (Coney Island White Fish Boy),' what the fuck is that?"

He told me, "When we all lived back on the East Coast, the big deal was everybody got high and drunk on Friday and Saturday nights and went to Brooklyn's Coney Island with chicks and fucked them on the beach. So, on Saturday and Sunday mornings, there'd be fucking used condoms all over the beach and under the boardwalk, which they called Coney Island White Fish."

One day I was talking to Steven when his wife Teresa Barrick and their son Taj came in. Taj was just an infant, so I squatted down while Teresa held him, and grabbed his finger and said, "Hi, little buddy!"

Steven looked at me and asked, "Do you have any kids?"

"Yeah, I have two: a daughter Valerie and a son named Ian."

A few weeks later, Val brought my five-year-old son Ian up to Vancouver, as we were all going to go to Whistler over the Thanksgiving weekend.

Ian was sitting in Little Mountain's lounge, just eating some grapes, when Steven came out of Aerosmith's studio, still scatting melodies running through his head, as was usual with him. Ian was very aware of Aerosmith even at that age, so when Steven walked in, Ian looked at him and excitedly shouted, "Dad, it's Steven Tyler!"

I was so impressed with Steven because after I had told him my son's name just that one time weeks ago, he walked right over to my boy and instantly said, "You must be Ian. Your daddy talks about you all the time."

Steven then put his hand out and said, "Gimme some!" motioning for Ian to slap his hand, high-five (or low-five) style. Ian took it more literally and simply put the rest of the grapes he was eating on Stephen's outstretched hand, and we all laughed our asses off.

Another day at Little Mountain, I was sitting in the living room area between Studio A and Studio B by myself, waiting to do a guitar track. While I had a little time to kill, I grabbed a guitar and while sitting on the couch in front of the TV, I started noodling around, playing "Bad Moon Rising" by Creedence, and "Over the Hills and Far Away" by Zeppelin. I then started playing some Aerosmith songs that I used to play in our tribute set years ago.

I played "Seasons of Wither" from the top and when I got right to the point where the vocals start, I heard Tyler's voice kick in. I swung my head around and saw that Steven had fucking snuck-up behind me. He sang the first verse into my ear, and then jumped over the couch in front of me, so I stopped playing.

He then told me the whole story of the night he wrote "Seasons of Wither." He said, "I was out, and I was kind of fucked-up. Walking home from a club to our band house back in Boston, I walked past a dumpster and saw a guitar neck sticking out. I pulled the guitar out and it looked like it was in reasonably good shape. I brought it home and gave it to Joe Perry. Joe cleaned it up for me, threw some strings on it, intonated it, tuned it, the whole bit."

Then Steven told me, "I went into our basement, and I pulled out a tapestry rug, lit some candles, smoked a joint, perhaps took a Tuinal or two, then just started fucking around with tunings. I'm not a guitar player, but I fucking tuned the guitar and I can play that whole fucking song with one finger."

He showed me the tuning, but again, I was so fanboyish about the whole fucking moment I didn't focus on the tuning, I was just focused on the story.

We then sat and played "Seasons of Wither," both of us singing it together!

At the end of the song, I turned around and Tommy's drum tech Clyde "Spidey" Duncan was videotaping us with my video camera. I said to Spidey, "How much did you get?"

He said, "I got all of it, dude. I saw Steven right when he walked up, so I grabbed your camera, and I filmed it all."

I couldn't believe it—how awesome! I thought to myself, "Fuck, that's killer. I've got that whole fucking thing on tape. Me and Steven Tyler doing 'Seasons of Wither.' I've got the story. Awesome!"

At one point during the recording session, Bob Rock wasn't happy with how we were playing, and he wanted us to blow off some steam, so someone called the Marble Arch and ordered about fifteen strippers to come to the studio.

The crew made sure our gear was completely covered in plastic. There were plastic mats all taped together on the floor, where fifteen fucking strippers rolled around before our eyes, wrestling in cherry pies, apple pies, and lemon meringue pies. It was pie wrestling, and we had a fucking blast!

We had a break over Christmas, and we all went back home to LA. I was spending some time with the kids and Val at her place in Thousand

Oaks one day, when I remembered I sung "Seasons of Wither" with Steven Tyler. I told Val I had it all on video, and she said, "Wow, no fucking way!"

I said, "Hold on a minute," while I went to my truck and got my video camera. I walked back in with it and my kids were sitting there on the lounge with Val and everybody was waiting with bated breath to see the video of Steven and me. I connected the cables and plugged them into my VCR player, then hit play.

The tape rolled, and it was pretty much a fucking orgy with chicks licking cherry pie out of each other's assholes. They're eating pie and throwing pie at each other's naked bodies. I quickly stopped the video camera, and Val said to the kids, "Go to your rooms!"

Our two kids said, "I think I just saw a naked girl with pie."

"No, you didn't."

Unbeknownst to me, someone took my video camera and duct-taped it to a ceiling fan shooting straight down and videotaped all the naked pie debauchery. To my horror, they filmed over the entire footage of Steven Tyler and myself doing "Seasons of Wither" together. I couldn't fucking believe it! The footage of one of the greatest experiences of my life was gone forever, replaced with tits, asses, and sweet cherry pie.

The kids went to their rooms. I was horrified. Val said, "Play the video."

I said, "Nah, you don't need to see that video. I'm not in it. It was just a case of boys will be boys."

She said louder, "Play the fucking video."

I hit the play button again.

Not even two minutes into the video, a male hand came into the shot and then its arm. The skull tattoo on the inside of my right arm was clearly visible, and then my fucking hand started squeezing and mashing pie into this girl's fucking titties. My separated wife said, "Yeah, you can get the fuck out of the house now."

I said, "Goddamn it. I just wanted to show you the video of Steven Tyler and me. I honestly had no fucking idea that somebody had taken my video camera, duct-taped it to the ceiling fan, and filmed that whole thing."

Somebody could have given me a heads-up. We were all excited about "Seasons of Wither," and I ended up with Marriage in Wither.

13
Nu Crue

There was a lot of contractual activity going on between Hollywood Records and Elektra Records to sever my legal ties from The Scream and have me in Mötley Crüe. It took about eight months of negotiating and legal arm-wrestling to sort it all out.

I was sweating bullets that whole time, because if somebody said something that somebody else didn't like, my gig with Mötley could all go to shit. The businesspeople would call me asking how I felt about this or that, and I told them, "Just sort it out and make it work."

I had already recorded that song "Young and Dumb" for the *Encino Man* soundtrack. Then a lot of money changed hands from Elektra to Hollywood Records, and Mötley was to take The Scream out on tour as our opening act, provided they had a new singer in place and their next album out in time.

I helped them out a bit with their album by singing some backups on a couple of tracks, one of them being "Miss Thang." I thought it was a cool record, but it was much different than the one I had done with the guys. They were getting more into music like the Red Hot Chili Peppers, so there were a lot more funk grooves in the sound.

They finished their album *Takin' It to the Next Level* and had advanced promo copies sent out to press and radio. I was on set the day they shot the first video, but just two weeks before the album's release, the label decided to pull the plug on the album and drop the band.

It was a devastating blow for the band, and I felt bad for the guys. The Scream essentially ceased at that point, and I copped blame, which inevitably caused some bad blood between some of us.

It was January 14, 1993, when Mötley finally announced to the world that I was their new singer. Then just a couple of weeks after the announcement, I made my first official appearance with the band, at the American Music Awards.

The band presented the award for Favorite Country Single, which made absolutely no fucking sense to me. Why was Mötley fucking Crüe giving a country award out? I wasn't really happy about it, but I had a little fun with it by wearing a cowboy hat.

The guys let me announce, "And the winner is: 'Achy Breaky Heart' by Billy Ray Cyrus." We stepped back on the Shrine Auditorium's podium as he made his winner's speech. I just looked at what crowd I could see on either side of his big mullet in front of me and laughed with Tommy while on stage.

As we left Vancouver's Pan Pacific Hotel for the Christmas holidays, management told us to not come back. So, this time we were staying at Pacific Palisades on Jervis Street in the West End District.

When Mick and I headed back up to Vancouver, we had a false start when our Delta Air Lines captain turned the 727 around on the LAX tarmac and kicked us off the flight because we were too fucking drunk and rowdy.

We were just fucking with each other the whole time in Vancouver, in a fun way. It started out when we arrived at the Pan Pacific the first time up there. Someone would knock on Mick's door and then run. That soon escalated to soaking the outside of his hotel room door with hairspray. They would then light it, knock on his door, and shout out FIRE before running off. Mick would look out through his peephole and see nothing but flames dancing in front of his eyes.

After doing that to Mick a good six or seven times, Mick went out and got a fucking twenty-pound bag of flour and literally covered the entire hallway floor with it. If anybody came to his door, he could then see exactly where the footprints came from.

After committing to sobriety, everybody would drink O'Doul's non-alcoholic beers, until somebody would get a hair up their ass and be off again.

Tommy and I hung out quite a bit. We would go out drinking and have four or five drinks, then go back to the hotel, sleep, get up the next morning, work out in the hotel gym, have breakfast, and go to the studio. It wasn't an everyday occurrence though. Somebody would say, "Oh, Pantera's playing at the Commodore, let's go out."

We'd have a good night, but it wouldn't get crazy.

Most of the time it was great fun, but Jesus Christ, there were also plenty of other times where so much crazy shit was going on, it was fucking hard work, too. I used to laugh about it, but a lot of times it was a very nervous fucking laugh, like I just want to get this record fucking done before one of these guys fucking offs himself!

While there may have been a bit of talk amongst fans that we were rerecording some old Mötley songs with my vocals while we were in the studio, we were just completely focused on recording our new music together…apart from the side debauchery that is Mötley Crüe, of course.

There was one song that we jammed a few times and wanted to cover as a bonus track, which was "Oh, Darlin'" by The Beatles. We asked Steven Tyler and Joe Perry from Aerosmith to play on the track with us, and they said, "Yeah, that'd be great. We love The Beatles, cool."

Our manager looked into the permissions to ensure we had a green light through the publishing company ATV Music. Michael Jackson had infamously bought ATV's extensive song catalog for almost $50 million in the mid-eighties, which made him the owner of about 250 Lennon-McCartney songs, including "Oh, Darlin'."

Our manager came into the studio one day and told us, "Guys, you're never going to believe this! I enquired about you guys tracking 'Oh, Darlin'' with Steven and Joe, and word has come back that Paul McCartney is interested in doing it with you guys!"

We freaked out at the thought of Paul, Steven, Joe, Mick, Nikki, Tommy, and myself all doing our thing on this track together. It all hinged on our schedules permitting it once we got back to Los Angeles.

Unfortunately, when the window of opportunity was there, Paul McCartney was in England and Aerosmith was out on their *Get a Grip* world tour. We just couldn't make it happen, so it never got finished—horseshoes & hand grenades! It would have been awesome though, I'm sure.

We were recording overdubs and some vocals on the song "Misunderstood" back in Los Angeles when Glenn Hughes came by to say hello and see what we were up to. Someone in the band said to Bob Rock, "Man, it would be fucking awesome if Glenn could sing something on this record with us," so Bob asked him.

Known as "The Voice of Rock," Glenn played bass and sang in Deep Purple, and briefly fronted Black Sabbath about a decade earlier. More recently, he had kicked his drug habits and released a solo album the year before called *LA Blues Authority Volume II: Glenn Hughes—Blues*, on which Mick played a couple of guitar tracks. I had met Glenn briefly when he popped into our rehearsal studio, as we were still rehearsing and writing.

Glenn agreed, "Yeah, yeah, yeah, I'll do something."

Bob said, "Well, do you want to do something on this song now?"

He said, "Yeah, okay, that's cool."

We quickly had the lyrics printed out and gave them to him. He went out into the control room, put the headphones on, and made some notes while he listened to it a couple of times.

He then stood up to the microphone, Bob hit play and record, and Glenn did two passes straight through, from top to bottom, while we all sat there listening and saying, "Holy fuck. That's not normal."

He just went boom and sang these parts that just worked on the song so well. Bob said, "You know what, do it one more time and try and change it up a little bit."

He did it once again, and Bob put his backing vocal track together with the best parts of those three quick takes. I don't think Glenn was in the building an hour, and he left.

I've never seen anything like it before. That's the difference between the old school guys and the guys now: he literally came in and just fucking nailed it.

Another day we were recording and wanted some Hammond B3 and some Clavinet keyboards on a song, so we were sitting there trying to think of who we could call in. Tommy and Nikki said, "Let's call Stevie Wonder and see if he would play on our record," but he wasn't available.

Then someone said, "What about Billy Preston?"

Billy had a great solo career but was a top session guy who played with the likes of Little Richard, Ray Charles, and then did so much work with The Beatles and The Rolling Stones. I'm talking fucking *Abbey Road*, *Let It Be*, *Sgt. Pepper's*, *Sticky Fingers*, *Exile on Main St.*, *Goats Head Soup*, *It's Only Rock 'n' Roll*, and *Tattoo You*. Need I say more?

The phone call was made, and the next fucking day Billy Preston was in the studio with us doing keyboard parts on "Babykills." We were like, fuck, this is badass! He played keys on a couple of tracks, and we hung out for a while, just bullshitting with him. Someone asked, "Dude, can you do the keyboard solo in 'Get Back,'" and he fucking did it note-for-note. It was the exact fucking tone as on the record.

One day Tommy and I were having a drink in the strip bar Crazy Girls, which was conveniently situated across the street from A&M Studios, when fucking Jimmy Page walked in. Another day as I arrived at Nikki's mansion, Ringo Starr was leaving with Harry Nilsson.

Another time, I was in a room of A&M when a beautiful Black girl came in and walked over, sitting herself down next to me. She was wearing jeans, a T-shirt, and had her hair pulled back in a ponytail with a baseball cap on. She didn't have a drop of makeup on and was just gorgeous. We chatted for a little while, and I flirted with her a bit. I ended up asking, "Anyway, what's your name?"

She smiled and said, "Oh, I'm Whitney…Whitney Houston."

Clueless Corabi said, "Oh, shit. Fuck. Hi, I'm John."

My whole time in Mötley was just surreal. I'm sure you're saying to yourself dude, c'mon, stop namedropping, but meeting all of these legendary performers was a constant mindfuck, and I was just some kid from Philly freaking out on a daily basis! I still have bruises from pinching myself back then.

Tommy and I were sitting at his house with guitar tech Bobby O, and Tommy's phone rang. "Yeah, dude, yeah, yeah, I know where you're at. Okay, yeah, we'll be down there," said Tommy, before he hung up.

He then turned to us and said, "Hey, Sylvester Stallone's right down the road. I golf with him all the time. Do you want to come down with me and say hi?"

We had no sooner headed out in Tommy's car when we crossed Thousand Oaks Boulevard and went into a small industrial area. We saw all these cameras, lights, and other gear set up around a pharmaceutical company's building, so we pulled in and asked someone where Sylvester was. They said, "Oh, he's over in his trailer, getting his hair and makeup touched up."

He was on the set of his latest movie, a science fiction action film called *Demolition Man*.

We went into his trailer and got introduced. We then sat there bullshitting for a while, as he told us about the movie in his familiar tone.

After a while, I asked him, "Hey, dude, do you remember when you were filming *Rocky*, you were doing a scene on the corner of Kensington Avenue and Tusculum Street in the Kensington area of Philadelphia.

That part where your brother and the guys were singing "Take You Back" on the corner around a burning fire barrel, and you walk up into the scene?"

Sylvester said, "Yeah, yeah, yeah."

I continued, "Well, I don't know if you remember but when you were doing that scene, there was a kid standing there while you guys were talking in between shots, and this kid asked you what the movie was about. You said it was a movie called *Rocky* about a boxer. The kid asked you if it was about Rocky Graziano or Rocky Marciano."

I could see Sylvester Stallone's brain ticking over as he thought about it for a minute. He said, "Yeah, yeah, I do vaguely remember that. It was like three o'clock in the morning, right?"

I said, "Yeah, that's right. Well, that kid was me!"

He said, "Fuck, no way!"

I told him that the location was just half a mile from where I lived on Silver Street, and we then talked for a while about Philadelphia, and all the old school boxers that we used to like watching on TV back in the day.

Tommy asked who else was in the movie, and Sylvester said, "Oh, there's this comedian guy Denis Leary, and a great up-and-coming actress named Sandy."

Earlier that year, Denis Leary released a live record of his comedy routine called *No Cure for Cancer*. The album opened with his single "Asshole," but I had played another track "More Drugs" to Tommy and Nikki, who had a good laugh at the part where he had a go at Mötley.

We left Sylvester to get back to work, and we walked up to the trailer Denis Leary was in and knocked on the door. He opened the door, saw it was me and Tommy Lee, and said, "God, I hope you guys have a sense of humor!"

We pissed ourselves laughing.

Denis invited us into the trailer and before long, Tommy and Denis were in one room while I sat in the main room with the other person in the trailer, the up-and-coming actress Sandy—a gorgeous woman named Sandra Bullock. She said, "Oh, so you're in Mötley Crüe?"

"Yep, I'm in Mötley Crüe," I said.

"Where are you from?" she then asked.

"I'm from Philadelphia, but I live here, like five minutes away."

She asked, "So, how long have you been in California?"

Kidding with her, I said, "What's with all the fucking questions? Are you a fucking cop?"

She was sitting there in a police uniform because her character in the movie was Lieutenant Huxley, and she just fucking came right back at me with some great retort that had me thinking, "Oh my God, I fucking love this girl." She was so funny, and I was immediately smitten.

Tommy and Denis headed out and were doing their thing while Sandra and I were hanging out, laughing like little school kids. Perhaps it was chemistry class because before long, I held her hand, and we started kissing a bit. We were getting to know each other when there was a knock on the trailer door, "Sandy, you need to film your scene now."

I walked over to the set with her and then watched as they filmed the scene in *Demolition Man* where Sylvester Stallone's self-driving car malfunctions and crashes through a window and rolls over, but it becomes completely covered in SecureFoam. When Sandra Bullock runs up, he punches through the foam and they pull the door off. He gets out, saying his car has turned into a cannoli.

They wanted to do it three fucking times, so in between takes Sandy would come over to straighten her police uniform, fix her hair, and have her makeup touched-up again. We would talk and hold hands, just bullshitting and goofing around telling jokes.

When they finally finished the scene and were done filming for the night, she needed to go back to her trailer, but she said to me, "Wait here, John, I'll be right back."

I said, "Okay, cool." I stood around there as crew started packing some things up on set. I waited and waited for probably thirty or forty minutes.

I started walking back toward where the trailers were when Bobby O came up to me and said, "Hey, Crab, that little actress chick—she's looking for you."

I said, "Where's she at?"

"She was over by the trailers," he said.

I walked over, knocked on the trailer, waited, knocked again, waited, looked inside, and saw nobody was in there. I knocked on the other trailer. Denis answered and said, "Nope, I think she left, dude."

I looked in all the trailers. I saw Sylvester again and asked if he knew where Sandy was. "No, I think she's done. I think she left," he said.

So, I walked back to where they were filming, where she told me to wait, and I saw Bobby there. He said, "Oh, Crab. That fucking little actress chick—she came by and asked me for your phone number before she left."

I said, "Well, did you fucking give it to her?"

He said, "No, dude, I didn't want to give her your phone number without asking you first!"

"Goddamn it, fuck!" I was so fucking bummed.

Demolition Man brought Sandra Bullock a lot of recognition and her next movie the following year was *Speed*. That's when she really broke-through and blew up. She eventually went on to win an Academy Award for Best Actress and became one of the highest paid actresses in the world.

What a fucking sweetheart she was. I was totally smitten with her that night. She was funnier than shit; she had the greatest sense of humor and was absolutely drop-dead gorgeous. Sandra was a lot of fun, and obviously talented. So, now I watch her movies and can't help but think: *What if?*

When Mick split-up with his wife Emi, he was really bummed and pulling his fucking hair out about it, as the lawyers got involved, and it was just a fucking nightmare for him. I said to Mick one night, "Come on, dude, you're fucking Mick Mars. Let's go out. Let's just go out tonight, and if you don't like it, we'll turn around and come home. Let's go to the Rainbow, get some dinner, have a cocktail or two, and come home. You need to get out."

In typical Mötley fashion, we were at the Rainbow and met a blonde girl who was a dancer at the club Star Gardens on Lankershim Boulevard in North Hollywood. She came over to our table and sat down and started talking to Mick. He started chatting her up, and she was making quite a fuss over him. I was thinking, "Awesome, thank you, God. Hopefully if nothing else, Mick, will just get fucking laid tonight and get some of the poison out of his system."

We had a good time at the Rainbow and the blonde asked us to come back to the strip club. I asked Mick if he wanted to go, and he said, "Yeah, I'll go for a minute." We fucking hung out for a little bit and then Mick and I bailed.

A day or two later, my intercom phone at the guesthouse rang, and Mick said, "What are you doing, you bastard?"

I said, "Oh, I'm just getting out of bed and having some coffee."

He said, "Well, throw some jeans on. We're going shooting!"

I said, "Nah, I think I'm going to pass."

Mick said, "I'm not asking you; I need you to help me out here, buddy. Remember that blonde chick from the other night? Well, she's coming up to go shooting with me, but she's bringing a friend. You're going to keep the friend busy."

I agreed and said, "Okay, anything I can do to help."

So, I put my guns in my Bronco and drove up to Mick's house, where we loaded up the back of my truck with targets, earmuffs, gloves, glasses, and enough bullets to fucking invade Iraq. I drove us north up into California's High Desert. As we drove up there, Mick told me that his brother and friend were coming, too; he was some sort of a bigwig with the California Highway Patrol.

As we were putting the goggles and gloves on, Mick was already loaded and fired off the first shots at the target from his .357 magnum revolver, with the blonde girl next to him and the two cops looking on.

Her twenty-four-year-old coworker friend was hanging out at the back of my truck, next to me as I loaded my gun. I hadn't even taken a shot yet, when the chick said, "Ow!" and put her hand on her stomach.

When she pulled her fucking hand away, her stomach was bleeding. I said, "What the fuck?"

She said, "I think I got stung by a bee!"

I said, "Ah, that's not a bee sting. You're bleeding, like quite a lot."

It was a fucking freak accident. There we were, all standing around wearing gloves, goggles, ear protection. Mick was probably fifteen feet in front of us and then the targets were probably another twenty-five feet ahead of Mick. He shot the metal target, hit it with a ping, then it swung back. He shot again as it swung, then shot it up a third time and the chick then grabbed her stomach. What the fuck?

We quickly packed everything up and rushed this chick to the hospital since it seemed she had somehow been shot. At the hospital, they spent some time digging around in her stomach, trying to find any bullet fragments. They finally found a fragment that was no bigger than your pinky fingernail, pulled it out and stitched her up. We were at the hospital all fucking day.

Mick had shot a defective bullet that exploded and fragmented when it hit the target. That little chunk ricocheted back between everybody and hit the exotic dancer right in the stomach—a freak accident that could never happen again in a million years.

Now, this is typical Mick Mars: he had her taken to the hospital right away and picked up the tab for the hospital bill. He sat down with her and said, "I'll pay your hospital bill. Now, how much do you make a day at work?"

She said, "Probably 500 to a thousand a day."

He agreed to give her an amount somewhere in between, like 750 a day.

He said, "I will pick up your bill until it heals; I will give you $750 a day for a month. I will also pay for a plastic surgeon after it heals to make sure you have minimal scarring. I will do this if you just let me handle it for you and don't go to a lawyer. Obviously, it's going to affect your dancing career, so I'll pay you to stay home until it's completely healed, so you're not going to miss a dime."

She took the money and got all the treatments they did for her. She then found a scumbag lawyer who found a loophole in their agreement, and she fucking sued the shit out of Mick. It cost him another truckload of money, which I thought was a piece-of-shit move on her part—total bullshit. That's typical of Mick's luck. I was like, "Fuck, the poor guy can't get a break."

The career of Tommy's wife Heather Locklear continued to rise with her joining the TV soap *Melrose Place*, but their marriage also came to an end. Tommy and I went out one night, a week or so after the split, commiserating being separated from our wives. We went to a Mexican place called Casa Vega in Sherman Oaks, which we called the darkest place on Earth, besides the Rainbow of course.

I was telling Tommy all the shit my wife was saying to me because we're splitting up, and Tommy was telling me all the shit that he was going through with Heather, then who came walking in and sat down right next to me? Fucking Slash.

Slash joined in our commiseration party. He had only married less than a year before, but his marriage was already in rough waters and headed for rocks. The three of us downed heaps of tequila and Corona as we were dishing our dirt, when who came walking in and sat down with us? Fucking Steve Lukather.

I always loved Steve's guitar playing in his band Toto, and he also played guitar on the bestselling album of all time: Michael Jackson's *Thriller*. A few years earlier, he had divorced from Marie Currie, twin sister of The Runaways' singer, and it was complicated as they had a couple of kids. So, Steve joined in our commiseration party and had some good tales as a subject matter expert while we drank and drank and drank some more.

Time flew by and the bartender finally came to our table and said, "Guys, it's four o'clock in the morning. You need to go. Go home!"

Still to this day, I don't know how they all got home, or if they actually went home after there. All I know is I drove home, which I should NOT have fucking done.

I drove home to Mick's guesthouse all the way up the 101 freeway to the Kanan Road exit, then through the mountains on the windy-as-fuck, two-lane road with no guardrail and a fucking five-hundred-foot drop. I pulled into the carport, got out of my fucking truck, and walked into the guesthouse, then crashed out on my couch, glad I hadn't crashed earlier.

When I came-to the next morning, I got up and saw my front door was still open and my truck was still fucking running. I never shut it off.

14

Pretty Little Poison Apples

In the middle of August, I went with Tommy, Nikki, and Bob Rock to Vancouver's Pacific Coliseum and saw Aerosmith on their *Get a Grip* Tour.

While we watched, Tommy turned to me and said, "Dude, I can't wait to fucking play Donington with Aerosmith. Man, that'll be fucking cool."

I asked, "What?" and he said, "Didn't anybody tell you? We're doing the Donington festival next year. We're supporting Aerosmith."

I freaked out, "Are you fucking kidding me?"

Unbeknownst to me, our management had started planning for us to go over to England and play Donington next year. It was going to be Aerosmith headlining, with Mötley Crüe as a special guest, and Pantera.

For years, I remember reading about all the Monsters of Rock concerts at Castle Donington in England. The annual hard rock and heavy metal festival started in 1980 and was always the biggest fucking festival in the world. I was super excited about it.

Then we got word that Extreme had been added to the bill. I guess at that point, Extreme was bigger than Mötley in Europe because there was talk of us going on before Extreme. That quickly led to Mötley pulling out of Donington. I was super bummed about it.

One early October day in Vancouver, Tommy said to us, "Hey, I've got us tickets and backstage passes to go see Robert Plant at the Orpheum Theatre. Who wants to come?" Given I had always missed out on seeing Led Zeppelin, Robert's *Fate of Nation* solo tour was the next best thing to me.

We enjoyed a great show, and it was awesome to hear the Golden God sing a handful of Zeppelin songs in his set, like "Ramble On" and "Going to California." Once he ended the show with "Whole Lotta Love," we headed backstage. His drummer Michael Lee told Tommy Lee that on show night, Robert likes to go to an English pub and jam some songs. "Why don't you guys come down?" he invited.

So, we went to this English pub, and I think everybody in Vancouver knew about it because there were probably five hundred people in this fucking pub; it was packed.

We made our way in and through the crowd, where we joined Robert in a booth. They motioned for us to sit with him. There we were chatting with Robert fucking Plant, and inside I'm screaming, are you fucking kidding me? It was surreal.

Robert's band went up on the little stage and started jamming. Robert went up and did a few songs, before Michael Lee signaled to Tommy and me to come up and jam. We stood up and as I headed to the stage, I turned around and saw that Tommy had sat back down again.

I got on stage with them, and they asked me what I wanted to play. They were going deep on blues shit—and I love the blues—but I'm not as well-versed with blues songs as Robert Plant and all his cats.

I didn't know what to suggest. I just looked at the band, then Robert asked, "Do you know 'The Lemon Song'?"

In a moment, there I was playing guitar to a fucking Led Zeppelin song on fucking stage with Robert Plant. I then sang a ZZ Top song "Tush" with his band, just to put a fucking cherry on top.

We had a song called "Evil D," simply because the opening riff that Tommy came up with was really fucking evil sounding and was in drop D tuning. We had the music down but hadn't come up with any lyrics for it. It was the last song we needed to finish writing for the album.

My mom called me one night while I was in my hotel room and as we chatted, she said, "Hey, I need to tell you that your Uncle Jack got arrested again."

I asked, "For what?"

She told me the whole story of how he had moved into a home in Philadelphia with a woman. He was renting a room from her, and she was single with two boys; it seems she was divorced. Then this woman was in a car accident and died after a while in the hospital. Uncle Jack looked after these kids for about six months, until the ex-husband got the estate and guardianship settled. When he moved back into the home, he kindly told Uncle Jack that he could continue to stay there.

After this guy moved back into the house, he eventually found out that Uncle Jack had been fucking molesting his two little boys, aged eight and three, the whole fucking time he had been living there.

I was fucking pissed. That motherfucker! He should still be locked away behind a cast-iron door after getting caught molesting my brother and sisters and so many other kids in the neighborhood all those years ago. They should NOT have let him out of jail because the inmates were threatening his life. Of course, you're a fucking target in prison if you have molested kids.

And then for him to be able to work as a janitor in a fucking Catholic elementary school—it was just ludicrous. And here we were: he had fucking done it again, the sick fuck! Who knows how many other victims were out there, too?

The authorities hadn't dealt with it, so I fucking wanted to—to end it once and for all. I wanted to run a razor across his throat and see him dead on a floor, because if he went back to prison, they'd probably just fucking let him out again. If he were in an unmarked grave, he wouldn't be able to take any more innocence. Even though he was my uncle, that monster didn't deserve to live; he wasn't human.[4]

It took me a long time to get to sleep that night after I got off the phone with my mom. I was so fucking pissed. I no sooner got to sleep than I had to get up again the next morning to meet in the hotel lobby. We got into the van and drove a mile or two to the studio, as usual.

I said to Tommy and Nikki, "That really fucking heavy song we have, 'Evil D,' I want to write this about my fucking uncle."

I told them the whole story about what he had done when I was a kid and what had just occurred again. They said, "Yes, yes!"

The lyrics were written, the song recorded, and we submitted the finished track titled "The Ballad of Jack Hayes." The record label came back and said we couldn't call him out by name. I said, "I don't really give a fuck. They weren't alleged crimes; he got caught for them. He's a piece of shit."

Their legal department held firm and said we couldn't call him out by name, so we simply changed the title of the song to "Uncle Jack," keeping all the lyrics as they were.

We took the proceeds from that song and donated them to organizations benefiting abused children.

There's a little rap that I do right before the guitar solo, and when I was in recording it, Bob Rock said, "Dude, come in here for a minute."

---

4 Since he was a repeat offender, Uncle Jack got sentenced to a life term in prison for these crimes, where he finally fucking died behind bars from a massive heart attack around Thanksgiving 2003.

He said, "Take the fucking gloves off, bro. This is your uncle, the one who fucking did all this shit to your brother and sisters. Let it out!"

Even though Bob pulled it back in the mix a bit quieter in the finished work, I went back in and screamed how I fucking hated him, the piece of shit, and how he's a fucking scumbag, and it really pissed me off, and I wanted to rip his goddamn heart out.

Tommy was sitting in the room and said, "Fuck, dude, that's intense."

Bob said, "That's it, that's the take."

Prior to submitting it, I called my brother and sisters and said, "Hey, I don't want to throw you under the bus, but here's the deal. I'm sure people are going to be asking me about this song. Are you guys cool with me talking about this in public?" They were adamant that I should do it; so we had their full support.

Whenever I have sung that song, anger is my overriding emotion. I fucking hate that guy so much, and I was angry that somebody was being allowed to get away with it by using government loopholes.

It was bad enough what he fucking did to my family, but for him to then be fucking set free from prison, go back to work as a janitor of an Catholic elementary school in Philadelphia for years, get free therapy as part of his release while my parents paid a small fortune, only to commit the same fucking crimes with two little boys again—that motherfucker! I was so fucking pissed about it all.

When Mötley hit the road and toured, we played "Uncle Jack" either six or seven songs into the set, depending on the night. My sister Anna came to see us play in North Carolina. Our tour manager took care of her and told me that he set her up with a seat at the front. I hadn't seen her up to that point, and as we hit the stage, I knew she was there, but I couldn't see her.

As we played "Uncle Jack," I just happened to look down for a minute, and I saw Anna was over in the corner in front of Nikki. She was fucking hysterical with tears rolling down her fucking cheeks. It was probably the most difficult time I've ever had getting through a song.

It made me think that we were grown people now, not the young kids anymore. At that point, I had just turned thirty-five and my sister was thirty-two and we were STILL affected by it. More than twenty fucking years later, his evil was still creepin'. That's when I knew it was never going to go away for us, ever.

We worked up about twenty-three songs for the album. "Ditch that Bitch" was one that pretty much sounded like a cross between Van Halen's "Hot for Teacher" and "La Grange" by ZZ Top.

Tommy's drums were insane with a very chaotic, fast shuffle double-bass, and we had really stupid, tongue-in-cheek fucking lyrics about a lot of these chicks that Mötley met through their careers, and were still meeting, who would do anything for backstage passes. We just had fun with it, but it never got released.

Our album was one of the last recorded at Little Mountain's 201 West Seventh Avenue location. At the end of '93, the twenty-year lease expired and the landlord wanted to double the rent. They chose not to renew it, so they relocated to Burnaby. They never reached the same heights second time around, though, just like when a famous nightclub moves locations—or a famous band gets a new singer.

Back in LA, Tommy had his limo driver swing by my place on the night before Halloween and pick me up. We then headed along Sunset Boulevard to The Viper Room, since one of its owners who Tommy knew, Johnny Depp, was going to play on stage that Tuesday night in some band. I'd seen Johnny act in movies like *Platoon* and *Edward Scissorhands*, but I'd never seen him play guitar. I didn't know at the time, but it was his new alt-rock band simply called P, which also featured Flea from the Red Hot Chili Peppers, Al Jourgensen from Ministry, and the singer from the Butthole Surfers.

We were running a bit late for their set, and as we got out of the limo and quickly headed into the club, we had to step over some young guy passed-out, face-down in the entrance way. The band was already into their set as we bellied up to the bar for cocktails. While we chatted away at the bar without even really watching the band, someone apparently said something to Flea after a song, so he took his bass off, left the stage, and the band finished up. We figured we had missed most of their set, so we chatted with Johnny Depp and others for the rest of the night.

When we left the club, we saw Christina Applegate outside leaning against the wall, bawling uncontrollably. Tommy knew her and asked what was wrong, and she sobbed, "A really good friend of mine, River, died. He came here tonight, and it seems he overdosed on drugs," so we just gave her a few words of comfort, best we could.

As Tommy and I sat in the limo headed back to my place, we put two-and-two together and fucking realized the guy we stepped over coming into the club was the young actor River Phoenix, who was actually overdosing. We were oblivious to what was going down while we were in the club, but after collapsing in the entrance and us stepping over him, he went into convulsions. His actor brother Joaquin Phoenix (then nineteen and known as Leaf) called 911, and Flea left the stage and went with River in the ambulance to nearby Cedars-Sinai Hospital, where they were unfortunately unable to resuscitate him.

River Phoenix was pronounced dead at just twenty-three years of age. Apparently, he'd been staying with Red Hot Chili Peppers guitarist John Frusciante in his final days, and they binged on smoking crack, plus shot coke and heroin.

Tommy and I couldn't believe it! River was apparently going to get up and perform with his buddy Flea that night but never made it on stage. The club remained closed for a week while mourning fans outside turned it into a shrine for him. Johnny Depp continued to close the West Hollywood club every year on Halloween for more than a decade as a mark of respect.

During the process of recording our album, Bob Rock commented, "God, you guys are so fucking different from each other musically, but it works."

Then as we were doing the mixes on songs for the album, Bob said, "I'd love to see each one of you guys, with no help from any of the other members of the band, just go into a room and write a song. I want to see what you guys come up with."

Not only was it Bob's way of seeing what we could come up with, I believe it was also a way of getting us out of his hair because we were always standing right behind him, asking questions while he was working away on the mixes.

With more than twenty great songs, we were having a hard time choosing which twelve would make it on the record. We knew there would be some leftover, so we came up with the idea that when die-hard fans in North America bought our album, there would be a bounce-back card they could fill out and send in with six bucks, and we would send them a limited-edition CD or cassette with songs on it. We were going to call it *Leftovers* but went with *Quaternary*.

We all went separate directions in the studio and grabbed an engineer. Initially, I had written a lullaby on acoustic guitar that I was going to record.

It was me fingerpicking on an acoustic in a style perhaps somewhat reminiscent of "Blackbird" by The Beatles. It was only a minute-and-a-half long.

I set the guitar down for a minute and started noodling around on a piano that was in the room, just hitting some chords. I hit the first chord and then the second chord. It was a total accident because I don't play piano much at all. I had no idea what the chords were that I was playing or what key I was in.

I started singing, sitting in this room alone, and started thinking of more lyrics as I put the song together roughly with the piano chords. I wanted to call it "Friends," so I wrote the first verse about being away and missing people, then I wrote the last verse as a retort, like someone saying, "Hey, I'm missing you, too."

Scott Humphrey was floating around helping Bob out with Pro Tools editing, and he was an amazing piano player, too. I brought Scott into the room and asked, "Hey, could you help me record this idea?"

I played it to him painstakingly slow, but he said, "Oh, it's great, Crab. Yeah, let's fucking do it."

I showed Scott what I was playing and after setting up some microphones, he played it all the way through. It would have taken me 150 fucking edits and punches for me to get it recorded. I then sang as he recorded my vocals, and I had Scott add some strings at the end.

When Bob heard the song, he loved it, saying, "It's very Beatlesesque, do you mind if I add some backing vocals?" We had these two guys that we used in Vancouver who Bob was very comfortable with, so they came in and recorded some backing vocals. We had a little fun with it.

Quaternary in America not only had our four individual songs, but a bonus track called "Babykills." The Japanese version also included "10,000 Miles Away" and some demo versions of songs, one of which was "Livin' in the No."

"Hooligan's Holiday" was chosen as the first single, and we needed to do a video for it. Tommy had seen Duran Duran's video for their song "Ordinary World," and we thought it was amazing. We got in touch with the director, a lovely English gentleman named Nick Egan, and started discussing a concept.

Our song's title came from the LA riots that stemmed from LAPD officers being acquitted of beating Rodney King. The TV news showed footage of people looting, burning, and fighting, and the news anchor said,

"It's a regular hooligan's holiday out there," which I thought was a genius phrase.

So we came up with a chaotic vibe of moving text and disturbing images of gang delinquency and themed it on Stanley Kubrick's 1971 cult classic *A Clockwork Orange* and the movie's droogs getting high and committing ultraviolent acts. It was a lot of fun doing that video, and I found out years later that a camera guy was one of the people who went on to create the TV show *South Park*.

In the lead-up to our album's release, an electronic press kit was made and distributed, which began with Nikki saying, "There were four ingredients. We took one fourth out and put a stronger fourth in. It's the first time we've been a band of four equal components."

We went on a short tour of Europe to do press and hold some listening parties in five cities, just before the album came out. I had only been to London with The Scream, so I was excited to visit mainland Europe for the first time.

As we headed to Munich for the first listening party, the label had already started printing the album artwork in preparation for release. Somebody at our label's office in Germany got an advanced copy of the album, opened it, and saw a photo inside of Nikki wearing a Nazi SS jacket with the red swastika armband.

The German label people caught it and immediately called the president of Elektra Records, and said, "We can't release this record. We're not going to release it."

In Germany, anything with a swastika on it is illegal. They had already printed a couple hundred thousand copies of it, which were destroyed. The quickest fix was to doctor the photo in the booklet to blackout all the SS regalia on his jacket, making it look all black.[5]

While they were at it, they also elongated Nikki's sleeve with black ink in a photo of him taking a piss, so you couldn't see his fucking dick.[6]

5 The swastika armband photo did manage to make its way into Nikki's spread in the 1994 tour book, though.

6 A Nikki dick-pic did seemingly make its way into the booklet of the numbered Collector's Edition CD version of our record, snapped by Neal Preston when we took two helicopters up to a Canadian glacier for a ridiculously freezing and expensive photo shoot.

After Munich, we headed to Paris, where the first fucking interview we did was a live television show at about nine in the morning. We had hair and makeup done, and then I sat between Tommy and Nikki on a couch, with the studio lights beaming on us. A little French interviewer came in and sat down and we got underway.

As we were live on TV, in his unfamiliar, thick French accent, the interviewer said, "So, John Corabi, I listened to this new record. You're a little man with such a big voice. I don't believe it's you singing on the record. Sing for me."

I sat there trying to decipher what he just said, and I looked at Nikki and whispered to him, "Did he just say sing for me?"

Nikki and Tommy leaned forward and looked at each other across me, then ended the interview. I never said a word on air.

We stayed at the amazing, upscale Saint James Paris, which is a high-end, luxury hotel built back in the fucking 1800s. The Arc de Triomphe was just a stroll away, and as a light snow fell, Tommy and I walked a few blocks to Trocadéro Gardens, where we took in a great view of the Eiffel Tower across the river Seine.

As we stood on the street, we heard somebody yell out, "Tommy!" We saw Dave Grohl running up to us. Kurt Cobain was sitting incognito at the café behind him. Dave said, "Dude, what are you guys doing?"

Following an *MTV Unplugged* performance a few months earlier, Nirvana were on a European tour and played Paris on Valentine's Day, before hitting up a few other countries. They played Munich on the first day of March, but Kurt was then unwell with bronchitis and severe laryngitis, so he went to Rome for treatment.

Kurt's wife Courtney Love found him unconscious on the floor of their hotel room in Rome after he had tried to commit suicide by overdosing on champagne and Rohypnol. He was rushed to the hospital, where he spent the next five days. The rest of their tour got canceled, and they had come to Paris for a day or two before they headed back home to America.

We chatted on the street for a while, and then the four of us went to a nearby café where we hung out and talked more over a coffee. I told them I enjoyed seeing them play in London when I was there with The Scream, and funnily enough Dave used to be in a band called Scream. While they talked a little bit about Kurt being sick and canceling the rest of their tour, I was unaware, as was the rest of the world, just how troubled Kurt was.

Just three weeks later, after he checked himself out of a detox facility following an intervention for his heroin addiction, Kurt Cobain was found dead in his Seattle home—he shot himself in the fucking head.

We flew from Paris to Milan. I was excited to be in Italy for the first time, even though it was the north and not the south, where my family came from. We went to our hotel and did all the press interviews at the hotel we stayed at.

The label ran a contest, and we attended a listening party at Rock Planet that night where the winners joined us. As we arrived at the club, there were probably 300 kids out front, waiting for us to show up. We hung backstage as they looped our "Hooligan's Holiday" video and played the album over the club's sound system. An Italian dude then introduced each one of us as we walked out and sat in a chair on stage for a Q&A session with Italian fans, done through an interpreter.

There was probably 600-700 kids crammed into this small club; it was so packed. After an hour or so of Q&A, we got up to walk off and fans rushed the stage and started tearing us apart, to the point where they were literally ripping sleeves off my clothing as souvenirs.

I got pushed so much that I fell and landed on the ground among all these legs and arms. One of the security guards managed to grab me and pull me out by my foot. As I was getting dragged out of the mayhem, Nikki looked down at me with a wide grin and said, "Welcome to the Crüe, dude!"

We got taken to another club called Shocking, where they had a party for us. We walked into the downstairs of this huge club that was pumping with dance music before being taken upstairs to a big horseshoe observation gallery that looked over the dance floor.

On this balcony area was our tour manager, us four band members, and about three hundred fucking models between the ages of eighteen and twenty-five scantily clad in miniskirts and hotpants. There were also ice buckets on stands full of champagne, vodka, and Jack Daniel's, conveniently placed every ten-feet along the balcony so we could help ourselves. They had beautiful platters of food laid out with shrimp, lobster, and pasta. I surveyed the scene thinking, "Holy fuck, are you kidding me right now?"

So we hung out and chilled, drank cocktails, and naturally started chatting up a few girls. I laid eyes on a stunning young lady and started a conversation. She barely spoke any English but told me her name was

Angelika. She was a twenty-one-year-old farm girl from somewhere in Poland who had only arrived in Milan a week or so ago and had never been out of her homeland before.

She asked where we had been and where we were going next. I said, "Tomorrow we leave Milan and go to Madrid, and after Madrid we go to London, then fly home to America."

This little Polish girl said, "Oh, London, London, London, I love London. I've seen photos of London; I've never been to London."

I kept thinking, "God, this girl is really cute." We hung out talking all night and when it was time for the band to leave, she stayed with the other models. Just before I walked out, I asked her, "Hey, would you like to come to London? We're having a record release party at the Hard Rock Café there."

She said, "No, I don't have the money to do that."

I said, "No, no, no. Give me your number, and I will call you, and I will get you a ticket to come to London and the party with me."

She couldn't believe it. The next day I made the arrangements to fly her out.

We got to Madrid and went to a radio station to do an interview. I swear to God there were about a thousand kids out front of the fucking station waiting for us. We needed the cops to create a fucking barricade line so we could get in and out of the station. It was insanity and felt like a little taste of Beatlemania.

When we arrived in London, it was colder than fuck. I've never been that cold in my life; it was fucking freezing.

We stayed at Conrad's Chelsea Harbour Hotel, which was another really swanky hotel. I checked in to my room and soon saw it was a huge fucking suite—it had a massive living room, massive dining room, a massive kitchen. There were two bedrooms, a massive bathroom, and sliding glass doors out onto a huge balcony right on the River Thames. I sat there looking around and thought, that Polish chick is coming tomorrow, and this is going to be killer.

We organized her ticket and had the Italian promoter's translator assist with the arrangements to get her on the flight from Milan. At Heathrow, a car service guy met her with her name on a sign, who drove her to the hotel, where I met her after doing press all day. I had the night off before our listening party the following night. I was perfectly set for a fun fucking night.

I met her in my hotel's lobby. This chick was absolutely stunning, a gorgeous girl. As we stood in the lobby, she got a phone call from her agent who said, "You've got to come back to Milan tomorrow." She had been booked for some fucking shoot, so couldn't come to the listening party. Fuck! We were both somewhat bummed, but at least we still had tonight, so I took her up to my suite.

She walked into my hotel room and looked around, and asked, "Ah, this room, just you?"

When I said it was just me, she told me in her really broken English, "This room, where I come from in Poland, a room like this, nine people lives."

She then looked at the big fruit basket and asked, "It's real?" I grabbed a couple of strawberries from it, threw one in my mouth, and handed her the other.

I was trying my best to communicate with this girl. She was stunning, and I couldn't take my eyes off her. After a while, I made a gesture with my hands like a fork and asked if she was hungry. I asked if she wanted to go for a steak. She looked at me with a frown and said, "I don't know this word, steak. I don't know this steak."

So, I started mooing like a fucking cow to try to get her to understand.

"Oh, no, no," she said as she reached into her bag. She pulled out a postcard of London's famous Piccadilly Circus and pointed to the McDonald's on it. "I want to go here."

I said, "No, no. Let's get steak."

"No, I want this," she insisted.

I caved, and we got a car to Piccadilly. We took in some neon sights and the famous fountain statue in the middle of the intersection and then she saw the McDonald's, just like on the postcard. Her face lit up as we went inside.

"What would you like?" I asked.

"Coca Cola…and apple pie." She didn't even want a burger. Cheapest date ever!

She ate her fucking apple pie and then asked me to sign its empty box. I signed it and passed it back to her. She neatly folded the McDonald's box and put it in her purse.

On the way back to the hotel, I suggested we hit the Marquee Club. I took her inside and asked what she would like to drink. "Coca Cola," she said. I got her a coke, and I got a Jack and coke.

As we sat there talking, she watched me drink and soon pointed at my glass asking, "What is this?"

I told her it was Jack Daniel's and Coca Cola, and she asked, "I try?" She took a sip and said, "This is very good." I got her one with the next round, and we hung in the club for a while, listening to shit like "Who Am I? (What's My Name?)" by Snoop Doggy Dogg.

We got a cab back to the hotel, and I opened a bottle of champagne. I poured us a glass each and gave her some more strawberries. I went to the bathroom for a minute and when I came back into the bedroom, this incredibly gorgeous girl was wearing a pair of black lace panties and nothing else—as she jumped up and down on the bed like a fucking five-year-old. She was excitedly laughing and squealing, "Oh, weee!" as she bounced up and down.

As much as I thought she was a drop-dead beauty, I could not fucking bring myself to fuck her. I felt like I would be taking candy from a baby. She was so sweet and defined innocence and had never been with anybody before. I just couldn't bring myself to damage this little girl. In that moment, jumping up and down naked on my bed, she just seemed so naïve and young. And this is the part of the memoir where you realize: I'M AN IDIOT!

I got her up the next morning and got her back in a car to the airport, then went and did press. I remained friends with Angelika and she lives in Berlin these days.

She emailed me some years later and said, "I can't believe you never even tried to kiss me or anything."

I said, "Well, I did earlier in the night, but I'm sorry, you were jumping up and down on my bed like a fucking five-year-old and as good as you looked, I couldn't do it."

She laughed about it.

Mötley's manager said to us in Europe, "I have good news, and I have really bad news. The good news is the album has come out and debuted at number seven on the Billboard 200 album charts."

We were stoked at the news and thought it was awesome. He said, "'Hooligan's Holiday' is in heavy rotation, getting a lot of calls and requests for it. The bad news though is everybody at Elektra is getting fired."

Mötley Crüe had resigned on a multi-album deal with millions advanced not long before I met them.

Three other huge deals had been signed by the label: Anthrax on a twenty-million-dollar deal before they released their *Sound of White Noise* album; Natalie Cole on a huge deal, and her record did nowhere near the numbers they needed; plus Anita Baker, and her record didn't do as well as expected either.

Elektra Records were under the umbrella of WEA, which was under the Time Warner umbrella. With the label's fortunes waning, the company's higher powers looked at the track record and apparently made it clear that if the Mötley record didn't come out and debut at number one, change would be swift!

So even though we debuted at number seven, they swept the proverbial broom through Elektra, sweeping out just about everyone at our label; some-thing like fifty-three people were clipped the week our record came out.

We didn't see anybody from the record label ever again from that point. There was nobody there to promote our album; they all got the boot. We were riding a nice little wave, getting tons of radio, still in heavy rotation, and debuted at number seven, but lost all our support at the label. The boardroom battles between senior Warner label executives, and the major structural changes carried out, really did damage.

Our record came out on March 15, and we were initially supposed to go out on tour at the end of March or the beginning of April. However, Nikki's wife Brandi was eight-months pregnant when the album was released, and Nikki didn't want to go on tour until she had their baby.

As a dad, I totally understood that, but it threw a wrench into plans. We didn't hit the road until June and the delay seemed to harm our promotional momentum, so we tried to use that time as best we could to rehearse, promote, and set the tour up.

We were aware that the climate of the music industry was changing. We talked about all the grunge bands like Nirvana, Soundgarden, Pearl Jam, and the effect it had been having in our industry. We had spent so much time recording the album in Vancouver, just 150 miles from their Seattle homes.

Pearl Jam was making a stink over ticket prices and service fees at the time. They were determined to keep their concert ticket prices very low, and waged a battle with Ticketmaster, taking them to court. I told the guys right from the get-go, "All these grunge bands are anti, so let's one-up them. As a music fan, do you know what I think would be cool? Why don't we just get one bus, one trailer, and a minimal amount of gear, and pick twenty American cities. We'll show up unannounced. The only people that will know are the clubs. We'll walk into places like the Whisky, CBGBs, and other legendary clubs, and set-up shop. The morning of the show, we'll walk into the local radio station, giveaway some records and tell listeners that we're in the city and playing at CBGBs tonight for free. Come on down!"

Nobody wanted to do it. Tommy looked at me and said, "Dude, you don't learn how to ride a horse by reading the book. You just get on the fucking horse, dude. Are you afraid to go out into the fucking arenas?"

I said, "No, I'm not afraid of the rodeo. I'm just thinking we should do twenty or thirty shows like that and film everything, like kids trying to get into the free Mötley Crüe show at The Station in Orlando or Trees in Dallas. While they're fighting about low ticket prices, we should just do free shows, get the radio support, and give something back to these fans. You don't need the money, dude. The mileage we'll get out of this will be great. We should do this one run for free, and then go into 3,000-seat theaters and just build it up from there."

They didn't want to do it, so we went out with ten or fifteen trucks full of shit, spent a gazillion dollars, and had an air of bigger, badder, and better. Nobody cared about bigger, badder and better, though. It was about $18.50 tickets and dudes on stage in shorts and anti-everything that Mötley stood for up to that point. I thought we took the wrong approach.

The last and final straw was the infamous interview with MTV. The interviewer asked what happened with Vince, and Nikki said we don't want to talk about that and nobody cares anyway. So the interviewer then asked if we cared that Vince sustained several broken ribs and internal injuries when his jet ski hit a coral reef a few weeks ago. Nikki laughed and Mick said, "My heart goes out to him. What happened to the coral reef?" before he started singing, "You're invited, but you weigh a ton."

Nikki made further fun of Vince saying something about 300 pounds of blubber landing on a coral reef. I knew we were doomed even before Nikki soon cut the interview short when they asked about girls, hairspray, and fire. We were doomed because they were drawing a line in the sand for fans, basically making them choose: you're either on Vince's side, or you're on our side.

It was a combination of the music climate, everything that was happening with our record label, and then our own ignorance and stupidity. We completely shot ourselves in the foot right out of the gate. At that point, we were like the Titanic with a fucking gaping hole and not enough buckets to bail us out.

15

Anywhere There's Electricity

I can't say that I never totally fit in with Mötley, but I never felt like I totally fit in either. They were always so over the top. Like, who takes a helicopter to a wedding? Who, on a whim, decides to buy a friend a Harley-Davidson? That's very Elvis-like to me. If you've got that kind of money and want to do that and that's what floats your boat, then more power to you. But I never totally understood that.

I knew some people in the Mötley business camp weren't big fans of mine. One day in particular, our tour manager sat down with the four of us and showed us the budget for one of the videos we were doing. At the end of the document, there was spot for the band to sign-off. Tommy signed it, Nikki signed it, Mick signed it, I signed it, and then it was faxed it back to the accountant.

The accountant called our tour manager almost immediately and started ripping him a new asshole, saying, "Hey, this is for the band's eyes only. Why the fuck did you have John Corabi sign it? He's not a member of the band. Why is he looking at our personal band shit?"

He told Nikki about it, and Nikki went to the phone immediately and said, "John is our fucking singer. Fucking deal with it, or you're fired."

As much as I appreciated Nikki having my back, the situation made me even more uncomfortable. There was Nikki telling a guy that's been with them since the early days that he either accepts me or he can fuck off and be gone.

Early on, Tommy and Nikki warned me of the trials and tribulations of being in a band of that caliber. "Everybody's going to say you're changing, but it's everybody around you that's going to change."

I told them, "It's never going to happen to me. My friends are too cool, and my family's way too grounded for that."

As sure as shit, though, so many people around me did change, and I fucking hated it. It made me feel very alone. I'm not talking about hitting me up for tickets. To give you an example, when the band took a break from recording for Christmas, I went back home to Philly for the holidays. I was at a party when one of my cousins (through marriage, whom I've known my whole life) grabbed a video camera and started filming me. For the first couple of minutes, it wasn't a big deal. But then I was eating a fucking meatball sub, and he literally had the camera two feet from my face. I said, "Come on, dude, put the camera down."

A bit later, I went up to the bathroom, and he followed me through the house, followed me up the steps, filming me. I looked at him and said, "Dude, if you don't fucking put that camera down, I'm going to shove it up your fucking ass! Enough."

That's when he got pissy with me, saying, "Oh, Mr. Fucking Rock Star now."

I said, "Dude, I have known you my whole fucking life, and you've never been this interested in filming me before." He had changed because I was in Mötley.

Then at the same party, I had a female cousin (again by marriage) walk into the room, while my wife stood ten feet away from us, and basically whispered in my ear, "Oh my God, I've always wanted to fuck you!"

As much as I had always wanted to be a rock star, there were a lot of things that took me a while to figure out how to deal with. I was learning at a rapid pace, instead of the more gradual pace the other guys experienced when they rose through the ranks. I just wanted to go and hang out with my kids and family and just relax, but once you're in that world, there is no fucking escaping it. It basically encompasses every fiber of your being. Everybody treats you differently.

I would go to the Rainbow and be taken to the best table in the house; no more waiting in line anymore. I would sit there thinking that I've been coming here for years, so why did you just bring me past everybody who's waiting in line? It took some getting used to, and I wasn't mentally prepared for the headfuck of it all after my whole life changed over a weekend.

I got into one of my first arguments with Nikki as we worked on the album. We were listening back to everything and getting off on how good the record sounded. I was excited about the record and made a comment along the lines of, "I love this fucking record, it sounds amazing. Whether it sells five copies or five million copies, I think we did a great job."

I swear it was like someone dragged the fucking needle across a record. Nikki looked at me and said, "Well, that's a really shitty attitude to have. This fucking record better not sell five copies. You need to fucking think a little bigger, my friend."

I said, "Dude, you know what I mean. At the end of the day, I'm just saying, I love the record and again, regardless of what it sells, I think we did a great job."

Nikki got pissed at me for having a negative attitude and felt I had low expectations and should be shooting higher. Obviously, I would have loved nothing more than the album to sell a couple more copies than *Thriller*.

As it turned out, the album sold over half a million copies in the United States and achieved gold status. I was given a framed gold album several years later, which sits somewhere in a closet. I have never hung it on a wall. I don't have a desire to hang all my accomplishments or awards on my walls. I'm not that guy, and I never have been. I still don't even have photos of myself hung. I'd much rather see photos of my heroes or grandkids, places I've been to, or my dogs.

The only album award I've ever hung on my wall for some time was a platinum copy of *Dr. Feelgood* that Mick gave me. He wrote on it something like, "Hey, Crab, Here's to many more of these with you... Mick Mars."

Around the time our album came out, Tommy said to me, "Hey, dude, the Pantera guys want me and you to come out to Texas. Dimebag is throwing a surprise party to celebrate Vinnie Paul's birthday, okay?"

"Sure," I told him. "That sounds like fun."

The guys in Pantera had visited us at Little Mountain Studio in Vancouver, and we wound up being friends with them. We played them songs like "Smoke the Sky" and "Uncle Jack," and they were freaking out saying, "Fuck, this is so heavy. This is great!" We went to their show at the Commodore Ballroom later that night, and as we hung out backstage, Phil Anselmo shaved all of Tommy's hair off. He tried valiantly to give me a buzz cut, too, but I told him to keep the fucking clipper well away from me.

Tommy and I flew out to Dallas and got picked up in a limo by Dime, Vinnie, and Rex. We started drinking as we headed to a radio station called 97.1 the Eagle.

Holding a bottle of Crown Royal whisky, they asked, "Hey, do you want to do an Excellent shot?"

I said, "Yeah, man, that's cool."

I downed the shot with them, and before long they asked again, "Hey, you want another Excellent shot?"

"Yeah, give me another one," I said.

We did an interview live on air, and they played some of our new record. While a commercial was playing and we were off air, they asked, "Another Excellent shot?" to which I obliged.

From the station, we went to a club called The Basement to celebrate Vinnie's birthday. We hung out backstage, fucking drinking more. "You want another Excellent shot?"

"Yeah, go ahead."

Suddenly, I started feeling weird. We had been sitting at a table for ages, so I got up and jammed on stage. Tommy jammed, the Pantera guys jammed, but everything started to become a little surreal. I started having a little bit of tunnel vision.

I walked outside to get some air, and this beautiful redhead came up to me and said, "Hi, I'm Jennifer and Lori told me to say hi to you."

Not knowing who she was talking about, I said, "Lori? Lori who?

She said, "Lori Kirkey."

Lori used to work at Hooters in Myrtle Beach, South Carolina, and I hadn't seen her since I was on tour with The Scream. I always thought she was attractive.

So, we started chatting, and I asked how she knew Lori. She called Lori on the phone, and we had a chat. Jennifer and I ended up going back inside the club, and we hung out for the rest of the night. I gave her my contact details to give to Lori.

As we sat there, I was getting hot and sweaty. I had had way too much to drink, and my head was starting to spin.

A gorgeous girl came over and sat down next to me. She was stunning and looked like that *Sports Illustrated* swimsuit model Kathy Ireland. As I sat there talking with her, one minute I was fucking wide awake, alert, and ready to go, then two minutes later I was nodding out. I told her, "I don't feel too well, so I'm going to head back to my hotel," and she said she would come back with me.

I said goodbye to Jennifer and headed back to the hotel with this other chick. I was all over the place. I'd been drinking all day on the plane, in the car, at the radio station, and at the club. I said, "Fuck, I'm pretty drunk. I just need to crash." I was hammered.

I got into bed, and this gorgeous chick took all her clothes off and got into bed with me. I said, "Goodnight," as I rolled over and passed out.

When I woke up the next morning, she was gone, and I had a temperature of about 103—I was fucking burning up.

Tommy and I were going to head back to Los Angeles that day, so we went over to Dimebag's house to say goodbye. Dime said, "Let's go get some fucking food, guys."

So, we went to a Japanese restaurant called Benihana where they cooked all this food in front of us on the grill. I didn't really eat much, as I felt like shit.

Then Dime asked me, "Hey, man, have you ever done a Hulk Blood?"

I said, "A what?"

He repeated, "A Hulk Blood."

"Nope, I don't know what that is," I told him.

He explained, "Well, there's two drinks, son: there's a Hulk Blood and there's a Black Tooth Grin."

The Black Tooth was a Crown Royal whisky and a little smidgen of coke, and the Hulk Blood was Japanese sake and Midori mixed together. We started drinking those, but I still felt like shit; the hair of the dog did nothing for me.

Once everyone had some food, we went back to Dime's house, and he said, "You guys need to stay another day. T-bone and Crab, I've got some jet skis, and we'll go out to the fucking lake."

Dime's partner Rita Haney and Rex's girl Belinda knew I wasn't feeling great, so they touched my head and said, "Holy fuck! You're really burning up."

I didn't want to be a fucking party-pooper or the guy who derails everyone's fun, so I just went along with it, figuring I'd start to feel better soon.

Once the jet skis were in the back of Dimebag's truck, I jumped in the back, too, thinking the fresh air on the drive out to the lake would help me feel better. It was like ninety degrees out, and I was wearing a sweater with a pair of leather pants. I was freezing my ass off while lying under a moving blanket on the black bed liner of Dime's pickup truck. I was so sick, and I couldn't get warm.

When they got to the lake, they apparently took the jet skis out from around me and I didn't budge, so they left me there. I had passed out asleep in the back of Dime's pickup truck and stayed there for three and a half or four hours. As cold as I was, I copped some fucking nasty sunburn.

Dime dropped us back at the hotel where I crashed again.

Tommy and I rode to the airport the next day, and I said to him, "Man, I still fucking feel like shit. I don't know what the fuck is wrong with me."

Tommy said, "Oh, it was probably just the ecstasy."

I said. "What the fuck are you talking about? What do you mean ecstasy?"

He said, "Well, dude, Excellent shot."

I got fucking pissed and said, "When have you ever seen me do shit like that? Fuck!"

I was told that the Excellent shots were a capsule that was half ecstasy and half heroin that was opened and put into a shot glass, and then they poured the whiskey in. Nobody fucking told me at the time, and I didn't see anyone do that. I was clueless to it, and I did six or more of those fucking shots.

I took another day or two to recover from the debauched weekend in Dallas, and a week or so later I got sent to Florida for a few days to do a guest spot on a local morning radio show in the Tampa Bay area.

My return flight connected at Dallas Fort Worth airport, so I decided to turn it into a layover so I could hang out with Lori and Jennifer again, then fly the last leg home to LA the next day.

The girls picked me up from the airport, and we went back to their home, where I dropped my bag since I was going to stay the night. They had another couple come over—a young, local singer named Dave Williams (who was also a friend of Dimebag) and his girlfriend, Cat. The five of us then went out for a steak dinner, and I enjoyed a glass of wine with my meal.

Soon after midnight we headed to The Basement again. The club's owner remembered me from a couple of weeks earlier and was very hospitable. I wasn't even through my first cocktail there when he called last drinks and kicked everybody out of the club so we could stay and hang out with him.

As the six of us sat there drinking, a couple of cops soon came in and raided the place. Lori and Dave didn't have their licenses on them, and Jennifer's was expired. Dave's girlfriend was only twenty, but for some reason the cops zeroed-in on me and arrested me. None of us knew what the fuck was going on, but I didn't want to resist, so I asked them what was happening as they led me to their police car.

At first, they wouldn't tell me anything, but then they said I was under arrest for public intoxication. It was total bullshit since I had not even had three drinks all night. I went fucking ballistic and insisted they take me to the hospital right fucking now for a blood test to prove that I was not intoxicated.

They took me to the police station instead of the hospital, where they put me in a cell and that's where I stayed for the rest of the night, and ALL of the following day. It was only when a different cop came and gave me a frozen burrito for dinner, he looked at me and said, "You look familiar."

I said, "Yeah, well, I don't know where you've seen me before. I'm the singer in a band called Mötley Crüe though, so maybe something to do with that."

"What are you doing in here then?" he asked.

"I have no idea. I was told I was arrested for public intoxication but I absolutely was not. I had not even had three drinks all night," I explained.

Moments later, the cops let me out and told me I was free to go, as they apologized and said they weren't sure what had happened.

I was pissed. "You motherfuckers! I missed my flight this morning back to Los Angeles. You've kept me in jail for the best part of a day for an absolute BULLSHIT reason. I'm going to sue the fucking shit out of you guys!" I never did, though.

Somebody told me that MTV News ran a short piece on me getting arrested in Texas, but I never saw it. I wondered if MTV got word once I told that cop I was in Mötley; I don't know how else they would've known about it.

I guess things happen for a reason, though, and I'm glad to have met and hung out with Dave Williams that night. He joined the band Drowning Pool five years later and as they rose to fame over the next few years, Dave was sadly found dead on the band's OzzFest tour bus after his heart failed from an undetected disease.[7] Whenever I hear their biggest hit "Bodies," I always think of Dave and that night.

Lori called me the following weekend and we chatted. I don't know how she felt, but I had a bit of a crush on Lori back then. I've always been friends with her, and she has been married to John Connolly from Sevendust for years now.

7 "Father, Mother, Son" and "Home Sweet Home" were played at Dave's funeral. Tommy Lee then joined OzzFest as a replacement for Drowning Pool since Dave had died, all of which happened soon after a boy had drowned in Tommy's pool.

I don't know what was going on at Lori's place but there was a lot of background noise. She had an old friend staying with her by the name of Robin, so she put her on the phone to say hi.

I was casually chatting with Robin, who told me she was there with Lori on vacation. She said, "I'm a model, and I'm in town doing some photos. I get out to LA quite a bit."

I said, "Well, next time you're out here, feel free to hit me up."

I got back on the phone with Lori, and we talked for a while longer.

About a week or two after that conversation, Robin called and said, "Hey, how are you? I'm coming into town. I'm going to stay with a friend but just wanted to see if you could perhaps pick me up at the airport, if you're not doing anything."

I didn't mind, so I picked her up at LAX, and her friend who she was supposed to stay with let her down and was a no-show. I said she could stay with me instead.

Robin was a really sweet Southern girl, a very pretty young girl about twenty-three-years-old. We clicked instantly and one thing led to another, and we started fucking dating. It's strange: it seems that every girl I've ever dated, I didn't pursue. They somehow just managed to fall in my lap, sent from up above for me.

We rehearsed in a little sweatbox room at a place called Studio D in Burbank, a few weeks on then a few weeks off, rinse and repeat. We would arrive about midday and rehearse until five, six, or seven o'clock each night, five days a week. Tommy was using his full drums with a complete PA around him and under him. Mick was using ten fucking amps, and Nikki was using five or six SVTs. I had my amps, but I only had two wedges in front of me, so it was usually very hard to hear as we played through our set twice.

Tommy had a new Southern girlfriend, too, Bobbie Brown. She was the blonde stunner in Warrant's "Cherry Pie" video, who married their singer Jani Lane after they met on the video set. They'd divorced in '93, though, and now she was putting a smile on Tommy's face ten miles wide.

Nikki and Brandi had their baby girl Storm in the middle of April, and then a couple of weeks later, we filmed a video for "Misunderstood" with Brian Lockwood directing, who the band had previously worked with on their "Anarchy in the U.K." video before he filmed us working and goofing off in the studio as we recorded our album.[8] For "Misunderstood," Brian filmed us playing on the front porch and inside an old Victorian house, which he sourced through the University of Southern California, close by on West Thirtieth Street in a bit of a rough LA neighborhood. There were young and old actors used to convey the lyrics, and it all came together in a great sepia tone.

Val visited the video shoot and arrived wearing a long coat and holding a huge bouquet of roses for my birthday. When she came onto my trailer, she opened the coat to expose her lingerie outfit underneath. At the end of the day shooting "Misunderstood," Val and I went with Tommy and Bobbie to the Sunset Marquis for drinks, and once they headed home, I got a room there with Val for the night.

Since the band had time on our hands, we paid Brian to also shoot a gritty, black-and-white, in-your-face–style music video for "Smoke the Sky" in our dark and smoky rehearsal studio. We used more of this time in Burbank to have Cindy Sommerfield come and take shots to be used in the tour program.

For our tour, we initially wanted to do a cool, all-day summer festival kind of event. We wanted to turn people onto different types of music. We were looking at having a heavier band like Pantera, plus the Ramones, James Taylor, and Johnny Winter for example.

It would be like a package from the seventies, when music was just music without all the labels as had become prevalent—throw five, six, or seven completely different bands on a bill and have a traveling road show.

As we tried to put it together, this artist didn't want to open for that one. Then somebody's manager didn't feel James Taylor should be on the same bill as Pantera. We grew tired of the constant infighting and didn't put it together.

We all loved King's X. Nikki brought in a band called Type O Negative, who I had not heard of. Type O couldn't start at the same time, so Brother Cane and King's X played the first three or four dates we did.

Given our album was self-titled, we wanted to come up with a strong name for the tour, as much as Nikki and the guys were very adamant that they just wanted the music to do the talking.

---

8 Brian Lockwood always had his camera rolling as we rehearsed, wrote, and recorded the album. The footage was intended for a "The Making of" home video that unfortunately was never finished or released.

As we did all the press interviews to launch the album, we naturally got asked if we were going to take our tour to wherever that publication or station was located. One of us had answered by saying, "Yeah, we're going to play anywhere there's electricity."

That stuck with us as a statement and "Anywhere There's Electricity" became the name of our tour. We had grand visions of the tour being very long, allowing us to play in all the rock-and-roll cities all over the fucking world.

Leading into our tour, though, we were told that ticket sales were well-below expectations. It was thanks to a culmination of losing our team at Elektra, some interview walkouts, and subsequent lack of promotion, plus the new musical climate of the grunge era.

We went to Tucson, Arizona, to do the preproduction rehearsal with the full show, since the first show of the tour was there. The sound was full-blown. Mick played through a dozen or so cabinets, standing in front of them probably ten or twelve feet away. He had his guitar sound coming out of the wedges at his feet, while Nikki and Tommy's sound came out of a giant wall of side-fill speakers to his side.

Then, on Nikki's side of the stage, he had his wedges and a big bank of side-fill speakers with Mick and Tommy's playing blaring out. At the most, I had three wedges to try and hear myself. Needless to say, I often strained my fucking voice trying to be heard over all the instruments.

While there were a few shows on the tour where ticket sales were really discouraging to say the least, overall the crowds were actually a pretty decent size. Due to the way it has been portrayed over time and in the movie *The Dirt*, I think some people have a vision of me walking on stage in high school gymnasiums to twenty fucking people, but it really wasn't that way. (Just watch any of the 1994 live concert bootlegs on YouTube to get a true feel for it.)

There were probably four thousand people who came out to our first show of the tour in Tucson. That's quite a lot of people—but the problem was that they were expecting ticket sales to fill out the 15,000-seat venue. For the most part, we were playing arenas that were generally a third or a half full.

Our fourth show of the tour was in front of 20,000 fans in Mexico City, which was not only my first time in Mexico, but it turned out to be the biggest crowd I ever performed in front of with Mötley Crüe.

After an intro tape played, which was sampled and looped from the band's "Primal Scream" video, we took the stage and opened with "Hooligan's Holiday" each night. Fans then got to hear me sing a few old classics in "Live Wire," "Shout at the Devil," and "Wild Side." We then usually played three new ones in a row, being "Power to the Music," "Smoke the Sky," and "Uncle Jack," but there were some nights where my throat was a little torn-up, so we skipped "Smoke the Sky."

I was enjoying myself on stage and also off stage during the tour. I can see how a person can easily become an alcoholic because of the company they keep. I was such a lightweight drinker when I first joined the band. I would have a cocktail or three and be fucking shitfaced. By the time we toured, though, I'd already been in the band a couple of years, and I was going through a handle of whiskey a day.

Tommy and I were drinking, so we were on one bus; Nikki and Mick weren't drinking, so they were on another bus. Our tour manager made sure that every day our bus got restocked. Tommy had a handle of vodka and all his mixers like cranberry juice and orange juice, plus a case of Corona. I had a handle of Jack Daniel's and tons of Diet Coke, along with a case of Heineken. Then we had a fifth of Malibu rum. That was our liquor rider for EVERY show.

Both Tommy and I smoked Marlboro Lights, so there was always a carton of cigarettes for me and a carton for Tommy. Not to mention trays of lunchmeats, potato chips, crackers, and whatever else our promoters would put on our buses for us.

We flew in from Mexico City the next day and for our next show we headed to Killeen, Texas, to play Fort Hood, one of the largest military bases in the world (and where Elvis commenced his basic military training). We saluted and participated in some official proceedings, did some press, and then they gave us a tour of the facilities, which culminated in them letting us drive some military tanks. Picture that for a minute…they let me and Mick in one tank, Tommy and Nikki in another, and we were just chasing each other around a fucking tank field!

Later that night, Tommy and I went out for drinks and got drunk as fuck at a bar. When we left the club to get a cab back, there was a totally gorgeous girl standing outside (who was also drunk), and we struck up a belligerent conversation.

She was also heading home, and it turned out her place wasn't out of the way, so she rode with us in the cab. When we got to her home,

I did the gentlemanly thing and got out and walked her to her front door, helped her to get inside, shut her front door, and got back in the cab with Tommy.

We finished our Fort Hood show the next night, and I walked from the stage back to my bus. Soaked with summer sweat, I got undressed and was toweling down when our tour manager knocked on the door.

I yelled out that I was getting changed, but he said, "Somebody here wants to say hi to you."

"Wait, I'm changing," I said again.

"No, seriously, somebody just wants to say hi to you real quick."

I caved and said, "Okay, but I'm in a towel."

He opened the bus door and a chick in military clothes walked on the bus. When I looked at her face, I realized it was the girl from the night before.

"Oh my God, thank you so much for getting me home last night; I was so drunk. I just wanted to thank you," she said.

She took her little fucking hat off and knelt down in front of me, opened my towel, and gave me the most amazing blowjob I've ever had in my life. I don't know where she learned how to do this, or who taught her, but she could've sucked a bowling ball through a garden hose and my balls through the shaft.

When I was done, she stood up, put her hat back on, gave me a hug, and walked off the bus, never to be seen again. As I went to shut the bus door behind her, my tour manager poked his head around and said, "What was that all about?"

I said, "Oh my God, dude. It's not just a job or a rock-and-roll cliché. It IS an adventure; your wildest fucking dreams can come true!"

When we arrived in Dallas to do promotion for our show, Tommy and I went back to the Eagle radio station for a preshow broadcast at a club. In typical, grand Mötley style, everything that could go wrong went wrong, and we wound up getting banned from the station forever.

You see, The Eagle came to our hotel and asked Tommy and I to go to a grand opening of a club they were broadcasting live from. The problem was nobody told us it was a LIVE feed. So we were dropping f-bombs left and right on the air, and still nobody said a word to us. At the end of the evening, as we were shitfaced drunk, I broke all the light bulbs in the back dressing room area of the club. Again, nothing was said.

After we did what we thought was a great show at The Starplex about a week later, everyone at the station was up in arms about our choice of lights and symbols on stage during "Power to The Music." A few days after we played our show in Dallas, I got a call from a DJ at The Eagle, and we got into a heated debate on air, at which point he told me they would never play another Mötley Crüe song again.

You see, we were using these lights called gobos that projected images on the wall behind the band and on the floor of the stage while we were playing. One of the images chosen was the swastika, an ancient symbol of divinity and spirituality in Indian religions like Hinduism and Buddhism that had been used for thousands of years. It was actually a symbol of good luck in the Western world until the 1930s, when Adolph Hitler adopted it as an emblem for his German Nazi Party, which basically changed the world's view of the symbol to one of HATE.

Now, you may be asking yourself, *Why would you use that symbol? Of all the symbols you could use, why this one?* Well, while we were rehearsing in LA for the tour, Nikki saw an article in the newspaper about a Hindu or Buddhist church in Malibu that had been vandalized because of some images that were on their property. The neighbors took offense to the use of swastikas and immediately started to destroy the church, even threatening to burn it down.

As we had just recorded a song called "Power to the Music" that lyrically discussed the cause and effects of censorship, freedom of speech, and mainly judging a book by its cover, we decided to try and make a political point. We were NOT condoning white supremacy or denying the atrocities of the Holocaust—what we were trying to make people understand was Hitler took this symbol and distorted its original meaning.

What we tried to say, and failed miserably at, was if you're not sure about something, ask questions. Don't jump to immediate conclusions.

While we could understand the Jewish community's outrage over the use of the symbol during World War II, we didn't understand the knee-jerk reaction and force to have it removed at the church. We felt that everyone should have discussed the origins, history, and meaning of the original symbol together and found a resolution.

So now I have a DJ in Dallas calling me a racist, a white supremacist, live on the air I might add, and verbally insulting all of us. The more he spoke, the more I tried to explain, and his reaction was EXACTLY what we were rebelling against. He didn't want to hear an explanation; his mind was already made up when he called. Nothing I could say would change a fucking thing.

I thanked him for his call, and his ignorance, and hung up. One more thing to add to the ever-growing list of reasons why our record and tour were failing miserably.

But while T-Bone and I were in Dallas for the preparty, we called Dime, Vinnie, and Rex from Pantera to come hang out. For reasons unknown, Vinnie and Rex had other commitments, so we went for drinks and then to a tattoo studio with Dimebag. He got the words Hulk Blood tattooed on his leg. Then Dime suggested we all get two little push buttons inked on our arms—one button that says "Kill" and the other saying "Reset," so we did. Needless to say, my tattoo is deeply special to me, and I'm having it recolored as a special little tribute to Dime. Vinnie and Dime will always be greatly missed.

I was sitting around tour rehearsals one day jamming on an acoustic guitar, teaching myself "Home Sweet Home." I just started playing it on guitar and singing to it, when Tommy heard me and said, "Fuck, dude, that sounds amazing! Why don't we do a totally different version of 'Home Sweet Home' this tour; let's do it acoustic."

That then led to us doing an acoustic segment, like Zeppelin used to do. They would go out and play a big heavy set, then break down and do an acoustic segment, and then come back for a heavy set again.

We worked up a great acoustic version of "Home Sweet Home," which I topped with a bit of harmonica. Onc of us suggested doing "Revolution" by The Beatles. (Mötley had already covered "Helter Skelter" and "Paperback Writer" by The Beatles over the years.) We then did "Loveshine" and "Don't Go Away Mad," which we always ended the acoustic segment with. We invited a handful of fans to come up on stage and hang out with us for the segment at each show, which gave them a real thrill. I can only imagine how I would have felt if I saw Aerosmith when I was a kid and they let me come up on stage with them like that.

For our first couple of shows, we also played "Black Country Woman" by Led Zeppelin and "Driftaway." However, everybody felt the segment was a bit too long, so we dropped those ones thereafter. We ended up adding an acoustic version of "Man in the Moon" toward the end of our tour, though. It was cool that Mötley played this live cover from my previous band, The Scream.

We played two cities in South Carolina leading into the Fourth of July weekend, and we earned ourselves a police escort out of both towns.

We knew we were going to have a little time off, so along the way to South Carolina, Tommy and I stopped at a fireworks place. Can you picture what $15,000 worth of fireworks might look like?

Our security guy walked into the back lounge of our tour bus as we hurtled down the highway, and he couldn't believe what he saw. Tommy and I were sitting there, shit-faced fucking drunk and smoking cigarettes, completely surrounded by fucking tire-sized rolls of firecrackers, Roman candles, M-80s, and all these other fireworks stacked up. He laughed his ass off but yelled at us, "Dudes, fuck, are you fucking idiots? Look around you! You're sitting on a case of dynamite and you're drinking and fucking smoking? Stop!" Bright sparks.

We played the County Fairgrounds in Greenville, and all these Marines from a nearby military base—Jarheads, as we called them in America—were doing security for the show. As we played, there was an incident on Nikki's side of the stage between a fan and security. The situation escalated to the point where all the security guys left. So, I walked over to the microphone, and I said, "Hey, listen: Security is gone. They're not going to harass you guys anymore. If you want us to play, we'll continue to play for you but don't make us look like assholes."

The audience was fine, and their Wednesday night seemed to get better without the Marines being present.

Problem was, when we got done playing our set, those Marines had gone back to the base and came back to the Fairgrounds with about fifty more pissed-off Marines that were going to tear us a new fucking asshole, due to the verbal assault we gave them from the stage.

Our tour manager covered us up with towels and had a bunch of cops walk us to the bus. They put us on the bus, and we got sent out of town with police escort to escape the Marines. We high-tailed it straight to Myrtle Beach. Not one of my happier moments.

We were resting in our bungalow when Tommy called me to say, "Crab, let's go into town!"

We got a cab to a little bar, where there was Tommy, his girl Bobbie, me, my girl Robin, the bartender, two guys at the end of the bar, and a band playing some crappy covers.

We ordered some cocktails and started sipping on them while chatting, when we saw the bartender grab his phone, dial a number, and then duck down behind the bar. We knew he was calling all his friends to tell them that Mötley Crüe was hanging out in his fucking bar. Within thirty minutes, the bar was packed.

The place was then pumping and jumping, and in grand fucking Mötley fashion, Tommy reached into his jacket's inside pocket and pulled out a little package of fucking firecrackers. "Hey, Crabby, watch this," he said with a wicked smile.

He lit a cigarette, then touched the cigarette to the fuse, and just chucked the fireworks back over his shoulder without even looking where he was fucking throwing them.

So, where did they land, you ask? I swear, you just can't make this shit up: it went into the packed crowd and landed right on the lap of a paraplegic guy in a wheelchair. Bang, bang, bang, bang! Bang, bang, bang! The dude was bouncing all over his chair trying to fucking dodge them.

When they finally stopped, he wheeled over to our table and said, "Jesus Christ, guys, you almost gave me a heart attack!"

Then the bartender told us, "Get out. Just get the fuck out."

We had been drinking whiskey and vodka, and Tommy had just ordered a bottle of Dom Perignon, so he grabbed the champagne, and we went outside. As bad as I felt, everybody was laughing about what just happened, as you couldn't do that again in a million years if you fucking tried.

We called a cab and a little Indian or Pakistani dude picked us up. The four of us were in the back of his cab, Robin was sitting on my lap and Bobbie was sitting on Tommy's as we swigged from the bottle of Dom and passed it around. Once finished, the empty bottle got thrown out the open taxi window.

So, where did it land, you ask? I swear again, you just can't make this shit up: it shattered on the road right in front of a fucking police squad car going the opposite way.

The cop turned around and with flashing lights and siren blaring, he pulled us over. He realized we were drunk, he realized we were in Mötley Crüe, so he asked us low long we were going to be in town for. He then told us to behave ourselves and let us go with a warning.

Once we got back to the hotel, Tommy said, "Let's go fucking skinny-dipping!"

Unfortunately, the indoor pool was locked and closed.

We called our security guy, who understood our predicament, and said, "No worries." He took out some kind of crazy Navy Seal knife, slid it between the doors, lifted up the lock, and opened the door. He then went around with a broomstick and pushed all the security cameras up to face the ceiling. He then held the door open for us and nodded with an at-your-service acknowledgement as we filed in past him.

We had fun skinny-dipping, going between the swimming pool and the Jacuzzi. After a while, Tommy and Bobbie started getting frisky with each other, so they said, "All right, Crab and Robin, we're out. See you later."

They got out of the pool, threw towels on, and jumped into a golf cart to head back to their bungalow. As he shut the door, our security guy said, "I'm driving these guys back, and I'll be right back for you guys."

Five minutes went by, ten minutes went by, fifteen minutes passed, and Robin and I also started getting frisky with each other, right there poolside.

Soon there was a knock on the door, so we stopped making out, and got back in the water. I yelled out to our security guy, "Come on in!"

Who came walking through the door? The same fucking cop who gave us the roadside warning earlier that night.

He looked at me and said, "Seriously? When I said behave yourselves, I didn't mean to break into a fucking pool house and disconnect all the security cameras. There's a silent alarm in here that's been going off since you guys did this."

Realizing Robin and I had been getting frisky, he then said to her, "Young lady, don't you have any more respect for yourself than to hang out with these fucking idiots?"

We took another hand-slapping from the cop and went back to our bungalow, promising to behave.

Next day we got up and over breakfast, we arranged that Robin and I would join Tommy and Bobbie for a walk down the beach later that morning, before we had to head to afternoon soundcheck. We hung out for a while, right by Second Avenue Pier, taking in the ocean view and people-watching, just chilling and enjoying some serenity.

Tommy then reached into the basket they brought with them and pulled out an entire bowl of firecrackers. "Watch this!" he said, as he went under the pier, lit the fuse, and came sprinting back to us.

Bang, bang, bang, bang! Bang, bang, bang, bang!

There were probably a thousand crackers in the roll that went off for about ten fucking minutes. Everybody around us laughed and thought the Fourth of July had come early. As the noise of the firecrackers died down, we heard a whistle getting louder, coming toward us on the beach.

Who was blowing the whistle, you ask? The same fucking cop who busted us skinny-dipping in the pool and gave us two warnings the day before. Fuck!

"Goddamn it!" he said, "Guys, fireworks are illegal in Horry County, Myrtle Beach. You can't set them off at all. Stop with the fireworks. Stop with the bullshit."

After we said sorry, he asked, "When is your show?"

"Tonight," we told him.

My father in his army uniform
Photo courtesy of the Corabi family archives

Uncle Jack on his confirmation day
Photo courtesy of the Corabi family archives

My sister Anna and I with our maternal grandparents
Photo courtesy of the Corabi family archives

All the Corabi kids—that's me on the left
Photo courtesy of the Corabi family archives

My first gigs were for my family in the late sixties
Photo courtesy of the Corabi family archives

Val and I with my grandmother at our (second) wedding reception
Photo courtesy of the Corabi family archives

In the warm California sun
Photo by Lynn Preston

Me with Chris Pisano, my guitarist and brother-in-law

Photo courtesy of the Corabi family archives

Angora promo photo

Photo by Lynn Preston

Doing my best Tyler in an outfit made by Valerie

Photo by Lynn Preston

Angora in Hollywood
Photo by Lynn Preston

Angora live at the Troubadour
Photo by Lynn Preston

One of the few Raggady Ann shows

Photo by Lynn Preston

Me with Bruce Bouillet of The Scream

Photo courtesy of Bruce Bouillet

The Angora days
Photo by Lynn Preston

On the set of Mötley's "Misunderstood" video

Photos courtesy of Brian Lockwood

On the set of Mötley's "Misunderstood" video

Photos courtesy of Brian Lockwood

Outside our tour bus

Photo by Bill Ragan

Photo with friends at mine and Mick's birthday party hosted by Tommy and Heather, April 1992

Photo courtesy of the Corabi family archives

A press ad for Mötley's show in San Antonio, Texas

Products from my Mötley Crüe album

Mötley Crüe at the Rock 'N' Roll Hall of Fame during its construction
Photo by Bill Ragan

Hangin' in the studio, working on their Hollywood Records debut, "Let It Scream", are renowned producer Eddie Kramer, band members Walt Woodward (SHARK ISLAND), John Aldrete (RACER X), band manager John Greenberg, and band members Bruce Bouillet (RACER X), and Philly born vocalist, John Corabi.

Magazine clipping from the Album Network

Photo courtesy of the Corabi family archives

Me and Debbie in our early years together
Photo courtesy of the Corabi family archives

Left to right: Fred Coury, me, Bruce Kulick, Tony Montana, and Rudy Sarzo
Photo by Denise Truscello

Beware of drumsticks
Photo by Denise Truscello

'onster Circus residency in Vegas
Photo by Denise Truscello

At the hospital with Mum when I became a dad

Photo courtesy of the Corabi family archives

Ian drumming in my band at Farm Rock 2016

Photo by Heather Warren

With my baby boy, Ian
Photo courtesy of the Corabi family archives

At home with one of my granddaughters
Photo courtesy of the Corabi family archives

Peforming at Farm Rock in Nashville 2016

Photo by Heather Warren

The Dead Daisies appearance at Hellfest in France 2017

Photo by Oliver Halfin, courtesy of The Dead Daisies

High in St. Louis, Missouri, at The Dead Daisies show

Photo by Katarina Benzova, courtesy of The Dead Daisies

The Dead Daisies UK tour 2016

Photo by Oliver Halfin, courtesy of The Dead Daisies

With a dedicated European fan at a Daisies show

Photo by Oliver Halfin, courtesy of The Dead Daisies

A Daisies full house in Belgrade, Serbia

Photo by Oliver Halfin, courtesy of The Dead Daisies

In a Nashville studio with Mick Mars for his solo music, 2016

Photo by Seraina Mars

With Mick Mars, 2016

Photo by Seraina Mars

Before the Daisies' first sold-out show in Havana, Cuba
Photo by Katarina Benzova, courtesy of The Dead Daisies

"Okay. Can you fucking maintain some level of civility and normality before you leave please?"

"Yep, we can do that for you, sir." Third warning.

Our show that Friday night was at an outdoor high school football stadium. We did our electric set closing with Nikki and I both smashing guitars at the end of "Kickstart My Heart" as usual, before coming out for our acoustic segment. We then plugged in again, played "Hammered" and said goodnight to the crowd.

When we went off, Tommy ran back behind the stage and lit a heap of fucking bottle rockets. It was boom over here, boom over there, boom everywhere. It was loud as fuck as the fireworks blew up and the crowd cheered and chanted for an encore.

Who came up to us behind the stage, you ask? The same fucking cop who busted us by the pier on the beach and gave us three warnings. He and the other cops with him said, "You're done. Clearly you guys have a complete disregard for rules. We told you guys that you can't do fireworks, you did it anyway. Show's over."

Nikki stormed back on stage and grabbed the microphone and addressed the audience, and before long, the crowd was chanting, "FUCK THE POLICE! FUCK THE POLICE!"

The cops decided to cave, rather than risk a riot. They let us do our encore song "Primal Scream" and as we came off stage, they grabbed each one of us by the scruff of our fucking necks and walked us right onto the tour bus.

They told our tour manager that we had to leave immediately. He said, "Well, we just need to wait for our crew guys and our gear." The cops said, "Fuck your crew guys. Fuck your gear. They need to be out of the city right now."

Having now earned our second police escort out of South Carolina, we rolled out of town with two squad cars in front of our two tour buses, and another two squad cars behind us, as they drove us right to the city limit. We crossed the line of no return and sat there and waited for a few hours as our crew dismantled all the gear, loaded it up, and caught up to us. The Anywhere There's Electricity Tour then headed north to Raleigh.

One of the places we played where thousands of kids certainly did not show up was in Atlanta. We were initially supposed to play the basketball stadium, but then it got downsized to The Fox Theater. We weren't happy about it, but we were happy to play the legendary venue where Lynyrd Skynyrd recorded their *One More from the Road* live album.

Unfortunately, they moved us again to a place called The Roxy. We walked in and saw the place could only hold a few hundred people, max. We were scratching our heads, saying, "What the fuck?"

It was one thing if people didn't like the record and decided not to come to the show that Fourth of July, but this reeked of they didn't even KNOW about the fucking new record or the show.

Before the show, our tour manager and some of the crew guys went to get something to eat from a little Mexican burrito joint right next door to the venue—not even thirty-five-feet away. The young dude behind the counter spotted a Mötley laminate hanging off a crew guy's pants, and he said, "Dude, I fucking love Mötley Crüe!"

He raved on about the band for a while, and then asked, "Do you tour with them?"

Our tour manager said, "Hey, let me ask you a question—do you know that Mötley Crüe is playing tonight here in town?"

The guy said, "No fucking way, dude. Where?"

He pointed and said, "Right there, right next door." The kid was flabbergasted; he couldn't believe it. He didn't even fucking know.

Back at The Roxy, the tour manager called the promoter in and said, "Hey, I want to see the fucking promotion you did for this show tonight."

The guy went and got a newspaper and showed it to him. There was a little strip classified ad consisting of three lines, "Mötley Crüe concert, Independence Day at The Roxy, Tickets at the door." That was it; there was no other advertising, nothing on the radio. No wonder the small venue was literally only half full!

I remember Tommy looking at Nikki saying, "Dude, how is it fucking possible that the last time we were in Atlanta, we sold-out the Omni Coliseum basketball arena—twenty-thousand fucking tickets? How is this possible that we can't even sell-out a place the size of the Whisky? How and why is this happening?"

I cannot say that 19,900 of those people that bought tickets the last time fucking hated me as the new singer or our record. It was a case of having a poor promoter, everybody at the label being fired and not working with the promoter, zero radio support from Elektra, and no support from MTV, thanks to ourselves.

However, five nights later we played an amphitheater in Nashville and there were thousands of people there. It was strange. It was so random and not what Mötley was used to.

A week prior to Atlanta, we played the Jacksonville Coliseum in Florida and about 2,800 people showed up, which looks horrible in a ten thousand–seat venue, especially when it's not curtained off. But that same night, Richard Marx played right across the street in a theater that held maybe two thousand, and he only had about six hundred people there; nobody was there for him either. The music scene was changing, and it was a weird time.

We got to Chicago and figured word had gotten out through the police that we had a little issue in Myrtle Beach with fireworks when we saw the fucking Bomb Squad show up at our show at The Riviera Theater.

Any tension was quickly relieved, though, when Tommy was handed a big brown paper bag of fireworks. Much bigger than an M-80, these were like quarter sticks called M-1000 or block busters or some shit. Tommy was keen to get back to the hotel after the show that night.

I was in my bed with Robin, trying to get my fucking groove on, and it sounded like we were in Iraq with all the whistling and boom of fucking missiles. All night, Tommy was lighting them and tossing them out the fucking window of the hotel.

I scratched my head and said to Robin, "How the fuck does someone do that and not worry about whether it's landing on someone's car or landing on someone walking under the hotel's window?"

When we got up the next day and met for lobby call, we saw divots in the fucking street where these things had landed and blown four-inch circular potholes in the ground.

We stood around outside looking at them and laughing, saying, "Oh my God, dude. Fuck, seriously? What if somebody would've been hit by them?"

Tommy got on the bus with Bobby O, while I stood outside it, smoking a cigarette and bullshitting with our tour manager and bus drivers.

I told them the story of when I was young and saw Aerosmith play in Philly during 1977. As they were coming back on The Spectrum stage for the encore, somebody threw an M-80 cherry bomb and it blew up and blinded Tyler in one eye, burning his cornea, and it cut an artery in Joe Perry's hand. They headed to the emergency room instead of playing "Toys in the Attic" as the encore.

I no sooner finished telling them when we heard a fucking loud explosion—BOOM! It was Tommy again—he lit another firecracker and threw it out of the back window of the bus. Our bus driver JB cursed and grabbed his arm. The explosion blew a hole in the ground and a fucking pea-size stone from the bitumen shot up and blew a hole right through JB's fucking arm. He couldn't drive; we had to get him to the hospital.

But this was typical. It was every fucking day or night. Just random, goofy, don't-give-a-fuck bullshit, every night of the fucking week. It was crazy some of the shit that would happen. Every night—every fucking night!

16
Big in Japan

For the last stop of our US tour, we played a hometown show at the Hollywood Palladium at the end of August. Glenn Hughes came down and joined us on stage to sing "Misunderstood" with us, and we had a bunch of friends and family at the show.

Mötley had previously done two sold-out hometown shows at the LA Forum on their *Dr. Feelgood* tour. Now we played the Palladium and it was half to three-quarters full, not even sold-out. The following month, Mötley's manager was fired and replaced with another guy.

A couple of weeks later, we were getting ready to go to Japan when I got a call. The gist of the conversation was essentially that I don't move around enough on stage. I was told, "Vince would jump up on the drum riser, and he would run all around the stage, and he would do all this shit."

Steve Vai was also at our Palladium show, and when he overheard a conversation complaining about my lack of movement at the show, Steve said, "John plays guitar, he plays guitar on everything. Just on that one song 'Power to the Music,' as well as singing, he played guitar, turned his guitar off, grabbed a harmonica, did a harmonica solo, then put the harmonica back, turned his guitar on, and played guitar again. He can't do that if he's climbing a lighting truss or if he's up on the drum riser." I was glad Steve defended me.

So when we went to Japan, they wanted to try me only playing guitar on the new songs that I recorded with them, and for the old Mötley shit like "Live Wire" and "Shout at the Devil," they wanted me to just front the band singing. No rehearsals, mind you, we'd just go over and do it.

We got to Osaka for the first show, and they gave me a straight stand and a microphone with a cord. It was a regular, heavy-weighted stand, not a wireless mic on a light, aluminum one that you see the likes of David Coverdale or Rod Stewart swinging around every which way.

Fuck, now I was starting to feel pressure. I felt that obviously I wasn't doing something right because they were now complaining. Mick also had to revert back to his old thinking and playing. He had a little more freedom when I was playing guitar as well. I just had to do the best I could.

Concerts in Japan start early, like six o'clock, so you're back at the hotel at 8:30 or 9:00 p.m. After our first show in Osaka, Nikki and I went back to our hotel and got some sushi. I then headed out to a club called Krug with two Japanese girls. It was my first time in Japan, and I was trying to communicate with these girls, and I was the only American person there and the English was very minimal—until an American model walked in.

Of course, I got talking with this blonde-haired, blue-eyed, really cute girl. She told me her name was Athena Currey and that she was from Portland, or Seattle. She also told me that she modeled in Osaka but goes to Tokyo every week. I told her that we had another six shows to play in Japan, the last of which would be in Tokyo in a week's time, so I invited her to come to the show. I told her we'd be staying at the Roppongi Prince Hotel.

We chatted the rest of the night until it was time to head back to the hotel at one or two o'clock in the morning. We got a taxi together and when the cab driver got to my hotel, I gave him extra money to take Athena the rest of the way back to her place.

Our Japanese promoter Mr. Udo had one of his staff take care of us as tour manager. His name was Takashi, but we called him Tak. When I walked into the hotel lobby, Tak was standing there, very annoyed with me. He said, "John Corabi-san, you don't go anywhere without letting me know!"

He was freaking out, so I told him, "Hey, okay, whatever, dude. I just went out for a couple of drinks, no big deal." I went to my room, but it was strike one with Tak.

We got the Shinkansen bullet train to Hiroshima the next day for our show, which was fun to do for the first time. Once we got into the hotel, our crew guys set one of the hotel rooms on fire as a prank. The craziness was not just contained to the band members.

We went to the venue and hung out backstage for a while as we got ready to perform. As usual, the preshow songs blared out over the speakers, then as the lights went out ready for show time, we walked from our dressing rooms to the stage.

As an intro tape played our sinister marching music with dog growling noises, we walked up onto stage as usual. We then routinely grabbed our guitars from their racks and put them on, before giving each other a little rev-up in a huddle, like sports teams do.

Once I put my guitar on and turned around, there was nobody else on the stage. I looked over thinking, "What the fuck are you guys doing." And I saw them laughing hysterically on the side of the stage. I looked at them wondering why they were laughing. As I was looking around, I noticed the dog growling and marching had swapped—they switched the fucking intro tape.

There they were pissing themselves laughing at me standing in front of a sold-out audience of Japanese people in Hiroshima and they were blaring through the fucking PA speakers The Gap Band's song "You Dropped a Bomb on Me."

I was mortified! Tak was not happy either, to say the least.

Strike two!

Given it was my first trip to Japan, and I had no experience with Japanese language, I had the crew guys write out a few key things phonetically for me and stick it on the stage floor next to my mic stand, so I could pronounce the city's name correctly, for example. I was keen to make a good impression on the fans.

After Hiroshima, we played in Fukuoka, so instead of writing "Foo-koo-o-ka" on my sheet, they wrote "Fuck-u-okay."

I said over the mic, "Hello, fuck you okay! I can't hear you, fuck you okay!"

Tak was on the side of stage yelling out to me, "It's Fukuoka," and I'm like, "Oh, fuck!" Strike three!

We headed north and played Sendai's Sun Plaza in Miyagi, where we stayed at the venue's hotel. Upon check-in, they told us that we couldn't go swimming in the pool. This is not uncommon in that country, as most public baths and swimming pools ban tattoos, since they are associated with the Japanese mafia Yakuza. "Please, no swimming in pool," the sweet little concierge lady said.

We got back to the hotel one night, and Tommy stripped off his clothes, and with his tattoos and black mane flowing, he jumped into the fucking pool. The next day, the hotel staff drained the pool, acid washed it, then refilled it back up again.

They had no sooner finished their treatment, when Nikki decided he would jump in the pool for a swim. The staff were not happy. They emptied the pool again, acid washed it, and filled it again. They were glad to see us leave Sendai.

You guessed it: Strike four!

Our last show of the tour was in Tokyo at the famous Budokan. After the indoor arena was built for the '64 Olympics, The Beatles were the first rock band to play there two years later. It has also been where many huge live albums were recorded, none better than *Cheap Trick at Budokan* and Deep Purple's *Made in Japan*.

A Yakuza tattoo artist named Horiwaka came and picked us up and took us for traditional hand-poked tebori tattoos, which was a trip. We then picked up some Kabuki masks and were messing around with them backstage before the show. I wore my white and black Kabuki mask backward as I walked on stage and looked out to 14,000 excited Japanese fans. It was a great show and compared to the size of crowds we played to in the US, Mötley was still big in Japan.

The promoter Mr. Udo took the band and whole crew out to a very nice dinner in Roppongi once we finished our last show. After all the antics, I was surprised he even talked to us at all. Mr. Udo went to great lengths to thank us all, and he picked up the whole tab in the fancy restaurant.

After dinner, Tommy, Bobbie, and I walked around the corner to this place called Pip's, a late-night bar in Roppongi where a lot of musicians and models used to hang out at. Takashi walked in as we sat there, and he ordered a pitcher of margaritas. His hand shook as he drank right out of the pitcher. The poor guy was trying to de-stress after we made his life complete misery over the last week. It was always thrills without a motive, and Tak had had to deal with it.

We stayed a while at Pip's before we headed to The Lexington Queen, another haunt where there was always rock stars and beauties partying up a storm. Tommy, Bobbie, and I sat at a table in the corner and the guys from Whitesnake were there, too, since they were in town playing on their *Greatest Hits* Tour.

We polished off a bottle of vodka and most of the Jack Daniel's bottle, so I went to the bar to get some more drinks. While I was waiting to be served, I met a model named Patricia and we started chatting. I brought her and the drinks back to the table where we continued to party.

When we closed out and got ready to leave, Tommy and Bobbie said they were going to head back to the hotel. Patricia said, "Do you want to go to Pip's?"

I said, "Yeah, sure. It's great there."

They had a blackboard by the door at the front of The Lexington Queen where they wrote all the names of the rock bands that were coming to Tokyo. I saw Mötley and Whitesnake on the board, then I noticed that Vince Neil was playing eight days later. I said to Patricia, "Oh, fuck, Vince Neil."

She said, "Oh, yeah, I'm going to see Vince."

I jokingly quipped, "Oh, cool, tell him I said hi."

I'd never met Vince in my life.

We went to Pip's and had a good time hanging out drinking, chatting, and listening to music. It would have been after 1:00 a.m. when Patricia said, "Let's get a change of scenery. My apartment's only two blocks from here."

As we left Pip's, I got my bearings so I could find my way back past the bar and to the hotel.

It was my first time seeing inside a Japanese apartment, and I noticed they are generally small, like in New York. Her one-bedroom apartment also had a bathroom and a combined kitchen and living room, with some dude who was a friend of a friend hanging out smoking weed in it. We joined him for a few tokes and a drink. The model then took me to her bedroom.

As crazy and fucked-up as life in Mötley was, I'd never seen anything as debauched as when we walked into her bedroom. There were three bunk beds stacked up to the left with a girl and a guy fucking in every single one of them. There were another two beds in front of me, and two people were fucking on those, and then I looked to the right. There were three more beds on the right wall and everybody in the lower beds was fucking as well—only the top bunk on that side was empty. I couldn't fucking believe it!

There I was in a room with about nine young naked model girls; there were girls with girls, girls with guys, and everybody was just fucking. It was like an orgy. We climbed up to the empty top bunk, hung out and joined the party.

I woke up the next day, and said, "Oh, fuck, I've got to go. I don't have long until my flight back to America. Hey, I had a great time. It was awesome. Thanks. Bye."

I scurried back to my hotel and walked into my room. My suitcase was already packed. I took a quick shower, changed, came downstairs, put my luggage in the van, went to the airport, got on the plane, flew home, got off the plane, and there was Robin waiting for me at the luggage carousel at the airport.

I greeted her with, "Hey, baby," and I went to give her a hug and kiss, but she kind of turned away from me.

She reached into her bag and pulled out an 8x10 photo of the model that I had just left in Japan. "Did you fuck her?" she asked.

"Nope. No, I did not. I hung out with her; I partied. I went back to her house and a bunch of people were back there. It was pretty much a party and I hung out."

She said, "Okay," and let it go. Fuck!

As we were driving and almost home, I asked Robin, "Just out of curiosity, how the fuck did you get that picture?"

It turned out that the girl I hung out with went to work the next day. Her agent took one look at her and said, "Holy Christ, you look like shit. Were you up all night?"

She said, "Yeah, I was hanging out with the singer in Mötley Crüe."

The agent said, "Oh, really? Okay, well go home and sleep. You look like shit."

She sent the model home, picked up the phone, called Robin, and said, "I'm faxing you a photo. Your boyfriend was fucking around on you last night with one of our girls." She then faxed Robin the photo.

So I got fucking pegged on the other side of the world, cheating on my girlfriend during the dialup age of the fucking internet. I am never going to cheat on my wife, ever. Fuck that. I learned a very valuable lesson that I'm just not meant to be a guy who cheats on his partner. In this day and age of internet connectivity, you couldn't fucking pay me to cheat on my wife!

A friend who was managing me for a while, Larry Morand, was also a tour manager. At that time in October 1994, he was working with Vince Neil. With a big smile on his face, Larry said to me one day, "You're a fucking asshole, Corabi. There I was sitting at a table in The Lexington Queen with fucking Vince when this blonde chick walked over and asked, "Oh, hey, you're Vince Neil, right?" Vince said, "Yeah, yeah, sit down."

So, she sat down at the table and said, "By the way, I was here last week and Johnny from Mötley Crüe told me to say hi."

Vince said, "Who?" and she reiterated, "John, the lead singer in Mötley Crüe. He told me to say hi to you!"

Vince fucking flipped the table over in a fit of rage. He started throwing bottles at her and cut his hand open in the process, while yelling, "I'm the fucking singer of Mötley fucking Crüe!"

I told Larry, "Sorry, dude, I honestly didn't mean for that to happen. It was just an off-the-cuff, passing joke as I drunkenly walked out the door."

She apparently thought I was serious and had tasked her with an important mission. Larry had to fucking tackle Vince to stop him from destroying the club and killing the girl, and then take him back to their hotel.

My first trip to the land of the rising sun was certainly memorable.

Arigato Gozaimasu!

17
Personality #9

After Japan, Nikki and his family holidayed in Thailand, while Tommy and Bobbie flew to Fiji. Mick came back to LA with me.

My girlfriend Robin had a roommate in New York City named Courtney Cross. We introduced her to my manager John Greenberg earlier during the tour, and they started dating and moved in together shortly before the tour was finished. They're happily married still, with two beautiful children and successful careers. So I guess something good did come out of the insanity.

I moved out of Mick's guesthouse into a house with Robin, Courtney, and Greenberg. They rented a huge four-bedroom house on a cul-de-sac in Thousand Oaks, so John and Courtney had a room, Robin and I had a room, and we had spare bedrooms for my kids to visit on weekends. We all lived together right after I got back from tour.

Our shows in Japan were the end of touring behind the self-titled Mötley Crüe album. We did play a little Christmas benefit at the Troubadour with some friends a week before Christmas, and then another small benefit show in Pasadena at the end of January with Billy Idol and a couple of guys from Guns N' Roses. That thirty-minute set turned out to be my last-ever live performance with the Crüe.

Before Christmas, though, we started writing and working on ideas for a new record to be called *Personality #9*, since it was the ninth Mötley Crüe record (counting our *Quaternary* EP.) We started rehearsing and writing at Mates Rehearsal Studio in North Hollywood, where we came up with riffs and parts of songs.

We'd start at Mates late in the morning and stay until six, seven, or eight o'clock at night. I'd be using my voice all day. Even if I wasn't singing words, I'd be scatting melodies.

The guys started giving me shit about my voice, as they'd done before on occasions, saying, "Fuck, dude, when we do the acoustic shit, you're singing great, but when we do the heavier stuff, you're kind of raspy, and you're fucking losing it."

I told them I couldn't fucking hear myself, as usual. Someone suggested trying in-ear monitors, so they went and got me in-ears that I used for a week. They said, "Oh my God, dude. That's like night and day," to which I replied, "Yeah, well, I'm not pushing as hard. I can actually fucking hear myself."

Thinking we had found the solution, I was told, "We're not going to pay for those, so if you want in-ears, you're going to have to pay for them yourself."

I said, "Well, unfortunately, we're going back to the wedges because I haven't really made any money since prior to my starting the last record."

As easy-going as the first record was, everything was tense this time around and getting more so as the days went by. We were coming up with some cool riffs, though. We had a song called "Backwash," another called "The Year I Lived a Day," and one called "La Dolce Vita." They could have been really cool songs, much in the vein of what we had done on the last record, but at that point, a combination of things started to happen.

The band's new manager came into the picture, and I felt right from the get-go that his vision was to get Mötley back together again with Vince and do multimillion-dollar deals so everybody would be rich, and therefore happy.

It seemed like the guys started to buy into it. Everybody was starting to doubt what we did on our last album, since it was the first Mötley record that didn't go platinum. Everyone was feeling the pressure, so they were looking internally at whatever issues they could pick, and externally at what was selling most in the rock world.

Not only were our buddies Pantera kicking fucking ass, Marilyn Manson was blowing up along with Nine Inch Nails. Tommy had helped them out a bit on their last album. Ministry was also a standout from a whole wave of bands coming through with an industrial heavy rock and techno metal sound. Nikki and Tommy listened to all this new music and were set on making themselves relevant and modern.

It grated on me, because I felt this wasn't what we were; it wasn't what I was. I've had a few times in my career where I thought I had to reinvent myself and then I caught myself and went, no, this is what I am. This is how I write, just stick with the program. As much as I tried to stick to my guns, I also compromised under the circumstances.

Tommy was going through a stage where he was drinking, doing drugs, and having issues between him and his fiancée Bobbie Brown. Encouraged to go to rehab, he was determined he wasn't going to go, so I ended up saying I would go with him, and he finally agreed to go.

The facility we went to was in Wickenburg, Arizona, where some of the world's best-known troubled celebrities had been before us. Pop stars and rock stars have traveled to Arizona for years; it's a primary rehab destination.

Even though Tommy was supposed to be in a rehab, he said, "I don't want to stay on the site. I want my own apartment." So they put us up in a two-bedroom condo a mile or so from the facility. I didn't know anything about rehab but presumed any treatment would just focus on his drugs issue.

We would get done with the day's program sessions at four or five o'clock in the afternoon. We'd go get some food, then Tommy would say, "Let's go to Tiffany's!"

We would then drive a fucking hour into Phoenix and hang out at Tiffany's Cabaret with strippers all night until one or two o'clock in the morning, then drive back up the fucking desert country roads to our apartment and show up for rehab at seven in the morning with bloodshot eyes and reeking of fucking vodka and whiskey.

I went with him, and it was the most stupid fucking week ever. It felt like a complete waste of fucking time and money.

Back in LA, I answered my phone one day, and it was Bobbie, hysterical and crying, sobbing, "Tommy just got married."

I said, "Nah, I'm in the band with him, so I'm pretty sure I would've heard if he got married. Somebody's just bullshitting you or something. Don't worry about it." I was so sure it hadn't happened that I told Bobbie I would give her a case of champagne if he did.

I no sooner got off the phone with her, when Tommy called and yelled into the phone, "Hey, Crab, I just got fucking married on the beach in Mexico to fucking Pam Anderson!"

Tommy had broken off his engagement to Bobbie, who unfortunately didn't get the memo, and flown down to Cancun, Mexico, with a couple of his buddies in pursuit of Playboy starlet Pamela Anderson. He caught her all right, and they married on the beach in their bathing suits.

When he got back to LA, they had a second wedding reception in the yard of his rented beach home in Malibu, which had a space theme to it. Robin and I didn't attend. He had a third reception at a club called Spice that Pam was part owner of, and we all made brief appearances at that. At this point, though, all of us—Nikki, Mick, and myself—were wondering what the fuck was happening and scratching our heads at Tommy's increasingly erratic behavior.

We got told that the Hard Rock wanted to buy some of our motorcycles to display in their establishments. The guys weren't into it, though. "Nah, fuck that," they said.

When I found out my mom needed more money as her cancer progressed, I went to our manager and said, "How much would they give for mine?"

He told me he would handle it, then came back and said, "If we get all the guys to sign the tank, they'll give you twenty-five for it," so I took the deal and sold the bike to them—I kept five and gave twenty grand to my mom.

Their intention was to display it inside their brand-new Hard Rock Hotel and Casino that was opening in Las Vegas. As you walk into the round, sunken casino section from the main entrance, they were going to have my bike displayed on one side, and another bike of Guns N' Roses drummer Matt Sorum on the other.

Nikki asked me how much I got for it. When I told him the amount, I saw his eyes light up. He called the Hard Rock and ended up selling one of his bikes to them. When they bought Nikki's and displayed it, mine got relegated and moved somewhere non-exotic. I believe it's still displayed in a Hard Rock Café, somewhere in the world, but I don't know where. I'd actually love to get that fucking bike back someday.

When I sold the bike to the guy from the Hard Rock, he invited me and Robin and Tommy and Pam to join them at the hotel's grand opening weekend. They said they'd cover our expenses if we just gambled and hung out. Knowing there'd be a red-carpet event with photographers and other grand-opening formalities, and as tight as my money situation was, I went out and bought a new pinstriped suit jacket, some new leather pants, and Robin bought a cool outfit to wear.

As we were getting ready to leave Los Angeles the day before, Nikki called me and said, "Hey, Crab, the people from the Hard Rock called, and they don't want you to come now—they want me and Tommy to come. They want the more high-profile members of the band to come."

I was fucking pissed. Robin and I had just spent all that money on new outfits and were totally looking forward to the trip and getting away for the weekend. I found out some time later that Vince was there as well, so it seemed to me they planned to get together and sort some things out for his return to the band. I was fucking angry.

Those last days in Mötley were rough. I was completely out of money. My mom died, my kid had been sick. Then the band terminated me. Shortly after that, my fiancée decided after three or four years that she needed space to focus on her acting career, so she dumped me. I was feeling low, tired, and beaten. It was one of the most miserable years of my life.

Years later, I was doing an acoustic gig somewhere, telling everybody this story. After explaining my misery, I embellished and joked, "I thought I handled it pretty good, until I pulled my gun out of my glovebox and realized there were no bullets in it when I put it in my mouth."

Everybody in the audience laughed, as I made light of my shitty situation and poked fun at myself. Well, somebody didn't get that joke. It fucking spread like wildfire that I tried to off myself, and I still get asked about that suicidal moment to this day.

People, it was just a joke—I love my life and family too much to ever fucking go out that way. Fortunately, through all the tough situations I've endured in life, I have never once thought about suicide. Please seek help if you do, though.

When the housing market in Southern California crashed and the recession hit, and everybody was losing money on their property values, I met a guy who wanted to sell me a house in Malibu. He had bought two plots of land right on the cusp of Malibu in the mountains, put a six-bedroom house on one and the other was still vacant.

He initially had the Mulholland Highway house on the market for something like $2.3 million, prior to the market crash. He then brought it down to $1.8, then down to $1.6, then it was about $1.1. He offered to me, "If we can do a cash deal right now for just what I put into the house, I'll sell you both lots, all 2.3 acres, and the house for $700,000."

I couldn't even afford in-ears to help my voice, let alone have that amount of cash.

So, I told Tommy about it. The newlyweds were living in a beachfront rental house in Malibu, and he was looking for a new pad. We went to the house, and I introduced the seller to Tommy, and we looked around the home. He brought Pam through it, and she loved it, too, so they bought it, getting the deal of a lifetime on the fucking house.

He had a giant basement/garage that got decked out as a rehearsal room he called Tommyland Studio, so we worked on our music there during the days as contractors carried out work on the house above us. That's when that fucking infamous home video tape went missing.

Tommy had a Neve recording console in the rehearsal basement, in front of a carpeted wall that had a five-hundred-pound safe as big as a fucking fridge behind it. Not only did the stolen safe contain an explicit sex tape from their boat trip on Lake Mead, it also had fucking watches, jewelry, cameras, knives, guns, ammunition, money, and other shit in it. They fought a legal battle for years and the sex video became the highest-selling adult video of all time.

We rehearsed at Tommy and Pam's for a while and started to record some demos. There were songs like "Let Us Prey," "Black Box," "Backwash," "The Year I Lived a Day," and "La Dolce Vita." There was also a song called "Personality #9," plus "Take Me in Your Wings," "Melody," and "Wrote My Name in Blood." We kind of formulated them at Tommy's house.

The house actually burned to the ground in the Californian wildfires of late 2019, years after Tommy had sold it; good thing he did.

When we were ready to start recording the album, Nikki wanted to have Scott Humphrey produce it. I love Scott, but I was always against having him be the producer; I always wanted to use Bob Rock again. However, they decided they didn't want Bob to produce because he'd be too expensive and over-produce it. Bob was the next in line to be fired, following their manager and accountant.

Scott was incredibly talented and really good at what he'd done, but my biggest fear of having Scott produce was he had never produced a whole record at that point in his career. Sure, he worked for Bob as an assistant engineer and Pro Tools editor on *Dr. Feelgood*, but producing and engineering are quite different roles.

We lived with the songs we tracked at Tommy's house for a while and then started recording at Nikki's house. Nikki was getting into technology more and bought gear to create a professional home studio he called Butt Cheese West.

I remember they couldn't get the headphone monitors to work very well, so they ran a cable into a LaserDisc player in the room I was doing vocals in and then plugged my headphones into the LaserDisc player, but I still only had partial fucking volume.

Nikki was still figuring out half his gear, so we'd start working on a song and then something would break down and nobody would know how to rectify it. So they'd have to organize for somebody to come out, and two days later they'd get it up and running again. Instead of just being themselves, they were hell-bent on trying to do something cutting-edge and different, so the mission of the album became: "Let's write a really cool song and then see how much we can fuck it up." They even had T-shirts made with "Just Wrenching It Productions" screen-printed.

Scott would record Tommy's drums, then the two of them would start tweaking the sound of them, trying different filters and effects. Tommy would find a sound effect that distorted his drums so they sounded like trashcans, and he would say, "Oh, dude, that's fucking badass!"

Nikki would then come in and say, "Oh, yeah, dude, that's fucking amazing. Here, let me grab my bass," and he would play a new bass line.

The problem was Mick and I had tapes of these songs that we were living with over the weeks, as I was trying to come up with vocal melodies and writing lyrics for them. Every time Tommy and Nikki would get with Scott, the songs drifted in a completely different direction.

I would show up with a melody or some lyrics in hand, and they would say, "Oh, dude, you've got to hear what we did to this song."

I would sit there and listen, then tell them, "This doesn't sound anything like what we demoed. What the fuck is this?"

They'd tell me, "Oh, dude, just play some guitar on this," so I would play guitar on it, but the song would be completely different in some cases than where it was. We now had a guitar, a bass, and a drum sound that was long removed from the original idea. That's when they would say, "Okay, dude, go in the studio now and let's see what vocals you come up with."

Tommy said, "Give me something ballsy, like fucking Pantera, but lush like Oasis."

I would be thinking Oasis and Pantera are two opposite ends of the spectrum. Then Nikki said, "Yeah, but like the Manic Street Preachers, Sisters of Mercy, and old Bowie combined," and then Scott said, "Yeah, dude, like Cheap Trick."

At that point, I didn't even know who the Manic Street Preachers or Sisters of Mercy were.

That was the producing I got, and I couldn't make sense of it. I'd tell them, "I'm sorry, call me an idiot, but you lost me at Oasis and Pantera. I don't even know how to do that."

It was just fucking miserable.

It felt like everything in Mötley's universe was completely falling apart. As enjoyable as our first record was, this era of the Crüe was dark, and felt as though it could all implode at any moment. We were looking at each other with disgust and none of us trusted the others.

Tommy said to me in the studio one day, "Exactly what do you do when you go home?" He was upset with me because I wasn't coming up with some genius fucking melody off the cuff.

I looked at him and said, "Well, you know what I do? I drive my kids to school. I pick up the dog shit in my yard. I do all the shit you pay people to do. I have a normal life, and the rest of the day I work on music."

We almost came to blows.

It deteriorated to the point where anything I played on guitar they thought was fucking amazing, but when I sang something, they hated it. During one of our arguments, I sarcastically said to Tommy and Nikki, "Well fuck, you guys love everything I do on guitar, and you fucking hate everything I do on vocals, so maybe I should just be a fucking guitar player," and I walked out of the room angry and frustrated.

Things got insane with the paparazzi for Tommy, and he couldn't fucking go anywhere without being completely harassed by the press. He couldn't even stay home and be left the fuck alone.

They had a ten-foot tall concrete privacy wall around their house, but they didn't have a pool yet, so one hot day they were running around in their yard squirting each other with hoses nude, and the press got photos of it. The photographers were up a fucking tree across the street capturing it all. Tommy grabbed a sawn-off shotgun, loaded it, pumped it, and aimed it at them.

Every time Tommy got into trouble, his name was all over the newspapers and TV. The Mötley band members were all really disenchanted with each other's behavior and busting each other's balls.

Pamela threw a huge surprise birthday party for Tommy in a remote field about a mile from their house on Mulholland in Malibu. I don't remember Nikki or Mick being there, but Robin and I went along. Slash was there and some guys from other bands, along with Tommy's friends.

It was so over the fucking top: there were midgets, confetti, and bubble machines; a Ferris wheel and rollercoaster amusement rides; lions and tigers in cages; contortionists and acrobats; fire-eaters and jugglers; a couple of dancers flown in from Cirque du Soleil in Las Vegas; and a large Arabian tent with a stage setup. It apparently cost about $300,000 to put on.

Robin and I hung out for a while, but it just wasn't our scene. When they started playing football and using a midget as the ball, we bailed, before the jam or getting taken home in a hired ambulance like the rest of the partygoers.

Nikki said in *The Dirt*, "Corabi was being treated like a criminal who had stolen our careers. Every day, we'd take all our frustrations out on him; we'd tell him that he needed to cut his hair or that he needed to sing in a completely different style. And every week we'd change our minds about everything."

I can expand on that.

I was told I was not up to par with the other three guys in the band, and I needed to cut my hair; I needed a wardrobe person; and I needed to get a choreography person. The situation was critical, and my back was against the wall. I felt I had to go along with it. I went to a fucking hair salon where I had all my hair cut off and peroxided white. I sat there looking in the salon mirror thinking, "If they want a blond fucking singer, they should just get their old fucking blond guy back!" It felt like another tactic to squeeze me out and force me to quit, but I was more pissed at myself for caving.

With my short, spiky Rod Stewart hair that was as white as fucking snow, I then found myself being led around stores by a woman (Madonna's wardrobe guru) trying to get me to buy fucking silver lamé pants and floral-print shirts. I ended up telling her, "Look, I'm a fucking jeans and T-shirt guy. I gave you the hair, but I'm not fucking wearing silver lamé pants. It's not ever going to happen."

Then it was time for choreography lessons. I was in a room with some chick telling me to look in the full-length mirror, while she told me how to be bigger than life on stage. I went twice and that was all I could fucking handle. I told them all, "This is NSYNC shit. No, I'm not doing a fucking pirouette in the middle of 'Live Wire,' that's not going to fucking happen."

Tommy started mocking me one day, saying, "Dude, what's with the trucks? Why do you always buy trucks?"

I said, "You own a truck."

He goes, "Yeah, I own a pickup truck. I have a Suburban, but I also have a Mercedes and I have a fucking Testarossa and a Harley-Davidson."

I said, "Okay, well I have a fucking truck. What's the big deal?"

Tommy said, "Well, you're the fucking lead singer, dude. You're the fucking man. You're the fucking lead singer of Mötley Crüe, dude. When you fucking show up, you show up!"

I didn't act like a rich motherfucker in a fancy car but it seemed everybody around me was belittling me now because they thought I should have been. Feeling the pressure, I took my truck and went to a Pontiac dealership. They hadn't made the Trans Am for a while, but they came out with a new one in 1996.

I bought a Pontiac Firebird Trans Am WS6 performance package. It was all black outside with black interior, big oversized tires, spoiler, six-speed stick, with a Corvette engine in it. It was faster than shit.

When I say I bought it, I mean I traded my truck in that I had another six or seven grand to pay off. They rolled over the balance onto the car loan, so I was now financing about fifty thousand fucking dollars.

I have to say now, in hindsight, that car was pretty badass! It actually grew on me, and as much as I hate to admit it, Tommy was right. When I pulled up to places in the car, people noticed. It's a shame that you have to have a flashy car or clothes to be taken seriously, though.

I was told there was a band meeting at Nikki's home studio on Friday the thirteenth of September. The night before, I had dinner with Tommy and Pam after Tommy and I had spent the day drinking beers, shooting pool, and talking about when we go on tour. When I walked into the meeting, I saw three or four people dressed in suits, along with the band manger.

After I took a seat, I was told, "Crab, sorry, I have some bad news. The record label is not going to support this version of Mötley Crüe. It's just not going to happen. So we're being forced to bring Vince back."

It felt like I was held behind a horse and it kicked me at full power right in the fucking chest. But at the same time, it also felt like a trainer at the gym had just grabbed the big barbell and lifted the weight off me that I could no longer bear.

For the last two years, I had been browbeaten by everyone around the band, being told, "You're not a star. You're not up to par with the rest of the guys. You need voice lessons. You need somebody to teach you how to dress. You need somebody to show you how to move."

To some, that may not seem like it would be that difficult, but it was fucking torture for me. I once made them laugh and smile just by opening my mouth; now they had been dissecting every fucking breath I took. I didn't know what to do to make them happy. I couldn't figure it out, but now I didn't need to anymore.

I tried not to be upset about it. I said to Nikki, "Do I need to get all my stuff now?"

He said, "Nah, don't worry about it, dude."

The manager said, "Why don't you come into my office on Tuesday, and we'll sort everything out?" to which I agreed.

I grabbed one of my guitars and walked out of Nikki's house to the new sports car I felt pressured into buying. Tommy followed me out, and he was pretty upset. He looked at me and said, "Fuck, Crab, I don't want to fucking do this. I don't want to fucking do this."

I told him, "Tommy, whatever. It's all good, dude. Don't worry about it."

I waved goodbye as I drove home.

I talked to my manager John Greenberg and his business partner Tim Heyne, and I told them I had been let go and what went down. They weren't surprised at all; everybody seemed to know it was coming but me.

The following Tuesday, I went with my managers to Mötley's management office to finalize my exiting arrangements. The only Mötley member there was Tommy. Just as when I joined the band, I was told, "Don't say anything to anybody. We're going to put out a press release, so just keep 'mum's the word' until we put out a press release with Vince, once we have sorted through some more details."

Amongst other things said, I agreed to help the guys finish the album in the studio. The managers then talked more of their management speak as Tommy and I left the room. We gave each other a hug, then he went one way and I went the other.

I think it was a few days later when I got the first phone call from Scott at 9:00 a.m. "Crab, what are you doing?"

"Nothing."

Scott said, "Can you come into the studio today?"

Tommy, Nikki, and/or Scott started calling me most days at eight or nine in the morning and said, "Crab, can you be here by ten o'clock?"

I asked them numerous times, "Are you sure Mick's cool with me doing these guitar parts? I'll do whatever you guys need me to do, so long as Mick is cool with me playing guitar."

"Yeah, yeah, yeah. It's great. We didn't get anything out of Mick. Come in, dude, we love what you do. It's fine, don't worry about it," they told me.

Over the next couple of weeks, I helped them out in the studio as needed. I was pretty much on call. I only went to the studio when they phoned and asked me to come in, but it was pretty much daily. I didn't see Mick, only Tommy, Nikki, Scott—and Vince.

The first time I ever met Vince was when we sat in Nikki's garage and had a few beers together. Vince said to me, "Hey, man, no hard feelings."

I replied, "Yeah, no hard feelings."

I also said, "Sorry about your daughter," since he had lost his little girl Skylar to cancer the year before. It's not like we became best buddies, but there was no animosity as people probably expected—we got along just fine.

I would show up at the studio at nine or ten o'clock in the morning with a coffee and a bagel. I'd sit down and play guitar while they hit record until about two o'clock. Vince would show up around noon and start singing. I'd be sitting in the back of the studio with Tommy.

We had written a song called "Kiss the Sky," and they had Vince in recording his vocals for it. They then said to me, "Crab, he's not singing that phrase the way that you sang it. Could you just go in and just show him how it should be done?"

I then walked into the vocal booth with Vince and sang the lines, "*Kiss it away, kiss it away, tomorrow*" and "*Wish it away, wish it away, the sorrow.*" They loved the way I phrased it, so after singing it to Vince a few times, he mimicked the way I did it.

It was a weird situation to find myself in, and I'm sure it was difficult for Vince as well, but I gave them this type of assistance for fucking weeks.

I thought I was handling the situation fine. Sure, I was scared at what was going to happen in the future, but I stuck it out and gave them the help they said they needed from me to progress the album. I went to the studio most days and played guitar and helped them finish the songs I had written with them.

One day Mick called as I just finished playing guitar in the studio. I answered the phone and he said, "Hey, Crab, what's going on? What are you doing there?"

I said, "Oh, I just played some guitar this morning, and I'm helping Vince with some vocals now."

He said, "What do you mean you played guitar?"

I said, "Well, I played guitar this morning from like ten o'clock until two, and now I'm helping Vince with vocals."

Years later, when Mick first moved near me in Nashville, we talked about it for three hours because he didn't really know what happened with me and I didn't really know what happened with him. There was friction and a coldness between us that harmed our friendship for a couple of decades, so we sorted it out.

Once we had talked it through, Mick just laughed, saying, "Now you know what I've been dealing with for the last thirty fucking years, Crab." I'm so glad I finally got to resolve it with Mick.

They were super fucking kind to me in the beginning, so that was the hardest part for me when I was ousted. It wasn't so much that they were bringing Vince back. These guys bought me a Harley-Davidson, they gave me guitars, and they gave me a Sony DAT machine. In the beginning, they had paid me more money to play music than I had ever received in my life.

It was a weird situation because I loved hanging out with those guys to a degree. I particularly adored hanging out with Tommy (as much as I could've done without some of the fucking drama at times). For five fucking years I saw those guys every fucking day, and then suddenly it was like, we don't need you anymore.

I had a really hard time processing how these people could be so nice to me in the beginning and then just dispose of me in this way and not give a fuck. I thought we were friends. I guess I was wrong.

In my earlier days in Mötley, my wife, Val, and I would go out to dinner with Nikki and Brandi, and sometimes another friend Ray and his wife Dominica would join us, too. Ray was VP of Rock Promotions for Elektra Records in the eighties before he went to Capitol Records. Another couple also joined us a few times, Kiss guitarist Bruce Kulick and his wife Christina.

A day or two after I was fired from Mötley, Nikki and Bruce were talking, when Nikki suggested to him, "You should fucking do something with John," since he knew Bruce was into similar bands that I loved, like Hendrix, Grand Funk Railroad, and Led Zeppelin.

Nikki then said to me, "You know, Crab, I was thinking you should put something together with Bruce Kulick. You guys are really similar as far as your influences go."

Bruce had joined Kiss back in September 1984, after original guitarist Ace Frehley had departed, and their next two replacements didn't last very long. Eleven years later, founding members Peter Criss and Ace came back to the band for an *MTV Unplugged* special, which led to the reformation of the original lineup in their trademark face-paint and costumes.

Bruce subsequently found himself sidelined during 1996 as Kiss sold-out Alive/Worldwide Tour dates across the globe. He was paid weekly during the tour and allowed to do other projects, so long as Gene Simmons and Paul Stanley approved of them. He stuck it out until December, when he officially left Kiss.

Not only did Bruce and I share some common musical influences, there was a current synchronicity in our disbanding situations—we were both ex-men. This joined us as a union.

The Universe has a very odd way of working for me: every time I've been down to my last fucking ten bucks in my bank account, some amazing unforeseen thing comes along to lift me out of the hardship. It'll be something completely random, like a great aunt or someone will pass away, and I'll get a check for ten grand, or some crazy gig will pay me an astronomical sum of money. It's always been that way for me. Call me superstitious or spiritual or whatever, but in tough times, it has given me faith and hope that everything will be okay; the universe shall provide.

And similarly, I truly believe in hindsight that I was given the Mötley Crüe gig for one reason and one reason only: to financially take care of my mother through her last years with lung cancer, and to take care of my son who had been diagnosed with diabetes.

When I was in The Scream, we were playing to growing crowds and making headway with a lot of positive vibes about the band. We had great press, great reviews, and all this wonderful shit. My mom then had two heart attacks and got diagnosed with terminal lung cancer and had financial trouble, and it wasn't long before Nikki and Tommy called me and asked me to join Mötley.

I'm super proud of the music that I wrote with the Mötley guys and I got to experience that wild and crazy fucking ride. As that was coming to an end for me and they brought Vince back, the lung cancer finally got the better of my mom, and she passed away in December of '96.

I'm actually quite proud of myself because I got a majority of that Mötley money in '92 and '93, then after that I didn't really get any money from them for a while. I had to stretch it out through '96. By decree of the courts of California, I was required to give my ex-wife Valerie support payments of $7,000 a month, and our son was in and out of the hospital with his diabetes.

I easily spent somewhere between $100,000-200,000 taking care of my mother, and I was only able to do that because I wasn't living extravagantly or high on the hog.

Now I was in a panic, though, emotionally freaking out about loss—the loss of my mom, the loss of my band, the loss of my income, the loss of my fiancée—and I was worried about how I was going to get through. I had started working a bit with Bruce Kulick but didn't know where that was going to go as I was figuring him out.

Christmas came and my soon-to-be ex-wife Valerie called and said, "We're all kind of worried about you. Why don't you come up and hang out with us for Christmas?" I accepted her offer but didn't even have enough money to just buy two cards for my kids and put twenty bucks in them. I was broke.

I had one of those big plastic water jugs from the top of an office water cooler. After getting home, I'd always throw any loose change and dollar bills in it.

Feeling I'd bottomed out, I looked at my jug that was almost a third full and thought I'd be able to cash it in for some money for my kids. At least I would have something to hand them when I walked in on Christmas Day.

I went to my local supermarket and turned on their coin-counting machine and started tipping coins in and watched the counter. Twenty bucks, fifty, a hundred, five hundred, a thousand—it just kept going as I poured more coins into the machine. Once it finished, I had nearly two grand and a huge sense of relief. The universe helped me out once again, allowing me to get through my next little hurdle. I bought Ian and Little Val some stuff, along with a bottle of red wine for Valerie. We had a great Christmas dinner together, sitting around the table talking.

Val was dating someone at the time, so afterward she asked me, "Hey, do you mind, can you stay here with the kids and watch them for a while as I have a gift I want to take over to my new guy?"

"Yeah, sure, no worries," I said.

Val left and I put a VHS tape on of some Disney movie. I laid on the couch and propped a pillow between my legs. Ian put his head on the pillow as he lay down and snuggled with me.

As we watched the movie, everything became clear, and I had an epiphany: Ian said to me, "Hey, Dad."

When I replied, "What's up, buddy?"

He said, "Thanks for coming and hanging out with us on Christmas."

I told him, "No worries, bud. I wanted to come up and see you guys."

He said, "I wanted to see you, too. I love you, Dad." A smile held back the tears.

I asked myself, "Why the fuck am I worried about Mötley Crüe and money and my ex-fiancée? Why was I worried that I wasn't getting invited to fucking parties anymore? Why am I concerned about Gibson guitars treating me like I have the fucking plague? Why am I worried about all this shit, when THIS right here is what is important?!"

I was feeling half-dead, but when my son said, "Thanks for coming and hanging out with us at Christmas, I love you," it turned my world around. Nothing really mattered but that. It was Clarity 101 for me, and it got me through the darkness.

18

Get Off My Cloud

I was at home with MTV on, when I heard them play a breaking news segment between video clips. They said something like, "Mötley Crüe has reformed with Vince Neil. A source from their management company says John Corabi is staying on as a fifth member of the band, as a guitar player." That was fucking news to me!

I called the band's management company and asked, "Just out of curiosity, what the fuck is going on? I just saw an MTV report that Mötley is now a five-piece band with me playing guitar. You guys told me not to say anything and I haven't, but they're announcing it on MTV that Vince is back and now I'm the rhythm guitar player. What the fuck?"

The woman replied, "That did not come from us. I'll get back to you."

She called me back a little while later and said it was just a false report. I said, "Well, they're still running it on MTV. I've seen it three more times since we talked an hour ago."

When *Generation Swine* came out, I didn't even know. I was working in the studio on Union songs one day when Bruce Kulick waltzed in and said, "Look, I got the new Mötley record."

The way he said it, though, was him indirectly giving me shit in a sarcastic joking manner, like, why didn't you tell anybody the record was out? When I looked at him with a what-the-fuck-are-you-talking-about expression, he realized I didn't even know it was out yet.

All these questions immediately came to mind: Why didn't they tell me the record was coming out in two weeks or whatever? Why didn't anybody from the management company call and tell me? Why didn't I perhaps even get a copy sent to me?

I said, "What? Wait, hold on, give me that fucking thing."

I opened the CD and looked through its packaging and songwriting credits, noticing I was only listed on "Let Us Prey." Bruce said to me, "Dude, you're not even listed on this record anywhere as an additional musician, but they have other people listed."

Aside from not being listed as a guitar player and backing vocalist on it, there was not even a Mötley Crüe would like to thank John Corabi for helping on the album, or for the last five years of his life—nothing!

At that point, I was like, "What the fuck? Seriously?" I was fucking pissed. I wasn't going to be a fucking doormat for them or for anybody.

I won't go into details of the songwriting publishing due to nondisclosure legalities, except to say things were far from what I had expected. I talked things through with my managers and decided to file a suit. I didn't want to sue them, but felt it was important to prove a point that I am not a fucking doormat, period. Once my lawyers took the case on, though, it seemed their eyes lit up with dollar signs, which meant I argued with my lawyers the whole fucking time while I tried to be firm but fair.

So while I worked with Bruce on putting an album together and then touring our new band called Union, I had to juggle trying to get that off the ground, while having commitments with the legal case against Mötley Crüe.

I fucking hated every minute of it. I couldn't understand how I could have farted into a microphone when I was doing the first record and they would've thought it was the greatest sound they had ever heard in their lives, to becoming my own walking leper colony. These were my buddies. I toured in a bus with Tommy and we were best buds; I lived with Mick, and I was at Nikki's house most days, writing lyrics as we busted each other's balls joking around and having fun. In some weird way, I fucking adored those guys. They were my brothers for five fucking years and then suddenly it was like, fuck off! There we were, staring each other down in legal meetings and not even talking to each other. I fucking HATED it.

Coincidently, much like me, Bruce Kulick had not only just lost his band, something happened with him and his wife Christina, and they were no longer together. It was an ugly situation for Bruce. He moved out of his place in West Hollywood and was living with a guy named Curt Cuomo in Woodland Hills, just renting a room from him.

Curt was a producer with a home studio called Cheyenne, and he had worked with Bruce and Paul Stanley on the Kiss album *Carnival of Souls*. The living arrangement was convenient, as Bruce and I would go into his room and write, then we'd walk to the other side of the house and show the ideas to Curt. The ideas were flowing easily for both Bruce and I as we both had a lot to get off our chest. We both had things to say about our relationships with our women, our bands, and people we felt just did us wrong. Some of the ideas even came accidentally.

The first song I wrote with Bruce was "Around Again." One day we were working on a song and trying to get a tone for the guitar, when I started playing a different riff that just came to me. Everybody said, "What is that?"

I played it again on guitar, Curt did some quick drums for it on his machine, and Bruce played a bass line. We laid the new idea down, so we didn't forget it, and then we went back and further developed that opening riff into the song "Love (I Don't Need it Anymore)."

Bruce and I recorded pretty much a whole album's worth of material at Curt's studio, with his drum machine providing the backbeat. I heard the words screaming in my head, while the melody was flowing from my pen. We had the majority of the record written and done before we got a bass player and a drummer for the band, and we initially dubbed the project Crablick—an amalgamation of my nickname Crab and the end of Bruce's last name Kulick—before we settled on the name Union.

As Bruce and I worked on music one day, Curt said he had to go out for a while and gave us a heads-up that Eddie Money was coming over; they were working on some new music together as well. Curt instructed us, "Just make sure Eddie doesn't smoke in my house, and make sure he doesn't drink and doesn't do this and that, etc."

Eddie was a rock singer who had success in the seventies and eighties but also had struggles with drug addiction and drinking. He was married to Laurie, a gorgeous but sweet lady who had to keep him under an iron fist for his own good.

Eddie walked in the front of the house with a baby in a capsule carrier—one of his five kids. He set the baby on the table, then walked back out to his car. From his trunk, he got these cans of premixed vodka and orange juice, came back into the kitchen, and popped the lid on a drink. I guess from being in the car on a hot day, some pressure built up, and when he popped the lid it exploded and sprayed fucking orange juice and vodka all over the kitchen. Mr. Clean Kulick yelled, "Goddamn it, Eddie!"

As Eddie freaked out and I laughed my ass off, Bruce ran around, grabbing paper towels and the tea towel to mop it up. I helped Bruce get it off all the kitchen walls and the fucking ceiling, and while we did that, Eddie walked away to a phone by the back door.

He called someone, and as he started talking business, he lit a cigarette. Eddie was standing right under the fucking fire alarm, so his cigarette smoke set off the alarm, which triggered a back-to-base alert for the fire department. The fire alarm was incredibly loud, and Bruce and I were freaking out, not knowing how to turn it off while remembering Curt had specifically said to make sure Eddie didn't smoke in his house.

We kept trying to shut the fucking alarm off but couldn't, so we tried calling Curt. After a few attempts, we finally got Curt on the phone. He quickly called the fire alarm company to tell them not to have the fire engines come, but they were already pulling onto the street by that time. They came in and reset the fire alarm after it rang for about fifteen minutes.

Eddie said he was going to go in a minute, so I walked outside. The fire department guys were leaving, and I walked all the way down to the end of the driveway by the street curb and lit a cigarette in the peace and quiet after that fucking tornado.

I watched Eddie walk out of the house and as he got to his car, he took his glasses off his head and placed them on top of the car. I must have looked away as I smoked because when I looked back toward Eddie again, he was in the car backing out of the fucking drive and his glasses were still sitting on the roof of the car.

I ran down the driveway, yelling out to him but he kept going. I threw my cigarette pack at his car and he stopped. I grabbed his glasses and handed them to him saying, "Dude, your glasses were on top of the car."

He said, "Oh, fuck, thanks. I would have got on the freeway and I wouldn't have been able to see anything."

He drove off down the street, and I watched until his car disappeared, while I finished my cigarette. I turned around and headed back to the house, and as I was about to walk in the door, what did I see sitting in the driveway right by the steps? His fucking baby!

I grabbed the baby and went inside, yelling out to Bruce, "Quick, call Curt! Tell him to call Eddie right now!"

From the kitchen where he was still cleaning up vodka and orange, Bruce said, "What's wrong?"

I said, "He left his fucking baby in the driveway and he's on his way home. If he gets home and walks into his house, the first thing his wife will say is where's the baby? She's going to fucking skin him alive!"

Bruce frantically called Curt. He said, "Curt, call Eddie Money and tell him that he left his baby at your house."

Curt called him and asked, "Eddie, you missing anything?" and he said, "What? No, I got my glasses. What are you talking about?"

He asked again, "So, you're not missing anything?"

Eddie was on the freeway, almost home. Curt said, "Dude, turn around and look in your car. Where is your child?"

Eddie yelled, "FUCK!"

He got off the freeway, turned around and came back after being three quarters of the way home before he was told he'd forgotten his baby.

In just half an hour, Eddie blew up a can of vodka orange juice, set off a fire alarm with a cigarette, left his glasses on his car in the driveway, and left his own fucking baby behind.

I loved the dude; he was always a sweetheart to me and fucking hilariously funny, but you could tell there were definitely some consequences from his substance abuse, and not just the permanent limp from his 1980 overdose that did nerve damage and took months for him to walk again. Now he's up in paradise somewhere, resting in peace.

It took me some time to recover from Robin dumping me. Somebody stole her heart away from me, but at least I got a new song from all the heartbreak, which I simply titled "Robin's Song."

I would head out to the Coconut Teaszer sometimes to help lift my spirits. I was there having a beer one night when the Vagabonds were set to play. Their singer Joe LeSte asked me on the spot to fill-in because his guitarist didn't make it, so I jumped up with his former Bang Tango band-mate Kyle Kyle on bass, and I followed along by watching his lead guitarist, Brian Forsythe from Kix. It was an hour of easy tunes, mainly covers and jam stuff with a couple of originals. Then other venues started asking us to play, so I did a few little gigs with them just for fun and some good times.

It wasn't long before I dated an LA girl named Annie Wood for a while, who was host of the nationally syndicated dating game show called *Bzzz!* That caused a little schism between Bruce and I because unbeknown to me when we got together, Bruce had also liked her.

You see, we were working away in the studio one day, and I was just wearing overalls with no shirt, flip-flops, and a headband—not prepared to go out anywhere. Bruce and Curt said, "Let's knock it on the head early. We've got to go down to Annie's house."

I asked, "Who's Annie?" to which they replied, "She's a friend of ours, and it's her birthday today."

Curt said, "Why don't you come with us? It's cool."

I said, "No, man. Look at how I'm dressed."

I was told, "Nah, dude, it's fine. Just come. It's good man. Annie's not uptight. She's really cool. It'll be no big deal."

So I caved in and said, "Okay, fine. I don't really have anything going on, so yeah, okay, I'll go. Let's go."

On the way to her place, I asked, "Hey, can we stop somewhere? I don't want to show up empty-handed, especially since it's her birthday."

I wanted to get something for Annie, so I bought a bottle of wine for her, and a bottle of Jack Daniel's for myself. While I was in the store, I also grabbed two packets of patchouli and Nag Champa incense, and a birthday card.

When we arrived, they introduced me, "Annie, this is John, our singer—John, this is Annie."

I said, "Hi, how you doing? Happy Birthday!" and I handed her a brown bag with the booze, card, and incense in it. Done.

I got a cocktail and went out on her balcony, where I was smoking and talking to a few different people for a while, just mingling. Annie came out a few times, and I noticed that not only was she very pretty, she seemed incredibly smart. I found it fascinating that she had her own TV show.

After a while, we all went inside. There were a couple of acoustic guitars there. Bruce had picked one up, sat down, and was going to start to play.

There was nowhere for me to sit on the three-seater couch, so I sat down on the floor in the corner, in front of the couch. Annie then came in from the kitchen, jumped over the couch and squeezed herself in right behind me.

Bruce played, and I was watching him as everybody sang along to Beatles' tunes. As I sipped my drink, I realized that as Annie was sitting behind me, she was wearing a skirt, and she had somewhat wrapped her bare legs around me, pressing them into my arms. That's when I noticed Bruce looking kind of annoyed. Things progressed as Annie started rubbing my head, and I then started leaning back into her legs more. I was really smitten with her. After a while, Bruce and Curt were ready to leave. Annie asked me, "Do you have to leave with them, too?"

I said, "Well, my car is at Curt's house, since I came with them."

Bruce and Curt's other housemate Jules offered, "It's okay, I can bring you back later."

There were still people at the party, and I was having fun, so we just kept hanging out and having cocktails. Next thing I know, Annie and

I were holding hands, and she asked me to stay. I clarified, "Like, you mean overnight?" and she said, "Yes."

I stayed the night and the next day I said, "Well, I'd better get back to Curt's house."

I showered, we ate a little snack, and then Annie drove me back to Bruce and Curt's and when I walked in, there was a thick tension in the air.

I cut to the chase and asked, "What the fuck? What's going on?"

Bruce said, "I fucking liked Annie."

I said, "I didn't know that, dude. How the fuck was I meant to know that? Nobody said anything to me. I didn't even know this chick; I had never met her before. What the fuck?"

Bruce and I have always had a kind of brotherly love/hate thing between us. I respect the shit out of him, but we're oil and water. I'm a tornado and discombobulated more times than not. I can walk into a room and it'll look like a bomb went off in it in five minutes—although I'll never be on the same level as Eddie Money.

Bruce is the complete antithesis of that. Everything has its place, which is fine with me—to a fucking point. The level of Yin and Yang competing forces went up a notch with us, not in a bad way, though. Bruce can be moody at times, as can I, but sometimes I feel he'll tend to talk down to me and when I sense that, I just don't take his shit. I'll just look at him like a brother and say, "Dude, fuck you," and he'll come back with, "Well, fuck you, John, fuck you, too."

Five minutes later one of us will then say, "Hey, what do you want to do on this song we're recording?" That's just the kind of competitive spirit between the two of us.

I had no idea who Annie was when I unintentionally hooked-up with her that night, and I had no fucking idea that Bruce had a crush on her and had taken her out to lunch or dinner before.

Annie and I dated a little bit, but it was a very short lived. We didn't argue or bicker, it was just that we were both busy working away on our own things. I really liked Annie a lot but our schedules didn't quite coordinate most of the time, so it just fizzled out, and that was my time dating the dating game show host.

Union didn't have to search for a drummer, as we had one coming around to Curt's and hanging out with us. Brent Fitz had drummed with former Shake Naked vocalist Lenita Erickson and met Bruce when he played some guitar for her. Bruce also saw him play drums at The Roxy with former Duran Duran backing singer Lamya, and when Bruce first heard Brent play piano, he invited him over to Curt's, and they became fast friends.

Brent had moved to Los Angeles from Canada and was trying to get established in the music industry. The more that Brent came by the studio, the more his talents impressed me. We had him play along to our "Old Man Wise" demo, since we couldn't get the right feel from Curt's drum machine, and he nailed it. I said to Bruce, "Fuck, this guy can really play the drums, plus he plays piano, and he can play guitar. Holy shit!"

Brent played the piano piece of my song "Friends" I did with Mötley, which helped form a connection between us as I sang along. Bruce agreed that he was really well-rounded and said he could also sing great.

With Brent on board, we started checking out different bass players. One night, Bruce saw a guy playing at the Hollywood Athletic Club and approached him. Jamie Hunting came into the studio, and we thought he had a cool look and was a great player, even if there was a little craziness about him. He had played with Eddie Money in the eighties and with David Lee Roth in '93 and '94. He turned out to be incredibly talented and the right fit for us.

We submitted all the songs that Bruce and I recorded with Curt to an East Coast independent label Mayhem Records. Their main man Paul Bibeau came over to California, and we did a showcase. They loved the band and gave us a record deal. Even though they were a small independent label, they had distribution through Universal.

With that secured, we went into Rumbo Records studio, where Brent played the drums along to what Curt had already created on the drum machine. We then had Jamie do the same thing for the bass lines on the songs before we mixed the album with Jim Mitchell. That whole first Union record is only a sixteen-track recording.

We recorded a few additional songs that didn't make the final cut for the album. One was called "Walking in Your Sleep," which I personally didn't feel was strong enough, so we held it aside. It eventually surfaced as a previously unreleased bonus track on the band's *Do Your Own Thing Live!* DVD.

Another was a song called "For You," on which Bruce sang lead vocals for the first time in his career (at that point as *Carnival of Sins* hadn't come out yet); it got released on the Japanese version of our Union album. We also recorded a great cover of "Oh, Darlin'" by The Beatles.

Union used a logo symbol of four diamonds symmetrically placed to form a larger diamond with an X through it. It was an emblem of the ancient Japanese Takeda clan, but we gave our version concave sides on the diamonds.

My dad asked me one day, "Well, how's this Union band coming along?"

I told him we had finished recording the album and the record label had it and we were starting to get some great initial reviews. Even though I had been in Mötley, I could feel things going great with Union, so I said to him, "I think this band is the one. I think my ship is finally coming in."

Dad wryly quipped, "Well, if your ship is coming in, don't be at the airport."

I have notoriously been the victim of idiotic judgement on my part. Sometimes, I just don't think. At least not with the head on my shoulders! I don't like throwing anyone under a bus, and I've always remained pretty good friends with a lot of women I've dated, but there are some exceptions.

This is another case of stupidity, poor judgement, and maybe a bit of falling for someone for ALL the wrong reasons, on both of our parts. I was alone and she was young and we were both figuring shit out. However, you reap what you sow.

I went out with Eric Singer and Ace Frehley to see Circus of Power from New York play on the Sunset Strip at the Key Club. While I was hanging out, I met Jizzy Pearl, the former singer of the Hollywood band Love/Hate, who also sang with LA Guns for a couple of years.

As I walked over to the side bar to get a drink, Jizzy was standing there so I said, "Hey, Jizz."

He said, "Hey, man, how are you doing? Say, I've got to ask you a question," and he started asking me about the label Union was on, Mayhem Records.

I said, "So far so good with them. It's been pretty cool. We've got our first album recorded, so I look forward to them getting that out."

As we were talking about that, he said, "Oh, I want you to meet my girl: this is Layla." I said, "Oh, hi. How are you?" and she shook my hand.

I chatted with Jizzy a while longer about Mötley and other things, and said, "I've always thought you had a great voice, dude. I'm a fan."

He was doing a solo record and wanted to know who at Mayhem he could submit his record to. I told him I didn't have the person's number on me, so I told him I'd give him my number so he could call me for it. Layla grabbed a napkin or something out of her bag and wrote my number down for him.

I said I would talk and hang with them some more before I left, but I went backstage with Eric and Ace then ended up splitting without saying goodbye to anyone.

A couple of days later, my phone rang. "Hi, it's Layla. I was with Jizzy the other day when you..."

I said, "Oh, hey, how are you?" We just started bullshitting, talking about music, talking about that concert we saw.

After a while, she said something like, "Oh, we should definitely hang some time."

I said to her, "Let me ask you a question: I didn't quite understand, are you Jizzy's wife or his girlfriend? What's the deal?"

She said, "Oh, no, we're just roommates."

I grilled her to a degree, "What do you mean roommates? Are you like romantically connected roommates or are you just two friends who are renting an apartment together?"

"We're just two friends renting an apartment together," she told me.

She again said that we should hang some time, so I said, "Well, as a matter of fact, on Tuesdays I always go down to this place called The Baked Potato in Studio City and jam with Teddy Andreadis from Guns N' Roses and others. It's a really cool place. So, if you're ever down there, stop by."

She said, "I've been there before. I love that place!"

The next Tuesday came and as I walked into The Baked Potato, there she was, hanging out with three or four guys that were her coworkers. She said, "Oh, this is so weird. I know that you said you come here all the time, but today my coworkers said they were coming here, and they asked if I'd like to come with them."

I said it was good to see her, and I bought her a drink. Next thing I know, we were making out. We got out of the club and hooked up in the front seat of my car. Afterward, she said, "I have to get going, as I have got to work tomorrow."

She gave me her number, and that was that.

We soon had a little party at Bruce's for something, and I asked everybody, "Hey, is it cool if I invite this chick over?"

"Sure. No worries," they said.

Layla came to Bruce's place and everybody met her, and told me, "Oh, dude, this chick is gorgeous. She's really sweet."

Bruce said, "Dude, good job. She's a fucking winner."

I don't feel bad getting duped, because everybody got duped in some way. My first clue that I missed was that I had not heard from Jizzy about the record label, at all.

I had an apartment, but I was somewhat hurting for cash. When I first separated from my ex-wife Valerie, my child support and alimony payments were seven grand a month. After a while, I kept telling her, "Val, I'm not making that kind of money anymore."

It got lowered to $4,500 a month, then $3,500 a month, and $2,500 a month, as my income dried up.

Val said to me, "Listen, I have a four-bedroom house in Thousand Oaks, and it's just me and Ian. Why don't you just split this rent with me? Financially, it'll be better for you, and it'll be better for me. Plus, Ian will get to see you."

It was a good arrangement that we entered into. Val was dating someone else, and she knew that I had started seeing a new girl. Val didn't give a shit what I did, and I didn't give a shit what she did.

One weeknight, I asked Layla to come over to my place, but she said she had work and couldn't come all the way up to where I lived. She didn't feel comfortable bringing me into her place, saying, "It's just a small place that Jizzy and I have, so I don't like having someone else in my place." There goes another clue.

However, I felt that I had a similar situation where I probably shouldn't bring a chick that I just met into my house, fuck in another room with my son across the hall and my ex-wife next door.

So I got a hotel room for us in North Hollywood. We went out to dinner, and she stayed until four or five o'clock in the morning, when she said, "I've got to go. I have to go home, shower, and get ready for work this morning."

There was no, "I've got to get back because Jizzy's going to find out and kill me!" There was none of that talk; she was very nonchalant about everything.

She called me the next day as I was doing some recording, and she said, "Oh, God, Jizzy threw me out."

I asked her why, then the whole plot twisted as she explained, "Well, we're roommates, but we used to date, but we're not dating anymore. It was just a platonic roommate kind of relationship, but he saw me coming in late at night from you. Since you used to be in Mötley, I think he's just really insecure about his career, and..."

"Fuck, man. Goddamnit," I said. By this point, we had been hanging out and fucking for a month and a half.

Layla then got a small apartment in Universal City, and after one thing led to another, or should I say all the clues I let pass by, we had a boyfriend-girlfriend thing happening. A little more time passed as I went on a promotional tour. But we talked every day I was gone, and we decided to move in together when I got home; we were a couple.

There was also a shitstorm online that we copped, nasty emails and ugly statements on the internet about her and about me. With the benefit of hindsight, my eyes should have been wide open to warning signs that I shouldn't be with her. It was one of those cases where my little head was doing all the thinking for my entire fucking body. My big head completely and stupidly ignored all the signs. I should've bailed but didn't.

So, how deep does this rabbit hole go, you ask?

She had a great job working as a manager for a post-production house in LA. She was young, about twenty-three, when she landed in my lap, gorgeous, and used her body like a fucking porn star. I wasn't smart enough or strong enough to tell her, "Hey, I like you. You're gorgeous. You're great and all, but call me when you're single, responsible, and grown-up."

The first Union show was at a strip bar called Pleasures in Pasadena. We played a few local shows in Los Angeles before we got a booking agent, mainly at the Coconut Teaszer on Sunset at Crescent Heights Boulevard. (The first of which was a benefit show for the late Guns N' Roses insider West Arkeen.) Our agent then put a tour together for us, and we earned decent money for shows. It wasn't Mötley money or Kiss money, but for a new band going out playing clubs, $7,000, $8,000, or $10,000 a show was great, especially considering nobody really knew about the band if they didn't read *Metal Edge* magazine. Gerri Miller, who edited the magazine, was championing us in her publication, and we took out the Best New Band award in it.

There was minimal-to-no radio support, and the majority of interviews we did were for small online sites and fanzines as the internet picked up steam. That first tour felt like pulling teeth to get people to come and see the band.

We had a tour bus and a crew, led by our tour manager (whose brother was John Lennon's lawyer), but right from the start, it was mutiny out on the road. The issues started out fairly small, like the crew guys didn't like the way Bruce talked to them or something. After we had been on the road for five or six weeks, I got a call from my manager Tim Heyne, who asked, "Dude, what the fuck's going on out there?"

I knew things weren't cohesive, but I asked, "What do you mean?"

He said, "We're not getting any of the deposit monies through."

Typically, when we were to play a gig, the club deposited half our performance payment into a bank account beforehand. Our tour manager was then picking up the remaining half from the club after we had played. Tim let me know that he wasn't seeing the other half payments from our tour manager.

I said, "What the fuck do you mean? We've been playing out here for six weeks and you're telling me you now haven't gotten any money at all?"

"That's right," he said.

I immediately went and told Bruce, and we sat down with our tour manager, asking, "Dude, where the fuck is all our money?"

He said, "Well, I've been sending it home. I'm wiring it, so I don't know what Tim's talking about."

We had an LA show at the Country Club coming up, so we said we'd sort it out once we got back home.

Union had a pretty solid turnout at the Country Club. To make it even better, the Kiss clan was there: Paul Stanley, Gene Simmons, Ace Frehley, Eric Singer, and Bruce's brother Bob Kulick. We obviously took care of them with tickets and backstage passes.

Once we finished the show, we headed back to our tour bus. Gene and Paul came on the bus, and we had a good time hanging out. Suddenly, our fucking tour manager came on the bus and started freaking out, yelling at everybody, "Get the fuck off this fucking bus!"

Bruce and I said, "Dude, these are our guests."

"I don't give a fuck. Get the off our bus," he spat back, still freaking out.

Gene said to him, "Excuse me, I'm Gene Simmons."

He replied, "I don't give a fuck who you are, get off the fucking bus!"

He threw everybody off. We were horrified, and I still don't know why everyone had to get off the bus. We talked with Union's managers, John Greenberg and Tim Heyne from my side, and Bruce's manager Larry Mazer, who were all working together. We relayed that the tour manager said he wired the money into the bank account, so they called him to ask to see the deposit receipts—perhaps the account number was incorrect or something.

He didn't answer the phone that first time or any other fucking time. There was no answer from him, and he didn't return any calls. We never heard from the fucking guy again! Not only were we paying him a wage, he decided to skedaddle with all our fucking halves of the performance money over all those weeks. He shafted us. Making matters worse, the stock counts of T-shirts and merchandise were off. It was a fucking financial bloodbath all round for us.

We went back out and finished the tour with me driving a van pulling a trailer, doing it the old-fashioned way. We didn't have a crew guy to help—it was just me, Bruce, Brent, Jamie, a trailer of gear, and some fans who kindly helped us along the way.

The first time the public heard us outside of LA was in the summer of '97 when we played the Detroit Kiss Expo. Since Bruce had been in Kiss for so many years and was now departed from the band, the organizers of Kiss conventions saw it as a great opportunity to expose him to fans at their events. They would look at our tour schedule and say, "Hey, you're going to be in Indianapolis on a Friday and then you're going there on Sunday, so why don't we have a convention here on the Saturday? We'll pay you guys five grand, and you can sell your merch and do whatever you like."

If it wasn't for the Kiss Army on the first couple of US tours we did with Union, we would not have stayed afloat. A lot of them invited us to their homes so we could shit, shower, and shave, and then they'd cook dinner for us.

As we arrived in Europe for the first tour, the Kiss convention people told us they had organized a tour bus for us. While it was appreciated, it was literally a box truck with some beds in it, around which we stored our gear.

It was so fucking cold in that fucking box truck driving through Sweden, since it was not insulated like a real tour bus. We would lie in our bunks with our fucking fur coats on and just laugh. As hard as it was, it was hilarious, and we had a really great time.

By and large, though, my days in Union were as regular as life is for a working musician. There were minimal crazy, dramatic incidents going on. There was no band member shooting my date with his gun, no Steven Tyler chatting with me, no helicopters, and no fireworks causing fucking mayhem. It was a breath of fresh air for me to have that sense of normalcy back.

We shared a lot of great experiences in Union, which was so much more real and down-to-earth than what I had experienced in Mötley. A lot of real blood, sweat, and tears went into the band. I do recall when we played in Nashville, though, I got very drunk after the show; I kicked on and walked into The Gold Rush bar and restaurant on the city's "Rock Block" with a couple of friends. We ordered drinks, and my glass seemed to have a hole in the bottom because next thing I knew it was empty again. I was trying to get the bartender's attention, without luck, so I stood up on the seat of our corner booth. I dropped my pants and started waving my dick at him. It worked; I got his attention. However, I didn't get the drink that I wanted—I got thrown out of the bar instead.

Shitfaced drunk, I headed to another bar and met a waitress. I brought her back to my hotel, where she walked into my room and took all her clothes off. I was so drunk, I just passed out, and when I woke up the next day, she had left with my sweater and all my cash. She even unbolted the fucking TV from in my room and left with that, too. It certainly made that night's drinks expensive.

I was on tour with Union in north New Jersey when my former drummer in The Scream, Walt Woodward, came to the show. We hung out backstage before the show, and he was hugging on me, and it was great to see him again after so long—he was the super-sweet, good-natured, funny dude that I remembered. And then he started drinking.

I hit the stage and about halfway through our set we started to play "Man in the Moon," so I dedicated it to Walt and the guys in The Scream. As I played the song, I saw Walt fucking elbow his way to the front. He came right through the middle of the crowd as I sang, stood right in front of me, flipped me off, and said, "You fucking ruined my life. Fuck you!"

That was the last time I ever saw him. Walt Woodward III unfortunately died on June 8, 2010, from alcohol poisoning and liver failure, at the young age of fifty-one—a similar fate as his hero John Bonham. People often ask me about reforming The Scream, and we've even been offered good money to play Loud Park festival in Tokyo, for example. However, it just hasn't felt right to me to do that without Walt behind the kit.

I started dating Layla while recording the first Union record, and then I went on tour. When I got home from Union's touring, we started living together. Once we started living together, her disease suddenly kicked in, and in time she lost her job. Our relationship got darker and darker as we progressed.

Since she was a kid, Layla suffered from a rare form of arthritis that is mainly endured by women over eighty. It would come and go, and at one point they thought she might have Lupus as well, but it was a form of rheumatoid arthritis. There were nights where she'd be lying in bed, and I would hear her crying. I would roll over and ask, "What's up?"

She'd sob, "I have to go to the bathroom, but I can't get up."

I would have to pop her toes, pop her ankle, pop her knee, and pop her hip, so she could move that leg. Then I'd have to do the other leg so she could walk to the bathroom. The disease affected all her joints, all the knuckles in her hands, everything.

I was making good money with Union, but not hand-over-fist, and my finances were tight. I was paying all the rent, paying all the utility bills, all the groceries, plus giving Val fifteen hundred a month now for Ian. I was just trying to fucking make ends meet.

Since Layla wasn't working and earning to contribute, she had an old Atlanta school friend named Deanna who said she wanted to move to LA and stay with us. So I found a house to rent in Granada Hills, with a yard for my dog Cody, a garage, and enough room for the three of us to settle in. I figured the house wasn't much more than the apartment we were in, but Deanna could contribute for a little while to help with the rent, but that didn't work out since I never got much money from her either.

Over time, Layla started feeling better. She was still having flare-ups every now and then with her disease, but she was okay for the most part. She decided to do some cheesecake modeling with Deanna and some other friends, modeling in bathing suits, bras, and panties, and sometimes topless with their hands over their tits. Layla asked me if I would mind, to which I told her, "Honestly, I'm fine if that's what you want to do. If you can make the kind of money that they're making by doing it and stay home and paint your art and do what you want to do, then I don't give a fuck. Do your thing. It's no big deal to me."

Of course, it gradually became more than that, as she progressed to working as a hostess in a topless strip bar. Then somebody there said, "You're really pretty, and you've got a great figure, why don't you dance?"

She asked me, "Would you be okay if I dance?"

I said, "Again, it doesn't bother me. Just be happy, make money, and don't get caught up in the bullshit."

She started dancing and then somebody said, "Why don't you do a website?"

Her friend Deanna had a website. There were companies needing girls to model in an outfit like a trench coat, then take it off and be wearing a bustier, panties, and stockings, then take the shoes off, take the stockings off, and guys will pay $9.99 a month to subscribe and watch them undress.

You see this shit all the time in Los Angeles, and it's not unusual for girls to make money that way in New York, Chicago, Dallas, etc. When she asked me, I again told her, "It doesn't bug me. It'd be like living with a Playboy bunny. Do what you want to do."

Union played shows with a lot of cool bands as we built an audience, but it just wasn't translating into any sizable sales and income. Our label Mayhem Records was really small, based out of Long Island. Paul Bibeau came in to run the fledging label for its owner, who was a guy that promoted concerts back in the day, like Led Zeppelin at Madison Square Garden. While we were out doing our thing on the road, we got word that Mayhem had gone belly-up, since they were losing more money than they were making.

When they closed the record label toward the end of our touring behind the debut album, we didn't know what would happen next. We were playing a West Coast run of shows with Cinderella at the time, and they got offered some money from a label in Los Angeles called Cleopatra Records to do a live album.

Cinderella was being managed by John Greenberg and Tim Heyne, too, who had managed me through The Scream, Mötley Crüe, and now Union. So they came to me and said, "Listen, we were talking to the record label today and when they realized Union is playing with Cinderella, they said they'd like to do a live album with you as well."

I said to them, "Oh, okay, but we've only got one studio album out. Isn't that kind of weird or premature to do a live album already?"

Since we didn't have a record deal, we thought it would be a good thing to keep momentum going for the fans and the band until we got another record deal. "Fuck it, let's do the record," we said.

Our last dates on the tour were in Los Angeles at the Key Club on the Sunset Strip, then the following night at The Galaxy Theatre in Orange County. They brought a mobile recording unit to the Key Club and the arrangement was we'd split the costs of that with Cinderella. Unfortunately, they had sound issues that they were resolving and did a really long soundcheck, which meant Union got no soundcheck.

That meant we didn't have anything recorded that night, but we were told not to worry about it because they'd make sure we would get a soundcheck the next night at The Galaxy; they would simply record that show instead. So we got to The Galaxy as Cinderella began their soundcheck, and they started having the same issues with the Studio on Wheels as the night before. An hour ticked by, then two hours, then three hours had passed, and they were still trying to figure out where some buzzing was coming from.

Greenberg was there, so I walked over to him and said, "Listen, man, if we don't get a fucking soundcheck, we're not fucking paying for our half of the mobile recording truck."

I was frustrated, he was frustrated, and I'm sure Cinderella was frustrated, too. They finally got it sorted. Cinderella got off stage, so we could do a soundcheck.

Union got on stage and quickly checked Brent's drums, tweaking them really quick. Bruce checked his guitar by strumming up and down a couple of times, "Yep. I'm good. I'm good."

Jamie plucked a few notes on his bass and said, "Yep, I'm good." We had no more than a thirty-minute soundcheck to record a fucking live album.

We took the stage that one night and played our set from top to bottom, and that is what you hear on the record. I remember there was one part during the first song "Old Man Wise" where a guitar was feeding back in the monitors.

That whole *Live in The Galaxy* album was just one show, one take, go! It came out pretty fucking good. (Incidentally, Cinderella called their album *Live at the Key Club* and used recordings from both nights.)

Since we only had the one studio album of Union material, we filled out our set with some songs from our previous bands, like "Man in the Moon" by The Scream, Mötley's "Power to the Music," and the Kiss song "Jungle." We also played Cheap Trick's "Surrender," which was always an audience favorite.

The label wanted us to include a bonus track, so we went into a studio and recorded "Hide Your Love Away" by The Beatles. We rehearsed the song and figured out all the parts each of us would play before it came time to record it. We basically walked into the studio and played it—we weren't in the studio for more than ninety minutes.

There are no drums on it, just tambourine and acoustic guitars. I think Brent may have even played guitar on that as well. We laid down the music, and then I sang it. We recorded the vocal harmonies, and we were done. "There's your bonus track. See you later, bye."

19

Do Your Own Thing

Over time, as Layla had some great photos taken by different photographers and danced at the strip bar, our own personal lives changed and, sexually, we got very experimental. One night in our Granada Hills home we were watching a TV series on HBO called *Real Sex* and the episode was about people who were not monogamous—they had open relationships and were swingers.

Commentating from the couch, I said, "Oh my God, I don't know if I could do that. Could you do that? I don't know if I could screw somebody's wife while her husband was fucking my wife. That's fucking weird!"

Layla said, "Yeah, I don't think I could do it either."

A month or so later, what I thought were just some flippant comments while chilling, came back when Layla told me, "Remember that conversation about open relationships we had? I have been really thinking about it, and I think I want to try it."

I asked, "Why?"

She offered, "It might be fun to have an open relationship. You can date who you want to date. I date who I want to date. Yet we still have each other."

This is how weak and idiotic I was, but it could've been because she was absolutely gorgeous and open to anything sexually (or maybe she was doing naked yoga while we were talking), but it made sense to me. I said, "Well, I guess the things that most people break-up over are either money or infidelity, so if you're being open about it, that gets rid of the dishonesty factor."

"Yes," she explained, "If you're on tour and think some girl is really hot and you'd love to fuck her, you can."

"Right," I said, "And if I'm cool with you fucking another guy while I'm gone and I know about it, then you're not lying to me."

So, it was decided, we now had an "open relationship."

A guy named Keith Leroux got Bruce and I to play acoustically at the Indianapolis Kiss Convention, which was one of the first of these events we did. Eric Singer was there, too, doing Q&As along with Bruce, talking about their time in Kiss and whatever else the Kiss fans wanted to hear about. Another guy Karl Cochran was there to do a Q&A, since he had played with Ace Frehley. There were dealers flogging their Kiss merch to fans, and Keith had arranged for a Kiss tribute band to finish the convention.

Throughout the course of the event, we got asked if we wanted to get up and jam. We thought it sounded like fun, so we huddled and figured out what songs we all knew and could play at a moment's notice. We ended up playing a couple of Kiss songs, "Beth" and "Rock and Roll All Nite," along with covers of "We're an American Band," "Tush," "Honky Tonk Women," and "Oh, Darlin'." Everybody was like, holy fuck, that was awesome!

It was my first time playing with Eric Singer, even though I had known him since the mid-eighties. (Union's drummer Brent Fitz was now living at Eric's place in North Hollywood, too.)

Soon after the convention, Eric told me, "Hey, I got offered this fucking deal with Keith. He wants to do a record where I put a project together. I want Bruce to do it and you."

Keith told him, "I'll pay you guys to do a record and then we'll go out and we'll sell it on all the Kiss websites and you guys will get a percentage of the record sales."

Everybody had to pick a couple of cool fucking tracks that we all grew up listening to. Eric picked "Razamanaz" by Nazareth, "Set Me Free" by Sweet, and "Twenty Flight Rock" by Eddie Cochran, which Elvis Presley and Montrose had also covered.

I picked "S.O.S. (Too Bad)" by Aerosmith, "Four Day Creep" by Humble Pie, and "Free Ride" by Edgar Winter. I also suggested "Never Before" by Deep Purple.

Karl Cochran picked "Still Alive & Well" by Johnny Winter and "Changes" by Buddy Miles and Jimi Hendrix.

Everybody threw in their song ideas, and we recorded them. They had initially started recording at Karl's place in Studio City, but then we went over to Curt Cuomo's studio where it just sounded better. The band was dubbed the Eric Singer Project (ESP) and the album was called *Lost and Spaced*. Keith released the first run of records as promised and made it available online only. It then started to spread throughout the Kiss Army worldwide.

We knew a guy named Kuni from Los Angeles, who was the head of Zain Records in Japan and was a massive Kiss fan. He released the album in Japan for fans. Then Universal Records wanted it for Europe, and it kept spreading.

Bruce knew a Greek guy Nicolas Kostadimas who said, "Bring ESP over to Europe!"

He put together a tour for ESP where we played about eight shows. We then went back and did eight more, then we went back and did ten more shows. It just kept getting bigger and bigger and bigger. Eric was smart about it, though: he would go in the dead of winter and at times when nobody else was touring in Europe. That way, we were the only game in town. I think the first four or five years we went over to Europe six or seven times. The last time we were there, we did great fucking business; it was awesome.

Along the way, Karl dropped out of the project, so we got Chuck Garric from Alice Cooper's band to play bass. There are videos everywhere of that band performing, including a DVD release of us playing *Live at the Marquee* in Sydney, Australia.

The four of us would tour as a band for three weeks and play fifteen sold-out shows. We had ESP records, ESP posters, and ESP T-shirts for sale, but we would also sell my CDs, photos, and pick packs. Eric Singer would have drumsticks and photos for fans to buy, and Bruce and Chuck would have photos and their solo records and merch as well.

ESP is so funny; it's like a rolling circus. I love watching Eric fuck with Bruce, though. He's a funny guy with a sarcastic sense of humor. Chuck and I would sit in the back of the van. Nicolas would get in the driver's seat, and Eric would then get in and say, "Hey, guys, watch this: when Bruce gets here, I'm going to wind him up."

We would start driving to the venue, and Eric would ask, "Hey, guys, just out of curiosity, does anybody else have the big jacuzzi tub and the fireplace in their room?"

We'd all say, "Uh, no!"

Then Bruce would let rip, "What the fuck? You have a fucking fireplace and a fucking jacuzzi in your room?"

Bruce would glare at our tour manager Nicholas, thinking he got shafted on the room big time, while we all laughed in the back. But Bruce would come right back at Eric as well. They would just wind each other up in fun ways the whole fucking tour, as they had done throughout their long history of touring together in Kiss since 1991.

We haven't done it for a little while, but I'm thinking now that Kiss is on their farewell tour with Eric Singer, ESP may well pick back up again in the not-too-distant future.

When Mayhem Records closed shop after going broke, Paul Bibeau founded a new label called Spitfire Records in September 1998 and brought across his best staff from Mayhem. He shopped around and partnered with London-based Eagle Rock Entertainment, which was looking to break into the American market.

Union signed on with Spitfire for our next studio album *The Blue Room*. They also signed other artists like Alice Cooper, Black Label Society, and Enuff Z'Nuff. We had more money from a bigger promotional budget, better marketing.

So, we immediately started writing songs for our next Union album. Eric Singer had a little building out the back of his North Hollywood house, next to his pool, which is where we used to do our ESP rehearsals. Bruce asked him if we could rehearse and write our album there, and he was cool enough to let us use it.

John Greenberg and Tim Heyne worked with numerous bands, including Ratt and Cinderella, and they also managed some record producers to help them source, negotiate, and secure contract work. One of their producers was Bob Marlette, who had just done Alice Cooper's *Brutal Planet* album. Bob came on board to produce our next Union album.

As we got into songwriting mode, I was lying in bed watching TV one night and a song idea came to me from out of nowhere. For me, once I start writing and recording in a studio, all the gears suddenly kick in and my brain is always thinking about music.

I got up and grabbed my guitar and went into the bathroom, where I sat down and played the earliest version of a song that became "Do Your Own Thing," as well as another called "I Wanna Be." When I got to Eric's place the next day, I showed them to the band, and everybody dug them. Bob Marlette dug them too, so we worked on them more. We worked away in Eric's place over two weeks or so, collaborating on the writing process, and then went into A&M Studios and recorded the drum tracks. Once we were happy with those, we shifted recording to Bob's house, where we built the songs up using Pro Tools software, so it was all recording, cutting, pasting, editing, and mixing.

We got to the point where it was time for me to write lyrics and then record vocals. Some of the songs came together very easy lyrically. "Dead" was easy, as were "Do Your Own Thing" and "I Wanna Be."

I wrote "Shine" about the Columbine High School massacre and all the community uproar following it. At that time, it was the deadliest school shooting in US history. Two twelfth grade students went into school, and they fucking killed twelve kids and a teacher, and then everybody in America was up in arms, saying, "Oh, God. Those two boys were totally corrupted by *The Basketball Diaries* movie and Marilyn Manson. They dressed like him, wore his T-shirts, etc."

If you listen to the lyrics for "Shine," I'm basically saying, "People, seriously! Stop pointing the fucking finger. Children are like computers: you get out of them what do you put into them."

The parents were like, "Oh, he listened to Marilyn Manson and that made him go on a killing spree."

My view was, "Okay, explain this Mom and Dad, in your wealthy affluent area in fucking Denver: how is it that your son had hand grenades under his fucking bed and pipe bombs, and you didn't even know?"

"Occupation alibis"—using the excuse that they were too busy with work to even fucking notice what was going on in their own fucking home.

The song "Everything's Alright" didn't come so easy, though; I was pulling my hair out because I didn't know what to say. I tried for days but hadn't come up with anything. Then I was driving in the car with my son Ian, when he said to me, "Hey, Dad, I liked that station that you had on before with The Beatles. Could you put that on again?"

An AM radio station in Los Angeles programmed The Beatles' songs twenty-four hours a day, seven days a week for about six months. So, I put that station on, and we listened to whatever Beatles songs they chose to play for us. As I sat there driving with my son next to me, I thought about how fucking cool The Beatles were and how I felt everything was all right in my world whenever I listened to them. Our parents listened to them, we listened to them, and now our kids are listening to them. I looked at Ian and thought it was amazing that my twelve-year-old was freaking out over them.

There will never-ever be another band like The Beatles—a band that can consistently, with each generation, continue to sell fucking records like they do and have such an appeal to so many different generations of fans. I'm sure that'll be happening for centuries to come, like how people still listen to fucking Beethoven and Tchaikovsky.

As I was thinking all this, the radio played their song "Good Day Sunshine." I started thinking of the song I needed lyrics for when it struck me that I should just write a lyrical tribute to The Beatles. When the rest of the band and Bob Marlette first heard my lyrics, they said, "What the fuck are these lyrics about?"

I said, "Well, if you actually read the lyrics, everything's about songs by The Beatles."

On second listen, they said, "Oh, fuck, that's awesome!"

The chorus then simply says, *"Hello, Goodbye,"* which was their 7" single I used to play to death with my cousin Andrew on his record player on Sundays when we were kids, and then, *"Good Day, Sunshine,"* for the song I heard on the radio that triggered this fun tribute to my favorite band.

Another song, "Hypnotized," was based on the porn star Savannah. I had met her before she committed suicide, although I didn't fuck her like Vince Neil. I thought she had a crazy life story, but somewhat typical of a lot of girls who endure some sort of traumatic incident in their young lives and then get into that whole scene. They start doing drugs and life gets fucking crazier and before they realize it, one thing after another happens and they get on a massive downward spiral they can't pull out of. People just open a magazine and say, "Oh, yeah, fuck dude, look at the tits on this one!" but don't know of all the bullshit that happened in their life prior to that moment being captured as a picture. Perhaps it's the same with rock magazines as well.

There were also quite a few songs on the record where I was indirectly giving a cathartic fuck you to people because I was angry. "Who Do You Think You Are?" is one that was fueled by all the music industry people who were writing Bruce and I off as passé, and also to past band management.

"Dead" was another one I wrote about such industry people and my recent experiences. For example, Gerri Miller from *Metal Edge* magazine was a massive supporter of Union. She was a huge fan of Kiss and a huge fan of Mötley and was naturally excited when she found out Bruce and I were putting a new band together.

She quickly contacted us for an interview, so we invited her down to hear the songs, and she absolutely loved what she heard. From that moment on, she gave us lots of ongoing positive coverage in her magazine, simply because she loved the band. Then we copped flack for it with all these people saying shit like, "John Corabi must be licking Gerri's pussy, and she's probably sucking Bruce's dick."

I got tired of people giving her a hard time and giving us a hard time so songs like "Dead" and "Who Do You Think You Are?" were directed at those motherfuckers as well, and lyrically it's basically me telling them all to fuck off.

There were a couple of songs I wish I could take back and work on, though, because I was under a deadline and got outvoted by the other three guys in the band. "Nah, dude, you're overthinking it. It's fine," they told me.

Well, I didn't want it to be fine, I wanted it to be fucking awesome! However, I do tend to overthink things, which is why it sometimes takes me longer to do shit than the next guy. I still think it's a great album, though.

It was a few days before we were to do a photo shoot for the new record, and I decided to get the word "Anti" tattooed across my stomach. The tattoo took up most of my stomach, but now it doesn't so much… and it's not because the tattoo shrunk.

Whenever somebody sees it, I invariably get asked, "Anti what?"

I realized I was anti-shit, and I still am! I'm anti-racism. I'm anti-envy; I'm anti-fads; I'm anti-unhappiness; I'm anti-today's radio programming. There's so much fucking great music, but really, why do we have to listen to the same twenty-five fucking songs on the radio all the time? I'm anti-negativity, as ironic as that could seem.

Perhaps I should have thought it through more. I thought the word was a statement, but apparently, it's vague. I do like its vagueness, though; it's like fill-in the fucking blank!

I'm not a mean-spirited person or a judgmental person, because I'm anti that, too. I fucking hate it when people judge other people. I know we may all do it in jest sometimes, but I don't like it when people are serious about stereotyping and judging other people.

"Oh my God, look at those two guys holding hands! Disgusting. Abomination."

It rages in my head. You know what, "Go fuck yourself. Who cares? Is it really hurting you?"

Maybe I've seen the best and worst in other people more than others because I travel so much, but one thing I'm really anti is the fact that a lot of people don't respect each other's viewpoints or opinions, especially today. They'll DEMAND respect, but can't give it.

Layla spoke on the phone with her dad one day, and she mentioned in conversation that things were tight financially as we tried to get ahead. So her dad invited us to come and live with him on his farm near

Minnesota, since he was now divorcing his second wife and living there alone. He said, "I've got the big old farmhouse and barn here on more than ten acres, so why don't you both come out here? You can stay for a while, and if you like it out here, we can just build you a house on the other side of my property."

I knew I could tour based from anywhere, and I really liked her dad, plus I was really looking forward to the cheaper lifestyle, but I told Layla it was up to her.

"Well, I do miss my family," she said.

I told her I would be happy if I could fly Ian out a couple of times a month to stay for a week or so, which would be straight-forward enough since Southwest Airlines flies from LA direct to Minneapolis.

We made all the necessary arrangements and left the Granada Hills house behind and moved to the state of Minnesota, an hour-and-a-half drive southwest of Minneapolis to a small town called Nicollet—population: 1,000. The town didn't even have a traffic light.

In all honesty, though, it wasn't bad in Nicollet. It was actually beautiful there, but it was fucking freezing. Even though I had grown up in so many snowy Philadelphia winters, it took me a while to get used to the cold temperatures there.

We selected and released our first single called "Do Your Own Thing" and suddenly Union went from getting no airplay at all to having the single added for play on more than a hundred radio stations across America. The bigger budget afforded us a promo guy named Rob Gill, who worked with all the radio stations and garnered great airplay. I flew out to LA as a low-budget tour was planned with Larry Morand as our tour manager, and he hired a driver who had never driven a tour bus before. It was an ancient, beat-up Eagle bus with a stick-shift on the floor.

We headed to San Diego for our first show and were to pick-up our bass player Jamie on the way. The bus driver forgot about Jamie and halfway to San Diego, we got a call from him asking, "Where the fuck are you guys? How much longer are you going to be?"

We told the driver to turn around and head to Pasadena to pick up Jamie as planned.

He got lost going to Santa Barbara and again going to Phoenix, Arizona. Once we eventually got to Phoenix, he raked the whole side of the bus and damaged it on something. That was his last straw, so Larry fired him and sent him home.

We replaced him with a badass driver named Spodey, who looked like Ian Anderson from Jethro Tull. As we drove from Phoenix to Denver, we were lying in our bunks and noticed the temperature really started dropping; it was fucking freezing. We looked at the air vents on the bus floor and there was fucking snow coming up through them.

We pulled the bus over in the middle of a snowstorm and realized that when the side of the bus got raked, the corners on two of the bay doors weakened and were now peeled back, like it had been through a fucking can opener. As we did seventy down the road, we were pulling the snow and cold air into the bays and up through the vents in the floor. We got going again but stopped at the first Walmart we saw and bought eight sleeping bags and some hoodies for extra warmth in our bunks.

As we rolled up to the clubs, though, the shows were now selling out—places like Pop's in St. Louis, and Birch Hill in New Jersey. We could feel the crowd numbers swelling as we sold out 600-, 800-, 1,000-capacity venues. Not only were we making more money from ticket sales, we were also selling more merch at the shows as well.

However, we weren't selling many records at all. We sent advanced promo copies of the full album out to all the radio stations, magazines, and press outlets during November and December 1999 and released a Happy Holidays advance CD of "Do Your Own Thing" for the festive season to help build the hype.

With the advanced releases, many industry people had lived with our album over the holidays; they had it for two or three months before Spitfire released it on February 22, 2000: 2-22-2k, it was all twos.

With all the radio airplay and promotion, album sales in the first week were respectable. We were getting great reviews, and were given the "heat-seekers" tag on the charts and moved about 7,000 units. Week two sales numbers came in and it was probably the most fucking severe drop in the history of records, down to something like a paltry sixty-three units. We scratched our heads saying, "What the fuck? How the fuck does that happen?"

As we then played concerts, fans came up to us after the show and handed us CDs with homemade covers, saying, "Nice to meet you, could you sign this?"

I would look at the CD and ask, "Where did you get this?"

The response was, "Oh, I burned it off the internet."

I could never say, "Well, fuck you, you fucking asshole. I'm not fucking signing that!" So I'd sign it and move along.

Bruce would say to me, "I signed nine fucking CDs tonight that were burned."

I'd ask, "Did you see my signature on any of the ones you signed? No? Well, yours weren't on the ones that I signed, so make that fucking eighteen."

We were signing twenty to twenty-five burned CDs a gig. Finally, I asked a fan, "What the fuck is this Napster thing that everybody's talking about?"

"Oh, it's just a website, dude. They have entire records on there. You can just fucking download the records for free."

So as sure as shit, I got home, went on Napster and saw our album was available, along with countless others. I could see the date it was first uploaded; our entire record had been on there for free from November, all of December, all of January, and half of February, all before our record came out. The fans who bought it on release were ones that wanted a physical product with all the packaging artwork. The rest didn't give a fuck. Napster and MP3 files changed the whole music industry.

We had only been on the farm for a month when I split and went on tour with Union in support of our new album *The Blue Room*. While I was on the road, Layla started having a rough time. Going through a divorce, her dad was miserable. He worked all day then came home and started drinking his blues away. I went back to Minnesota for a few days in between concerts to give her some support and then went back out on the road.

Now, living a relatively mellow country life away from Los Angeles, I thought everything with Layla and I had settled down. I felt our fucking wild, experimental days were now behind us. It was a quieter life on the farm.

She got the Union band symbol tattooed on her lower back in the tramp-stamp position, and I was feeling she was being more dedicated to me. I'm not sure if it was something in the water there, but something fucking possessed me to start talking about getting married. Layla then mentioned it to her mom, who said, "I think it would be great! You should get married on the beach here in Pensacola, Florida. We'll have the whole family down, and John can bring his kids down."

We started making wedding plans.

Union went back over to Scandinavia in the summer of 2000, thanks again to the local Kiss Army who set up a tour for us. We played a show in Stockholm at Pub Anchor and by the time we left the venue it was probably 2:00 a.m., so we headed straight to a TV station to set-up for a live acoustic performance on a morning show called Nyhetsmorgon. After being up all night, we sound-checked at six in the morning. A few hours later we played "October Morning Wind" to open the program, then waited another two hours to play "Hypnotized" to end the show.

We then loaded the van up with our gear and drove from the TV station to Sweden Rock Festival, where we played in a delirious, sleep-deprived state on the main stage with Saxon, King's X, Alice Cooper, and Dio.

The Kiss Army guys made lots of fucking calls to make it all happen and made sure we got paid well. They drove us around everywhere, and even made sure our riders were right. They went above and beyond the call of duty for us, which was greatly appreciated. We saw our following had really grown from our first tour of those countries, but unfortunately it wasn't sustainable. We just weren't making a decent living financially.

20
Round and Round

As touring with Union slowed to a crawl, I bounced back and forth between my Minnesota residence with Layla and doing a Union gig or two. We could feel the band was near the end of our road.

Bruce auditioned for Grand Funk Railroad. They offered him a great salary to go out and do a show on Friday, a show on Saturday, maybe one on Sunday, and then he'd be home. For those two or three shows a week, he would make more than he was making lugging with us in Union for ten or thirteen weeks on the road.

While Bruce was waiting to hear if he got the Grand Funk gig, I went to the Key Club one night to see Metal Skool play, who are known as Steel Panther these days. Ratt's drummer Bobby Blotzer was there and said to me, "Hey, dude, we're looking for a singer."

Ratt enjoyed some real commercial success through the eighties, when each of their four studio albums went platinum. They were a significant early Hollywood band in that Sunset Strip scene and now they needed a singer to replace Stephen Pearcy.

I told him, "Not interested, dude. I don't want to be your singer. I bought that shirt with the fucking Mötley gig. I'm not wearing it again."

He said, "If you change your mind, give me a call."

I was then talking with their bassist Robbie Crane and told him about my exchange with Bobby. He said, "Well, we need a guitar player, too, since Kerri Kelli is leaving to go play in Slash's band and they're going on tour with AC/DC. Do you know any guitarists?"

I said, "Well, I'll do that. I can play guitar."

Word got back to their lead guitarist Warren DeMartini, and he invited me over to his house to jam. He asked me to learn the guitar solo to "Round and Round" and do it with him. I went to his house to play electric guitar, and we sat there with no amps. I started playing the song with him, and progressed to do the solo together, before he stopped and said, "Yeah, that'll work. All right, good. You're in!"

Bruce then told me he got the Grand Funk Railroad gig. I said, "Good, because I'm now in Ratt."

Union's bassist Jamie and drummer Brent wound up joining Vince Neil's solo band after a while. It sure is strange how life works out sometimes.

Warren called me a few days after my successful audition and said, "Hey, dude. I've got to ask you a question: do you have an issue with our singer?"

At that point, I didn't even know who would be singing. I asked, "Is Pearcy back? I don't know who your singer is."

He apologized and said, "Oh, shit, dude, it's Jizzy Pearl!"

I was upfront with Warren, "Here's the deal, dude, I don't have an issue with Jizzy at all, but you may have to go and talk to him. I don't want to hear anything about my girlfriend Layla; I don't want to discuss it. I'm just here to do my job. I'll learn the songs, play the shows, get my pay, and leave. That's it. So I'm good with him, if he's cool with me."

I hit the road with Ratt and there were a few incidents on the first tour where Jizzy and I rubbed each other the wrong way. One night he had a little too much wine, and I had some whiskey under my belt, when some shit started between him and another guy Joe Anthony on the bus. I grabbed Jizzy and said something like, "Hey, dude, just chill out," and he started on me about Layla.

"I'm not going to do this with you," I told him, and refused to get into it with him.

We used to jokingly call him Jizzilla because he was fine until he started drinking red wine, then he would turn into a monster and start slapping people. Jizzy and I had some issues to begin with, but we got through it.

A Ratt fan was giving Jizzy shit one night about being the new singer, mouthing off and flipping him off, just like I used to get when I replaced Vince in Mötley. As we played, Jizzy came over to my side of the stage and the guy flipped him off again from two or three people deep from the front.

I reached into the crowd and grabbed the guy by his fucking hair and pulled him almost up onto the stage. I said to him, "Dude, seriously, do you really want to do this? Are you here to have a good fucking time or are you here to be a fucking jerk off?"

He backpedaled, saying, "Nah, I'll be cool. I'll be cool."

I told him, "Stephen's not here, so Jizzy took a gig that was offered to him. Come on, dude, let it go."

The guy was fine after that, and so was Jizzy, after he saw me sticking up for him.

Jizzy and I have been good friends with each other ever since that show.

In the first year I played with Ratt, if I didn't have any shows with them and Bruce also had a break from Grand Funk, we'd play some Union shows. This included some very successful shows in South America—Argentina actually being Union's last show with the four of us together. We also went over to Japan for four shows, but with a fill-in drummer, as Brent couldn't make it.

During another break between Ratt shows, Layla and I got married in Pensacola, Florida. I flew my son Ian in for it, while Layla went down ahead of me with her mom. I flew in, drove into town, met Layla, and got the marriage license.

We married the following day on March 10, 2001. I stayed one more day and had a shrimp and crawfish boil with her whole family, then flew out the next morning to go back on tour with Ratt. Ian flew home to LA, and Layla stayed in Pensacola with her mom and stepfather a while longer before she flew back to Minnesota.

Her grandfather on her mom's side of the family had recently passed away, so there was a decent inheritance that her mother, aunts, and uncles got. Her mom paid for the Pensacola beach house that we stayed in; she wouldn't take a penny from me for it. She even paid for the wedding photographer and the shrimp boil, then gave us a wedding card with $10,000 in it as a gift. It was extremely generous of her to do that, and I'll never forget her generosity.

Us newlyweds were still talking with Layla's dad about splitting his parcel of land and selling about half his acreage to me, but we ran into a zoning issue that was preventing the sale. We were living in her dad's house and couldn't build another house for us on his land.

By this stage, though, Layla was over the country life as there was absolutely nothing for her to do on the farm or in the small town, and her health was waning again. On top of that, she felt she was just babysitting her dad who was fucking miserable as he fell apart going through another divorce.

She definitely wasn't happy and didn't know what to do, so I said, "Well, we can go back to California if you'd like."

My friend Bernadette called to talk about my dog Cody that she was looking after. She had just bought a huge ranch house in California's High Desert with about ten acres of land, closest to a little town called Acton. It had plenty of room for her thirty Alaskan Malamutes.

There was no significant other in Bernie's life, so she said, "If you and Layla want to move back to California, I have a huge apartment on the whole top of the building that the previous owner built for his daughter. It has a separate entrance and is self-contained. It'd be good to have somebody around for a while, since it's just me and the animals."

She continued, "You two can just live rent-free in the upper apartment while Layla gets her health back on track. You'll be close to Ian, you can have your dog back, and there's no financial burden at all."

Layla and I saw it as a ticket out of rural boredom hell, so we loaded up a trailer again and headed back west to California.

Somebody from Mötley's management company called and said, "Hey, we're doing an autobiography on Mötley Crüe called *The Dirt* with an author Neil Strauss. We weren't going to include you in the book, but he feels like you are a big part of their history, so he wants to interview you for it. Are you cool with doing that?"

When I said I was fine to do it, I was asked, "Well, what do you want for doing the book interviews and being a contributor?"

They were going to pay me, but like a fucking moron I said, "No, it's fine. I don't want any payment. The only thing I would like for doing these interviews is if I can be sent five or ten copies of the book when it comes out. If you can have the guys sign them, then I'll sign them, too, and give one to my son, my dad, my brothers and sisters, and maybe a few close friends."

"Yeah, sure. No worries. How about a dozen books then?" they offered. "Yep, that'd be great. Cool, done."

I did my interviews with Neil Strauss, probably three or four of them for about four hours each time. Strauss said, "This is awesome, thank you, buddy."

"Okay, great," I said, before I reiterated with Strauss, "Hey, can you just make sure that when it's done, I get my twelve copies of the book?"

"Sure, no worries. Cool," I was again told.

So, *The Dirt: Confessions of the World's Most Notorious Rock Band* came out in hardcover during May 2001 and spent the next month on the *New York Times* Bestseller list. No package arrived for me. Then the paperback edition came out—still nothing on my end. I felt I had been stiffed.

I got asked about Mötley and the book during all my media interviews at the time, and one day I griped about it a bit. One of the band members saw the interview and sent me an email and wrote something like, "Crab, why the fuck would I give you a copy of the book? I don't even have one. Dude, they're only thirty bucks, go buy one!"

It annoyed the shit out of me, and as of this writing, I do own one copy of *The Dirt*, given to me as a gift by a friend. I refused to buy it simply on principle, and I have signed thousands of them for the fans that were kind enough to include me and ask for my autograph.

A friend of mine, Leanne, took some headshot photos of me, and then took some great swimsuit and topless *Playboy*-esque modeling style shots of Layla down on Venice Beach. The idea was to use them on a website they were building to get modeling assignments at events like NAMM shows or other trade shows where it was commonplace to have a couple of hot chicks at the Bose speakers stand, for example.

Due to her rheumatoid arthritis, Layla couldn't sit at a desk all day, but she couldn't stand and be on her feet all day either. So shift assignments like this were something where she could move around to the degree she needed to. It was almost impossible for her to sit for an hour, because her joints would lock-up in that position and hurt.

We also started a website for her that was a play on the Candyland board game, and in obvious fashion she named the website Laylaland. I didn't mind the photos and making money that way as it was done tastefully, plus it gave her a lot of free time to dedicate to her art and maybe getting some of her paintings sold online as well.

I was out of town playing shows when Layla got a call from a guy at a liquor company who said, "I really love your look. My company is sponsoring tours with a brand of Scotch called Cutty Sark. We're doing a concert series all through America called the Rock the Boat Tour. We're going to have two or three bands on the tour, headlined by Cold from Jacksonville, Florida. We're going to sponsor the whole tour and want to put together a bunch of sexy Cutty girls to go out and emcee the shows, wearing black shorts and form-fitted tight Cutty tops. We want you to give Cutty Sark cups to people and throw out promotional wristbands, hats, blinking buttons, and other items. You'll travel on your own bus with three or four other girls. We'll take care of a lot of your costs, and you'll be paid about $1,500 a week. I'd love you to join us on the road for it."

At first, Layla said to me, "I don't know about this. What do you think?"

I asked her, "Other than being in Atlanta, Minnesota, and LA, have you ever been anywhere else? Have you ever toured before? Have you ever traveled?"

When she said she hadn't, and thinking the opportunity ticked all her job health constraint boxes, I said, "Well, honestly, I could use a little help financially, plus I see this as an opportunity for you to get on a tour bus and travel all over the United States and have some fun."

They also talked about going over to Europe. She met with the organizer who called her back a week later and said, "We'd love to have you on board."

Layla asked me again, "Are you sure you're cool with me doing it? We just got married, so how are we going to see each other?"

I reassured her, "Hey, if I'm on tour and you're on tour, when you have a break, you come and see me. Or I can come see you. We'll figure it out. I'm going to be making very good money with Ratt. You'll be making really good money, too. This is good; it's awesome actually. Let's do this!"

I was in Arizona on tour with Ratt when I woke to hear our sound guy, Randy Meullier, running up and down the bus, saying, "Dude, dude. Oh my God, you've got to fucking see this. We're being attacked!"

I got out of my bunk and saw everybody in the front of the bus watching live TV—it was September 11, 2001, and planes had flown into the World Trade Center twin towers and the fucking Pentagon.

I stood watching in disbelief; we were all stunned. Layla called me, freaking out, saying, "Oh my God, I've got to go to NYC in a week to meet all the Cutty girls and have a photoshoot with them. I don't know if I want to go."

I talked her off the ledge and calmed her down so she didn't quit before she began. Their plan was to do a bunch of press and hit all the New York radio stations, then get on a tour bus and head to Allentown, Pennsylvania, for the first of about forty shows.

Ratt decided to cancel that night's gig in Tucson. Everybody was really somber after the day's horrific events, and the rest of the tour just had a weird fucking vibe to it.

I was still out on the road doing my thing a couple of weeks later when Layla flew to New York. She called me every day saying, "Oh my God, this is going to be so much fun. We went to the *Howard Stern Show*, we did this, and we did that. The posters from the photo shoot look awesome."

I was so happy for her and somewhat relieved.

The day their promotional work in New York was done, they got on the tour bus to head to Allentown, and she called me again later that night. This time she was a mess, hysterically crying to me, "God, I don't know if I can do this, babe. I just saw our tour schedule. We're going to be out on the road until December—it's only the end of September! I don't know if I can do this."

I reassured her again, telling her that she needed to do it for a multitude of positive reasons. She said, "I love you. You're so important to me. I don't want to lose you. You're the love of my life. I can't breathe without you."

Then she pleaded, "Just promise me we'll talk every day, and if we can, we've got to make sure we make time to see each other, and you'll come and see me, right?"

I said, "Yes, I will call every day and we will see each other. I promise. It's all good, no worries."

Then the following day I didn't hear anything from her, so I gave her a call. I tried numerous times, but each time it just rang and went to voicemail. I sent her a text, asking her to call me when she got it, but I got no reply.

I tried calling again the next day, but it still kept going to voicemail. I started getting worried, so I left a message, "Layla, what the fuck? Is everything okay? Are you alive? What the fuck is the deal? You were so insistent on us talking daily."

She called me after a few days and explained, "Oh my God. You don't understand. We're getting up early in the morning; we're going to radio stations or fucking TV stations, then we've got to do promos and meet and greets with the band. Then we've got to go and set the room up and hang banners because we don't have a crew. The bands have their crew, but we don't have one. We're setting everything up including the merch tables with all these wristbands, blinking buttons, and hats, plus three different T-shirts. We've got a backdrop that needs to be hung at the back of the stage. I literally haven't gotten any sleep at all."

The way she explained it, it made sense to me. It sounded like a lot of shit she had to do.

I played a few more Ratt shows and then had a little break of about two weeks from my tour. Layla's tour was coming through LA at the time, so I met her at the House of Blues. She talked with the other Cutty girls and asked if it was cool if I joined them on the tour bus for a little while, so I jumped on for three shows in San Francisco, Sacramento, and Portland.

I took all the Cutty girls out for dinner one night, as well as the guys from the support band Dope. Those guys were fucking scrimping, so I said, "Come on, come with us. We'll go get some food." I was happy to pick-up the tab for everybody's dinner and drinks that night. We had a fun night out.

Layla and I noticed on our tour schedules that we would both be in Cleveland, Ohio, on Thanksgiving Day, staying just six blocks from each other. We also saw that Layla's tour would be playing in Chicago two days prior, and I would also be in Chicago on a day off.

As we said goodbye to each other on the West Coast, we looked forward to seeing each other in Chicago in two to three weeks' time, and then enjoying our first Thanksgiving together as a married couple. I thought it was going to be awesome.

Once I got into Chicago the night before her, I called but didn't hear back. I tried again four or five times during the next day that I had off but heard nothing back the whole day—no fucking answer and no fucking reply to any of my voicemails and texts. Nothing!

I knew her schedule said she would be in Chicago, but I didn't know what hotel she was going to be staying at. I called her mom and asked, "Hey, have you heard from Layla? I haven't heard from her in a week and I'm not real happy about it."

Her mom just made some off-color joke about it, so I didn't get any help from her.

I stayed up until two o'clock in the morning, watching TV and fucking stewing. This whole not calling thing had been sporadic all through the whole fucking tour, and I was particularly pissed that she had left me high and dry during the opportunistic time we planned to be together.

Something was not right, so I called her again and said, "Layla, this is your husband. If I do not hear from you by morning, I am going to call a fucking lawyer, and I'm going to proceed to file for a divorce. Something is going on. Something's not right, and I'm pissed. This is fucked up." Then I went to bed.

When I woke the next morning, I checked my phone and saw no messages. I called her again and said, "Okay, it's John. I'm fucking done with this shit. I'm just fucking telling you right now, you and I are through. I don't give a shit. I'm fucking done with this bullshit. Don't fucking call me. I don't want to hear from you. I don't want to see your fucking face. I'm done. I'm filing for divorce," and I hung up.

I wasn't sad though, I was angry.

I got to the venue for that night's gig as the crew were loading in. Our tour manager Caesar came over to me inside the venue and said, "Crab, I think you should go out to our tour bus."

"Why?" I snapped back at him.

He said, "Your wife is on the bus."

When I walked into the bus, everybody else who was in there got up and walked out without saying a fucking word.

Layla was bawling. "I just got your message. I'm so fucking sorry. I'm such a horrible wife," she sobbed.

"I'm not going to argue that point with you because you're fucking right!" I told her.

"You had two days off, and I had two days off. Why did I not hear from you on the days that we were supposed to hang out? I even called your fucking mother trying to reach you. What the fuck, Layla?" I shouted at her.

Wiping the makeup from her eyes as she sobbed, she said, "I charged my phone and it was in my bunk. When we arrived in Chicago, I put my things in my suitcase and grabbed my shoes, but I left my phone on the bus. Then when the bus driver dropped us off at the hotel, he took the bus and parked it somewhere else; it was in a different lot. He only brought the bus back this afternoon when he picked us up, so I just got your messages now. I'm so sorry."

As pissed as I was, it was plausible. I can't say that I haven't done something like that on the road before. It also made sense because I know there's not a lot of parking for tour buses in New York City and Chicago.

I backpedaled and said in a calmer manner, "Okay, that's fine, but why the fuck am I not hearing from you for four or five days at a time?"

Still crying hysterically, she said, "I told you the schedules are fucking crazy! I can't wait for this tour to be over. I just want to go home and lie in bed with you for a week."

She got up and started hugging me tight, while sobbing, "I'm so sorry; I'm so sorry."

"Okay, okay, calm down, calm down," I told her.

Minutes later, she locked the fucking back lounge door of the tour bus, took off her clothes, and quickly made me forget what we were arguing about.

I played my gig, and she did hers, and as we parted again, I said, "See you in two days for Thanksgiving in Cleveland, baby."

I called my wife when I got into my Cleveland hotel, keen to meet up for a nice Thanksgiving dinner. Layla answered this time, but said, "I can't come and meet you for dinner, unfortunately. I'm just slammed here. I just can't do it, sorry."

I asked what time her show was, and then said, "Well, I'll be finished with my show a little earlier than you, so I'll come over. I know you're leaving later tonight, but I'm not leaving until tomorrow morning and I'd love to see you. We're literally six blocks from each other, so I'll come to you."

After Ratt's set, I headed over to the Aragon Ballroom where Cold and Dope played. I went in and said hello to all the Cutty girls, and Layla said to me, "They let me get done a little early since we're moving on tonight. I just want to spend a few minutes with you on the bus."

We went on the bus and hung out for a little while, with the rear lounge door locked of course.

I then heard the front door of the bus open, then shut, followed by an argument that seemed to start outside the bus. Someone was getting dragged back in the club, while yelling, "You fucking bitch. Fuck you."

I looked out but couldn't see who was arguing and making noise. By the time I opened the bus door for a minute, I faintly saw some people in the distance scuffling, but it felt like it was just the tail end of whatever just happened.

At the end of the night, the girls were packed-up and ready to roll on, so I gave Layla another hug and kiss goodbye until I was to see her next in New York in early December.

I was scheduled to arrive in New York the day of her last show of the tour, before I played with Ratt the following night. She was going to come to my show before flying home, and I said she could bring the other Cutty girls along and they would be welcome to hang out at the show.

You guessed it: the same old situation. I didn't fucking hear from her again, all day.

When she finally called me before I hit the stage that night, she explained, "Oh, we had to do final counts on all the merch that was left, so I was counting all the T-shirts and the hats and the blinking buttons. Then they gave us our last pay and for a job well done, they also gave us a bonus, and took the four of us Cutty girls to a day spa. So, we've been at a day spa all day."

"That's fucking nice, but a text or something would have been fucking appreciated," I snapped, feeling that something just wasn't right, and I was fucking angry again.

"I know, I'm sorry," she said.

I performed in New York City with Ratt that mid-December night in a foul fucking mood. None of the Cutty girls came to the show, including my wife. The next morning, Layla got up and flew home to LA and started calling me again—five fucking times a day, every day.

"Oh my God, I'm so glad that tour's over. Now I have time I can talk to you," she said.

I figured she probably just wasn't cut-out for tour life and couldn't handle the demands of it all. It seemed things were starting to get back to normal between us, now that she was home again.

I was to arrive home from tour on December 20, and as it got closer, Layla said, "I hope you're not mad at me, but Aubrey (one of her Cutty friends) is working at a convention in Atlanta that weekend, and she asked me to do it with her. They said they'd fly me out and pay me a thousand bucks for the two days. I hope you don't mind. I'll only be gone for the three nights, then we'll have Christmas together."

Prior to being one of the Cutty girls touring with my wife, Aubrey had done *Playboy* and a lot of other modelling work, eventually being one of the models holding a briefcase on the TV show *Deal or No Deal* with Howie Mandel.

I said, "Sure, no problem. Instead of me flying home from the tour, do you want me to fly down to Atlanta instead, and then we could fly home together once you've finished your job with Aubrey?"

She said, "No, it's cool. I'm going to be working the whole time at this convention thing anyway, so you may as well just head home, get a Christmas tree, and I'll see you there a few days later." We said our goodbyes, hung up, and she texted me all her hotel information and schedule.

So I flew home to LA as intended, probably crossing paths with her in the sky as she flew to Atlanta. I had no sooner started to unpack when I got a call from my friend Lisa Jansen, who used to manage Sass Jordan and Vince Neil at one point. After exchanging pleasantries, Lisa asked, "Do you like Alanis Morissette's music?"

I said, "Yeah, that fucking *Jagged Little Pill* album is great! Why?"

Lisa said, "Alanis is looking for a guitar player, but she wants somebody who can also sing. Would you be interested in doing it? It's a stadium tour, and it's extremely good money. I know her manager, and I know they'll take good care of you."

"I love it, sounds great," I said.

She instructed me, "Put a resume together, email it to me, and I'll forward it to her manager for consideration."

I'm perhaps the most computer-illiterate person you'll ever meet. I knew how to turn on my big old CRT monitor and do some basic things online with my computer setup, including printer and fax. The concept of "windows" and them minimizing and maximizing and fucking disappearing on me would do my fucking head in, though.

I don't think I had ever put together a proper music resume in my life before, but now was a great time to do it. I added my name on the top of the blank computer document. Then I listed all the bands I've played with, and all my albums recorded. It was a challenge, but after a while I felt it was shaping up well. However, I thought it could do with a current picture of me, so I tried to find a decent one of me with my long black dreadlocks.

I eventually found one I liked and dragged it onto my resume. I managed to email it off to Lisa, and then I wanted to print myself a copy of it. I scrolled to hit the print button. I don't know what the fuck I hit instead over on the top left-hand side of my screen, but my resume disappeared, and some other window opened and was then showing me the entire history of the printer.

I said to myself, "What the fuck is this window?" As I thought about how to get rid of it from the screen, I also wondered what it was and why it was there. I clicked on the first line-item file and a picture opened on the screen.

It was a nude photo of my wife with a note, "I miss you. I can't wait to be in your arms again." Unfortunately, I had never seen this photo; she didn't send it to ME, so I hit print. I double-clicked on the next one and it was another nude photo of her. The third one was a photo of a familiar looking guy with his cock out, print. I went through this whole fucking print history, then started digging into more history on the computer. Recent events in our married life suddenly became much clearer to me.

Layla was fucking around on me with Simon from the band Dope, with whom she'd just been touring with for months. What pissed me off even more was it wasn't the singer. It wasn't their guitarist, and it wasn't their bass player—fuck, it wasn't even their drummer. It was their fucking keyboardist/programmer!

The fly on the wall saw me say to my monitor in disbelief, "Seriously, the keyboard player? You fucking left me for a fucking keyboard player? The guy can't even play the fucking keys! He was just hitting simple buttons, triggering fucking samples!"

I found out that she was not working at a convention in Atlanta, she was hanging out in a hotel room there instead. Then I found out that she had fucking bought him an airline ticket from New York to meet her in Atlanta, using my fucking debit card.

I opened a bottle of wine and started checking back through my bank records, saying, "Motherfucker, you're fucking kidding me," every time I discovered something. I read everything I could, from a stack of fucking emails, to chat room records that had saved. I sat there reading the correspondence between them and was fucking livid.

An idea came to me from my almost empty wine bottle about midnight. I called the hotel in Atlanta where it was 3:00 a.m. and asked to please be put through to Mrs. Corabi's room, as I am her husband.

The phone rang a few times before I hung up, then called the hotel back again. I said, "Excuse me, could you do me a favor please? I just called my wife's room, but she didn't answer. I know it's late, but if you get a minute, could you just knock on the door please, and slide a note under it to advise her there's a pressing issue at home, so can she please call back?"

Twenty minutes later my phone rang. Layla said, "Hey, babe, is everything okay? What's wrong? I got a note saying there's an emergency at home."

I said, "No, no. There's no emergency. I just wanted to let you know that I'm coming out there."

All flustered, she said, "What, to Atlanta?"

"That's right, I'm coming out. I'm on my way to the airport now."

She said, "Well, I'm working. I'm not really going to be able to..."

I calmly cut her off and matter-of-factly said, "Layla...I'm coming out there, and I'm going to kill everybody in your hotel room."

There was a moment's silence.

"And you can tell Simon the Dope, if and when I ever see him that I'm going to cut his throat from ear to ear, and I'm going to pull his tongue out through the hole—I'm going to give him a fucking Sicilian Necktie," and I hung the phone up.

I then sat there and finished the last drops of my wine, then went to bed. I slept like a fucking baby that night.

The next morning, she called me and started another sob story, "I'm the worst wife ever."

I said, "You're a fucking whore. I'm fucking done with you, fuck you. Here's the deal: I'm packing every fucking thing that you own. I'm packing it up, and I'm going to have it at the door. Here's what you're going to do: you're going to come home on December twenty-third. You are going to spend Christmas at this house because everybody has already planned to come here for Christmas Day, and I'm not ruining their plans. You're going to smile, and you're going to act like everything's okay. And then on December twenty-sixth, you're going to get your shit and get the fuck out of the house, period!"

21
Here Come the Brides

Layla came home from Atlanta, and we got through the holidays. With the festive spirit around us, she spun me another story, saying she didn't know how she had put us in this situation. She said, "I love you, John. I fucked up, and I'm truly sorry. Please don't file for divorce, please! I don't know what the fuck I was thinking. I'm going to go to Florida and stay with Aubrey in Flagler Beach."

I caved again, to a degree, and said, "Okay, you do whatever you've got to do, but I'm telling you right now, I don't want to talk to you. If you're seriously trying to get shit sorted out and you need to go to Florida to think and figure it out, don't call me. Don't call that other prick either. Don't call anybody. You need to go and sort your fucking life out and figure out what it is that you want out of life because you're all over the fucking map."

She said, "All right, I'm going to do that then."

Aubrey was supposedly splitting-up with her boyfriend as well, so she was going to leave Oregon, come to us in Acton, pick-up Layla and all her possessions, while I was away working, then go to fucking Flagler Beach to live with Aubrey's parents for a little while.

Since I was going to be away recording with Bobby Blotzer on his side project at the time, I gave our friend Bernadette a heads-up but didn't fill her in on all the details. I just said, "Layla's going to go to Florida for a little while to sort her life out. Aubrey, and most likely Aubrey's guy friend, are going to come over to pick-up all Layla's stuff, and they're all going to drive cross-country together."

Before I left, I made sure all Layla's shit was packed. Where she had any photos hanging on the wall, I even took the fucking nail out of the wall, taped it to the back of the photo frame, then wrapped it in brown paper. I didn't want any fucking remnants of her in the house. I gave her the furniture and just packed everything to be easily picked-up so she would get the fuck out. Everything was ready to go.

When I got home from recording, Bernadette asked, "Can I talk to you about something? Are you getting a divorce? What's the deal?" so I explained a little more to her.

Bernie insisted that something was odd, telling me, "I met Aubrey and her boyfriend when they came here with Layla to get all her stuff. There were only three people here, but unless Layla was watching a movie or something upstairs, I swear to God, it sounded like two people were upstairs having sex."

"Oh, I doubt that. That would be fucking beyond brazen," I said. "I'd say it would have been a movie." I dropped it, thinking there's no way she would've invited a guy to my house.

About a month later, I got a call out of the blue from Layla. She said, "Hey, I was just driving down the road, and I know you told me not to call, but, God, I miss you. As I was driving, I heard a song that reminded me of you, so I just wanted to call and hear your voice."

She continued with, "I know that you're mad at me, and I know I deserve it, but God, I really don't want to get a divorce. I've really been thinking about everything, and I want to come home and be with you. Even if it's just for a visit, can I come home and just see you for like a few days?"

I was torn because I was still fucking mad at her and did not want her to move back in, but I thought perhaps she was genuinely making changes for the better and some time away had done the trick. She said, "How about if I come out for Valentine's Day?"

I stupidly agreed to it, and we made the arrangements for her to come out for a long weekend. She began texting me five times a day, things like, "Miss you," "Love you," "Can't wait to see you."

Valentine's Day came, and I picked her up at the airport and brought her home. I didn't want to say much, so I let her do the talking. She told me that she'd really been doing a lot of thinking and it had helped. She said, "When I leave here, I'm going to go back to Florida and take a little more time to keep thinking, but I would really like to be able to come home. We should go to counselling and do whatever to make it work between us again."

I said, "Well, I'm definitely going to need some counseling after this, but I'm not committing to anything. Let's just take it slow, take it easy.

I don't think you should talk to me though, and I don't think you should be talking to the Dope."

I looked at her and asked, "Have you talked with him?"

She said, "I'm going to be honest with you. Yes, we've talked a few times on the phone."

I wasn't happy about that, but it was what it was, and at least she was being up-front with me about it for once.

I told her, "You've got more to do to sort your life out, so let's just have fun while you're here and then you'll go back to Florida to keep working on things."

Over the course of that weekend, she kept having little breakdowns, and she'd sob, "God, I miss our apartment, and I miss our life. I miss this, I miss that. I miss you."

I saw that my buddies Sevendust were playing at the Palace in Hollywood, so I suggested we go to the show to get us out of the house for an evening. Layla said, "Oh, okay, that's crazy: they'll be headlining the next tour I've lined-up to do for Cutty Sark."

I wasn't sure that going back out on the road would be the best thing for her, but I didn't say anything.

After the show, we went to the bus to say hello and thank you for the tickets, and I introduced her to all the guys in the band, "This is my wife, and she's going to be on your upcoming tour for Cutty Sark."

"Oh, awesome," they said, and we proceeded to have a great time hanging out, which reminded me of the old days when she and I would be out together.

We sat around at home the next day, and her mom called. After talking with Layla for a while, the phone got passed to me and her mom said, "How are things going? I hope you guys can work everything out. I would really like that."

At the end of her time with me in California, I drove her to the airport where she flew back to Florida to sort her life out more. After dropping her off, I went back home and her mom called me again, keen to understand how it went between us.

We chatted, and I told her about some of the things we discussed over the weekend. Her mom said at one point, "Sometimes, I just don't understand my daughter. She gets so mad at me, 'cause my husband is really upset with her right now and won't let her in the house, and she doesn't understand why."

When I asked why her husband was angry with Layla, she explained, "Well, after all the money that we spent on your wedding, not even a year ago, only to have her show up at our house on the way to Florida with that other guy, it just wasn't good."

"What do you mean Layla showed up at your house with another guy, who was this guy?" I asked, thinking she was perhaps talking about Aubrey's boyfriend.

"His name was Simon," she said.

Motherfucker! Are you fucking kidding me?! Layla and Simon drove across the country together and stayed in hotels together, again using a debit card connected to my fucking bank account. I thought the hotel rooms were for her and Aubrey, but they were for her and Simon. Now I suddenly remembered everything Bernadette had said about a guy staying in my house, and it sounded like someone was having sex in my apartment. No fucking way.

And she had the fucking audacity to take the Dope to her mom's house. Her mom had shelled-out thousands of dollars for our wedding, and there she was taking him to her place. Her stepfather asked, "Who the fuck is this guy?"

When Layla said it was her friend, he told her, "Well, you and your friend can get the fuck out of my house!"

Layla went to Flagler Beach but wasn't living there at Aubrey's parents' like I was told, she only stayed there for a week or so. Simon had quit the band Dope and moved from New York City to Melbourne, Florida, about forty minutes away. So the whole time she was in Florida sorting her life out, she stayed with Simon and his father at their fucking house.

I immediately called Layla in Florida and left her a message when she didn't answer, saying, "You're a fucking cunt! I can't fucking believe you. You had better fucking call me. We are so fucking done!"

I gave it a while and heard nothing from her. I then dug out her phone bills and looked through the call details until I found a number with the right area code. I called it, and it was Simon's voice on the recorded message.

I said, "Simon, John Corabi. Hey, motherfucker, tell my wife to fucking call home," and I hung up.

She soon called me at home and yelled, "Don't you fucking call Simon! You're a fucking asshole. I can't fucking believe you would do that to him! And by the way, Simon and I are moving back to LA to live together, so fuck off, you're a loser!"

I couldn't believe in a matter of hours, she went from apologizing, begging to come home, and now was calling me an asshole and a loser because I accidently caught her in another handful of lies. I never understood why the fuck she came to LA and spent Valentine's with me. I never heard a peep from her in the months to follow, which was absolute bliss.

Ratt hit the road for a summer tour called Rock Fest 2002. The lineup was Dokken, Ratt, Warrant, Firehouse, and LA Guns. One of the shows on the tour was in Dubuque, Iowa, at a club called The Pig Pen. The owner had built an outdoor summer venue behind the place that probably held two thousand people. As Ratt played, I looked out at the paltry crowd of only about three hundred people that showed up, and it gave me a fucking panic attack.

I freaked out thinking, "Fuck, I think I peaked in 1994. I've got to reinvent myself. Even five or ten years ago, these bands would have sold this place out on their own. Now there are five bands here that can't even draw three hundred people." While I was overcome with anxiety, I decided I would seriously work on a solo album.

I had written a few songs that I had up my sleeve, so I went to Dave Darling from the band Boxing Ghandis, and played him two songs: "Meet Me on the Moon" and "Open Your Eyes" and said, "Rock isn't happening anymore. Can you help me to reinvent myself? I need to totally do a makeover."

We recorded and created these two songs that were cool; there were lots of drum machines and loops. Dave did a great job on them.

I kept listening to them over and over and over again. After I lived with the songs for a while, I realized they weren't quite what I was thinking. They weren't right. When I then played them to people, I could see their head tilt like a puppy as they listened. They'd say things like, "What the fuck is this, dude? This isn't you."

My manager John Greenberg said, "Yeah, dude, I'm not hearing it."

I got a little indignant about the negative feedback, so I stopped working on the album for a while and filed the tunes under "Songs that People Will Never Hear," and went back to focusing on doing my job with Ratt. I'd been looking for a guiding light to appear and show me the new musical direction I needed to go in, but it just didn't fucking happen. Sometimes I'm my own worst enemy.

On that summer Rock Fest Tour, LA Guns played their set first, and then when I played mine with Ratt, Traci Guns usually sat on my side of the stage. I had my cabinets behind me, but off to the side I had a case with my two amp heads in it, which I used as a table. It usually had a pack of my Marlboro Ultra Lights, a lighter, an ashtray, and a cold can of Guinness or two from my cooler that sat alongside it. As Jizzy spoke with the crowd between songs, it was my little refuge where I grabbed a cigarette and had a chug of stout. You do know that if you dip a crab in Guinness it will walk straight, right?

Traci sat there as I played most days and hung out. I'd look over at him, and he'd point to my cooler like, hey, can I have a Guinness, and I'd say, "Yeah, dude, help yourself." He would always have a bottle of Jack Daniel's, so he'd share his Jack with me.

As we hung out more and more, he said to me, "Hey, dude, I hope this isn't weird or anything but I'm putting a new band together with Nikki Sixx."

I said I thought that was cool, and he continued, "Oh, man, you've got to hear this fucking singer we've got. God, dude, he's fucking great! I'd love for you to be involved as a guitar player with backing vocals, I think it'd be killer."

He played me their cover version of the Sweet song "No You Don't" and I said, "Holy fuck, it sounds great."

He asked, "You dig it?" and I told him, "Yeah, dude, it's fucking awesome."

Traci went and talked to Nikki, telling him that he thought I would be a great addition to the band and would fit-in great. Traci was all about the image and dug my waist-length dreadlocks, and he really loved my guitar playing. He had watched and listened to me so much on the Ratt tour, and he thought I was a very solid rhythm guitar player.

I then got a call from Nikki Sixx one day, "Hey, dude, I've obviously been talking to fucking Traci, so do you want to join us in this band?"

I said, "Yeah, that's cool," and he joked with me, "I guess we have to put up with each other again."

I don't recall if Nikki or Traci already knew Stevo Bruno, but I think I referred them to him. Once I was home from the Ratt tour, we went down and checked out his Klown Studios together. Everything felt right, so we started rehearsing and putting songs together and then went in to record demos. The name of the band was going to be Cockstar, then Motordog, before eventually settling on Brides of Destruction, as suggested by our friend from Brooklyn, Dano.

The first song I started writing with them was "I Got a Gun." As we worked on various songs, I started recognizing that they were all very different sounding. Individually they were great songs, but I never totally understood what was going on musically with the band. I felt there wasn't a thread that tied all the songs together on the record. Traci and I had a bit of a disagreement about it, but we worked through it and resolved our differences over a whiskey.

I played the first two gigs in Brides of Destruction, one in the middle of December '02 at the Ventura Theater before Taproot and Mudvayne, then another at the House of Blues in Anaheim.

When I arrived for the Anaheim gig four hours before showtime, Nikki was there with his wife, Donna D'Errico. Traci and our drummer Scotty arrived and when it came time to soundcheck at three hours before showtime, our singer London was still yet to arrive. With an hour and a half to the gig, we finally reached him on the phone. He was fucking stranded on the side of the road because his car had broken down.

We certainly didn't want to cancel our performance, even though it was somewhat of a secret show, so I got in my car and drove north on the fucking freeway doing a hundred. I spotted London on the side of the road in the middle of two exits, so I had to go past and exit, then get back on and come back down the freeway again to him.

As I headed for Anaheim, London changed into his stage clothes in the front of my car, banging my mirror and knocking things about in the process. I skidded to a halt in the carpark before we ran inside and took the stage. We played our short set that ended in Mötley Crüe covers "Shout at the Devil" and "Live Wire," then hit the freeway home again. It was a headfuck playing Mötley songs on stage again with Nikki.

As I sat at the front desk of Klown Studios one day while we worked on Brides songs, Layla walked through the front door with Aubrey. I hadn't heard from her in months, so I'm sure I looked surprised when I said, "Hey, what are you two doing here?"

She said, "Can I talk to you?"

I went outside with them so my bandmates couldn't hear any conversation, especially since I was waiting for her to tell me that she had filed for divorce. Instead, she said, "I moved here with Simon. He quit playing for Dope, and we have an apartment just five minutes from here."

"You're fucking kidding me," I said.

"Nope, but I made a huge mistake. He's got a drinking problem, and he gets really violent and beats me up," she told me.

Aubrey added, "Yeah, he's really rough on her. He's mean to her, pushes her, and gets really aggressive."

They kept divulging all this shit about him and his behavior, until I asked, "What the fuck do you want me to do about it? The last time

I spoke with you I was the fucking asshole because I phoned him and gave him some shit. You made this bed and now you don't want to lie in it?"

I felt bad for her, though, and something inside me wanted her to believe that I had always been the right guy and that she had made a huge mistake.

She started showing up at the studio almost daily. Simon got up every day and had his morning coffee, gave her a kiss goodbye, and went to work at a place that designed video games in Culver City. She'd wait about twenty minutes, shower, and throw something nice on and then come to the studio and wait for me to show up. It didn't take long for her to get really flirty with me, saying, "Oh, gosh, you know how much I miss you."

Nikki said something to me like, "Dude, careful, have you really thought about why she is back? It's because she's seen pictures and stuff online that you and I are back together again in this band."

"Yep, I'm not disagreeing with that assessment," I told him.

The guys in my band would comment to me, though, "Dude, she's fucking hot. Man, your wife is so hot."

I got in the mood for a piece of ass one day and justified it to myself by telling the voice in my head that I didn't trust her and probably wasn't going to fucking live with her again, so I'm just going to fuck her. If she wants to come to the studio and fuck around, then that's fine. Once I'm done, I'll just send her right back home to him. The shoe was now on the other foot—I'm the other guy now! Two can play this fucking game.

It got fucking stupid. She would ask if we could go get some lunch, and then sit there hysterically crying, telling me he's an asshole, and he does this and he says that. "I made a huge mistake leaving you, and I don't know what I was thinking. You were such a great husband, and I fucked it up," she'd say as I passed another napkin to wipe her face.

One day she said, "I was serious when I said you were a great husband. Is there any way to work things out?"

"I don't know," I told her.

Her extreme hot and cold mood swings were so fucking draining on me. I didn't know if she just enjoyed playing fucking head games or if she had some sort of mental issue like bipolar disorder.

She kept saying to me, "I'm going to leave him. Can we get an apartment together? We can go to therapy together and try and salvage our marriage."

As she was telling me that she wanted to work things out, she went back to work on her next Cutty Sark sponsored tour, headlined again by Seven-dust. One of the supports on that tour was a band from Alabama called Trust Company, and it didn't take long for her to fucking hook-up with their singer. She did the exact same thing to Simon as she did to me, except she upgraded from the keyboard player. At least it got her out of my fucking hair.

It was a very strange time in my life. I was trying to write music for the Brides of Destruction. I was doing shows with Ratt, and I was doing my estranged wife again, and it was all doing my fucking head in. It was unbelievable; it was fucking insanity.

Every aspect of my relationship with Layla was, in hindsight, fucking delusional on my part. I can't even blame anything on her because I allowed her to do it all to me, everything. I bought every fucking word she said, hook, line, and sinker.

We continued working on the Brides of Destruction record *Here Come the Brides*, but it was all over the place to me. There was "Shut the Fuck Up," which I thought was punk metal. Then you had the song "2x Dead," which was something that could have been on one of the Mötley records that I recorded with the guys. Then there was a ballad "Only Get So Far," which I thought was very reminiscent of a big eighties power pop ballad.

I thought the best song on the album was "Life," which Nikki wrote with some guys Kevin Kadish and Justin Nichols. When we were done with it, it sounded like a snotty but poppy tune Cheap Trick would do. It seemed that everybody concurred that it was the best song on the record, but London couldn't sing it, so our drummer Scot Coogan sang it. Scotty hit a home run with it; he sounded great.

With the songs being all over the place, and having no public identity at that point, my biggest concern was there was no thread that tied our first album together. Over the years I had heard some of my record labels and industry people say in regards to The Scream, Mötley, Union, etc., "It's really eclectic, but it's got a thread that runs through it." Like, Bob Seger can do "Turn the Page," then he can do "Kathmandu" and "Her Strut" because it's Bob Seger's voice that ties it all together. That's the thread.

I felt the Brides' music was not only drastically different from song to song—"Shut the Fuck Up" didn't sound anything like "2x Dead" or "Only Get So Far" or "Life;" they were four distinctly different tunes—but the one song everybody was pegging to be the best song on the first record was sung by the drummer and not the front man London, who they were saying was the greatest thing since fucking sliced bread. It didn't make any sense to me, so then it just started getting tense.

We played our demos for Bob Rock, who was the first choice to produce the album, but in so many words, he reiterated my views on the songs. He basically said, "I'm going to pass on this one and not produce it. I think you guys need to go and write."

Next thing I know, I got a call and was told I'd no longer be involved in the songwriting and would just be taught the songs once others wrote them. I thought about it for the five minutes after hanging up; it didn't sit well with me.

As I walked over to my phone to make a call and quit, it rang, and it was Traci, who said, "Hey, Crab, what are you doing?"

I said, "Thinking, and before you say anything more, I just want to tell you that I'm quitting. I don't want to do this anymore. If I can't write and contribute and be a part of something, then I'm out because I'm doing exactly that in Ratt. I'm a hired bitch with Ratt, and I'm fine with that. That's the road I chose with them. I don't want to be just some dude that plays guitar with you guys, though, sorry."

Years later, I did a run of shows with Traci, and he seemed a little upset with me, so I sat down with him and realized it stemmed from my departure from the Brides of Destruction. We talked about a lot of shit. There seemed to be a disconnect between Traci and Nikki and the things I was told. So however it came to be, I pulled the fucking pin, and it was the end of another fucking band for me that I thought was going to be huge. There went the Brides, no world domination.

22
Space Truckin'

After all the shit I went through with Layla, and all the shit with Brides of Destruction, my head needed a fucking break—big time! I was mentally burned out and needed some space.

Somebody told me of an old spiritual belief, where if you're going through a lot of turmoil, the negativity remains in your hair as it grows. My long dreadlocks weighed probably seventy pounds when wet, and the weight didn't help with all the headaches I was dealing with.

I went to my ex-wife Val and said, "Cut it all off, please." She got her scissors and went to work, leaving me with an inch of hair all over my head. It was a weight lifted off me, but I knew I needed more change.

I had lost faith in the music industry given the current climate, plus I had my fucking confidence beaten out of me to the point where I felt like I was a passé has-been, ready to be put out to fucking pasture.

I had worked my way up and through the Mötley peak and didn't have money at the end of that. I started up Union and barely made any money from that either. I had just tried another new band in the Brides but was still living hand-to-mouth. I was a hired gun in Ratt and now they were going to be taking some time-off from playing shows, most likely a year or so, so I knew my bank balance would be heading south.

There I sat in my forties, with kids, still struggling, so I asked myself if I wanted to keep doing this rock-and-roll shit for the rest of my fucking life. If I couldn't reinvent myself in the music business, I needed to try a different industry. Everything pointed to it being the right time for me to try something different in life. Maybe it was a mid-life crisis, or maybe I was being adventurous.

I opened the day's newspaper to the Wanted classified section, closed my eyes, and I put my finger down on the page. My finger landed on an ad for OTR Drivers, which stands for "over the road"—basically drivers who haul all types of goods over long distances. The ad said something like: "OTR Drivers needed. Make money, benefits, home on weekends." It sounded perfect.

I've always been enamored with the thought of driving a fucking freight train across America, even as a kid. I think that would be the coolest fucking thing ever, but it requires five years of schooling. Truck driving school is so much less, so this was a better option for me, since I love driving and had always wanted to drive a semi-trailer truck, too.

With the little money I had in my bank account, I decided I was going to go to school and learn how to drive an eighteen-wheeler. I've always been a "Gypsy" at heart, so this traveling life felt right to me.

I went to a truck-driving school in San Bernadino for three weeks, where I learned how to back-up, parallel park, drive forward, reverse, sideways—you fucking name it!

I stayed with my dear friend Leanne out in this town called Redlands, which was only ten minutes away from truck school. Since I had a 6:30 a.m. start at school each morning, it made it a lot easier than driving sixty-plus miles each way to and from my home in Thousand Oaks. After class, I read a textbook and took notes, and had to complete a written assignment.

As I studied one night, I got a text message from Layla saying, "I love you and really miss you." On my birthday the very next day, I got another text from her saying, "I want a divorce." I couldn't make sense of it.

I said to Leanne, "I showed you my text from Layla last night. Will you look at this text that I just got?"

She read it and immediately said, "What the fuck? Is that girl on drugs?"

I stayed focused on my schooling and graduated after passing all my written and driving tests. Once I got my qualifications and license, I began the arduous task of creating and submitting my resume to lots of different companies, which I'd only done once before when I applied for Alanis Morrisette's band—unsuccessfully, I might add—and you know how that fucking experience turned out.

Although I was burned out from making a living in the music industry, I thought there was no harm in going to gigs sometimes and having music as my hobby. I couldn't just sit at home and become a hermit crab. I went to the Cat Club in LA on Thursday nights, where I'd walk in through the back door and hang out, sometimes even jam with the band. Kenny the bartender would see me and say, "Hey, Crab, how you doing? What do you want?"

I'd say, "All right, Guinness, thanks."

After the familiar pop and fizz of the can opening, I would take a sip and walk back to the rear door again and sit on the chair they always had there to prop the door open. I was happy sitting on the chair by myself, drinking my Guinness, and smoking my cigarettes.

At some point, the jam band called The Starfuckers started playing. It was Dizzy Reed from Guns N' Roses on keyboard, Ryan Roxie from Alice Cooper's band on guitar, Eric Dover from Slash's band on guitar, Stefan Adika on bass, and Slim Jim Phantom from the Stray Cats on drums. Sometimes Eric Singer would play drums instead, depending on who was in or out of town, and sometimes a VIP guest would get up and jam, like Brian May.

Those guys got asked to play a private party in Eddie Van Halen's backyard, so they asked me if I wanted in. I played guitar with Dover singing, Adika on bass, Derek Sherinian on keyboards, and Brian Tichy on drums. The decadent party in the Hollywood hills celebrated the release of his friend's movie *Sacred Sin*, which was actually a porn movie Eddie had written a couple of instrumental tracks for.

We rehearsed at Eddie's massive house—the 5150 Estate—the day before, as he worked on music. There were bottles of Smoking Loon wine all over his house, and a mattress with a massive burn spot on the family room floor near his grand piano. I asked, "Ed, what's with the fucking mattress here?"

"Well, I go to my studio and work there all day. I have a little bit of wine, and if I can't make it up the steps to the bedroom, I just crash here. A few weeks ago, I fell asleep with a lit cigarette, and it caught on fire."

"Oh, shit," I said, "Lucky you managed to put it out."

"Yeah, I just pissed on it," he casually remarked.

After the rehearsal, I played bass as we jammed on Zeppelin songs with Eddie.

At the party the next night, we played a bunch of covers like "Rebel Yell" and "You Really Got Me," then Eddie got up with us and played "Jump," "Panama," "Ain't Talkin' 'Bout Love," and "Eruption." It was surreal playing guitar with Eddie Van Halen on Van Halen songs in his fucking backyard! RIP Eddie.

Another night back at the Cat Club, a cocktail waitress came over to me and asked, "Do you need anything, John?"

I looked at her and said, "What's your name?" to which she replied, "Ashley."

I asked, "Oh, how do you know my name?"

She said, "I know who you are," to which I replied, "Wow, I've never seen you before." I thought she was cute.

She laughed and said, "I know who you are because I've been working here for a year, you asshole," before walking away.

As The Starfuckers played, Ashley came by me again, so I apologized, and we started bullshitting. Our conversation got interrupted when the band called me up to sing "Helter Skelter," "Oh, Darlin'," and "Sweet Emotion" with them.

Once off stage, I resumed chatting with Ashley again, who soon introduced me to her bass player friend Stacy and another friend named Ashley. They told me they were all taking music lessons and had a band called The Hot Chix. They only knew one song and wanted to play it while The Starfuckers had a break between sets.

Ashley was the drummer, and she said they didn't have a lead guitar player. "Could you play lead for us?" she asked.

I said, "Well, I don't know your song, and I'm not a lead player either."

The other Ashley was their guitarist, and she said, "Can't you just make something up?"

While laughing, I said, "Okay, I'll figure something out and do a guitar solo for you girls."

Their singer Sarah arrived, and they got set-up during the break. I borrowed Ryan Roxie's guitar and joined them on stage, when they began the one and only song they knew: "Highway to Hell."

It was fucking hilarious. I laughed so hard I backed up from the front of the stage all the way back past the amps and sat on the back corner of the drum riser to let them have their moment in the spotlight. I played a solo in the vein of Angus Young, and when the song ended, they took a bow and walked off the stage. The band and the audience all pissed themselves laughing—it was such a funny moment.

Ashley went back to work behind the bar, and I told the girls I wanted to buy them a round of drinks. Ashley said, "I'm not allowed to drink while I'm working," so I bought myself a shot and ones for the three other girls.

I turned around to pay for them and when I looked back, my shot glass was empty. I said, "What the fuck?"

While I was paying for them, Ashley had reached in between everybody, pulled my shot out, slammed it, and put the empty glass back.

She got done with work, and we sat there for a while, talking while Ashley had a couple more drinks. As the night drew on, everybody left, and I was a little concerned because Ashley seemed a bit buzzed. I didn't drink that much over the course of the evening, I paced myself.

I asked Ashley, "Hey, can I give you a ride home?" She invited me in once we got to her place, and that's when I realized that she was roommates with the other Ashley, her guitarist.

We hung out talking until four in the morning and started kissing and making out. Ashley stopped and said, "No, this ain't going to happen. If this happens, you're never going to call me back or see me again."

I assured her that wouldn't be the case, but she still said, "No, you won't."

I was smitten with her. I knew she was young, but there was something about her that seemed very worldly. Here we go again. I was kind of fascinated with her.

Her dad was a lawyer in the South, so she came from a well-to-do family and grew up in a huge home. The family even had a plane when she was a kid. She was well educated, having gone through an all-girls boarding school and then college in Paris. She spoke a couple of languages fluently and struck me as very intelligent and mature.

I called her a couple of days later to see what she was up to. She invited me down to her apartment again, where we sat around drinking wine and chatting for hours. I wound up staying overnight.

A week or two after meeting Ashley, I got the call I had been waiting for. I got myself a pair of work boots and got a job working for a trucking company called Werner Enterprises. I grew a big fucking beard and put a baseball cap on. I was a fucking truck driver now!

For my first three hundred hours behind the wheel, I had to have somebody with me in the truck, shadowing me and showing me the ropes. My cabin buddy was a guy named Shane Ahrens, and it was his truck.

Everyone at the company knew me as John, and from paperwork, Shane knew my name was John Corabi. I didn't put my music history on my resume, so people were none the wiser. Shane's truck was a ten-speed Peterbilt, the one with the really long nose in the front. It was much sweeter than the old beat-up truck that I did my lessons in, and it had nice beds in the back of the cabin.

I pulled into a truck-stop one day near Amarillo, Texas, and went to the restroom before getting some food for us. When I got back in the truck and passed Shane his burger, I noticed he was fucking staring at me awkwardly.

He said, "Dude, while you were gone, I heard a trivia question on the radio station. They asked listeners what was the name of the singer that replaced Vince Neil in Mötley Crüe, and then they said your name. Is that you? Or was that a cousin or something?"

I started laughing and said, "Yeah, it's me."

With a perplexed look on his face, he asked again, "So, you were in Mötley Crüe?"

"Yep!" I confirmed with a grin.

"What the fuck are you doing driving my truck then?" he asked. He couldn't figure it out.

"It's a long story," I told him. "I just needed a change of scenery, and I've always been fascinated with trucks, and the truckers' lifestyle," as we went back to eating our food.

I must have been driving about ten hours a day, since I clocked up my three hundred hours in about thirty days and felt comfortable behind the wheel of Shane's truck.

Someone from the office called Shane to get his take on my progress. "He's great, he's got it," he told them.

When they asked if he thought I'd be good in my own truck, without hesitating he told them, "Absolutely, he looks fine. He's ready for that."

Shane dropped me off at one of Werner's main offices in Dallas, where I spent a few hours getting a truck assigned to me, including getting a batch number, a gas card, and a map of all the truck-stops they had accounts with.

I asked them, "Hey, I don't know how you guys do this, but is there any way I can have a Peterbilt? That's what I'm used to driving."

They gave me my own Peterbilt truck to drive, which I did month after month and had a lot of fun doing it.

I hauled all kinds of loads across the United States, everything from explosives to army rations for shipping overseas to Iraq and other bases. Werner had a military contract, so I had to pick-up trailers in Lincoln, Nebraska, from Purina (their dog food plant also made the fucking K-ration packs for the military to eat—yeah, I know what you're thinking!), and I would take them to a ship in New Orleans.

While I was out doing over-the-road trucking, Ashley and I called each other regularly during the first couple of months. We chatted on the phone and the talk started to get a little more heated and then it became pillow talk, and it kept escalating. I guess we were dating.

After two months of constantly being on the road, I contacted Werner's office and said, "Your ad said weekends off and that hasn't happened yet. I want to go home and see my kid."

I also wanted to see Ashley.

Instead of continuing as an over-the-road driver, they changed my role to a dedicated run, where I picked-up a trailer in LA and drove it to Phoenix, Arizona, and dropped it off. I then picked another trailer up in Phoenix and drove it the five or six hours back to LA—about thirty miles east of LA actually, in the Ontario area.

The change of run suited me, and I enjoyed having some weekends off. Some days I'd get back to Ontario at six o'clock at night and wouldn't need to start my next run until nine or ten o'clock the following morning.

Whenever we could, Ashley and I would go to dinner, hang out together for the rest of the night, and she'd often stay over and get up early the next morning to drive back to LA in time for work.

After five or six months of this routine, Ashley rode with me in the truck to Phoenix one day. We listened to music as I drove, and she said she wanted to hear some of my stuff. I played her some Mötley, some Union, and The Scream, which she had never heard of.

I could see her out of my peripheral listening intently and after a while, she turned to me and asked, "What are you doing?"

I said, "What do you mean, what am I doing? I'm driving a fucking truck."

She said, "John Corabi, what the fuck are you doing? I don't understand. You're so fucking talented, you're so good with words, and your voice is so good. Why are you driving this truck?"

I tried to explain, "I was mentally tapped-out and tired of dealing with too many phony, plastic people in LA. I needed a break from the music industry and wanted to get out of town for a while, get out of a rut, and escape all the shit life kept throwing at me."

She said, "I'm sorry, I get that you want to make a living, and I get that you want to have insurance, and I get that you needed a break and you needed to get out of LA. However, people are put on Earth to do things. You were put on this Earth to play a guitar and write music and sing songs. You were given that talent, and you're not using it. That's a real shame to me."

She got me thinking.

I had a blast driving an eighteen-wheeler across America. I actually saw more of the country in my eight or nine months on the road than I saw in twenty years of touring. I took in so much beautiful scenery throughout America, which was my perfect therapy for a complete mental break.

Ratt still wasn't touring, as Warren DeMartini wanted to take some substantial time off, but they did a few weekend shows here and there that I played with them. I quit my job with Werner Trucking, but got another driving for the *LA Times* newspaper to keep making ends meet in the meantime.

My usual round consisted of driving up to the Valencia area of California, past Santa Clarita and the Magic Mountain amusement park, arriving about 1:00 a.m. They loaded a truck with the day's newspapers, and I drove all the way down the I-5 to my designated area, Orange County.

My OC route consisted of pulling up to little paper stands and stores, where I'd get out of the truck, open the back doors and toss the right amount of newspaper bundles out.

By the time I finished delivering all the journalists' words and stories on my route, it was six or seven o'clock in the morning, and every fucking bone in my body hurt, especially my fingers and arms. Each bundle of newspapers weighed about twenty pounds, which doesn't feel like a lot until you fucking move 2,000 of them—then your body will know all about it. I'd wake up and have to do it all over again, every fucking day. It was brutal because it was very physical, as well as driving the truck.

I did the over-the-road trucking, but the novelty wore off when I was never home. I tried a dedicated route, which was better, but I was still only home maybe one day a week. I then did the more local route delivering the news, but the hours and physicality sucked.

Then I got a call from the Ratt camp, "Hey, we're going to go back out on tour again, and we want you to play with us."

"Sure," I said, and thank God, I thought.

It didn't take me long to realize that in one night of playing music, I could make what would take me a week to earn driving the truck, even though it was steady income with benefits. I could make way more money on stage and be doing something that I loved, once again.

I just needed to get away from everything to truly appreciate my talent, my gift of being able to walk on stage, play the guitar, and sing for an hour or two. I had to step away from it, to get my love of it back again. I had realized my path to true happiness was in music.

Mind you though, in a pinch, if I could never sing or play guitar again, or if nobody gave a fuck about me anymore, I know I could go and drive a truck again and be content doing it.

Ashley and I went to The Viper Room one night to see some friends of mine play in their band Blacklist Union. I had known their singer Tony West since I was in Mötley.

Not long after we walked in, I heard somebody say, "Hey, Corabi!"

I turned around and saw it was Billy Duffy from The Cult. He asked me how I've been, and we got to talking. He said, "Hey, I was just thinking that I've got this fucking side thing that I'm doing with some friends, and I'd love to have you come down and jam with us. It's just a real kind of easy, low-key thing. We're just having some fun doing some covers."

So, I said, "All right, cool," and we swapped numbers.

I talked with him on the phone a few times, and then he asked me if I could come down and sing "Draw the Line" by Aerosmith, AC/DC's "Back in Black," and "Helter Skelter" for my audition. When I said, "No problem," he said I'd also be playing with his buddy and bass player from The Cult, Chris Wyse, as well as Jerry Cantrell from Alice in Chains.

That sounded pretty cool to me, so I sang those three songs, and they thought it was fucking great. "Let's do this," we all agreed.

Jerry named the band Cardboard Vampyres after his cats, as they had chewed a few cardboard boxes of unpacked things he had not yet put away when he moved into his new house.

We put together a list of songs comprised of some Alice in Chains, some by The Cult, and some cool cover songs like Black Sabbath's "Hole in the Sky" and "I Wanna Be Your Dog" by The Stooges.

It didn't take long before we started playing some shows at the Troubadour, and it was great fun. After a dozen or so shows on the road, plus some corporate events in New York and other cities, we felt some momentum building.

We then played a couple of opening spots for ZZ Top in fucking Texas and Oklahoma. While playing in front of ZZ Top's sold-out audience at The Zoo Amphitheatre in Oklahoma, I walked over to Jerry mid-set and yelled in his ear, "Dude, this is fucking crazy! We're a cover band playing in front of seven thousand fucking people!" and he gave me that Cantrell smirk and we laughed.

Backstage, I met ZZ Top's tour accountant, a guy by the name of Pete Merluzzi. We connected and while I didn't realize it at the time, Pete would become a helpful guide in my career moving forward. Unfortunately, the Cardboard Vampyres became not-so-fun for some of the members, so we stopped playing. It's a shame it didn't last longer because it really was a lot of fun for me. I needed to really enjoy playing music again, so it was a great tonic.

Ratt toured around the United States during the summer of 2006, and at the end of June, we played a show supporting Vince Neil at a venue in Tampa, Florida, that was called the St. Pete Times Forum at the time. I believe the concert was already a makeup show because Vince had canceled one prior to this.

I had previously met a young girl who lived in the area and thought she was super attractive. Ashley and I were in an on-again-off-again relationship, so I invited this girl to the show in Tampa and set her up with a backstage pass so we could hang out. We were backstage after I finished my set with Ratt, when I heard the familiar sound of "Helter Skelter" starting. As I listened with one ear while chatting, I thought there was a delay happening in the room because I heard the music, but the vocals weren't quite in sync, it just seemed slow with a lag.

I poured my guest a wine and grabbed myself a Guinness, all the while listening and noticing that Vince did not sound in good form. It sounded like he was out of time and out of key, but it may have just been where we were hearing it from.

So we grabbed our drinks and headed out into the crowd. Taking up position on the floor seating near the front, we were on the left-hand side of the stage in front of bass player, Dana Strum. As I was talking to this girl, she turned sideways and interrupted me and said, "I think somebody's trying to get ahold of you."

I turned around and saw Vince's tour manager, Jack Carson, up on the side of the stage, flashing me with his flashlight. I knew Jack from way back in the Union days. I pointed to myself, and he nodded his head yes and motioned me to come up. I headed forward, showed the security guy my pass and went backstage.

As I got to the top of the backstage steps, Jack met me and asked, "Do you remember any of the Mötley songs?"

I said, "Well, yeah, what's going on?"

He pointed to Vince positioned behind a scrim where nobody could see him. Vince was on the edge of a plastic chair, half-slumped over a card table, clutching a bottle of vodka, and throwing up in a bucket.

Jack said, "He's gone, dude. He can't sing. Can you go up and sing a few?"

Happy to help out and knowing that contractually they had to put on a show, I said, "Yeah, sure, dude. Whatever you need."

Dana came over to me, "Hey, dude, I appreciate your help."

I told him, "Sure thing, we can get through it."

I walked on stage while Vince's three-piece band finished playing some Led Zeppelin songs. When guitarist Jeff Blando saw me enter, he started playing "Live Wire."

The audience responded very favorably and just as I took the microphone, Vince was suddenly there. He wrapped his arm around me, kind of hanging on and propping himself up. I sang the first verse and chorus, then Vince gave the second verse a shot before I helped on the chorus again. Vince told the audience, "You know what? I love this motherfucker," and he hugged me.

My mind raced: once Vince came back out, I didn't feel comfortable being up there. I didn't want to piss Vince off, or anybody else. I fucking stood there with Vince hugging on me, wondering if he wanted me to sing, or if I should exit. It was a touchy situation. I finished the song, handed him the microphone, and left the stage.

I went back to my guest down in the crowd. They only got through another couple of drawn-out songs, and as hundreds of people were booing and leaving, they assisted Vince off stage and brought his show to an end.

When Jack asked me to help, I was under the impression that Vince was so intoxicated he couldn't even stand up, let alone make his way to the fucking stage. However, if Vince could get up off the chair and come out, then he was on his own—it was his show, his train-wreck. Little did I know at the time that the two of us were being filmed by fans and the video would be fucking uploaded to YouTube. Our side-by-side singing is seen by some as proof for the Mötley fan debate that still seems to rage on: John's better, Vince is better, John is better, fuck John, fuck Vince. Jesus fucking Christ, people!

Some have even gone so far as saying that I set Vince up to look like an asshole, like I spiked his fucking water or some shit. That couldn't be further from the fucking truth. It's not like I was getting paid to sing or anything, I just got asked to help a couple of buddies out, that's all! I will never understand how the fuck I was the bad guy for wanting to help some friends in need.

I saw Aerosmith and Mötley Crüe on their coheadlining Route of All Evil Tour a few weeks before Thanksgiving in '06. I don't exactly recall how I got the tickets; I think Tommy Lee invited me down to the Hollywood Bowl.

Sitting in the audience when Mötley took the stage first, I watched their bombastic set with heaps of pyro, female acrobats, Nikki spitting blood, and all this shit. Looking past all that to the musicianship, other than Mick and Nikki, I felt like Vince and Tommy were just phoning it in, going through the motions. Tommy spotted me in the crowd and threw sticks at me from his kit, kidding around with me.

It was actually my first time seeing Mötley Crüe perform. I had never seen Mötley prior to joining the band, and obviously I didn't see Mötley when I was in the band because I was on stage.

I had seen Vince sing before, and he usually sounded really good, but that night honestly wasn't Vince's finest hour. Of course, it was nothing like earlier that summer when I got asked to help him out during his solo show, but he certainly wasn't in his best form. But watching them play, I understood why Vince was right for them on all their music they created before I was in the band; I got it. While they played "Home Sweet Home" halfway through their set, I watched people leaving their seats to go get a beer or take a shit or whatever. I stood there looking around thinking it was crazy.

Once all Mötley's stuff was off stage, Aerosmith came out with no frills, just a row of amps, a set of drums, a long catwalk, and they just destroyed. In contrast to Mötley, halfway through Aerosmith's set, Steven Tyler and Joe Perry sat on two chairs and played "Hangman Jury" that went into "Seasons of Wither." The whole band then kicked in during the guitar solo and snow fell from the ceiling—their only production prop. Tyler sang his ass off. The band sounded great and was fucking badass. They then did "Dream On," and it gave me goosebumps.

I was left an after-show pass, so I went backstage and the first person I saw was Nikki, who came over and gave me a hug then left. I didn't see Vince. Mick saw me from a distance and gave me a bit of a wave as he walked out—he didn't talk to me, as I think he was still not sure about what went down with me and Mötley during the *Generation Swine* recording.

I went into Tommy's dressing room. He soon looked at me and said, "Honestly, dude, what did you think of the band? He knew it was my first time seeing Mötley play.

I said, "Honestly?" and he said, "Yeah, dude, be blunt, honestly—how was the show?"

So, I said, "Honestly, dude, I thought you guys just got your ass handed to you on a plate by a bunch of sixty-year-olds. Aerosmith had nothing on stage but amps. I'm sorry, you asked, and that's my honest answer," I told him. "It seemed you guys just phoned it in. If you didn't have the acrobats and the fucking fire, it would've been a fucking massacre."

I would have never said a word, but Tommy asked and told me to be honest. I think my words cut too deep, though, and I stepped on a toe or two. Perhaps that is a reason why Tommy doesn't really speak with me anymore. I don't think I've talked with him since.

I got asked to go down to a resort in Sandestin, Florida, and play two nights with The Starfuckers, as part of a three-day celebrity charity golf tournament event hosted by the country band Trick Pony. After guests played golf during the day, we played sets of cover songs to entertain them into the night on the main strip in the resort.

I sang "Oh, Darlin'" by The Beatles with the legendary Steve Cropper, some Cheap Trick and Aerosmith songs, including "Walk This Way." Darryl McDaniels from Run DMC joined me on stage, so we did that rap-rock version, which the guests loved. While there, I met a local guy named Todd Armstrong, whose regional gasoline distribution company was the major sponsor of the event.

We played at a place called Hammerhead's at one end of this walkway in the Village of Baytowne Wharf resort, and then walked to another bar Rum Runners at the other end, where I kicked on drinking with Todd and Rum Runner's owner, Mark. Steve Azar, a country artist and a frequent guest at charity golf tournaments across the country, joined us, along with his percussionist, Jason. We all had a fun night hanging out drinking, joking around laughing. After exchanging battle stories, we exchanged phone numbers.

I didn't know it at the time, but the lady who would eventually become my wife was there as well. We didn't meet that night but were probably only a matter of feet away from one another.

In the weeks following the event, Todd searched me online and heard me singing slower songs from my catalogue like "Father, Mother, Son;" "Loveshine;" "Driftaway;" and "October Morning Wind."

He called me in LA and said, "Hey, man, when you said you were in Mötley Crüe, I didn't realize you wrote and sang slower acoustic songs, too. You've got some pretty great slow songs. You know I have my gasoline distribution business, but I also have a music publishing company. I've got a couple of artists who I work with in Nashville, so I'm wondering if you would want to come and write with some of my guys?"

Todd sent me a ticket, and I flew to Nashville. Once I landed, he and another guy Marcel picked me up from my hotel in the Green Hills area and took me to another celebrity golf tournament. I told them I didn't golf but tried hitting a couple of balls anyway. After witnessing my swings and misses, Todd suggested, "All right, why don't you just drive the cart?" so I drove the cart around the course all Friday while drinking beers and passing cold beers to the ones who could play.

We went for dinner afterward at a place called Carraba's, and then rolled on to this place called The Red Door Saloon in the midtown section of Nashville by Music Row. I fell ill suddenly and told them, "Oh, shit, I don't know what I ate, but something is not agreeing with me."

I spent the rest of the night in my hotel room dealing with food poisoning and the flow from my top end and bottom.

They had tickets for me to join them the next day at Nashville's famed steeplechase horserace event. When they called me in the morning, I said, "I need to just hang in my room today. You'll have to enjoy the spring racing and watching everybody in their big hats drinking mint juleps without me, sorry."

I was between the bathroom and TV in bed all fucking day long, which was a shitty way to be spending my first time hanging out in Nashville.

I felt a little better on Sunday, but not much, so I eased my way through the day. I finally managed to get together with Marcel and once we started working on a tune, it was basically time for me to leave and fly back to LA.

Finishing what I had started, I ended up going back out to Nashville a few more times, where I completed the song with Marcel, and I wrote with a multiplatinum songwriter named Gary Hannon.

When not writing, I went out with Marcel, Gary, and Steve Cropper and hit up different bars and pubs around town. Steve introduced me to a producer Eddie Gore, who had a studio right by Music Row in Nashville. We recorded a couple of my songs there one day, and I was so pumped because I had laid down three tunes with Steve Cropper and Audley Freed on guitar. Everything sounded amazing!

It started to rain, and we could hear thunder outside when all of a sudden the lights flickered off, then back on immediately. That's when Eddie turned around and looked at Steve and me. His face was beet red, and he was beyond pissed. Apparently when the power cut off for a second we lost all of the files. He thought he had saved it all throughout the recording process but it unfortunately was somehow lost with the brief outage.

After we finished recording and trying to recover the files, we headed for the bar down the street, midtown's The Red Door. As we sat there, a lady, Debbie Sorenson, walked in and said hello to Eddie, who introduced us, "John, this is Debbie—Debbie, this is John."

She was only there briefly as she had to leave, which was a pity because I thought she was very attractive. Eddie said she was his next-door neighbor, and she owned the condo next to his. So Eddie and I went back to our drinks and laughing at ourselves for losing the entire session for the day.

Another night I was out with Gary Hannon, country artist John Michael Montgomery, and another writer buddy of theirs. We went to a Longhorn's steakhouse, ate, and had a few drinks. After dinner, we decided to head down to Broadway, which is the main strip in Nashville, and have a few more cocktails. John said he was leaving to go on tour that night, so he was calling his tour manager throughout the evening.

We started at the historic honky-tonk bar Tootsie's, and John jumped up on stage and played a few songs with the band. He tore the place up, which meant everybody in the place bought us more drinks.

Then we went to The Stage where they had a band playing a bit of everything. John went up and did his thing again, and then I went up and sang "Oh, Darlin'." When I was done, I joined Gary and John at the bar, who now met a few more friends. Gary introduced me to the gang, and I nodded and said hello, but I didn't really hear the names because the band was playing—I didn't have a clue who these new friends were.

A girl was sitting at the bar, and she was drinking whiskey shooters and longneck Budweisers. She had a cool hippie country thing going on, and she excused herself for a second to use the bathroom. I sat down on the stool she was on and continued drinking, figuring I'd give her the seat when she got back. After a few minutes, she came back, and just jumped up onto my lap and started drinking again, which I was not upset about as I thought she was cute.

I started to notice that people were taking photos, but I thought it was because of John, thinking nobody here knows who I am, or Gary for that matter. We sat there for about ten or fifteen minutes when the band took a break. I apologized to the girl for taking her seat, and not hearing the introductions, so I asked her what her name was.

She nonchalantly said, "Oh, hi, I'm Gretchen."

Then it dawned on me, as I almost choked on my whiskey; it was country star Gretchen Wilson. I told her I loved her "Redneck Woman" song and video, and welcomed her to the party that was slowly growing out of control.

By this time, we were all drunk and aimlessly bar hopping all along Broadway, and John's tour manager was growing more irritated by the minute. We would call and say we're back at Tootsie's, and he would tell us to wait there, but we would do a couple of shots, pick up more friends, and head to another bar. The tour manager would call back screaming, "Where the fuck are you guys? I'm at Tootsie's,"

We would say, "Oh, we're down the street at Cadillac Ranch."

We did this all evening. John was supposed to be on the tour bus by 8:30 p.m. to drive to Oklahoma the following day. So when the tour manager finally found us back at The Stage at midnight, he was fucking fuming!

Gary and I opened the bus door, and John crawled onto the bus while his manager called the rest of us ASSHOLES! He was definitely not a happy man, but off they went to Oklahoma.

I thanked Gary for a great night as we pissed ourselves laughing and waited for cabs. I told him, "Man, this town is really fucking cool. The people here are genuinely nice. I like it. The musicians are talented; there are songwriters who are talented. Maybe I'll move here."

Whenever I went to Nashville, I stayed with friends Laura and Henry Seligmann and their daughter Alyssa. I had met Laura and Henry through Cinderella when I was on a Ratt tour. They were in the process of buying a new home in Lebanon, Tennessee, and they casually mentioned that they were going to rent their place out once they moved into their new home.

Ashley and I were in our on-again-off-again relationship. She would break it off with me, go away for a while, and then come back again, saying, "I missed you, but this doesn't mean that we're together again." Even though she was unsure of what she wanted, she was as clear as she could be with me.

I visited Nashville around Christmas and then Ashley asked me if I wanted to come down to Georgia and visit her at her folks' place for the holidays. I said, "Yes, of course," hoping something positive would break with us. I went and hung out with her and her family for the festive season, and then went back to Nashville to work on music.

There was certainly something about the Southern charm that was drawing me in. I just liked it and the difference became even more apparent when I went back to Los Angeles in the new year of 2007.

It was a mid-March day as I sat in my car on the 405 freeway, not going anywhere. It took about a fucking hour to go one fucking exit. Unhappy that I was wedged bumper-to-bumper, I thought about how my relationship with Ashley had broken down and how that wasn't going anywhere either. It felt like Los Angeles was fucking eating me alive again!

I called Laura from the middle of the traffic jam and asked, "Just out of curiosity, are you serious about renting your Nashville house out?"

When she said she was, I asked, "Well, when are you planning on moving into your new home?" to which she replied, "Not long to go now, probably around the first week of April."

"And just out of curiosity, how much rent do you want for the house?" I enquired.

Somewhat hesitantly, she said, "Maybe eight hundred and fifty dollars."

I clarified, "Eight hundred and fifty dollars a month?"

"Yeah," she said.

Having stayed at the two-story house a few times before, I knew it had three bedrooms upstairs, two bathrooms upstairs, and one downstairs, plus a dining room, living room, kitchen, and garage. There was a screened-in back deck that needed a little love, but it overlooked a massive backyard the size of three soccer pitches with a creek running through it.

I was currently paying $1,500 for a small cottage in Burbank that I shared with my drummer buddy Troy Patrick Farrell. I thought, now I can have a whole fucking house to myself for $850.

So, I committed to Laura, "Okay, I'll be there the first week of April."

The traffic jam was beneficial to me after all. I was moving to fucking Nashville!

PART III

THE END: NASHVILLE, TENNESSEE

23
Back for More

When I got to Nashville, Laura and Henry were still in the house for the first couple of weeks getting ready to move, so I put all the packing boxes full of my shit in the garage. I then got a phone call from Warren DeMartini who told me, "Stephen Pearcy is back, and we're going out on a massive tour with Poison and White Lion, so you need to be in LA for Ratt rehearsals."

Once Laura and Henry moved, I spent the next week unpacking and setting up my new place with new furniture. A guy named Topher Nolen who lived down the street came by, knocked on the door, and welcomed me to the neighborhood. I had met him briefly through Laura and Henry, and he asked if I needed a hand with anything.

"Are you any good with a hex key?" I asked, then he helped me put my new furniture together as we smoked some cigarettes, drank Guinness, and bullshitted while trying to decipher the instructions. Topher has been the bass player in my solo band ever since.

No sooner was my house set-up, I flew back to Los Angeles for two weeks of Ratt rehearsals before embarking on a huge tour. I was gone all through May, June, July, August, September, and I think it got extended into October and November as well. I didn't get to enjoy my new Nashville home for quite some time.

I had been stockpiling songs I was writing, not exactly sure what sure what I was going to do with them. One of the first was a Led Zeppelin-ish acoustic song called "Danse de Papillion." Another was a song I called

"Crash," which I heard in my head as having a Stones-y, Black Crowes kind of vibe.

I got together with Brent Woods after playing it for him on acoustic guitar. He thought it sounded awesome, so I started working on it with him, trying to get it right. Brent is a great guitarist who was in Wildside (named after the Mötley song) and played in Vince Neil's band with my Ratt bassist Robbie Crane.

We laid it down, but I wasn't totally sure if it was right or not. Sometimes as a musician, you don't really know if a song's going to go as you hear it in your head. It may be something simple like the mix, where maybe the bass is too loud, the guitars need to come up, or the drums need to come up, or the bass and guitars need to come down, or whatever it is. I couldn't get the electric version of "Crash" right, so I put the song to bed and didn't wake it up for a few years.

I was listening and dissecting, perfecting, as I tried to find my new musical way. I tried to move forward, but I was stuck because I was trying to reinvent myself and do something that was going to make me relevant, instead of just being me. At the same time, I got frustrated with John Greenberg and Tim Heyne from Union Entertainment Group, so I split from them. They were my managers from the beginning, with me all through The Scream, all through Mötley, and through most of my Union days. While I was playing in Ratt, I was keen to get my own music happening, and I felt they weren't very supportive of my efforts.

They snubbed the two songs I did with Dave Darling, and when John Greenberg listened to what I was working on with Brent Woods, he mumbled, "It's okay. Sounds very Beatles-esque."

At that point they were no longer managing Ratt, but they were handling Cinderella, Oleander, Saliva, Nickelback, and other big rock bands. They were also managing some producers and songwriters. I called them a few times and asked if they could hook me up with one of their producers to help. It would take them a week or two to call me back and then they weren't very forthcoming. I started to feel like I wasn't important to them anymore and they had better things to do.

I was hanging with Pete Merluzzi and he said, "Well, since you don't have management anymore, I'll help manage you." It had been a few years since I met him backstage when Cardboard Vampyres supported ZZ Top, and I felt I could trust having him in my corner. Pete stopped me from being my own worst enemy when he told me, "Crab, seriously, just do a fucking record, stop overthinking it. You are who you are and there are people out there who appreciate what you do. And you need to just stop overthinking. Stop being a fucking idiot and just go out and do your fucking record."

It took me a while to heed his advice, but I eventually said, "All right, I'm going to do an acoustic record."

I listened to the song "Crash" again, and transposed the key, making it about five steps higher than it initially was, and played it with a capo. Daniel Karkos (a local musician I started working with), Topher, and I arranged some beautiful harmonies for it and when we laid it down, it turned out great. It's a song about the end of a relationship, and I used my experience with Ashley as inspiration. She was young and wasn't sure what she wanted, and it was an expression of how I felt after she gave up and let go and my world came crashing down again.

Ratt's 2007 summer coheadlining tour with Poison was meant to include White Lion as support, but they had to drop out due to some legal issues over their band name, so they were subsequently replaced by young Swedish rockers Vains of Jenna.

Ratt's founding singer Stephen Pearcy was back in the band after a six-year absence, displacing Jizzy Pearl in the process. I knew Stephen from my time in Mötley and loved having him back again. At times, he's been accused of being short or rude to some people, but I've always had nothing but great experiences with him. You never really knew which Stephen you were getting on any given night, though, so I also think he gave Ratt that dark, rock edge that it was lacking with the rest of us. Stephen loves rock music and epitomizes the lifestyle completely. The only drag about having him back was that the daily disagreements between Bobby and Warren became a three-headed monster, but the debauchery and I-don't-give-a-fuck level was definitely raised a bit with Pearcy's return.

We knew a guy who met us on the road and would bring us hash and weed, which sometimes got smoked out of apples by Stephen. He brought us a two-inch-thick blueberry muffin cake in a pan, which came with his warning, "Take it easy with cutting yourself a piece of cake because I greased the fucking pan with hash butter and added weed to the cake batter. I also glazed the top of the muffin cake with more fucking hash butter."

I took a piece of hashberry muffin cake and ate it, as did Warren and Robbie Crane. Stephen must have been hungry since he took two pieces.

I yelled out to the Vains of Jenna guys, "You've got to try this!"

They grabbed a piece of hashberry cake and split it between the four of them and about forty minutes later they were fucking obliterated, sitting and lying on the ground, trying to make sense of shit.

Sitting on our tour bus, I said to Robbie, "Holy fuck, dude. I'm beyond fucking high right now!"

Robbie replied, "Dude, me, too. Fuck. This is unbelievable. That hashberry muffin cake is SO fucking potent!"

I sat outside the bus for a while, smoking cigarettes, drinking Guinness, and laughing as I watched the fucking Vains of Jenna guys just fumble and fall over themselves. With my sides aching from the hilarity, we rolled on toward the next town, and I got into my bunk.

I watched half of *The Big Lebowski*...well, just stared at the TV screen really, not knowing what the fuck was going on. I was that high. I finally turned it off and managed to get to sleep, when I stirred at five o'clock in the morning, disturbed by the sounds of loud acoustic classical music.

As I opened my bunk's curtains, I heard Robbie also open his. I looked down at Robbie under my bunk, and then we both looked across the fucking aisle of the bus to the top bunk opposite us. There was Warren lying in bed, still in his leather stage pants, watching an Andre Segovia video with a huge shit-eating grin on his face. He had no idea that Robbie and I were waving and yelling at him, "Dude, turn your fucking TV down! Goddamnit, fuck!"

We got up the next morning and were still high. Stephen emerged from his bunk and ate the last two pieces. He scraped all the remnants of the hashberry cake off the bottom of the fucking pan and licked his fingers clean. "Dude, you're a fucking machine!" I said.

It was definitely fun and nonstop foolishness.

Border crossings were always a trip, and they still are, as far as I'm concerned. One time crossing into Canada we had to wake up at like 5:30 in the morning and take our passports into the office, so we made sure we got rid of any illegal substances beforehand.

As we were getting our shoes on to go in, some of the officers entered our bus with dogs. It was funny watching the drug-sniffing dogs nearly go into convulsions as they sniffed their way through our bus. We didn't have anything but I'm sure the curtains, carpet, and the bowl full of apples that Stephen converted into pipes sent the dogs into sensory overload.

I fucking hate crossing the border into Canada, or back into America for that matter. I can't figure out which side of the border has the bigger dicks protecting it. Every fucking time I cross, they're fucking assholes about searching me. You'd think by now, after having pulled me over to search twenty or thirty times, they'd figure out that I'm not smuggling drugs or humans across the border.

Another time, coming back into America on a tour with Cinderella, Quiet Riot, and Firehouse, I got into a screaming match with a border agent. Everything was going fine. We pulled over, and everyone got out of bed and went into the office with our passports. After checking our credentials, they sent us back to our bus with instructions that agents would be checking the vehicles as well.

About thirty minutes later, Cinderella's bus was cleared to split, and these two young agents came onto our bus, gave it a quick once over, checked our passports again, and told us we were good to go.

Suddenly, this grumpy fucking asshole who obviously didn't get laid the night before came onto our bus and screamed at the two younger agents, "Nobody is cleared to go until I say." He told us to stay on the bus and left.

So we waited thirty minutes…forty-five…an hour…you get the point. He's taking his good-old time. He pulled over another bus full of these little old ladies coming back from a gambling excursion, and he made them all pull their luggage out from under the bus and sit in the summer morning sun while he took his time searching all of the buses on our tour.

At this point, we'd been waiting for about three hours for this guy to finish his search. We'd all had coffee, cigarettes, food, and hadn't been allowed to use the bathroom facilities inside the building, and we couldn't do ANYTHING on the bus. So I went outside to the trailer, where the idiot was going through all the cases, and I asked if I could help him expedite the process. The guy turned and yelled at me, "GET ON THE FUCKING BUS!"

I lost it. I said, "Excuse me? Who do you think you're talking to?"

The guy was livid with me and told me he's an officer of Homeland Security and I need to return to my bus. I really just wanted to explain the bathroom situation we were in.

He said, "I don't give a shit! Get on your fucking bus!"

So I told him he was a fucking moron, making us all wait for three hours. We had to use the bathroom, we had a schedule to keep, and he was keeping the old ladies in the sun. We were all afraid they were going to have fucking heat strokes waiting for this prick.

Now, as I mentioned, he had let the Cinderella bus go through at 6:00 a.m. On the bus was Tom Keifer, Fred Coury, Eric Brittingham, Jeff LaBar, Gary Corbett (their keyboard player), and their pyro guy JT. So, while this guy was yelling at me and telling me he has an important job to do, blah, blah, blah—I screamed at him and reminded him how fucking stupid he was, as the one bus he did let through had on it: one guy from the Middle East, three guys with police records, and one explosives expert.

That's when I felt Larry Morand's death grip on the back of my neck, as he walked me back to the Ratt bus. He was laughing at me, as were the

Ratt guys, but they all advised me to shut the fuck up and not make the situation worse.

After our long tour with Poison, we took a little break, and I tried to get settled into my house. On the night of December 12, 2007, I was lying on my couch when Eddie Gore's wife Lorie called me and said, "Hey, I'm supposed to go to a Christmas party tonight. My husband is out of town, so do you want to go to this Christmas party with me?"

Lorie is an attractive woman, and I must have paused for a while as I processed her question, wondering if there was some ulterior motive happening. I was immediately thinking all the wrong shit, and I think Lorie picked up on my hesitation. She said, "Eddie told me to call you, because he thought you might be at home alone. I'll meet you at the Tin Roof, and we'll go to the party."

I said, "Okay, but I can't stay out too late as I have a flight to LA tomorrow."

I threw on a pair of leather pants and a black tank top. I put on a little bit of guy-liner and quickly tweaked my short, spiky hair. I put on a sweater and a coat, grabbed a bottle of champagne and a bottle of red wine to contribute, and headed to the Tin Roof where I met Lorie. From there, we headed to the party at a house in East Nashville. We walked up to the front door and knocked. A familiar looking woman answered the door. She had a black cocktail dress on with a neck bow. It was Debbie, Eddie, and Lorie's very attractive next-door neighbor who I had met briefly the year before. As Debbie motioned to us to enter and I walked in, there was a quick little exchange between Debbie and Lorie that I somewhat noticed.

Once inside this beautiful home with beautiful furniture, I instantly saw all the men wearing vests and suit jackets, while the ladies wore long evening dresses. Even the food was upscale. Holy shit, I thought to myself, I do not fucking belong here at all.

I took a seat and after ten minutes Debbie came by with a tray of shots and offered, "Hey, do you want a blowjob…Jäger?" chuckling as she handed me a drink.

We did two blowjob shots together, and I asked, "Is it cool if I take my coat and sweater off? I'm wearing a tank top underneath, but I'm covered in tattoos."

She said, "Oh, yeah, we're tattoo friendly here; no big deal," as she led me to a bedroom where I could put my things.

We then headed back to where Lorie was, and I tried to mingle with some of the other partygoers. I asked Debbie about smoking a cigarette, and she said to head out the back of the house.

I lit up a smoke in the backyard and this guy Richie Lee came out. He said, "Hey, man, what are you doing here?" so I told him my friend invited me.

I asked, "What's your name?" and he said, "I'm Richie."

I said, "Hi, I'm John," and he said, "I know who you are, you're John fucking Corabi."

Debbie came outside, and I offered her a cigarette. I could tell she didn't smoke but tried to smoke a cigarette with me. She tried her best to look like she had been doing it for years, and we still laugh about that today. I later found out that Debbie had just split-up with her boyfriend and had been commenting to Eddie and Lorie, "Hey, when's your little rocker friend coming back to Nashville? I'd really like to meet that guy again." They took her up on it and brought me to the party, so when Debbie opened the door and saw me there with Lorie, she couldn't believe it. We were set-up by our friends Eddie and Lorie Gore.

Debbie was also thinking, "Fuck, when it rains it pours," because her ex-boyfriend was also there, plus she had called some other guy who she liked, and he was riding into town to come to the party, too.

As the party wore on that night, I said to Debbie, "You know what, why don't you sit down? Let me make YOU a drink. What do you want to drink?" That apparently left a very favorable impression on her.

When most of the people had left the party, Debbie said, "Hey, let's go to The Red Door."

Wanting me to hook-up with Debbie, Lorie said, "Yeah, let's go!"

So, I went with Debbie and half a dozen of her friends and we bellied up to the back bar, listening to music, and talking. Debbie and I kissed each other a few times, but it was getting late and I had to get home because I had a flight to Los Angeles the following morning, so I tried to get Debbie to come home with me, to no avail. I even tried my best pickup line on her: I asked her, "Have you ever played post office?" She didn't know the game, so I told her, "That's where I take you home, and lick you like a stamp, and put my MALE in your BOX!"

She laughed and said, "In all of my years bar tending, I've never heard that one!"

As she was leaving with her girlfriends, I said to her, "Hey, wait here, I'm just going to walk Lorie to her car."

When I came back, everybody was gone. What the fuck? Maybe it was too soon with the joke?

I overslept and almost missed my flight the next morning; I was so fucking hungover and miserable. When I arrived in LA just after noon, I tried calling her and left a message, "Debbie Sorenson, this is John Corabi. I love you but I fucking hate you. I'm so fucking hungover right now."

Debbie had just ended a relationship, and I had also split with Ashley. My modus operandi in the past was to get out of one relationship and very quickly jump into another one. I didn't want to do that again and neither did she.

I eventually went on a couple of dates with her, and as we talked, I told her, "I honestly don't know what I want."

I told her later that part of me was sitting there looking at her, recognizing she's very attractive, but wondering why this gorgeous chick in her early thirties was not dating someone, or why she wasn't married or had been married before. I was so burned from experience that I was trying to figure out what was wrong and what I was not seeing.

She owned a couple of residential properties in Nashville, and she not only had her hair salon business, she owned its commercial property as well. Maybe her focus had been on her career more than finding Mr. Right.

I was being cautious, and I think it was good for both of us. I was completely honest in saying I wasn't sure what I wanted, as much as I definitely loved hanging out with her.

She said, "That's fine, go figure yourself out. Go do what you've got to do, but at the end of the day, don't come by my house unless you call. And I'm just letting you know now, if you're going to date other people and do what you're going to do, then I'm going to date other people and do what I'm going to do. We'll figure it out and see if it works in time. Time will tell."

I knew Debbie was seeing other people, as I was seeing other people, but every time I was back in Nashville, I wanted to see her and hang out.

In April, I had a few days off at home around my birthday, and she had just been to her best friend's wedding in Jamaica and cut her trip short so she could be home some of the time when I was in Nashville.

Debbie called and asked, "Hey, are you still in town?" to which I replied, "Yeah, I'm leaving tomorrow night."

She said, "I know your birthday's coming up, so I have something for you. If it's cool, I'd love to come by your place and drop it off."

She showed up to my house that evening with a huge tray of sushi and a giant chocolate birthday cake. I thought that was really sweet of her, and it made a big impact on me. She hung out and stayed the night before I headed back to Los Angeles for rehearsals with Ratt for a European tour.

I dated a few other women, but, with no disrespect, I felt like I was getting shit from everybody. Like, "You didn't call me yesterday? Why didn't you call for two days? What were you doing?"

Ashley still called me on occasion, too, and it just got to the point where I had a long, hard think about it. I didn't know if I had an issue communicating my thoughts to these ladies or what, but I did not dig getting reprimanded or fucking yelled at since I thought I was being very clear in the relationships.

Everybody I'd been dating had been on my ass. The only person who was totally honest with me and hadn't given me any shit about anything was Debbie.

While on my European tour with Ratt, I called her from Ireland, and we had a big, long conversation. She said, "I was going to talk to you about this, and I don't want this to sound like a threat or an ultimatum, but I just need to know where we're at, if this is going to go any further or if I'm just a booty call when you come back to Nashville."

I respected that. It had been about eight months of uncertainty, and it was time to decide. I asked her, "Can you wait until I get home? I'd really like to take you out to dinner and sit down and talk about all this more."

She said, "Absolutely, fair enough. No decision needs to be made in the next week." So I really thought about my situation with Debbie and some of the other girls I had met or dated along the way, and I came to the conclusion that I really liked being with her, and I may be blowing something really cool if I'm too cautious. With my newfound perspective, I finished the Ratt tour, and headed home to Nashville.

After I got home, I called Debbie and asked if she wanted to go get a bite to eat and hang. We had a great dinner at a place called Virago, and I told her that I wanted to be with her in a monogamous relationship. She was happy; I was happy. It had been eight or nine months, and we had both dated some other people, but nothing panned out. She told me later that she really wanted things to work out with me.

Being a hairstylist, a lot of her friends and clients will come in and complain about their dating experiences. I have no qualms in telling them, "Listen to Debbie when she gives you dating advice, because when we were dating, she didn't play me per se, but she played me like a violin. She knew to not give me shit. I was going to do what I wanted, and she was going to do what she wanted. There were rules, though: don't come by my house unless you call, and whatever you're doing, I'm probably going to be doing the same thing. So long as you are clear on that, then go do what you've got to do and figure out what you want."

Other than the one time to give me my birthday gift, she never called me, and never complained if I didn't call her. She just let everything play out the way it should play out, with no pressure.

It took a moment of clarity in fucking Ireland for me to realize and say to myself, this chick is not giving me any grief. What am I still looking for? I've been married twice, and I've had my fill of fucking girlfriends, but perhaps my paranoia may be keeping me from the one. Maybe Debbie is the one!

So, I gave into it and took the next step.

A year or so after I moved to Nashville, my son Ian came out and lived with me. I was really happy he came, because I missed him. He wasn't a little boy anymore, but I still missed my kid!

I was dating Debbie, and shortly after Ian moved in, his mom Val came out and stayed at my house with Debbie and I to help celebrate his twenty-first birthday. I remember it was right before midnight when I said to everybody, "Let's go and get the birthday boy his first legal drink in a bar."

Debbie, Val, Ian, and I got into my car and went to this place about a mile from my house that I used to frequent called Big Tony's. When I walked in, the DJ saw me and asked me how I was, and I told him we were there to celebrate Ian turning twenty-one at midnight. He made an announcement over the PA and every person in that bar bought Ian a shot of either Jäger or whiskey.

Ian got so fucked up. We wrote the number twenty-one on his forehead with a black sharpie, and had to pour him into my car, and then his bed. He was so ill the next day for his actual birthday party with his friends that he didn't touch a drop of booze. Good times!

He did really well at first living in Nashville. He eventually got a job at Pearl drums, but also started hanging out with a crew that just sat around smoking weed as much as they could. He and a work buddy constantly went in late, or did not show up at all, so they both got fired. Having lost his job, Ian sat around the house doing nothing except smoking weed, getting involved with crazy girls, sitting on the computer up in his room, and doing stupid shit. I got fucking pissed about it.

At one point, I'd told him to not smoke in my house or to clean-up after himself, and we had a falling out. Another day, he was on the computer for eight fucking hours straight. I yelled up to him, "Fuck, get out of your room and go out and get some fucking sunlight. Do something, anything other than what you have been doing for the last eight hours!"

Twenty minutes later, he was still up in his room on the computer, so I yelled out again. Another twenty minutes went by, and he still hadn't moved, so I said, "If I fucking tell you this one more time, shit's going to get stupid!"

Yet, another twenty minutes went by and he still sat there on the fucking computer. I thought to myself, fine, well, if you want to be a little prick about it, watch this, as I walked over to the main power box and shut off the all the fucking power in the house. Fuck you. Now you're getting nothing, was my mindset.

He came downstairs in a huff and as he walked out the front door, I said to him, "Listen, if your foot touches the tar in the street, I'm going to fucking end your life at the curb."

He came back in, and we started talking.

I said, "Listen, dude, I'm not trying to bust your balls, but you have to go get a fucking job—do something! Help out around here."

He didn't like what I had to say, so it wasn't long after that day, he said, "I think I'm going to move back to California. I miss my friends."

I got him a ticket, and he flew back to California to live.

I was still in Ratt, and I still loved those guys…individually. I'd sit and talk with Warren, and he would be completely mellow and easy to get along with—Mr. Guitar Player. Even if it was a room full of people and Warren, it was fine. But as far back as when I joined the band, when Bobby Blotzer was inserted into the situation, the whole thing became a pissing match between him and Warren, who would say, "Bobby, you're playing the songs too fast."

Bobby would tell him, "No, you're playing too slow," and so it would go on, back and forth. If Bobby said left, Warren would say right.

I love Blotzer, but he could be stubborn and hard to deal with. He didn't think about the feelings of anyone around him. When he had a thought, he immediately acted on it or said what was on his mind, oblivious to whomever he offended.

He was notorious for getting on the bus at the end of the night, usually buzzed, taking all his clothes off, and walking around the tour bus in his underwear and the occasional T-shirt. At that point, Robbie Crane would usually have a go at him, by busting his balls about his "flat ass." So he'd go into the back lounge of the bus alone, while we were all trying to sleep and listen to fucking Journey and Heart with the volume cranked to thirteen, triggering more fucking comments or arguments. The frustrating part of it all is, deep down, he's a good-hearted lug, but most of the time he doesn't even realize he's doing something that you want to kill him over.

When Stephen rejoined the band and came into the mix, it was a pissing match between all three of them, and then Stephen would shout, "Goddamn, just shut the fuck up. Let's just rock out. Jesus Christ!"

It was the most functioning dysfunctional family ever—dare I say probably even worse than Mötley, if that's actually possible. I've never been in a band that fucking argued between themselves so much.

They'd say, "Rehearsal at noon," so I would make sure I was there by noon. Then we would fucking sit there for an hour and a half or two hours while Bobby and Warren argued because they couldn't fucking figure out what tempo the song was supposed to be.

So I started showing up at 1:30 p.m. every day, just to be more efficient. Robbie and I would sometimes get back in the car and drive to Subway, eat our fucking sandwiches, take a shit, smoke a cigarette, drive back, and Warren and Bobby would still be arguing about the tempo of the first fucking song we were going to play. I got so tired of it.

I played my last show as a member of the band at the House of Blues, and Ratt's manager organized for some people from a record label that was a subsidiary of Roadrunner Records to see us perform. We leveled the club that night; the band was sounding tight, and definitely firing on all cylinders. The label people came backstage into the dressing room and said, "We love the fucking band. You guys are fucking awesome. We're offering you guys a record deal. Let's do this!"

I had never recorded any music with Ratt, but when I got home to Nashville after that run, I gave it some more thought, then picked up the phone and told them, "I quit."

They said, "What? We just got a record deal!"

I explained, "Yeah, I can't get through a fucking rehearsal without you guys wanting to kill each other and driving me crazy. I'm not going into a fucking studio in another state to write and record this next record *Infestation* and live with you guys for three or four months."

Especially after my experience with Blotzer doing his *Twenty 4 Seven* solo record.

After playing rhythm guitar in Ratt for eight years, I had enough and quit the band. They got Carlos Carvazo from Quiet Riot to replace me. And although I had just left Ratt, they asked me to come back for one weekend run of three shows that Carlos Carvazo couldn't do. Oddly enough, their first show was in Nashville, so they came here and rehearsed with me at SIR studios. We played the Wildhorse Saloon, then a gig in Upstate New York, and then the last show I ever played with Ratt was the M3 Festival in Maryland.

24
Taste of India

My buddy Pete Merluzzi, who was great for giving me some advice and trying to help steer me away from some of my usual neurotic bullshit, told me about an opportunity. He said, "We've got some backers and want to do a showcase for this new residency event in Las Vegas called Monster Circus. I'd like you to be a part of it."

They put together a very elaborate showcase at the Las Vegas Hilton with Cirque de Soleil aerialists, costumed dancers, and freaks, pyro, and an amazing light show. For the showcase, it was Bobby Rock, Bruce Kulick, Tony Montana, Rudy Sarzo, Dee Snider, and myself. All the buyers from the city's casinos came along to check it out, and offers came in over the festive season to put the show on early in 2009 and the managers decided to go with the Hilton, where we did the showcase.

We signed our deal with the Hilton and settled on our regular band lineup and made some changes to the show overall. Barry Manilow would play the early show at the venue from 7:00 to 9:00 p.m., then after a quick changeover, our ringmaster Sicko the Clown compèred Monster Circus from ten-midnight as we played rock and metal anthems from the seventies, eighties, and nineties. It ran on Thursday, Friday, and Saturday night, two weekends a month. It was a sinful carnival-and-rock residency in Vegas before other bands started doing them.

The lineup of the band was now Bruce, Fred Coury (who replaced Bobby on drums), Rudy, Tony, and me. Brent Fitz ended up playing keyboards and some guitar with us, and when Dee came out as a special guest and sang, I switched to guitar with Bruce and Tony. The core band would play the usual set, and the idea was to then bring in a new guest star each weekend, like Ted Nugent for example, and we'd back the guest for four or five songs in the middle of the set, ending with a grand finale that included everybody. We had a list of guests lined-up like Sammy Hagar, John Waite, Robin Zander, Ann Wilson, and the Nuge.

We opened the show with "Shout It Out Loud" by Kiss and went into "Back in Black." For the third song, all the lights were dimmed, and they lit the theater to look like hundreds of stars floating around as Brent sat at the piano and started "Dream On." While I sang the Aerosmith classic, two girls came down out of the ceiling and performed graceful acrobatic spins and moves just five feet above my head.

We also played "Hot for Teacher," and given it was Vegas, all the girls wore white shirts, and fishnet stockings with their ass hanging out from under plaid skirts.

The residency numbers were a bit slow in the beginning, but as it built momentum over the four months of shows we played, there were too many people who got involved in decisions. All the artists had managers giving their input, plus the financial backers, the Hilton staff, and they all thought they knew better than the next guy—everybody was a chief and there were no fucking Indians. It became super cutthroat to the point that Fred and I would just go and hang elsewhere to escape the politics and bullshit. We would go shopping, go for lunch, work out together, whatever we felt like to keep our noses out of all the bickering.

Since our work was at the Hilton hotel and casino, we stayed there the whole time. We had a 24/7–access pass where we could go to a massive cafeteria buffet area for all the casino's employees. I could get up at 3:00 a.m., go downstairs to the employee's cafeteria, and eat a free fucking chicken salad or whatever the fuck I wanted.

The Hilton certainly looked after us, even when I celebrated my fiftieth birthday there. Debbie flew in for it, along with a bunch of my buddies from Nashville and other parts of the States. Everybody stayed at the hotel, which gave me two cabanas right at the pool. I partied with my friends and some of the people from the show from noon until six the following morning.

Monster Circus could have been awesome, but it just became a fucking battle of egos—who could do it better, who could do it cheaper, who could do it bigger. The whole thing just imploded. I believe Dee Snider's manager, Phil Carson (Jack's father), ended up telling the Hilton management that they should just lose all the guys in the band and Dee could put on a better show without us, so we took time off for them to sort it out.

I think at that point, the Hilton certainly started asking themselves why they needed any of our people involved. They put it to bed for a couple of years and then launched a scaled-back version called *Raiding the Rock Vault*, which is still going on today.

Turning fifty wasn't all fun, though: I had been sick around this time, so I went to the doctor, who did a chest X-ray and put me through a bit of a physical. I got a scare when I went back and was told, "You've got a little spot on your lung. I'm going to give you some antibiotics and send you home for two weeks, then we'll do another chest X-ray and hopefully it's just bronchitis or something."

What the fuck?!

Naturally, I started having the most horrible thoughts that it was the dreaded C-word, so I decided to quit smoking. I took CHANTIX, which is a prescription medicine used to reduce nicotine cravings and the pleasurable effects of cigarettes. It worked; I managed to quit the cigarettes, but unfortunately started substituting smoking with other shit.

I'd sit and watch a movie with Debbie and instead of lighting a fucking cigarette or a joint, I would get up and eat half a bag of fucking Oreo cookies. I wound up gaining all this weight and had to go on a fucking diet. Dealing with such issues, I was feeling bad and down, reflecting on my life and also thinking, "What the fuck do I have to show for all of the shit that I've done in music?"

My dad called, and we had a real cool heart-to-heart. While we had a strained relationship when I was younger, it did improve as we got older. I was boo-hooing and feeling woe is me, and my dad stopped me dead in my tracks during this great conversation. He picked me up when I was feeling low.

He said, "You have a lot to show for what you've done if you think about it: you got married at nineteen to a woman who already had a daughter. You went to California to chase your dream. You put The Scream together, then you joined Mötley Crüe. At the same time, your mom was diagnosed with cancer and your son was diagnosed with diabetes. You made all that money and you took care of your mom, your kids, wives, and girlfriends in between. You've even taken care of your Uncle Gene, who passed away."

Turning the focus to himself, he explained, "When I graduated from high school, I wanted to be an artist. However, I joined the military instead. I did my time in the Korean War, then got out of the military. I met your mom, fell in love, got married, and shortly after, you came into the picture. I still wanted to be an artist, but I put everything aside, and I put on a suit and a tie, and I pushed the pencil, and I jumbled numbers, and I did what I had to do, because that's what you did."

He continued, "I had four kids, and I did well for myself. I've got money in the bank, I own a house, and I did lots of other shit in life.

Now you have taken care of your whole family, and you're not hurting financially for anything. The difference is: you did it all doing what you love to do, being an artist—a musical artist."

Dad then told me, "So, that makes you a bigger man than I'll ever be."

I couldn't finish the conversation with him. I was so emotionally blown away by what he said, I had to get off the phone.

Our relationship improved to the point where my dad and I called each other to talk at least once a week, twice a week sometimes. He called me when he retired, and when he was so excited to tell me, "I bought an El Camino, my favorite car that I've always wanted to buy!"

It was cool to sit and listen to him go on and on and on about it.

Unfortunately, his excitement wouldn't last much longer.

My former housemate Troy Patrick called me one day in Nashville and told me about the shows he played in India, drumming for White Lion, in front of 42,000 people at one concert. He said there was an opportunity for me to go there and play two shows, since former Guns N' Roses guitarist Gilby Clarke could no longer do it with him. I had never been to India before, let alone played there, so I told him to count me in.

Troy's band was called Lost Angels and included guitarist Eric Dover, who had played with Alice Cooper and fronted Slash's Snakepit. There was also Muddy Stardust on bass, who had played with LA Guns and Chris Robinson's Brotherhood.

I was senile by the time I got to India because I flew from Nashville to Dallas, Dallas to Burbank, then went to Troy's house briefly, showered and dressed, and got into a car and went to LAX. We flew from LAX to Moscow, then Moscow to New Delhi. Then it was a flight from Delhi to some small town in India where we got into a car and drove another three hours up into the mountains before we finally arrived at Dimapur in a district called Nagaland. Our shows were in northeast India—the part of India that is wedged between Bangladesh, Bhutan, and Myanmar (Burma).

I knew I was in a completely foreign land when I noticed tiger crossing signs along the roadside. I was so fucking tired from traveling for fifty fucking hours though.

It was a hundred degrees in New Delhi with probably a hundred percent humidity. I got hot in my stingray leather and denim jacket, so I took it off and put it on the back of my chair and fell asleep. I don't know if somebody took my fucking jacket off the chair or if I just forgot it in my delirious state, but when we finally got to our destination, I realized I didn't have my jacket. I made a bunch of phone calls to the airport and airline, but they couldn't find it—there went two grand down the drain.

India is a very intense and amazing place. It seemed like all the people there were either really rich or beyond dirt poor, with nobody in the middle. I went to a restaurant and watched a goat be born right in front of the window while I was fucking eating. What freaked me out more was hearing about the restaurant's bathroom. Muddy left the table to go to the bathroom to take a shit and looked around for the toilet paper. Not only was there no toilet paper, there wasn't even a fucking toilet paper holder or dispenser. We wondered if they wipe their ass with their fucking hands and then wash their hands. Muddy said the guy before him in the restroom was the cook, so luckily we hadn't ordered yet and obviously didn't order anything off that menu.

We stayed at a guesthouse called Aiers' Enclave that was like a big house in Simi Valley with a wall around it. While I laid on the bed in my air-conditioned room, I turned the TV on but couldn't find a channel in English. While I watched it anyway, out of my peripheral, I noticed something move on the wall. I looked over but there was nothing there. I watched the TV again and some movement again caught my eye. This time I quickly looked over and saw a big fucking lizard running on my wall.

My body clock was totally ass backward from the jetlag. I found myself wide-awake at 5:00 a.m., so I got up and walked down the hallway. On the second floor, there was a window that opened. I sat on the window ledge with my feet dangling over and lit a cigarette (yes…as a professional moron, I had started smoking again).

I thought about how The Beatles had taken a spiritual journey to northern India in '68 to be trained in Transcendental Meditation at Maharishi's ashram, on the lead of George Harrison, and how their stay turned out to be their most productive period for songwriting.

I wondered if such songwriting inspiration may come to me while there, but got distracted as dawn broke, and I started to see that right next to this 4,000-square-foot guesthouse with a wall around it, was a fucking makeshift plywood box building with a rusty corrugated tin roof. A woman emerged from the ramshackle home with a vase-shaped vessel. I watched her walk down a path to a little creek running the murkiest orange-brown water that looked like it would have also smelled pungent. She filled up this vessel, walked back, lit a fire, and put two pots on the flames.

She poured water into the two pots and started cooking something in one of them. Once it was fully daylight, the man of the house and five little kids popped out, and they all bathed with the warm water from the other pot.

It was fascinating for me to watch these everyday events of such a different lifestyle.

Once Troy and the other guys were up, they said they wanted to go to an internet café to send a message home that they had arrived safely. We had an escort of military guys with rifles and machine guns taking us where we needed to go. It was like a convoy of police and army, the whole nine yards. The local host took us to a place where Troy put some rupee coins in a slot. I said, "Fuck, this is dial-up, dude. It's going to take forever."

I went outside to smoke a cigarette and saw that right next door to this internet cafe, if you could call it that, was a guy sitting down reading a newspaper in his shed-like shop. It was a wooden shack with a corrugated tin roof, just like the one I saw earlier that day, from which chickens and other dead animals hung from hooks.

A dead pig that looked to weigh a couple of hundred pounds was laid on a front table with its side filleted open. It felt like it was 120 degrees outside with stupidly high humidity, and the flies buzzed all over these fucking carcasses.

Customers came up from time to time and interrupted his morning read. They talked in their local language while he grabbed a knife and cut chunks off the pig, then wrapped it in paper and exchanged money. I had a hard time thinking about consumption of that pork from such sweaty, fly-infested, shit conditions in the blazing high-noon sun.

After forty minutes, my four bandmates came out of the internet café frustrated that it took them so long to write an email and send it home to their loved ones to tell them they made it to India. Nobody ever got the emails either.

Our hosts then took us to a hospital and school where we took some time to bring a smile to the faces of some less fortunate Indian kids. We also went to a mall, where we almost got fucking mobbed, so we didn't stay there long and headed back to our living quarters to just rest and get over the jetlag.

When we got up the next morning for breakfast, one of the servants asked me, "Ah, Master, would you like some bacon and eggs?"

I respectfully replied, "I'm going to pass on that. I saw your fucking bacon yesterday. I'll just have the toast, thank you very much. And when you brew the coffee, please brew it twice."

We went to Dimapur's DSSC Stadium for our soundcheck. The first thing I noticed was the entire stage—the trusses, the floor, everything—was made of bamboo. It was extremely strong, but the sight kept messing with my head.

I watched two guys walk around the grassed area where the crowd would be watching us from. One guy had a long sickle that he used to cut the long grass while the other guy caught fleeing snakes and stuck them in fucking hessian bags. There I stood outside wearing jeans and fucking flip-flops, thinking that nobody sent me the fucking memo there could be fucking King Cobras. It's funny now, but I wasn't laughing at the time!

Twenty-six thousand people showed up to the concert, and we had a great fucking night. The next day was a seven-hour drive to our show that night in Shillong, where our promoters couldn't pay us our performance fee up-front as agreed, so Troy called another promoter, who also happened to be a prince who he met when he was there with White Lion. Suddenly, the prince and an entourage that included cops showed up in force.

Guns were drawn on our promoters and their parents, as they were told, "We're going to pay the band on your behalf, but you're going to fucking sign your house over to me. And if you don't pay me back within a month, I will keep your house and everything that you've ever worked for in your life."

I stood there astounded.

I was in India for about eight days and lost fifteen pounds from sweating and not eating much. I was afraid to eat in case I got sick, so I only ate bread and grilled corn on the cob with fucking lemon juice and spice.

I drank bottles of iced tea, and a few Diet Cokes, but without ice; I had to make sure they were refrigerated. I didn't drink any water unless it was in a bottle and the seal was intact. At one of the places where we stayed, we asked for some cases of bottled water, and Muddy noticed one case where all the lids had been cracked. He yelled at the guy, "I'm not drinking these fucking refilled bottles. You're fucking with us now. You need to make sure we have unopened bottles of water. We will fucking check."

We used the bottled water to brush our teeth and rinse our mouths out. Thankfully, with such precautions, I got out of there with no health issues. I would go back again but would prefer to play the bigger cities like Mumbai, New Delhi, and Bengaluru. I appreciate why people can either love it or hate it over there. It's so confronting in many ways, but it seems even the poorest of the poor find happiness in the simplest of things and not the material things in life. There's a lot to appreciate about that.

Back in Nashville, I felt it was time for me to put together a band to do some solo shows—electric, not acoustic. I had my neighbor Topher Nolen on bass, Sean Hughes on drums, and a great guitarist named Phil Shouse to play lead while I played rhythm guitar.

Sean was a solid drummer, but it was one of those situations where I'd look at him play and wonder, "God, this guy's so fucking good. Why is he not in a bigger band? What's the fucking deal?" It didn't take long before I thought he started to look kind of pasty, and I was wondering if he was into drugs.

We did a couple of local shows before Phil scored a well-paid gig with a country artist, so he had to take that opportunity.

With a run of three or four shows coming up in Canada, I auditioned guitar players. Sean suggested a guitarist named Eric from back in his Maryland hometown. He said, "This guy's a fucking crazy guitar player. He can play blues; he's great on acoustic guitar, too—whatever you need. If you want him to play Yngwie, he could."

Coming with such a big recommendation, I called Eric and he seemed nice enough on the phone, so I set it up where he was to come to Nashville, stay in my guest bedroom, and rehearse with us for a week before going to Canada. I asked Eric, as I had asked Sean and Topher previously, "We're going to Canada, so do you have any issues with border crosses?"

"Nope, everything's good," they all told me.

When it was time for Eric to come to Nashville, he called me and said, "I don't have a car, so a friend of mine is going to bring me down."

Eric rolled up to my door and on first impression he seemed a little goofy. His driver friend looked like he should have been in the Sex Pistols, and he ended up staying the night on my couch.

Debbie woke up the next morning and walked into our living room to get something. Eric's friend had got up, made coffee, and was sitting on my couch wearing only underwear briefs and nothing else—no pants, no shirt, no shoes, nothing. As he sipped on his coffee, Debbie said, "Put some pants on, please. I don't need to see your skinny fucking ass."

As we rehearsed, the visas came through for Canada. I said to my band members, "I've got our visas, but it doesn't mean you're getting into the country. Does anyone have a police record? Are you sure there's not going to be any fucking bullshit when we get to the border?"

"Nope, everything's good," they all told me once again.

I asked again at another point during our rehearsal week, and Sean said, "Dude, I fucking told you I'm good. Stop fucking asking! There's no problem, we're going to be fine."

So, I told them all, "Okay, I hear you, but here's the deal: I know I can get into Canada because I've done it many times before. I'm just telling you now, if I drive all the way to fucking Canada and I can't get in because one of you motherfuckers didn't tell me what's up, you're going to be very grateful there are border security officers there with guns, because I'm going to fucking kill you guys at the border."

We drove for eight hours all the way up north through America to Detroit and reached the US Customs and Border Protection checkpoint about 1:00 a.m., in order to cross the Ambassador Bridge over the Detroit River into Canada.

We handed the officers our passports. They left, then came back and told us to pull the vehicle over and come into their office. They asked where we were headed, so I said, "I'm the guy in charge. We're coming up to play a few shows. There's my paperwork, in order, so there shouldn't be a problem. There are no drugs or contraband in the car. Everybody reassured me that there are no police records, so run the passports and do whatever you've got to do. I'm sure we're good."

After fifteen minutes, the officer came back over and said to me, "Mr. Corabi, here's the deal: you and Christopher Nolen (Topher) are fine. The other two guys weren't completely forthright with you, and they've got issues."

I'm sure the officer could see the instant rage in my face, as I turned to Sean and Eric and said, "You two motherfuckers can talk to this guy. I fucking told you guys that if your bullshit prevents me from getting into Canada, you'd better pray that motherfucker has his gun drawn because I'm going to fucking kick your asses right here, right now."

I sat down with Topher, and we laughed in futility at the situation. Topher said, "Dude, I can't believe it. How many fucking times did you ask those motherfuckers?"

Things had already started getting fractious with me and Sean, but it went completely sour at that point.

The officer eventually called me back over as Sean and Eric walked away from him. He said, "Mr. Corabi, I apologize but this is the only way you're getting into Canada. Those two now must pay three hundred and fifty dollars each to get into Canada since they weren't honest and tried to say that they didn't have a record. So, here's what I'm going to do: there's no reason for you and Mr. Nolen to be penalized. If they can both pay me the three hundred and fifty bucks, we'll let them into the country. When is your last show?"

I told him it's as my paperwork stated. He asked if I was leaving the night of my last show, and I told him we were going to be leaving the following morning. He clarified the date we were going to leave and confirmed it with me, then said, "There will be an alert at every border crossing in Canada. If you don't leave the country and go back to America by two o'clock the day after your last show, there will be a warrant for the arrest of all four of you."

"Fair enough," I told him, and at about five in the morning, we finally crossed into Canada and began the four-hour drive to Toronto. I was so fucking tired that I had to pull into a rest area on the side of the road at one point for a forty-minute nap.

I shut the car off, shut all the lights off, and was sitting there falling asleep when Sean opened the back door of the car and decided to start rifling through his luggage with the door open, so the lights were on. Nobody could sleep.

"Shut the fucking door!" I shouted at him, "I'm trying to catch some fucking sleep." We just butted heads the whole fucking time as our relationship had deteriorated.

We finally got to the hotel in Toronto and had a bit of sleep. When Topher came down to the lobby, he saw Sean there, who started getting in his ear saying, "Man, I think it's really fucked that we had to pay that 350 bucks. I think John should pay me and Eric back."

At that point, Topher was pouring himself a coffee as he saw me coming down the steps. He told Sean, "Well, here comes Corabi. You can go ask him, but I'm just going to say good luck because it isn't going to end well for you, bud."

When it came time to play the shows, Eric was a train wreck. We played songs like "Dead" by Union, and he started doing the guitar solo in the wrong key. I said, "Dude, what are you doing?"

He said, "Playing the guitar solo."

"Don't you hear you're playing in the wrong key?" I asked, to which he tried to tell me that it was the right key. I said, "Dude, the song is in the key of D."

"No, it isn't; it's in F," he argued.

I said, "Listen motherfucker, are you fucking kidding me? I wrote the goddamn song, fuck off and play it in D." Topher just laughed at us.

We played the shows and got out of Canada on time before any warrants could be issued for us.

Back in Nashville, Sean and I kept butting heads, and Topher said, "I think you two guys need to talk."

I told Sean, "Dude, I feel like if I say go left, you'll go right. I fucking told you about going into Canada. I warned you multiple times. Now I just feel like you're doing shit to just fucking spite me, and I don't dig it. I'm about to book a US tour, and I'm questioning if you can do it."

Sean reassured me he could.

Replacing Eric with a guitar player from New York named Kevin Hunter, and with Sean's reassurance that he'd be fine behind the drum kit, I went ahead and booked a US tour with Faster Pussycat and LA Guns, dubbed The Triple Threat Tour.

Ten days before we hit the road, though, Sean told me, "I'm kind of having an issue with drugs and need to go home. I need to get my head straight and figure everything out."

Just what I fucking needed!

I called Troy Patrick, and thankfully he was able to do it at short notice.

Then I found out Kevin couldn't drive to Nashville—he had a license, but no car—so I drove to New York, picked him up and all of his gear, before I drove back across the country from New York to LA to rehearse with Troy for a few days. We finally got to Sacramento to begin the tour.

Troy worked with an agency I'll call "Shitshow Worldwide," who was booking the tour. When I signed on to do the tour, I got a sheet from them that listed all the dates with a fee at the end. At the first show in Sacramento, I got paid fine, but the promoters skipped out on LA Guns and Faster Pussycat. They didn't get paid, so they didn't play.

The next show was in Vegas, so I drove the nine-hour loop back down south through Bakersfield practically to LA, before heading east and north again. When I finally got into Vegas, I found out LA Guns and Faster Pussycat were to play at one venue, while I was to play at a separate venue on a door deal.

Even though Troy worked for these guys at the agency, he said, "Fuck, sorry dude. I don't know what's going on here."

One of our next shows was a festival in Oklahoma. An owner of the Shitshow Worldwide agency I'll call "Fuckwad" is a musician from a fucking eighties glam band who was also on the festival bill. I approached him to complain about the door deals. The motherfucker had the audacity to look me in the face and say, "Hey, dude, door deals, whatever, bro, it's called paying your dues!"

I spat back, "Who the fuck do you think you're talking to? I was the lead singer in the band that your band emulates. I don't do fucking door deals, so that shit's going to stop. If there are any fucking door deals on my schedule from here on out, just take them off the list because I ain't fucking doing them—I don't do fucking door deals, jerkoff!"

We had fun on the rest of the tour through the United States, hanging out with my former bandmates Traci Guns and Jizzy Pearl, who was singing for LA Guns. We had a blast with the Faster Pussycat guys, too, as always. We finished in Montreal, so dropped Kevin off with his gear in Upstate New York, where he rented a vehicle to head back home.

A few weeks later, we flew out to Sweden to play the Stockholm Rock Out Festival on September 11, 2010, which was my first solo performance in Scandinavia.

Once we got there, Troy got into a fistfight with Fuckwad from Shitshow Worldwide, so I went with Topher and Kevin to go meet Ryan Roxie. He lived in Stockholm and invited us to come to a club that Friday night to help him DJ. The owner said, "If you show up, I'll give you and your band friends free cocktails."

It sounded like a good deal and it was—we had a blast!

We got a train from the club back to our hotel. I sat with Topher, Kevin, another drummer named Seven Antonopoulos, and a girl at one end of the car. Three Black guys got on and sat at the other end. Seven and the girl got off, and we went one more stop.

We stood at the train door waiting for it to come to a halt, and as soon as it did, the three Black guys opened the door down their end and ran along the platform to confront us as we got off.

One of them started pushing me and yelled, "You called me n****r?"

Confused, I said, "Excuse me?"

Again, he said, "You called me n****r!"

I looked at my guitarist Kevin, who by the way is African American, and he was looking at me, and we both wondered what the fuck was happening.

"Dude, what the fuck are you talking about?" I asked.

He pushed me again, so I pushed him. Topher got pushed and before we knew it, an all-out brawl started on the fucking subway platform, and as we scrapped, we ended up in a pile at the bottom of the steps.

The frightened station worker selling tickets at the lower level called the cops, who saw the whole thing on CCTV cameras. They told me, Topher, and Kevin to leave and detained the three Black guys. We laughed our asses off as we made the short walk back to our hotel, saying how crazy that was.

We had another drink with one of the promoters at the hotel, and I went back to my room after an hour. As I started getting undressed, I went to take my glasses off the top of my head, then yelled, "Fuck! I've lost my fucking glasses."

I put my fucking clothes back on and started retracing my steps. Down the hallway, into the same elevator I came up on. Nothing. The bar downstairs was closed, and they didn't seem to be there. I went to the front desk and asked, "Anybody find a pair of glasses?"

I walked out the front door of the hotel and down the same side of the street we took along the block to the train station. I remember where we crossed the street and checked there, but still nothing by the time I got to the train station. As I looked around the bottom of the steps where the fight finished, the ticket seller saw me again and said, "Hey, what's going on?"

"Fuck, dude," I said, "I lost my glasses. I had a pair of glasses on the top of my head, and I lost them. Is it cool if I go back upstairs and just look around the platform a bit in case I lost them in the scuffle?"

"Why don't you wait a minute? The train hasn't come yet, so wait here with me because I'm not sure if those guys are still up there."

I waited until the next train came and went, until he said, "Okay, it should be all clear now."

I walked back up the two flights of fucking steps, looking all along each one until I got to the top platform. As I looked around the glass walls of the stair's entryway and through to the platform spot where we got off, I looked up and saw people sitting a ways down the platform. Without my glasses, it took me a while to try and focus.

"YOU!" I heard shouted and saw the guy who started the whole fight was now running right at me, while his two buddies sat there wondering what the fuck was going on.

I backpedaled through the glass door at the top of the steps, which closed after me. The guy ran full steam at me, taking his jacket off on the approach. When he made it to the glass door, both his arms were behind him, still stuck in his jacket sleeves, and he tried to get his jacket off before reaching me. The glass door opened, and I fucking punched him right in the face.

The stupid idiot toppled backward and landed on his ass while the doors shut again. His two mates started running toward me, as did two cops who jumped the tracks from the opposite platform and loudly blew their whistles.

So there I sat on the train platform at 3:00 a.m., telling the arresting cops, "This whole thing started because he said I called him a n****r. Officer, I just came here from America to play a rock show tomorrow night. My guitar player is actually Black, so I'm hardly the racist that guy is making me out to be."

The cops went back and forth and after another hour passed, one of them asked me, "Do you speak any Swedish?"

I said, "I know *tack* for thank you, and I can order *pyttipanna* in a restaurant, but other than that, I don't speak any at all."

He said, "Okay, here's what we're going to do: I'm going to walk you back to the hotel, where you're going to give me your passport. We'll review all the surveillance tapes from the train that you were on and from the platform. If everything they're saying is right, then you're going to have an issue tomorrow. But if you didn't do anything as you say, I'll be more than happy to give you your passport back. I'll be at your show."

"If you want to come to the show, I can put you on the guest list."

"Okay, do that," he said. "I'll bring your passport back to you at five o'clock tomorrow. I don't think you're going to have an issue because I've been talking with them for an hour and their story has changed five times. They're now saying that you called them a n****r in Swedish."

After some sleep, the band met in the lobby to head to the venue Gamla Tryckeriet for the show. Troy was banged-up a bit from his fight, Topher's watch got broken, and we all had cuts and scrapes.

Ryan Roxie busted our fucking balls during the rest of the trip, saying, "John Corabi, the last act of crime we had here was like twenty-four years ago. There's been no crime since, nothing. I don't even think our police have a phone. There was no crime in Sweden until you fucking showed up here to play!"

Once home again, Troy sent me an email from the owners of Shitshow Worldwide. As I've said before, the industry standard is that half of my performance fee always gets sent up-front from the promoter to the booking agent as a deposit, while I pick-up the other half at the show.

Troy had sent a message to Fuckwad from Shitshow Worldwide to get the rest of my money, and he forwarded me the reply from them that basically said, "Fuck John Corabi. I'm using John Corabi's deposit money to offset my band's losses. Fuck him."

I looked into legal action but would have needed a Californian lawyer. Once I tallied up the amount of money they owed me for the North American tour and the show in Stockholm, and weighed that up with what it would likely cost me to sue them and file a complaint with the Better Business Bureau, I decided it wasn't worth it. I decided I would wipe my hands of it, but I did tell Fuckwad from Shitshow Worldwide and his partner that if I ever see them in a dark alley, shit's going to get real. I don't like getting ripped off!

Shortly after I had it out with the booking agency, Traci Guns called me to chat, and I told him what transpired. They then had the gall to call me back and say, "We don't appreciate you telling Traci Guns that we ripped you off."

I said, "You did rip me off. I have a fucking email that tells Troy that you're going to rip me off. What part of this am I not understanding? You did fucking rip me off!"

"Well, you'd better fucking stop," he said, "or I'm going to sue you for slander."

I said, "Go ahead and sue me for slander because then I will countersue you for fucking not paying me!"

It was a fucking shit show...hence the name "Shitshow Worldwide."

25
If I Had a Dime

My dad sent out cards in the mail formally inviting everyone to his seventy-fifth birthday party to be held in his backyard. When we next spoke on the phone, he asked me if I received the invitation that he sent to me and Debbie. I told him I wasn't sure if I could make it and would have to check my performance schedule, but I really wanted to be there for it. He said, "Okay, no worries, but I'd love for you to be there, and bring Debbie of course."

A week or two before the event, I finally committed and told him, "Dad, I'm definitely coming. We're going to drive up."

He said, "All right, awesome! It'll be great to see you there."

When I spoke with him again a couple of days before his big event, he told me, "It's funny, so many in the family didn't RSVP until they found out you were coming and now everybody wants to come to my party. I told them if they didn't RSVP, no catering for them. They get a peanut butter and jelly sandwich."

Debbie and I stayed at a hotel in Philadelphia then drove to my dad's house for the party. We walked inside and saw my dad had a lot of catering out on the main table. He had another small table set-up next to it.

The big table was laid out with an array of delicious looking pasta, meat, and salad dishes. The little table beside it had just the one dish of about twenty peanut butter jelly sandwiches.

He was true to his word: if you didn't RSVP, you weren't allowed to have the fucking pasta and meat. He enforced it! I heard him say to a guest, "I don't give a shit, you didn't RSVP! You didn't give a shit about my seventy-fifth birthday until Johnny was coming, so now you can have a peanut butter and jelly sandwich."

Debbie and I still laugh and joke about it to this day. Dad was such a funny guy.

I parted from Pete Merluzzi's management and met a Canadian guy named Jay, who had a record label and management company in Nashville. I don't remember how we met, but he was a fan of the Mötley record I did, and as we got talking more, he said, "I've got my own studio, and I've got a record label with a few acts on it. I think it'd be great if you would do an album with me."

I told him I had been thinking about doing an acoustic record to which he replied, "Even better, since it'll be cheaper to do."

I got together again with Daniel Karkos, who everybody calls DA. He was a guitarist who had moved to Nashville from Rochester, New York, and had done some production and writing work with Jerry from King's X and was also a whizz in the studio. I brought Topher in to play bass and Matt Farley for percussion, since there would be no drums on it. It took us about three months to record all the songs, predominantly at night and produced by Chris Henderson, the guitarist from Three Doors Down.

During this time, I got a call from tour manager Larry Morand, who asked if I'd go out and do a tour with Cinderella. Tom Keifer saw me perform an acoustic show somewhere, and he wanted me on their bill. Tom didn't want to have shitty cover bands that the local promoters would choose to open for them every night. He was fine if they wanted to put a third band on first as a local support, but he wanted the schedule to be the local band, then me doing a thirty to forty-five-minute acoustic set, then Cinderella to come on and knock it out.

I was a little nervous about it as I hadn't done any solo shows in larger places; I didn't know how it was going to go over with me standing there with an acoustic guitar by myself, opening for Cinderella. It turned out great, though, and the Cinderella camp was incredibly generous and helpful. They allocated me a bunk on their crew bus and all my gear traveled with theirs. I did the whole tour around the US with them and played probably forty to fifty shows.

We finished laying down the acoustic songs in the studio, right before I had to leave on that tour. Daniel said he'd sit with Chris Henderson to help mix the record while I was gone, so I told him to send me the mixes. I talked with Daniel every day while I was on the road and gave him feedback, "I like this; I don't like that." Overall, DA spent more time in the studio working on it than I did; he did a great job, being very particular and thorough.

Daniel sent five or six finished songs to me that I downloaded to my phone. I told Larry Morand, "Oh, dude, you've got to hear this record I did. It's pretty good."

He had a listen and said, "Fuck, dude, this is great shit!"

Since I didn't have a manager, I asked Larry if he ever thought about managing, and he said, "Yeah, I actually manage a couple of bands."

I offered, "Well, if you want to take me under your wing, I'd be more than happy to," and he obliged.

When I got home from the tour, Larry asked if I signed a deal with Jay. I said, "Nah, I kept asking for a contract from the guy, but he didn't want to. He said we should just do a handshake. We never discussed money, percentages, or anything."

Larry said, "Listen, give me his number. I want to sit down with him because I played the record for somebody at Universal, and they love it. They want to do something with you. Even if it's on this guy's label, we can likely come to an arrangement where Universal does the distribution and cranks their publicity department machine. That would mean performances on late-night shows, like David Letterman and Conan O'Brien."

Larry and I both spoke with Jay, and he refused to come to the party and work with the major record label. I explained, "This is better for everybody, including you. It will be worldwide distribution with Universal, and they're going to put it through their machine with all the right advertising and videos. They love the record!"

He refused to budge, but then eventually came around a bit and said, "Let me think about it, and I'll tell you what I want."

Two months went by, then three months. I got hold of him and said, "Dude, seriously? What's going on? I want to sort this out because Universal's getting edgy, asking if we're going to do this or not."

Finally, he said, "All right, I'll back out of it and sell you the masters for $25,000 plus I get fifty percent of the record for life."

"You're fucking high! That's ridiculous!" was Larry's response.

Larry asked me about where and how it was recorded. I told him, "We did it in this guy's studio—at least, he said it was his studio. There were no session musicians. We played everything between like six and ten o'clock at night, over three months. There was no tape involved, it was done with Pro Tools, so any costs would have been really low."

A while later, I went with Debbie and a few friends to a Mexican cantina called Chuy's in Nashville. As we drank our tequilas that evening, somehow the story of my lost record deal got brought up and how its future was now in limbo.

When I finished telling them about it, Debbie took a sip of her tequila, looked at me, and said, "John Corabi, you know I love you, but all I can say is you need to stop being a fucking pussy. Call that motherfucker and either give him an ultimatum or tell him to go fuck himself once and for all. This is your life. You're not twenty years old anymore, so you can't sit around and fucking wait for this guy to decide whatever. He's ruining your fucking career, and he's ruining your fucking life."

"You know what? You're right," I confessed.

Debbie asked me how much it would cost to record the fucking record again, so I said I'd figure it out. By then, I was jamming with Cheney Brannon, who had been the drummer in Collective Soul. I called Cheney and DA and asked them, "How much would it cost me to rerecord this *Unplugged* album in my house?"

They each ran some numbers then got together and did some math, before they told me, "Dude, this thing should not cost you more than five grand."

I called Jay the following Monday morning and said, "I'm fucking sick of calling you and not getting calls returned, so here's the deal: you've got until five o'clock Friday to give me my masters. Agree to the counteroffer and give me my fucking masters, or come Monday, I'm rerecording the entire fucking record myself."

Five o'clock Friday came and went, and I didn't hear a peep from him. Saturday came and went, and I didn't hear from him either. Yep, Sunday as well. On Monday, Cheney brought up a heap of gear from Atlanta, and we set up a studio in my fucking house and recorded the entire acoustic record in my living room. I sang the vocals in the second bedroom with the bathroom door open for a little reverb. My other spare bedroom was the control room. We recorded the entire record in a week and then Cheney and I took it to Atlanta and mixed it in a day and a half.

We started that record on a Monday and finished recording on Sunday. We mixed it Tuesday and Wednesday, and we were done. I sent it off to Larry Morand, who gave it to Joe O'Brien at Rat Pak Records. They took it to mastering, where the guy said, "I really don't need to master anything. The record is awesome as it is."

I booked a supporting tour in Europe as Rat Pak started pressing the records and printing the artwork.

The original guy, Jay, eventually responded after a month and said, "All right, I'm willing to negotiate," to which Larry said, "Hey, buddy, here's the deal: John's already rerecorded it and the album's coming out in a few weeks, so you can save your copy for your fireplace mantle. Talk to you later."

He was pissed. When he started threats of legal action, Larry told him, "Good luck. You have no agreement. There was no contract, and we both called you about thirty fucking times, and you were an asshole and didn't call us back. Have a nice life."

I got asked by Gibson guitars to visit Moscow and attend and perform at their biggest music industry trade show, Musikmesse Russia 2013, akin to California's NAMM Show. I went over and played with Ryan Roxie, Greg Smith (who played bass for Alice Cooper and Ted Nugent), Bobby Rondinelli, and former AC/DC drummer Chris Slade.

Individually, we did music clinics, then came together as a celebrity panel of judges for a Battle of the Bands. At the end of that competition, they invited us to get on stage and jam some tunes, which we did. We had fun and then headed back to America.

Bobby Rondinelli was then approached by a hulking Russian dude who everybody called Big Al. He walked around in a fur coat and had his fingers in everything. He put an offer in to Bobby for us to come back to Russia and play ten shows, so Bobby asked me to sing on the tour. Instead of Ryan Roxie, Craig Goldy of Dio and Geoff Nichols from Black Sabbath were recruited for the tour. The band was called the Classic Rock All-Stars.

Time was short to submit my passport and visa application, so I was pushed to the wire to have it back in time. As the visa-processing period came to an end, I flew from Nashville to New York's La Guardia Airport and got a cab into Manhattan. I went into the office, quickly picked up my passport and visa, jumped back into a taxi to JFK Airport, and barely made my Aeroflot flight to Moscow.

We did a ton of press from the minute we got there. They then took us to a very nice, upscale restaurant where we enjoyed a great meal, and as soon as we finished eating, all these photographers suddenly appeared and started taking photos of us individually, then with the restaurant owner, then with the staff, and then people in the restaurant. I could see that Big Al had side deals going with everybody.

We played in towns like Chelyabinsk, Magnitogorsk, and Omsk, which were down near the border of Kazakhstan and fucking closer to Mongolia than Moscow. We were driven around in an old beat-up fucking Greyhound bus, and I didn't get good vibes in some of the outlying parts of Russia—to the point where I couldn't wait to get out of there.

The agreement had been that all funds or fees for the tour would be direct deposited into all of our bank accounts before we left America.

We each had contacted Big Al about the money, as it hadn't appeared by the time we left home. While we were in Russia, we were all checking our accounts to no avail, and each day Big Al or someone from his camp would say, "Oh, it's probably just taking a bit longer for the money because it's coming from Russia."

We were getting nervous and angrier by the minute. The last show we played on the tour was in Minsk, Belarus. We had a sold-out crowd of about three thousand kids in the audience, ready for us to take the stage, when we actually locked ourselves in the dressing room and yelled to Big Al on the other side of the door, "We're not coming out until we get paid in fucking full. We're not playing a fucking note of music until we get fucking paid!"

The strong-arming worked, and he came through with our pay, so we went on and played our final show. We all went back to our hotel and sat in the lobby where we drank a TON of vodka, then packed our suitcases so we could get the fuck home and chill.

Once back in Nashville, I got a phone call from a buddy named Kevin who had been one of the investors in the Monster Circus show in Vegas, and he offered me the opportunity to be a judge on a new TV show called *American Super Group*. I received the contract, and it seemed to have similarities with *American Idol*.

The show eventually ended-up falling through, but while I was considering the contract and offer, Bobby Rondinelli called me. It had been a few months since we toured Russia together, and he asked, "Hey, do you want to go back to Russia? They've got another eight or ten shows for the Classic Rock All-Stars."

Two things came to mind: 1) if this TV show kicks into motion and I commit to it, I'm going to fuck everybody in the band since I was the main singer, so I wasn't totally sure that I'd be able to do it, and 2) I didn't really want to do it to begin with because everything seemed too fucking shady last time.

I declined the second Russian tour since my gut told me it just didn't seem right. Everybody else went back over to Russia, and they replaced me with Tony Martin, the guy that sang with Black Sabbath for so many years. They did the tour and unfortunately nobody got paid; they all got fucked on their cash. Thank God I fucking listened to my intuition and didn't go back to the USSR.

During one of my weekly calls with Dad, he told me about a medical issue. He went to the bathroom to take a piss and noticed there was blood in his urine. He immediately went to the doctor and they first thought it might be kidney stones. He had a CT scan, and they diagnosed him with cancer.

Initially, it was near his kidneys and at the base of his spine. It eventually got up his spinal cord and into his brain. Nobody realized it had progressed that much as he was doing okay and was talkative, until he got up one morning and they thought he had a stroke. But it wasn't a stroke—the cancer had spread into his brain and affected his motor functions. His speech became somewhat impeded, and he couldn't see very well, while his movements became smaller.

I called him often, and I'd go to New Jersey and see him when I could. On one visit, I put him in a wheelchair, covered him with a warm blanket, and we walked around his neighborhood for a little while. We talked, and even though we'd been making up for lost time from years earlier, I felt like I said everything to him that I needed—and wanted—to.

He got treatments like chemo and all that shit, but watching him with the cancer in his brain, it was like he had a computer virus. At first there was something that wasn't right, then next thing the computer starts running a little slower, then it gets really, really slow before it gets to the point where you just get the spinning pinwheel of death or blue screen of death.

I played some shows that finished in Ohio and then had four or five days off, so I drove to New Jersey and hung out with my dad for a few days. By this point, he was at home, bed-ridden with hospice care. He couldn't talk, and he didn't know who was in the room, he just kind of stared. I knew he was nearing the end of this journey, and I wanted to see him one last time. When I left to go play some more shows, I was pretty bummed, as I knew it was the last time I was ever going to see him, and it was.

Dad passed away five days before my birthday in 2014, at seventy-nine years of age. I was not in the best of spirits, but I was scheduled to play the M3 Festival on my birthday that year, so Topher, Ian, and a buddy named Josh Dutoit packed into a van and headed to Maryland to do the show.

We arrived the night before, and I remember having way too many Jameson's and getting a bit trashed at the hotel bar, as I tried to forget the death of my father and knock a bit of the dust off from the long trip from Nashville. We played early the next day, much to my hungover dismay, on a side stage, right after Heaven's Edge, and the band played great! We went right back to the hotel bar and had more cocktails, then caught up on some sleep for the long drive back the next morning. Overall, it was a great trip considering the circumstances.

At different points in our relationship, Debbie and I flirted with talk of getting married. Initially, she was of the opinion that it was unnecessary and said things like, "What do you need to get married for? Who cares about getting married? It's just a piece of paper. I don't give a shit. I don't want a ring."

Her tune changed over time. Eventually she said, "I've never been in a relationship this long and well, if I was going to marry anybody, it would be you."

When my dad got sicker with cancer, he said to me, "I know you've been married twice before, but have you ever thought about getting married to Debbie?"

"I don't think we're going to get married. What makes you ask?"

He replied, "I think you should marry her! I really like her. I really respect the fact that she's a hard worker and achieved so much on her own."

Debbie and I went back to New Jersey for my dad's funeral. It seemed like everybody said to us, "Oh, God, Nick really loved you and Debbie, he really loved you both," with some even telling us that he told them that he wished we would get married.

It made us think that life is short, so why not get married! "Let's do this. Let's just fucking do it," we agreed, but we never made any plans together or talked about when we might get married. I guess we were just engaged at that point.

I had some gigs coming up in Las Vegas and Phoenix toward the end of that 2014 summer. Debbie wanted to come to Vegas with me for the shows as a getaway to spend some time chilling and hanging out, just lying by a pool.

In the weeks prior to the trip away, she saw a nice white dress online that she liked and showed it to me for my opinion, thinking she could perhaps wear it to the beach over her swimwear. I thought it suited her and said she could even wear it poolside when we go to Vegas, so she bought it, tried it on, and it fit well and looked great on her.

I secretly bought Debbie a wedding ring, and as we left for Vegas, I ensured she had packed her new white dress. I knew I would have to tell Debbie at some point about my plan to get married in Vegas, since we would have to get a marriage license there first.

We had two tickets on Southwest to fly from Nashville to Vegas and for some unknown reason, they didn't have us seated together. We went up to the airline desk at the gate to see if they could change it. Debbie said hello to a male staff member that she knew, who was behind the counter as well.

I asked the lady serving us, "Is there any way you could you change this please, so we can sit together?

She said she didn't think she could, so I explained, "Listen, we're going to Vegas right now to get married."

I saw Debbie out of the corner of my eye quickly turn and look at me. The guy that Debbie knew who worked for Southwest asked, "Are you serious?"

So, I pulled the ring out of my pocket, opened the case, and I showed it to them and said, "Yes, we're going to Vegas to get married."

Debbie was stunned—she went fucking white, looked across at the ring box I held and looked back at the dude, and said, "Holy shit! I guess I'm getting married!"

Once we got seated together on the plane, I showed her the ring properly and told her we had an appointment booked to get our marriage license, as well as my other wedding plans.

We stayed at the Las Vegas Hilton, since I knew everybody there from when I did the *Monster Circus* residency. I got a sweet deal on a great hotel room right at the pool, so we could open the sliding glass doors, walk through a little patio, and slide right into the pool.

We arrived in Vegas and after getting our license, I then went and played my gig at a place called Vamp'd, owned by Danny Koker (of Count's Kustoms fame) and his wife, Korie. My buddy David Stonich flew in and while I headed to Phoenix the following day, he took Debbie to see Olivia Newton John's residency concert at the Flamingo and took her to dinner—he was essentially our witness, best man, and maid of honor.

After I played in Phoenix, I got the first flight out the next morning back to Las Vegas and back to Debbie. We hung out by the pool for a couple of hours. At two o'clock we got dressed and drove to one of those little Vegas chapels. We got married at four o'clock, went out to dinner, and stayed up 'til about four in the morning, hitting a bunch of different bars, restaurants, and clubs. It was awesome!

I got up the next morning, had some coffee, and went to the airport with Debbie and David, where we ate some Mexican food with a couple of tequila shots. David and I walked into the smokers' lounge to have an after-snack cigarette, when the ever-present slot machines enticed me. I'm not usually a gambler but I put twenty bucks in a slot machine, pulled the lever, and won five hundred bucks. Good to go, I tapped out; we walked onto the plane, and I flew home as a married man. Vegas: See ya later, baby!

Prior to Dad's passing and my getting married, my son Ian called me from home in Los Angeles out of the clear blue one day and said, "Hey,

Dad, I've got to talk to you. There's something I need to tell you. I know you're not going to be happy with me, but I want to tell you."

I knew it wasn't going to be good, but then he dropped the bombshell on me and said, "I've been doing heroin for the last year."

I could not fucking believe it! Trying to make sense of it or help me understand, I asked him how he came to be hooked on smack. I thought it might have stemmed from his fucking car accident. He went out drinking with a couple of friends one night about a year and a half prior, and his friend who drove them home was drunk. She was doing sixty-five miles per hour in a residential street when she plowed headfirst into a Chevy Suburban.

The cop who came to see his mother Valerie told her, "God, when I first showed up at the scene, I walked up to the car and didn't call an ambulance—I called the morgue because I thought they were all dead."

Ian was unconscious and had a broken collarbone and broken ribs. The three kids were all hurt pretty bad, but thankfully there was no fatality. I knew he spent time in the hospital where they reset his bones and gave him pain pills, but he told me that he started popping more and more pain pills, then one thing led to another. He met a girl and dated her, and she and her crew were doing pain pills and whatever else they could get their hands on. He told me he graduated to heroin and had been shooting the shit for the last year. He also told me that his girlfriend had overdosed a couple of times, and Ian had also OD'd a couple of times. He was caught in the vice, rollin' the dice, and I was fucking astounded!

For the next four or five months, I constantly had late-night phone calls with him on the other end of the line in LA completely out of his fucking gourd, crying, "I can't believe I'm doing this. I can't believe I got to this point. What's wrong with me? I'm just going to kill myself," and then he'd hang up the phone, leaving me hanging.

I had no idea how to handle the situation. I flew out to California to try and talk with him and do an intervention on the two of them. That idea went out the window; they didn't hear a fucking word I had to say.

I came back home to Nashville and told Debbie, "I don't have a good feeling about this. This is not going to fucking end well."

Memories of Birdman dying from an overdose when I was a kid flashed in my mind, and I kept thinking about the lyrics to "Father, Mother, Son" that I wrote twenty fucking years ago. I would go to bed at night and be woken by my phone ringing at two o'clock in the morning, sure that it was somebody in my family or the authorities to tell me Ian was gone. I would pick up the phone to answer it, and it would be Ian, upset, crying, and freaking out. At least he was breathing, I thought.

"Well, what do you want me to do, Ian?" I asked repeatedly. "Do you want my help?"

"I don't know," he would always say.

This went on for four months, five months, six months. However long it was, it felt a thousand times fucking longer. Then I got the call.

"Dad, I don't want to do this anymore. Can I come and live with you and Debbie? I have to get my shit together, or I'm going to die," Ian told me.

His call surprised the shit out of me but was most welcome. I said, "Ian, in all fairness, let me talk to Debbie and sort this out. If she's cool with it, no problem."

His talk of impending death was nothing new to me, and I thought talking with Debbie was the right thing to do, as having a heroin addict around you at home is not a common circumstance. I didn't know how she'd react, when I asked, "How do you feel about this?"

She was instant in her response, "Yes, absolutely. If he needs help, let's help him."

So I called Ian back, and he said he wanted to come as soon as possible. Then I felt like I had to be the tough-love guy and say to him, "If you're going to come out here and just continue doing what you're doing, then stay where you're at. If you really want to come here and get clean and get your life together, then I'm all about it. I'll do anything I can to help you."

He said, "No, I want to come out to get away and change."

I emailed a couple of my former bandmates who I knew had dealt with such drug addiction in the past but sadly got fuck-all advice back. So I called a buddy of mine, Gary Corbett, who was a touring keyboard player with Cinderella and also had some experience with addiction. When I filled Gary in on the situation and told him that I didn't know what to do, he talked with me on the phone for three hours and said he would get me some prescription medication called Suboxone.

"If you need anything, let me know. I'm only a phone call away. I'll come down, help you out, whatever you need," he kindly offered.

He got me the Suboxone and told me how to distribute it to Ian. He explained, "It's basically like an opiate blocker and is used to treat opioid addiction. It'll help wean him off the narcotics."

I picked Ian up when he arrived in Nashville, drove home, and gave him a quarter of a Suboxone strip. There are four bars in a strip, so I gave him the first one to dissolve under his tongue. He slept the first day and when he got up, we talked later that night out on the porch.

I gave him another quarter bar the next day, and he slept again, a lot. Later that night, we talked some more and when he got up on the third day, he said, "I don't want to do this anymore."

"I take that stuff and all I do is sleep the day away, so I don't want to take it anymore," he said, as he took the rest of the Suboxone and put it in an envelope. He mailed it to his girlfriend in LA hoping that she would get off drugs as well. That didn't quite work out, as her addiction journey was longer than Ian's.

Ian cleaned his shit up by just getting through each day best he could and staying clean. Debbie was at work one afternoon when Ian and I sat on the porch having a cigarette. He said to me, "You know, Dad, I've been so angry with you because you were never there for my birthdays, graduations, and all the other important events in my life."

We talked through it all for hours.

Once we worked through that, he told me, "You know, I've always just wanted to be in a band with you."

So I told him to hold on a minute as I ducked inside the house. When I returned, I handed him the Mötley record I did and said, "If you can play this album note for note, then the gig is yours. This is probably the hardest stuff that I recorded, but if you can play this album from top to bottom, note for note, then you're my drummer."

I played the tough love card again and said, "Here's the deal: you want to smoke a little weed? Fine. You want to have a drink with me and the guys in the band? That's fine. If I ever see you do anything other than that—cocaine, methamphetamine, any sort of pills, any hallucinogens, smack, whatever the fuck it is—you're out! I will literally fire you on the spot and send you back to California."

I feel like he's been Ian again since that talk. He's been great. He really wanted to be in my band and at the time, I had Cheney Brannon drumming with me. Cheney understood and said, "The kid's a great drummer. If you want him in the band, then I think you should do it."

So, I let Cheney go, and Ian joined my band, and we went out and played shows together. We did well out there playing the Mötley '94 album. We did a ton of gigs all over the country. Knock on wood, Ian's been fucking awesome. His work ethic has improved greatly, and he's just moved into a new home with his girlfriend and twin daughters. He managed to kick the hard drugs, and he still plays drums with me, as well as bands like Tantric and Rehab. As a dad, I couldn't be prouder of him right now for doing all the positive things he's doing.

26
Revolucion

I got back home one Sunday in January of 2015 from a run of US shows, and had some more dates coming up in Canada. I got up the next morning and went to the store to pick up some groceries and when I drove back into my driveway, my phone rang. I looked down and saw Marco Mendoza's name on my screen. I had not talked with Marco in forever.

I switched my engine off, sat there in my car, and chatted. Marco said, "Hey, bro. Listen, I'm jamming with this band, and we need a singer. I know that you've got something going on of your own, but I would just like to see if this is something that you'd be interested in."

My initial reaction was, "Thanks, but no thanks." I wasn't interested, since I was happy just playing in my own band with my son.

Marco said, "Do me a favor: just talk to the manager David Edwards, who used to manage INXS."

When I asked who was involved, he said, "It's me, Brian Tichy, David Lowy (who started the band), plus Richard Fortus and Dizzy Reed from Guns N' Roses. We're called The Dead Daisies."

I had played with Dizzy a million times before and always enjoyed it. I had also played with Brian a bunch of times. I had jammed with Marco at one of the local Hollywood jams. I didn't know Richard, but I knew of him, and I didn't know David at all.

When I went inside after the call with Marco, I asked my friend Darron Meeks, who was living with me, if he had ever heard of a band called The Dead Daisies. Darron said, "Oh, yeah, I've fucking heard them. They're from Australia or something. I saw them play when they were on tour last year with Kiss and Def Leppard. I think they've released just the one album, and Slash played lead on their single from it."

My interest piqued as I noted they were playing arenas. My manager at the time, Larry Morand, also checked them out for me. I wondered why they needed a new singer, and what happened with the previous guy. From what I gathered, a lot of it had to do with a messy incident that their singer Jon Stevens had with his fiancée, Jodhi Meares, who was an Australian model turned fashion designer and divorced from a billionaire, which turned into an ordeal involving charges and court.

The Dead Daisies' manager David Edwards soon called and said, "We'd love for you to come out to LA and meet everybody."

I kept saying I was happy doing my own thing, so he pitched at me, "Well, we're only going to need you about twenty-six weeks a year—half a year—and the rest of the time you're on your own to do whatever you like. My band can probably help your band, and your band can help my band."

I agreed that could work, so he said, "All right, I'll send you a plane ticket then, so you can fly out to LA and meet everyone."

Right out of the gate, they flew me first class and put me up at the luxurious Sunset Marquis in West Hollywood. I checked-in and met David Edwards, then later that night we went out to dinner, where I met David Lowy and Richard Fortus. As we talked into the night, I thought it could be pretty fucking awesome if I could juggle my own thing and theirs.

When I told them I still needed a little time to think about it, David Edwards asked, "Would you at least be interested in going to Cuba with us?"

He told me they had a trip lined-up that was to be the first for an international rock band. We would perform as guests of the Cuban Ministry of Culture, Institute of Music, and the Cuban Rock Agency. President Obama was lifting trade sanctions, so we'd be heading there with the blessing of the American government and the Cuban government. I thought it sounded like a once-in-a-lifetime opportunity, and if they were having issues with their singer, I could fill-in for ten days to get them out of a bind. In hindsight, though, I think they had already moved on from Jon and going to Cuba was a trial period for me.

I flew back to Nashville, then played a few Canadian dates performing Mötley '94 material. When we arrived in Canada, the temperature in Montreal was minus forty, and we almost didn't make the show due to a massive blizzard. We then traveled to Ottawa, London, Ontario, and ended in Toronto. After the show in Toronto, the guys in my band stayed that night, and drove back to Nashville the following morning, while I went to the airport at 5:00 a.m. and flew to Miami.

Bleary-eyed, I transferred in Miami to a terminal for private jets. Richard showed up with photographer Katarina Benzova and a vanload of others, including the manager, Bernard Fowler and Darryl Jones from The Rolling Stones, who were going to play with us as well. We boarded our chartered private plane and flew from Miami to Havana, Cuba.

We checked into our hotel then headed right to Abdala recording studio, where we did a press conference. We certainly fucking hit the ground running.

The first of our Cuban shows was at a massive club called Maxim Rock. It was a sold-out, over-capacity, hot-and-sweaty show in front of probably 1,500 people, and another 1,500 outside who missed out on getting inside. The atmosphere was intense, in a positive way. Everybody was walking around in band T-shirts from the likes of The Beatles, Led Zeppelin, Guns N' Roses, and Iron Maiden. They loved this kind of shit there.

That was on Wednesday and then we had three days until our next show. We visited hospitals and schools, including music schools where local musicians sat in and jammed with us. We also recorded a couple of covers in Havana with producer Ben Grosse (who had worked with Red Hot Chili Peppers, Sevendust, and Stone Temple Pilots) behind the boards at Abdala studios.

At my suggestion, one was "Midnight Moses" by The Sensational Alex Harvey Band—the song that I first heard covered by Dead End Kids back in Philly. We included some Cuban-style percussion in it during the breakdown section. Richard suggested an old blues number by Howlin' Wolf called "Evil" that was written by Willie Dixon, so we covered that as well.

Our second show was in this historic old open-air amphitheater called Salón Rosado de la Tropical. That place was a legendary beer garden where Cuba's famous musician Arsenio Rodríguez tore it up as a salsa and mambo pioneer back in the forties, when the mafia ruled. This show was called the Cuba Rocks for Peace concert and there were six or seven thousand people there; it was packed. Before we went on stage, David Edwards told us, "There are some government people here, so after the show, don't go anywhere. They'd like to come backstage and say hello."

We thoroughly enjoyed performing for the crowd and once we finished our encore and headed backstage, everybody waited for the dignitaries. Miguel Díaz-Canel, who was the vice president of Cuba and currently the president, came backstage and met us. Raul Castro, the country's president at the time and Fidel Castro's brother, didn't make it, but his son Alejandro Castro Espín was at the show and came backstage to say hello and express gratitude for us coming.

With assistance from a translator, these political dignitaries essentially said, "You've done a great thing here. Thank you for coming and playing your music for our people. You're now like a family. You're a friend of Cuba. If you ever want to come to Cuba, we welcome you." Ernesto

Guevara Jr., the youngest son of Che Guevara, watched us play, too, and enjoyed taking some photos backstage with everybody. It was awesome meeting him and having a good chat about Harley-Davidsons.

Harley's were very popular there in the fifties before the Cuban Revolution, but then they had to stop selling them. Many Harley's from that era still exist, having been lovingly restored and maintained by "Harlistas." *The Motorcycle Diaries* is a best-selling memoir that traces the early travels of Ernesto's famous father, as a coming-of-age adventure through five South American countries for nine months in 1952, whose experiences sparked his future revolutionary ways. Ernesto now runs a motorcycle travel agency business La Poderosa Tours (named after the nickname his father gave to his Norton 500cc motorbike), where he rents Harley-Davidsons and takes you on a seven-day or ten-day tour around the island of Cuba, taking you to all these places of importance in the revolutionary war. He said I should come with him and ride around Cuba some time, since there was no room in the schedule to do it on this trip. I'd like to take him up on that one day, as I can be a bit of a history geek and there's a lot of interesting history down there.

Sights on the streets aren't just limited to old Harleys, though, as there are also many American cars from the fifties there, all lovingly restored and maintained. I saw immaculate old '57 Chevys and '55 Cadillacs, leftover from an era when Cuba was the vacation paradise for mobsters.

The trade embargoes placed on Cuba meant they have not been able to import parts for all these vehicles, let alone new vehicles. So if they need a new driveshaft, instead of ordering one, they take the old driveshaft to a machinist who fabricates a brand-new driveshaft exactly the same as the old one. Every part of those old cars, even down to their fucking lug nuts, are fabricated and made by hand in Cuba because they could never import parts. It's amazing!

The embargoes also mean that Cubans can't go to a store and buy things like guitar strings. People have guitars there, but they can't get strings because most are American made. One way around this, though, is to send money to a family member or somebody they know in America, who buys some guitar strings and sends them back through the mail.

When it came time for us to leave Cuba, Marco gave a bass away, and we took boxes and boxes of picks (or plectrums, depending where you're from), strings, and other gear, and gave them to the music school.

We had a blast in Cuba; it was a great trip. We played two unbelievable sold-out shows and saw so much of Havana. The people were amazing, it's cheap, and the food was amazing, too, although David Lowy will argue that point: we all ate grilled octopus during one meal, and he had some kind of reaction from it that made him as sick as a dog for a couple of days.

Since Bernard and Darryl were there playing with us, fans kept asking them, "When are you going to come back here again and bring the Rolling Stones with you?"

Darryl told them, "Oh, trust me, when we're done here, we're going back to New York and we're going to tell Mick and Keith all about this trip."

Whether or not it was because of our trip, I don't know, but a year later the Stones went there and played a free outdoor concert at the Ciudad Deportiva de la Habana sports complex that was attended by an estimated 500,000 fucking people, as documented in their *Havana Moon* concert film.

Unfortunately, President Trump reversed so many of the changes that Obama started, so we're right back to square one in many ways and all the embargoes are back on again. Time will tell if that changes under the Biden administration. If you can get past the politics, I highly recommend visiting that pretty little island.

A week or so after I got back to Nashville from Cuba, I got a call from David Edwards, who asked, "Hey, man, would you like to come to Australia and finish The Dead Daisies' record?"

I postponed and rescheduled some gigs and shuffled my schedule around so I could depart on March 10. We had exactly one month to write, record, mix, and master the entire record before I flew home on April 11.

The first week was spent writing before we started recording tracks. Brian Tichy couldn't make it to Sydney, so we had Jackie Barnes come in and do the drums. Jackie's dad is Jimmy Barnes, who fronted Cold Chisel and has the highest number of hit albums of any Australian artist ever.

Jimmy came by the studio and heard what we were doing. He said he had a tune called "Empty Heart" that would be a great fit for the band. We thought it was a great song, so we recorded it as a duet.

Jimmy sang the song all the way through from top to bottom and then I did, too. With the miracle of Pro Tools, they edited it to start with Jimmy's verse, followed by a chorus with both of us, then a verse from me, and mixed it up and pieced it together from there into the version you hear on the album.

The guys already had some songs that Jon Stevens had written with them, namely "Mexico," "Something I Said," "Make the Best of It," and a tune called "Critical."

I brought in a song called "Sleep," while for the rest of the songs, we sat in a room together that week and came up with "Devil Out of Time," "You and I," "Looking for the One," "Get Up, Get Ready," and "My Time." On the album, we also included the two covers of "Midnight Moses" and "Evil" that we recorded in Cuba.

While in Havana, we met the Buena Vista Social Club, an ensemble of Cuban musicians who revive the music of prerevolutionary Cuba. They happened to be in Australia as we were recording, so David Lowy invited them to, "Come out on my boat, and we'll have some lunch."

We took a break from work and got on a water taxi. As it turned a bend, I looked out from the side of the water taxi and noticed a ship in the distance as they said, "Oh, look, there's David's boat!"

As I looked at the size of the ship, I told them, "Okay, wrong terminology guys. A boat has oars, that is not a boat, that is a fucking ship!"

We all boarded the vessel and there were about thirty people on the back deck of his pleasure craft, with plenty more room to run and play tag without bumping into anybody. There was staff walking around the deck serving food and wine. I was astounded.

Smiling, David said to me, "If you want to take a dip, feel free to."

I told him, "Dude, I've been to Australia before, and I love Australia, but I have also read about Australia and seen TV shows, so I know you have sharks, lots of sharks."

He explained, "Oh, no, it's totally safe. I've got this device on the side of my boat that we turn on and it emits an electrical impulse that keeps all the sharks away. So feel free to jump in—it's safe."

I said, "No, thanks. I'm not going in the water here, buddy. That's not going to happen, not on your watch or mine. I'll just stay here and get another whiskey with these shrimps, or prawns as you Aussies call them, thanks."

I declined his offer to go fucking swimming in Sydney Harbor.

As I spent more time with my new bandmates, I got to know more about them. David Lowy is a very private person, but has an incredible story of his own family, who are one of the most successful on Earth—yes, Earth!

Not only is he the guitarist and driving force behind The Dead Daisies, as the eldest son, he is the principal of the family's finances and runs a private investment business Lowy Family Group with offices in New York City on Wall Street, plus Los Angeles and Sydney. It's not like he has sat back in life with a silver spoon in his mouth, though—he is THE hardest working person I have ever encountered in my life!

David received a Member of the Order of Australia for his services to aviation. He pilots his own Gulfstream 550 business jet but can fly aerobatics, even getting chosen to represent Australia at the World Aerobatic Championships, but turned down the opportunity due to business commitments.

You could say the Lowy story started from humble beginnings, but it was more like extreme hardship. You see, David's father Frank is a Hungarian Jew who was born in Czechoslovakia and forced to live in a ghetto in Hungary during World War II.

Members of his family were in concentration camps, including Frank's father Hugo, who was beaten to death at Auschwitz for refusing to leave his Jewish prayer shawl behind. The Nazis typically instructed the Jews to leave their belongings behind by having them throw them onto a pile.

Somehow, Frank escaped the Holocaust and got out of Auschwitz, making his way to France where he boarded a ship in 1946 that was headed for Palestine. He was caught en route by British authorities and interned in a detention camp in Cyprus. Two years later, he was serving in the military for Israel and fought in the Arab-Israeli War in the Galilee and Gaza. Eventually, he made his way to Australia to start a new life.

Frank and the rest of his family didn't know what had happened to Hugo. He was grabbed and taken away, and young Frank never saw his father again. The mystery was only solved a couple of years before I joined the band, and it happened by a complete fucking fluke. David's brother Peter was staying at a Ritz-Carlton hotel in Arizona and when he got up one morning to do some business, he was perturbed because he didn't get his *Wall Street Journal* delivered to his room like he had requested.

On his way out of the hotel, he stopped at the concierge desk in the lobby to let them know he didn't get his newspaper. There was a guy in front of him in the line of people checking out, so they chatted a bit. When this guy went to the counter, Peter overheard the concierge worker ask his name, and he said it was Lowy.

Peter went over and tapped the guy on the shoulder, and said, "Hey, excuse me, but I just overheard you say your last name is Lowy. That's my last name, too. Where are you from?"

They struck a conversation and figured out they were distant cousins. One thing led to another and this guy in line told Peter that his grandfather Hugo was praying and wouldn't give up this prayer shawl, so the Germans beat him to death.

Peter asked him, "Would you do me a favor? I've got to call my dad, Frank, because he's been wondering what happened to his dad for his whole life. Can you please explain this to him?"

Once Frank was informed of the story, the family commissioned the restoration of an old cattle car rail wagon that had transported Hungarian Jews to Auschwitz and had it placed in the vicinity of the spot of where he was murdered at the concentration camp. They put a plaque on it as a mark of respect to Hugo Lowy and all the other Hungarian Jews who endured the Holocaust.

That story is fascinating to me, but it's only one fucking part of it.

After Frank made his way to Australia, he started a fruit stand at a farmers' market. He did well with that and expanded to buy the stand next to his. Then he bought the stand across from his, and then another one and kept going. He kept reinvesting the money he made into growing the business for himself, and he soon owned the entire farmers' market.

He then bought a piece of subdivided farmland property and turned that into a shopping center in Sydney's western suburbs. Then he turned that into another mall, then another mall, then another, until he owned malls across Australia.

After the atrocities he experienced in Europe and the Middle East, he started from scratch in Australia and built the mall empire Westfield Corporation. Frank became the richest person in Australia with one of the largest mall businesses in the world.

In December 2017, Westfield accepted an AU$32.8 billion takeover from a European commercial real estate company called Unibail-Rodamco. Sir Frank Lowy, or Big Frank as I used to jokingly call him, started it all with a fucking fruit stand in the fifties!

The business was built on qualities like hard work, determination, and smart decisions, and each of Frank's kids have this same drive.

Therefore, it has always fucking irritated the shit out of me when people flippantly dismiss The Dead Daisies as just some billionaire's hobby or a billionaire's fucking midlife crisis. I will say this right now: David Lowy will work ANYBODY under the fucking table!

We would come home to a hotel from playing a concert at say midnight. He would sit with me and the guys and have a couple of cocktails and talk. Then he would go up to his room, lie down for two hours, get up, and conduct calls with Australia or Israel or fucking Japan, doing business until five or six o'clock in the morning, at which point he would go back to sleep until eight o'clock, then get up, have breakfast, meet us in the lobby, and we'd travel to the next concert.

I don't know how the fuck he does it, but I respect and adore David; he's truly a great dude.

After our month recording in Sydney, I played a few solo shows in the US before I flew to LA and met up with The Dead Daisies again. We shot a fun video for "Mexico" at Jumbo's Clown Room, a famous burlesque club on Hollywood Boulevard, and then rehearsed and flew straight to Europe for a huge arena tour with Kiss in June, when our album *Revolución* came out.

It was surreal touring with Kiss. I've known Gene since the eighties, when he wanted to sign my band Angora, and I knew Eric Singer very well, too, of course. I also knew guitarist Tommy Thayer for some time, having met back when he was playing in the Kiss tribute band Cold Gin.

The only member of Kiss who I kind of felt intimidated around was Paul Stanley. I don't know why that was, but I felt that Paul didn't really like me for some reason. He seemed really outgoing with Marco and Richard and David, but with me he would just put a little fist bump out to me. The more I hung out with him and we talked, though, I felt he warmed to me.

I had so many hilariously surreal moments on that tour where I found myself sitting there, pinching myself. While I sat there talking with the Demon and the Starchild, the voice in my head would tell me, fuck, this is so surreal. This is the band when you were a kid that you fucking freaked out over, and spent money on their records and concert tickets…and now look at you: you're sitting in a backstage cafeteria sharing a fucking steak with Gene Simmons and Paul Stanley, and we're just talking about family and everyday life things, interspersed with Gene telling me crazy fucking Jew jokes.

In 2015, I finally got the opportunity to perform on the hallowed ground of Castle Donington, where the legendary Monsters of Rock concerts were held each year. After Mötley pulled out of the 1994 event and was replaced by Sepultura, I was stoked that my time had finally come!

We had Tommy Clufetos, who had been playing with the reunited Black Sabbath, on drums. David Lowy had a competing commitment and couldn't perform with us. Somebody suggested a guy from LA to fill-in for David, but he was a bit of a train wreck, and the day he was to fly out there was an issue with his passport, so he couldn't make it to England either.

The day before our performance, our manager came to me with Richard Fortus and asked, "Do you think you could play guitar tomorrow for our Download set, and sing?"

I told them I'd give it a college try, so I spent the entire day with a guitar learning all the parts and trying to figure out if I could sing and play the songs at the same time before I did press all night.

Debbie came over to see me at our shows in England and Paris. Her family is from outside of London, so she visited family and had dinner with her cousins and aunts while I practiced and did press.

I had another quick run-through of the set in our hotel room, early on the morning of our show. We were the first band to play on the last day, and it had rained that whole fucking summer weekend and was freezing cold. It came time to soundcheck at about 11:00 a.m., just an hour before our set. I didn't have any of my own guitars there, so I had to use David's guitar and amp. I walked out onto the stage and looked out at an empty field with the cold rain falling.

Downhearted, I thought to myself, it's my first fucking trip to Donington, and I'm going to play to a muddy lawn. There's nobody fucking here. It's cold. I'm not supposed to be playing guitar. What else could go wrong?

Back in the dressing room, I ran through all the last-minute shit for our short thirty-minute set then walked back to the stage. When I looked out from the side of stage, ready to go on, I saw 30,000 to 40,000 people waiting for us. I don't know where they fucking came from but in less than an hour, it went from twelve stragglers on this massive field to about 40,000 people.

We played "Mexico," "Midnight Moses," "With You and I," "Devil Out of Time," "Lock 'n' Load" and killed it. I came off stage, put the guitar down, and said, "Next time can I get a little more notice?" as everybody high-fived me and said it was awesome.

We then went back to the hotel, where I packed and got on a bus with my wife for a nine-hour trip to Paris, during which I reflected on my first Donington experience. It was certainly memorable.

We finished our run in Europe and toured a leg the following month with Whitesnake, consisting of fourteen shows down the east coast of America through Florida and across into Louisiana and Texas. It was an awesome tour; we had such a great time with those guys.

David Coverdale was another guy I grew up listening to, from his time fronting Deep Purple through to Whitesnake's *Ready an' Willing* album, so it was surreal to be spending time with him, especially up in the air.

We all traveled together on David Lowy's plane between some of the shows, and David Coverdale and I sat at the same table. David would walk on the plane and say to me in his English accent, "Oh, Johnny C., how are you today?"

After playing New York, we headed south to Florida. I arranged with Debbie for her to drive with our friends Lisa Fry and David Stonich down to Florida to come and see some of the shows there and hang out. We were scheduled to play in Melbourne, Florida, where her mom lives, and intended to make good use of the day off I had there.

Debbie came backstage after our first Florida show and said, "Oh my God, that was so great!"

She hadn't seen the band since Download, where she watched the short set from side of stage, not out in the front.

As we talked in the hallway, she asked, "Out of curiosity, where are the Whitesnake guys? I see your dressing rooms, but where are theirs?"

I pointed and said, "David Coverdale's room is right there, two doors down from ours."

Just as I said that, the door opened, and David came out.

He saw me and walked over. "Ah, Johnny C., how are you mate? I hear Mrs. C. is in the crowd tonight. Am I going to meet her?"

I said, "David, this is Debbie—Debbie, this is David," and he took her hand, looked into her eyes and said, "Oh, Mrs. C.—ravishing!" as he leaned in and gave her a kiss. I saw my wife go weak at the knees.

A few days later, Debbie headed home, and I got on the plane for the next show. David said, "Ah, Johnny C., it was lovely meeting your wife," to which I snapped back, "Yeah, fuck you, David!"

The whole plane suddenly went quiet.

David glared at me, and I continued, "Yep, you said my wife was ravishing and kissed her, so then I had a follow her around with a mop for three fucking days."

He started laughing.

"Now when I want to get laid, I've got to sing 'Here I Go Again,' so fuck you!" I told him.

The whole plane was roaring with laughter.

We then came home for a moment before going to Australia and New Zealand with Kiss. Word came in that Richard Fortus was in a motorcycle accident. He broke his shoulder blade in two places, his collarbone, six ribs, a big toe, plus lacerated his liver, and bruised his lung, then rode two hours back home with a concussion. He had never missed a show during his career, so he was bummed to have to sit out the entire trip down under.

We called Doug Aldrich to see if he could fill in for Richard, but he had prior commitments with Glenn Hughes, so we got Dave Leslie from Baby Animals to help us out. There were a few shows that David Lowy wasn't able to play, so we had Randall Waller fill in, who had played with Rose Tattoo, Keith Urban, and Shania Twain. We had to arrive in Australia a few days earlier to give us time to rehearse with Dave and Randall.

For half of that fucking October run through Perth, Adelaide, Melbourne, Sydney, Newcastle, Brisbane, and Auckland, I stood on arena stages with two other guitarists who I'd never even played a show with before. I had a killer time with those guys, though; it was a lot of fun.

Before the first show, we performed "Empty Heart" on a morning TV show in Sydney, and when we came back to that city, we did a secret location show at Fraser Harley-Davidson Motorcycles for fans who won the opportunity to attend. We gave away a Harley as part of a charity fundraiser.

Those shows were the end of The Kiss 40th Anniversary World Tour. We had just a week or two at home, so I played a Mötley '94 show at the Basement East on Woodland Street in Nashville with the intent of releasing it as a live album one day.

A few days later, I met up with The Dead Daisies on the Norwegian Pearl ship for the fifth annual Kiss Kruise, where Kiss performed *Alive!* in full. That was fucking great to see, since it was the first Kiss album I ever heard and it had such an impact on me as a kid.

After the Kiss Kruise, we went back through Europe again in December with Whitesnake. Richard was playing with us but still healing and in a bit of pain from his accident, so he wasn't doing as many of his trademark jumps and windmills on stage during that tour.

There was a show or two in Germany that we played with Judas Priest on that European run as well. Their drummer Scott Travis, as you remember, was my original drummer in The Scream. When Scott and I get together, it's anything goes, so it was good seeing him.

I didn't really meet any of the other Priest guys, other than a brief hello with Rob Halford. Once our support set was done, we watched them play. Halford is seven years older than me, and I remember thinking, "He sounds just like the fucking records—he's unbelievable!"

When we finished our European shows with Whitesnake, we went to Israel for a week where we did a bunch of press and played a great show at Zappa in Jerusalem, and an even better one at the Barby Club in Tel Aviv.

Playing Israel's capital Jerusalem, which is one of the oldest fucking cities in the world and holy to Judaism, Christianity, and Islam, was quite an amazing experience. We had a few days to do some sightseeing around Jerusalem, too, which was even more special given it was the week before Christmas. There's so much history there. It was great to travel around the city and outside the city walls near the Damascus Gate to see the Calvary, a rock-cut Garden Tomb in a skull-shaped hill that is the site of the burial and resurrection of Jesus Christ—where he was fucking crucified. I went in the tomb where they laid him out.

We went to Masada, an ancient desert fortress in Israel that's a thousand feet up on top of a rock plateau overlooking the Dead Sea. Herod the Great built a couple of palaces for himself up on the mountain somehow, thirty years before Christ.

We took a cable car to the top, and there were stairs allowing us to walk around and down. Apparently, there was a siege there in the year seventy-four where nearly a thousand Jewish men, women, and children were completely encircled in the fort, and instead of being captured by the Romans, they all just committed mass suicide.

As I walked around these historical sites, I thought about life in America, where cities have been around for 200 or 250 years. You look at a house and say, "Oh, fuck, man, your house is old; it was built in the 1960s," and there I was sitting in the Tomb of Christ from over 2,000 years ago and it's still intact. That was unbelievable.

We went down to the Dead Sea on the border of Israel and Jordan. Richard brought his daughters with him, and they went floating around in the water while we had lunch. His girls got out of the water and had some weird skin irritation from the high salt content, so I was glad I didn't go in.

I'm not really a fan of water anyway and have a bit of an issue with sharks. If I can't see the bottom, I ain't fucking swimming in it. I emailed Debbie and told her I didn't want to swim in the Dead Sea because of sharks, and she replied, "You were at the Dead Sea. It's called the Dead Sea because nothing lives in it. It's just saltwater, you fucking idiot."

My first year in The Dead Daisies was a lot of fun, although it did take some getting used to the fast pace the Daisies work at. Even back on my first tour with them, I was thinking, "This pace is just crazy, it's grueling touring." I understand and appreciate with everybody's scheduling, they've got to cram in as much as they can, but I questioned if I wanted to do this as much as what was happening. I had already started thinking if it was something I wanted to do for a long period of time because I didn't see any slow down at all. There was no pacing. It was just the show must go on, let's move!

27
Make Some Noise

Richard Fortus and Dizzy Reed parted ways with The Dead Daisies as we moved into 2016. The previous October, they gave us a heads-up about rejoining Guns N' Roses. They soon went out on their Not in This Lifetime…Tour, which was the first time since 1993 that Axl, Slash, and Duff had performed together. It went on to become the third-highest grossing concert tour of all fucking time.

There was talk about getting Doug Aldrich in the band, and I assumed we'd go out and play more shows with him and another keyboardist for a while in support of our *Revolución* record then eventually work on our next album. As they thought about it more, they decided, "We're getting a new guitar player, but not another keyboard player. We'll just go right into the studio and make a brand-new record."

We started getting material together in January, then went into the studio at the start of February, writing and recording our next album. We were in Sienna Recording Studio on Nashville's Music Row, working with Marti Frederiksen, who had bought the studio with Josh Gruss less than two years prior.

It was cool for me to get up and go to work in the studio every day then go back home instead of living out of a hotel, and we finished recording the album in March, after about five weeks, and then released singles in June and July before our *Make Some Noise* record came out in August on Spitfire Music.

When we toured Europe the year before, we experimented with some covers in our set. We played "Helter Skelter" a lot and "Sick as a Dog" by Aerosmith a few times. We also started playing the Creedence classic "Fortunate Son" and it just stuck. It's one of those songs that you can play in America, Germany, France, Italy, Japan, and even Israel as we did, and people love it.

You can play it for an older crowd that went through the Vietnam War, and they know every word from when it came out at the end of 1969. You can play it for a younger crowd, and they know every word, too. It's just one of those songs that everybody loves—it resonates all over the world. So, we recorded our version for the *Make Some Noise* album.

Songwriting with The Dead Daisies was largely a collaborative effort. Sometimes the words don't come so easy, so if I got stumped on something, everybody was willing to help. A lot of the album's lyrics came about by me sitting in a room with Marti tweaking things. I would write some lyrics and Marti would change the direction of the song a little bit or add something in or pull something out, and then I'd further tweak it to suit. Marti is not just a great producer, he's a talented songwriter as well.

As an example of the collaboration, I had some trouble with the song "Mainline," not knowing what I wanted the lyrics to be about, and I said to Marco, "Fuck, lyrically, I'm hitting a bit of a wall here."

He started writing shit down and gave me two pages of lyrics, thoughts, and sentences. There was one line that he wrote down in his pages that grabbed my attention and sparked an idea. "Mainline" was a double entendre that could be talking about riding a train or it could be about doing drugs. It made even more sense to me and Doug, since we're both from Philadelphia, because Main Line is another name for the western suburbs of Philly that follows the former Pennsylvania Railroad's once prestigious Main Line out from the city.

There's an odd chord progression in the song's chorus that was throwing me a bit, so Marti scatted a melody at me. I couldn't hear a melody over those chords being used but I totally heard where he was going with it, and it all just came together easily from there.

For me, lyrics are the hardest fucking thing to do because you've got to tell a story but in the constraint of a rhythm. Then you have to rhyme within the sentence, or the first sentence and the second sentence have to rhyme, then the third and the fourth, or the second and the fourth. There's just all these patterns and variables that you need to factor in while trying to have universal appeal, great rhythm, and a catchy melody.

"Long Way to Go" was another song I had some trouble writing; I didn't even have a title or anything. I stepped out of Studio C to get away from the song I was working on lyrically, and as I walked back toward the room, the Studio A door opened and David Lowy walked out after doing some guitar tracks with Marti.

As we passed each other, I asked, "How's it going with your guitar parts, dude?" and he said, "Got a long way to go but no time to get there."

As he walked away, he stopped, turned back and said what I was thinking, "That might be a song title." So we put together "Long Way to Go" from there.

It was cool that if I ever got into a pinch, one of them would come in and say something or throw something at me, anything. Even if it was just a word, it would sometimes spark something for me to finish my thought and get the lyrics down. It was very collaborative in that way. I love working with different people and bouncing ideas off others.

As we were finishing the album, we struggled to try and figure out another song to do. I had always wanted to do "Join Together" by The Who because it's so powerfully heavy. When that fucking heavy opening riff comes in, it has always grabbed me.

We talked about covering it and Marti loved the idea, so Doug ran with it, heavied it up even more and made it his own. "Join Together" then came together easily in the studio and wound up being a mainstay in our set. That was a crowd-pleasing singalong wherever we went.

Just prior to the start of 2016, as we started getting material together for The Dead Daisies' next album, I had some time at home. Mick Mars called one night and said he was in a bit of a bind with his recordings. I got together with him again to work on songs for his solo album. I was a bit confused as to what was going on with his record, because the previous year, a musician friend Jeremy Asbrock asked me if I'd heard Mick's new stuff. I said, "What are you talking about?"

He said, "Oh, Mick's recording with Tommy Henriksen from Alice Cooper's band and some new singer, and they recorded with Michael Wagener." Mick first worked with Wagener when he mixed Mötley's debut album *Too Fast for Love*.

"Oh, cool. Okay, great, awesome," I told them, thinking Mick must have decided to go in a different direction from when he initially wanted me to sing on his album. It was no big deal to me.

A few months later, I played a festival in Europe with The Dead Daisies, I ran into Mick's guitar tech, Bobby O, who said, "Hey, Crab, what are you doing? You know, Mick really wants to talk to you."

We started bullshitting, and I said, "Okay, what's up? I heard he's got a new thing going with another singer. I'm excited to hear the record. How's it sound?"

He said, "No, that's not the case," so I told him to tell Mick to call me.

About four months went by with no word from Mick, and I was fully embroiled in the Daisies as we changed from Richard and Dizzy and prepared to write with our new guitarist Doug Aldrich. It was shortly after the Christmas holidays when Mick called and asked me to come into Blackbird Studio in Nashville. He gave me a tape of two songs: "Gimme Blood" and "Shake the Cage." The latter didn't have any lyrics other than repeating the title for its chorus, so I wrote some quick lyrics for it. They were two songs he had recorded with Tommy Henriksen, but he didn't like the vocals or something, so he was rerecording them. I liked the song "Gimme Blood," but I'm not a big fan of "Shake the Cage."

We talked again about doing a new record and what style it would be. My view was Mick should do an album with old-school, big, heavy blues riffs, like "Hair of the Dog" by Nazareth or "Mississippi Queen" and "Never in My Life" by Mountain—something like that, just very blues structured, but with Mick's touch on it.

"With your guitar tone and playing, and my vocals, let's just do a huge rock blues record!" I said.

Mick didn't want to do that and wasn't able to convey to me what direction he wanted the music to go in, but I was prepared to work through it with him more, since I was as excited as everybody else for Mick to finally put a fucking solo record out. I did the vocals with Mick on his two songs, and he put a couple of video snippets of the songs out online. The footage showed us working in the studio together and having fun. Immediately, there was a positive buzz about Corabi and Mars working together again.

In the weeks after, though, Mick sent me a link to a Swedish magazine interview that spoke very negatively of my songwriting abilities. I listened to my gut and put two and two together as I went over to Mick's house, and we discussed the project and situation some more. I told Mick that as much as I would love to keep working on his solo album, I truly believed in my heart that if I did his record, it would invoke many more business issues he'd have to deal with, and I didn't want my involvement to be detrimental to him.

I love Mick to death and hope he finds a way to finally release his long-awaited solo album.

The Dead Daisies kicked off our touring in 2016 by being the special performers at Musikmesse, Europe's biggest trade fair for the music industry. We were there in Frankfurt for about a week in April and did a bunch of press.

Our video for the album's first single "Long Way to Go" was shot on one of a few shows we did with the Hollywood Vampires, the band featuring actor Johnny Depp on guitar, along with Alice Cooper and Joe Perry.

Kiss wanted us to do their whole Freedom to Rock Tour, but given we had commitments in Europe, we could only do the second month of it with them.

We did a bunch of European festivals again through the summer, like Wacken in Germany, Ramblin' Man in England, and Steelhouse Festival in Wales, with solo shows scattered amongst them.

When we flew back into Chicago, the tour bus picked us up at the airport and took us to Wisconsin. We started the tour in Green Bay, then performed the following night in Fort Wayne, Indiana, and played eighteen great shows through the Midwest and along the east coast of America with Kiss.

During breaks with the Daisies, I would do shows of my own. Either acoustic solo or full band shows. On the first June Saturday that year, Vince Neil headlined the second day of Farm Rock at Nashville's Marathon Music Works. Before Vince on the bill was Kix, Steelheart, Vixen, and me. I saw Vince there, and he invited me on his tour bus, where we had a long talk. We even had a photo taken of us on his bus, which we both posted on our Facebook pages.

Vince and I laughed as we talked about how everybody assumes that we hate each other. Vince said, "Oh, man, I love you, dude. We should do some shows together."

I said, "Honestly, Vince, wouldn't it just be a pisser if we just fucking went out and did a bunch of shows together? I'll open for you and do forty minutes, then you do your thing. I think every fucking music fan on Earth will come just out of sheer curiosity."

He said, "Yeah, that's a great fucking idea, dude. Let's put that together!"

The next time I ran into Vince was in October 2018 at Sammy Hagar's beach party and car show in Huntington Beach. When I spotted him there, I walked over and said, "Vince, how are you doing, buddy?"

He looked at me with a blank stare, like he didn't have a fucking clue who I was. Maybe my hair was different or my beard longer, but it was like he had a big "who the fuck is that guy?" thought bubble above his fucking head. He didn't say a word to me; not a single fucking word. I didn't take it personally, however, 'cause I'm totally used to strange things happening with characters in this industry by now.

John Greenberg and I started talking more frequently a couple of years ago, and he asked me why I left Union Entertainment Group. We had an in-depth, heart-to-heart conversation. I explained to him, "You were twenty-three or twenty-four when I took you on as my manager, having just got off the road with Richard Marx, and you were working as an intern. So, I brought you on with The Scream and although you got us a record deal, you had never really managed a band on your own before, which is why we chose Tim Heyne to be a comanager with you.

"We started picking up quite a bit of juice in The Scream and then I got the Mötley call. I didn't need a manager at that point, but I wanted you guys to be in my corner as a form of insurance, so I paid you twenty percent of those big payments I received at the start of my tenure in Mötley. I didn't need to do that, but I was okay with it. I never had that much money in my fucking life, so I didn't give a shit. When I later renegotiated your twenty percent rate to ten, Tim even said, 'If you didn't give us that money, the company would've gone bankrupt.'

"Then I started dating Robin, and you were introduced to her roommate, whom you've been married to for decades. Then I had a barbecue at my house, and Bryan Coleman told me he wanted to be a manager, so I gave him your number and suggested he could possibly intern for you and Tim. Bryan is smart and a good dude. You all made lots of money from him signing and managing the likes of Hinder, Nickelback, Oleander, and Saliva.

"But when I asked you guys for a little help for a songwriter or producer to help me possibly reinvent myself, you guys always made me wait two weeks or three weeks for a return call. It's not as if I was asking for money, just some fucking assistance from my management team. That was my beef—I got tired of fucking waiting."

I talked to John and Tim about it separately and they said, "You know what? You're right, fair enough. Our bad."

I told John, "I don't need you to call me every day, let's just talk once or twice a week. I'm really a low maintenance artist who doesn't need a lot of shit from anybody, but when I do, don't make me wait."

I love both John and Tim, and we've shared a lot of history together. I'm loyal to a fault at times and never wanted to leave the "family." I've seen John get married. I witnessed his kids growing up, and vice versa.

We're all like family again, and I couldn't be happier to say John Greenberg is my manager again.

The Dead Daisies went to Japan for the first time that October, when we played Loud Park Festival in Tokyo. I had a great time in Japan, as always, and we then headed to South Korea for a USO Tour in front of American troops across four or five different camp bases. One of them was Camp Casey in Dongducheon-si, where we checked out the Korean Demilitarized Zone (DMZ) line. We looked through binoculars at the chain-link fence and guard stations less than a quarter of a mile away in North Korea.

That military base is on high alert all the time, so it was pretty intense. They asked us to mingle with the troops, so we sat in a big mess hall and had lunch with these young military kids, talking with them, signing stuff, and taking photos with them. It was somewhat amusing to me because half of them probably didn't even know who we were, they were so young. The staff sergeants and the major may have known who we were, but I'm sure half the troops asked one another, "Who the fuck are these old longhaired guys?"

We entertained troops by playing a show in Camp Casey's Hanson Field House. We gave everybody guitar picks, took photos, saluted, and did our meet and greet. With a sense of patriotism, we added Grand Funk's song "We're an American Band" to our set for the South Korean shows. As we played it, I thought back to when I first played it at my Stetson Junior High assembly. I had come a long way.

We went to Osan Air Base where we took some photos next to bombers and fighter jets, like the F-16 Fighting Falcons. They invited us to try a Blackhawk helicopter simulator. Obviously, David Lowy got in the simulator and flew the chopper like a fucking fighter pilot. I got mine off the ground but at about twenty-five feet up, I nosedived the helicopter right into an animated barracks, so I was glad it was only a fun simulation.

One of the last bases we visited was Yongsan Garrison. It's in a mountainous region in Seoul, and it serves as the headquarters for US military forces command and control of all Special Ops Forces stationed in South Korea. As part of that visit, we went to Camp Kim, which was like fucking NORAD.

We toured through all these fucking deep tunnels and underground rooms where the intelligence operates from and saw all their computers and shit. If there was a nuclear attack from North Korea, all the highest-ranking military officers would descend on this place with its tunnels gated by multiple reinforced steel doors. There were even some rooms where they said, "That's classified. I'm sorry, you can't go in there."

We flew home and the very next morning boarded a cruise ship to play on the next Kiss Kruise, as we sailed between tropical island paradises. Talk about a fucking contrast of environments.

28
Burn It Down

Once again, we no sooner got home than the following month we were back over in Europe touring, this time with Irish rockers The Answer. The entire tour was sold out before we even left America. They are great dudes, so we had a blast with them on the road. Swedish all-girl band Thundermother did a few shows with us, too, when we were able to have a third band on the bill.

When The Dead Daisies first played London, they played Camden Underworld, which holds five hundred people, and now on our return visits we played Electric Ballroom and KOKO that both hold about three times that, so the shows kept getting bigger.

It was a coheadline tour with The Answer, so one night we would go on first, then we'd flip it and go on second the following night. It was a very successful tour for us with great audience turnout each show, plus we had a lot of fun.

On that European tour, we recorded about ten shows including Paris, Vienna, London, and Hamburg. We came home and took the holidays off while management went through all the recordings. Doug Aldrich was tasked to listen to every single song of each performance and pick out the best version.

Instead of working on another studio album through the winter like the past two years, they said we would release a live album instead, giving us all a much-needed creative break. We had a guy mix a live track but none of us really liked it, so we contacted Anthony Focx, who comixes a lot of Marti Frederiksen's work with him. Anthony took our materials and ran with it. He mixed the shit out of it, sent it back, and that became our *Live and Louder* album that was released in May 2017. It was great to have a double live vinyl album out, after being a fan of so many live records from the seventies.

Needless to say, we went right back out on tour again, after rehearsing in New York City for a little while, and hit the European circuit hard once again. We flew back to LA for just a couple of days rest, then we hit South America for the first time, playing in Brazil, Argentina, Chile, and a sold-out concert all the way down in Mexico City in front of about two thousand people.

In August and September, we did The Dirty Dozen Tour throughout the US in August, then went back in the studio in October. We started writing in Alicia Keys' personal studio called Oven in New York City for what became our *Burn It Down* album. We recorded it in November and December, and then took off for the holidays. I absolutely needed that break.

In my time off the road, I enjoyed the NFL playoffs even more than usual because the Philadelphia Eagles had made it through.

Even though the Eagles were the hometown team playing in their own stadium, they had a back-up quarterback and other injured players, and everybody had them pegged as the underdogs and could not see them beating Minnesota in the NFC Championship game to make it through to the Super Bowl. Consensus was there was no way they were going to win; there was no way that was going to happen.

To everyone's shock though, they won 38-7. I was pumped, and I spoke with my brother Nick on the phone after the game; we were both so excited our team was finally going to the fucking Super Bowl!

The following day, my half-brother Todd called my phone. I was busy doing things for Debbie at the time since it was her birthday, so I chose to ignore his incoming calls, thinking he probably just wanted to talk about the Eagles' great win yesterday and I'd catch up with him later.

As I was in the kitchen, I then heard Debbie's phone ring and she answered it. "Hi…what? You're kidding me!"

Debbie started crying, and as she handed me the phone, I asked her, "What's wrong?"

She said, "You're brother, Nick…he's gone."

I was crushed. I had just talked with him last night, and he was in such a happy mood. What the fuck happened? Apparently he got up in the morning and was getting ready to go to work. He showered and was dressing when he sat down on the end of his bed, had a massive heart attack, and instantly dropped dead.

Two weeks later, I sat at a bar in Nashville watching the Super Bowl with a bunch of friends. I was so happy that the Eagles beat the Patriots, but on the flip side, I had to excuse myself and go into the bathroom where I fucking lost it. I broke down and cried hard, so upset that my dad and my brother didn't get to see their victory.

I'm glad my fifty-two-year-old brother was happy the last time I spoke with him, though. In recent years, it seemed his life was finally going quite well after so much struggle, which I've always attributed to pedophile Uncle Jack. You see, Nicky was the sweetest little kid, but after Uncle Jack molested him, he seemed to go through life being a train wreck. Nicky was a happy-go-lucky person, but very dark. During career day at school, when they asked, "What do you want to do when you are grown up?" he gave a considered speech about how he wanted to be a hit man. And he was serious.

There was an old textile mill—the Bromley Mill—that stood five stories high in our Kensington neighborhood. My mom called me in tears one day while I was working and said, "Your brother's in intensive care." For a ten-buck bet, he was dared to go up onto the roof, jump onto a skylight and run across it. As he started running, it caved in, and he fell about two stories, hitting every pipe on the way down. He broke bones and was concussed and went into a coma.

Two or three days later, Mom called me again and said, "That son of a bitch brother of yours: his friends that dared him to go on the roof were at the hospital when Nicky finally woke up from his coma, and he looked at his friend Kevin and the first thing he said was where's my ten bucks?"

Nick was fucking crazy. If you pissed him off, he would rip your fucking head off, skin you alive, and wear you as a shirt.

I remember him getting into a fight with three guys once. They fucking beat the shit out of him. It was just like in the movie *American X* with Edward Norton, where his face was put on the curb and he was kicked in the head and a bunch of his teeth were knocked out. Nick stood up, spat his teeth out, put his fists back up, and said, "Is that all you've got? Let's go, c'mon!"

He did sweet things, like buy me cool crucifixes that I could wear on stage, but he had a switch that would flip and he just didn't give a fuck.

One time, my dad called me in a panic, as he was on the way to the hospital because Nick had been stabbed in a bar fight. Nick was a gay man, and he was out that night with his gay friend in a downtown Philadelphia bar, when three Italian guys came walking in.

Nick's friend briefly glanced at them as they entered, then he looked away, but one of the Italians said, "What the fuck are you looking at, faggot?" as he walked over and slapped him.

When Nick stood up and tried to separate them, the guy grabbed a fucking knife off the bar and jammed it into my brother's side. It went in through his ribs and punctured his lung. My brother was so fucking enraged by it, he beat all three of the guys to within an inch of their lives with a barstool. He then walked himself to a nearby hospital, with the knife still sticking out of his lung, and passed out in the lobby on arrival. He was pronounced dead in that hospital lobby, but thankfully, they managed to revive him.

Nick was much more together toward the end of his life, and he was finally getting his shit together. He wasn't doing drugs anymore; he went to school to be a hairdresser and was then teaching people hairdressing when he suddenly dropped dead that morning. It was a real shock, and I still miss him dearly.

On the previous year's Make Some Noise Tour, we played Woodstock Festival, an annual free rock music festival running since 1995 in Kostrzyn, Poland, inspired by the original Woodstock Festival. It's said to be the biggest open-air festival in Europe, drawing more than 600,000 people on average in recent years.

We filmed a live video for "Join Together" and the promoter said, "Fuck, I love this band. You guys are great. You should come back next year!" So as we toured *Live and Louder*, David Edwards told us, "Hey, the Woodstock Festival wants you to come back and close the evening."

We went from being the fourth or fifth band on the bill, to the headlining spot on the first night, in one year. They also asked us to perform with the Polish Gorzów Philharmonic Orchestra, and since it is the Woodstock love and peace charity concert, they also wanted us to play some songs that relate to happiness. We obliged and included John Lennon's "Give Peace a Chance," Neil Young's "Rockin' in the Free World," The Beatles' classic "Let It Be," and a bluesier take on Louis Armstrong's "What a Wonderful World."

We recorded a rehearsal and sent it to the orchestra. They charted everything out before we arrived in Poland, ready for a few days of rehearsals with them. The first day we got together was a fucking mess. They charted our songs to the exact measure of how we did it on the tape. As we started a song like "Helter Skelter," they counted it off one, two, three, four, but I decided to wait a little longer before I started singing than I did on the tape, thinking they're not going to start playing until I started. They said, "Yeah, no, it doesn't work that way."

Thank God we had Brian Tichy, "Mr. Berklee College of Music graduate," with us. He explained to us, "You have to understand with orchestra arrangements, they read the sheet music and start counting from the very first bar. Our taped version of "Helter Skelter" that we gave them probably has 370 bars of music, and we can't vary from that. We have to play the same 370 bars of music."

So, Brian went through the whole tape and counted it out and charted everything for each one of us. "Crab, you can't wait. As soon as that guitar starts, it's a bar of one, two, three, four, and you come in after five bars because that's when you started singing on the tape."

"Okay, I've got it," I said, as I walked around, kidding around saying, "This is bullshit. I didn't realize there was fucking math involved in rock-and-roll."

It was tedious but a very cool experience in the end. The fact that we actually pulled that entire set off without a hitch was amazing. Once we sorted it out, we had two full days of rehearsal, and we did the show the following night in front of the estimated 300,000 fucking people.

As far back across the outdoor field as I could see from the stage, it was just a sea of fucking people. It was definitely the biggest show that I've ever played in my career. It was fucking massive!

At the end of 2017, I took a bit of time out. Debbie and I had two homes, so we decided to sell one and move into the other that we refurbished. Debbie's mom stayed at our place for a few months, and once I was done recording *Burn It Down*, we took Mom home to Melbourne, Florida, and hung out there between Christmas and New Year to chill out for a week's vacation.

While on vacation in Florida, though, I actually got ready to finally release my *Live '94—One Night in Nashville* album. It was supposed to come out in December, but the vinyl wasn't ready for the preordered fan bundles, so it was delayed by about ten days until it was released in the first week of January.

Along with Topher on bass and my son Ian on drums[9], my solo band also features a great Nashville guitarist Jeremy Asbrock, who has been with me since I started doing those Mötley Crüe album shows. He was already playing with us when I joined The Dead Daisies.

I had another guitar player named Josh Dutoit for a little while and the guy that played on the *Live '94* record is Tommy Daley. He played just

9 Ian's first concert drumming behind me was coincidently on the twentieth anniversary of the self-titled *Mötley Crüe* album release.

that one show with us and did a great job. He didn't do more as he has other commitments with his clothing store Black Shag Vintage in an old East Nashville fire station, plus his own band, also called Black Shag.

That album was recorded live from our show in 2015, and every time I was going to release it, the Daisies put out a record. I didn't want to do something that was going to jeopardize mine or jeopardize theirs, so I kept holding mine back, waiting for the right time to put it out. By the time it finally came out in January of 2018, the record had been sitting on the shelf for two and a half fucking years. Already, those limited-edition vinyl albums are worth quite a bit in the collectors' market.

I was excited to get it out and hopefully get some sort of a 2018 schedule from The Dead Daisies where I could go out and play some shows with them, as well as make plans to go out and play shows with my son again.

"Let me know when you're going to need me and when you're not going to need me," I asked. As much as I hoped that would be the case, I knew the Daisies' schedule would be so maniacal, I'd be lucky to play any fucking solo shows.

I'm very passionate about what I do. I got into it with Marco a few times over things. I got into it with Doug a few times when we were in the studio, simply because Doug is Doug, and he's got a certain way of doing things, and I'm me and I have a certain way of doing things, and then Marti was involved in the equation as well. So, naturally there were times where we all butted heads, we disagreed and fucking made a point or stated a case, then walked away from it. No big deal.

I loved the band and got along with everybody for the most part really well, though.

I didn't know Brian Tichy wasn't in the band until I got to rehearsals and found out he wasn't coming. He had some prior engagements that were set up and the guys wanted somebody who was going to do the *Burn It Down* record and the tour.

Brian loves to stay busy. He was doing the Daisies, but he had done some shows with Steven Tyler and Joe Perry. He was doing some stuff with Don Felder from the Eagles and his solo band. Last time I talked to Brian, he was in Japan with a band called B'z, who are a massive Japanese band, the biggest rock act in all of Asia.

The Dead Daisies brought in Deen Castronovo to be the new drummer. I knew of him from his time playing in Bad English, Ozzy, and

Journey, but I had never met him before. Doug had played with Deen in their Revolution Saints project, so he called Deen and he flew in.

It was me, Marti, Marco, Doug, and David doing the songwriting, and as we put shit together, we accidently tripped on the tone of the record. It came about from a guitar pedal that Marco was using, lent by the engineer. Marco wanted an old Geezer Butler, Grand Funk Railroad–style bass tone, a little distorted. The engineer said, "Oh dude, I've got a pedal for you. It's going to change your life!"

He plugged the fucking pedal in and started playing the riff for what became "What Goes Around." It was all heavy and kind of dark, and we said, "Oh, that's fucking badass! It's like old-school seventies."

Once we put that song together, Doug said, "I didn't really think we were going to be that heavy, but since we are, check out this riff," and he pulled out the riff for "Rise Up."

He started playing this fucking riff, and we excitedly said, "It's like old Sabbath." That set the tone for the rest of the record.

I wrote the lyrics to "Rise Up" as a call for people to wake up and start taking action, instead of just being passive. It isn't a Rise Up Democrats or Rise Up Republicans message. It's Rise Up EVERYBODY and hold all those asshats in Washington accountable. Why can't people see that our leaders are dividing us with hate? It's not just happening in the United States either.

After stockpiling songs and riffs in Alicia Keys' New York studio for a week or so, we came back to Nashville where they set-up this studio for us to work out of and record the *Burn It Down* record. We were still writing and tweaking songs as we went.

For example, "Resurrected" was in a different key that sounded more like an Aerosmith *Draw the Line*–era track, like "Last Time I Saw the Sun" from our previous album. Marti spoke to me one night and said he felt the song wasn't quite there as it was, so we decided to take another look at it. As we played with it, we retuned it, and it came together in one night; it became one of the lead tracks for the album.

I met Deen for the first time in New York when we were writing. Aside from Doug, nobody really knew him, but we knew he had some prior legal troubles. He got booted from Journey in the summer of 2015 when he was indicted on drug-related felony charges. He took a plea bargain instead of going to trial and got four years of probation and counseling for his addictions and domestic violence incident.

While in New York, he was asked to join us in Nashville. Until we got started in Nashville, I hadn't heard him play a fucking note of anything. We gave him tapes that we made in New York, which he took home and listened to. He then went in and recorded the drum tracks, which he nailed—he fucking crushed it!

As I got to know Deen, I felt his infectious energy. He's always upbeat and funny; he's got a great sense of humor. We hit it off immediately and became really tight. I just fucked with him the whole time.

I've always been very self-reflective and always try to be as conscious and aware as I can be. I don't want to hurt anybody's feelings or tread on their toes, especially when I have a point to make. The guys in Mötley used to give me shit for this all the time, and they yelled at me because I always prefaced my differing viewpoint with, "Hey, I'm not trying to be an asshole, but..."

Even when I disagree with somebody, I always try and look at their point of view, but if I have a point that I want to make, I always try to keep my temper in check and say, "Listen, I totally understand your point. I'm not trying to be argumentative, but have you ever looked at it this way?"

Sure, I've lost my temper before, but I do try to always remain as calm as possible. Even if I'm fucking livid with somebody, I can still have empathy going into the argument. I always try to look at things from every angle, including theirs.

However, the older I've become, I'm more frustrated because I really don't see a lot of empathy from others. I especially don't see it in America, which is why if you look at my lyrics since The Scream record, I think I started getting a little more worldly, as I experienced things that say eighty-five percent of people honestly won't see the way I've seen it.

I've had the great fortune to travel the world for the last thirty years, so I've seen some of the good and bad of different cultures and the governments of other countries and how they work. Don't get me wrong, I'm by no means saying I'm an authority on government, but I've seen things and asked questions that most people won't ever get the chance to see or ask. Sure, you can go on vacation to any foreign country for a week, but you most likely haven't gone there and worked, year after year for a couple weeks at a time, which gives you a deeper understanding of that culture.

You haven't actually worked in Brazil, Japan, England, or Russia, and sat with a promoter and had a drink with him and asked him about his life there and what it's actually like. I have, and such experiences help shape my views on the world and people, outside of what social or mainstream media force-feed us.

For example, people here in the US violently argue about guns, global warming, abortion, gay marriage, religion, racism, corporate greed, and health care. Everything has become political, including wearing a mask during a global pandemic. It's become completely ridiculous, idiotic, and devoid of all empathy.

It all stems from ignorance, in my honest opinion. People nowadays know it all, but don't actually want to know what they don't already know. They don't realize that the media in all forms has become weaponized to make us do what we're doing. People have figured out how to use the news, Facebook, and Twitter to push their agenda. When I was growing up, news was just that: NEWS! Walter Cronkite reported the news, truthfully and unbiased, without any political catering.

I loathe the fact that millions of keyboard warriors have become simple know-it-alls, virologists, biologists, and political analysts, and even have the gall to tell people like myself what they like or don't like about the way we look, dress, sing, etc. It's annoying and actually quite rude. I feel like saying if your life is so fucking perfect, maybe you should write a self-help book, or maybe be a fashion designer, or actually earn a PhD in science.

I'm not angry, but it is sad, and I'm just stunned at the lack of empathy and manners, and how people's common sense is not so common anymore. So many seem to be blind, deaf, and angered by varying opinions, and just because they heard or saw something they believed, they've become immovable; nobody puts themselves in the other person's shoes anymore. So, basically we subscribe to the articles or news that matches our train of thought, because we've been programmed to not think for ourselves. It's all algorithms, kids, and somebody smarter than us has figured it out. Perhaps this is what governments want, though.

The older I get, I don't like that there is no humanity anymore, and everything is driven by self-serving greed. Everything has become black or white, there's nothing acceptable in the middle. Governments have become self-serving businesses and are not at all there for the people.

I think about such things and wonder what kind of world our children are inheriting, and what their kids will have to endure over their lives.

When I initially talked with The Dead Daisies' management about joining, they told me, "It'll be twenty-six weeks per year. We're going to need you for half a year."

But the time I had for myself was never January to May, or May to December, for example. It was a month and a half here, a week or two there, then nothing. So, I couldn't actually get any steam with anything of my own.

My son sat there asking me, "Fuck, Dad, when are we going to play next? Are we ever going to play again?"

He was working in a restaurant passing time, "Dad, I love you but I fucking hate you. I came out here to be in a band with you and now you go and join this other fucking band."

He was disappointed, and I can't say I blame him.

The Daisies were forging ahead with momentum to the point where, especially in Europe, we were constantly being offered opportunities and a lot of them would come in last minute.

On one occasion when I was actually able to be out doing some solo shows, somebody from the Daisies' management company called and asked, "Hey, can you get on a plane tomorrow and fly out to LA?"

I said, "Dude, I'm on tour. NO! I'm doing shows. No, I can't."

A NASCAR team wanted to use our song "Rise Up" as a theme song, so they asked us to come to Los Angeles and hang out to get to know everybody. Doug, Marco, and David went out and schmoozed everybody. I couldn't go, and Deen couldn't go either.

So, there were always scheduling issues, which I understand. The Dead Daisies became an entity that really took off, and I just couldn't find time or a gap in our schedule to do my own thing.

The *Burn It Down* album came out, and we went back over to Europe in April. We started the *Burn It Down* World Tour in Scotland and went out with a bigger crew and a bigger production.

We got into London and played the old Camden Palace that's called KOKO these days, which was sold-out; the entire UK tour was a sell-out before we even got there. We ended up going back to London later in the year and played another two sold-out shows.

There was no question it was really fucking taking off. From my point of view though, I was concerned about all the promo events we were doing and the amount of shows that we were playing in a row. The train was rolling at full steam, so my concerns at that point were irrelevant.

I therefore felt the best thing for me to do was to focus on myself. I knew on my own, I could make the same amount of money and work at my own pace that I'm comfortable with vocally and physically, so I thought it was the best thing for everybody if I left The Dead Daisies.

In mid-September, when we did the last show on our American leg at The Roxy in Hollywood, I told them, "Come January, I'm out!"

I came home after our US tour, hung out for a few weeks, and thought about my future.

We then did Kiss Kruise 2018 on the Norwegian Jade in the first week of November and went right back to Europe again for yet another tour. I played my last show with The Dead Daisies in front of 1,500 people in Frankfurt, Germany, a week before Christmas and that was it. I said to the guys, "I can't do this anymore. I'm just going to go do my own thing now. I'm out. Everything is all good. Thank you for the opportunity."

It wasn't because of anything with the band; I just didn't want to keep going at THEIR pace anymore. I even said to the guys when I left, "Hey, if you ever need another band as an opener or a double-bill some time, give me a call. I'd love to do it."

29

Life Is as It Should Be

I began 2019 by heading out on my own acoustic tour of Europe. Over the course of a month, I played fun shows in Norway, Finland, Sweden, Poland, Holland, Germany, Switzerland, England, Scotland, Austria, France, Italy, and Spain.

Mötley's bestselling autobiography *The Dirt* finally got turned into a movie by Netflix and was being hyped as I toured Europe. Honestly, I didn't think I was going to be in it. I was sure I wasn't going to get mentioned at all in the movie, and I was totally fine with that.

When I watched *The Dirt* movie in March before I headed back out on a tour of Australia, I thought the way I was fleetingly included as a grinning, mute character was actually worse than if they would have just left me out of it.

I told the *LA Times* when they interviewed me about the movie, "Personally, I just want to be my own guy and enjoy life, and I've accepted the fact that Mötley is Vince, Nikki, Tommy, and Mick. So, I expect nothing from that camp at all. I was actually surprised I was even mentioned in the movie at all. I didn't expect it. I am a bit disappointed that they couldn't lockdown Morgan Freeman to play me, though."

I then smirked as I thought of the poor sucker that had to load and unload all those newspaper bundles containing my words in the *LA Times*, just like I used to years ago.

I toured Australia with my full band, since the promoter Silverback Touring wanted me to perform the 1994 self-titled album that I did with Mötley Crüe—from top to bottom. The album reached number three there when it came out, which was its highest chart position of any country. In fact, it's the highest Australian position that ANY Mötley release has ever reached.

I'm still able to sing all the songs from that Mötley record, but if you really analyze the way I sing it live now to what I did on the record, there's definitely some spots where I don't go up too high, and I'll do some bluesy little thing instead. I know my voice and my capabilities, and I know my limits, so I'll play with the melody a little bit, but for the most part, probably eighty percent of what I do live is like the record.

When it was originally recorded, I sang a verse ten or twenty times and then Bob Rock would say, "Wow, man, I really liked how you sang this line better than the other."

"Okay, well let's use that one," I'd say.

He'd then map it out and put it all together, and we'd listen to it for a day or two, then come back in and correct or tweak. If something was a little sharp or flat, I would fix it.

So I had the luxury of singing a verse and then I could stop, sip some tea, or go smoke a cigarette, come back in and sing the verse again. When you're doing the record, you're doing it in pieces, but when I get on stage, I've got to sing "Hooligan's Holiday" live from top to bottom in one take.

At those shows in Australia, not only did I have to do "Hooligan's Holiday" from top to bottom, I had to do the entire record from top to bottom in the order it appeared on the album, plus some songs from *Quaternary* as an encore. Then do that over four shows in four nights, with jetlag. That is not an easy thing to do at sixty.

I declared the Adelaide show of that tour as my last time playing that Mötley album top to bottom like that, simply because I have so many other songs from my catalogue that I want and love to play, and I'm not going to just limit myself or be pigeonholed to just one fucking album.

Following the Australian tour, I was headed to Florida in my motorhome with some friends for a getaway celebration of my sixtieth birthday. Just prior to that holiday, I was in Denver doing acoustic shows with Ian, so I bought some weed for the festivities. These days, you go to these fucking dispensaries and it's just like Baskin-Robbins or Ben & Jerry's, where there are 900 different flavors to choose from!

Fuck, when I was a kid, you walked up to whoever was dealing in your neighborhood, handed him a five-dollar bill, and he passed you a little Manila envelope. "Here's your nickel bag for five bucks, now go smoke the sky!" Times change.

The Dead Daisies announced Glenn Hughes was replacing me and Marco by issuing a statement that said, "From the band's inception, the idea was for members to bring their own ideas to the table but also have the flexibility to come and go when working on their other projects. Both John and Marco are, and always will be, a part of The Dead Daisies musical family, but at this point in time they have decided to do some work on their own solo projects."

Fair enough, from my point of view, but I felt bad for Marco since he was in the band from the beginning. I left the band, but I don't know what the deal was with Marco. I saw him when I was in LA, but we didn't really talk about it; we just hung out as friends, which we hadn't done the whole time we were in the Daisies together.

My manager John belongs to a cigar club, so we went to the club right on the harbor by a marina. I had some whiskey and a cigar, while Marco drank soda water and smoked a cigar. We ate some food and just talked about other stuff, like our wives and families. He told me about his tour of Europe, and I was talking about my tour in the States, and we never really mentioned The Dead Daisies. It was cool to just hang out as buddies. However, I do feel really shitty that my decision negatively impacted him, and he didn't see it coming. A consequence for me was losing the luxury of knowing I had that money coming in. It was more of a guaranteed income stream and that security also went with my decision to leave them. So it was a big decision for me to say I didn't want to do it anymore. I didn't want to kill myself for it, preferring to just go at my own pace now.

I really loved being in the band, but at the same time, it was a little scary leaving that financial cushion, and now I've got to go out and hustle. Well, I made my bed, so I'm fine, and I certainly believe that as one door closes in life, another one opens.

The bottom line is that if I do have to be replaced by somebody, it's not bad being replaced by somebody in the Rock and Roll Hall of Fame, a legendary singer I grew up admiring. That's pretty fucking awesome.

My zodiac sign is Taurus, and they say one of the main traits about Taurus is you fucking dig your heels in, and you're stubborn. I think there are some aspects to the wandering bull that I do associate with, like being practical and grounded, but I don't really consider myself a stubborn human being. I don't think of myself that way because just being in a band, you must learn to fucking compromise. So I've never been a my-way-or-fuck-off kind of a guy.

Like my situation with the Daisies, for example: I wanted them to understand the physical aspects of being a singer, and some things in regard to our schedules, and we just didn't quite see eye-to-eye on it. So instead of sitting there saying, "Fuck off, it's my way or the highway," I thought about the situation for a length of time, and then I said, "Okay, well maybe it's time for us to go in different directions."

Taureans are notoriously stubborn, but I don't think I'm that stubborn at all.

When I recorded my *Unplugged* solo album back in 2012 and Larry Morand was managing me, he asked if I would like to play the Monsters of Rock Cruise. Having played on Vince Neil's cruise before, I had an idea what it would be like, so I signed on.

That first year, it was just me by myself with my acoustic guitar, doing my thing. I told my guys DA and Topher about it, so they bought tickets and came on the boat, too. There's been a couple of times when those guys sat in and played with me as I came back on the cruise year after year.

The Monsters of Rock Cruise became an annual event on my performance schedule, and I have done every year since, except 2020 and 2016. I was supposed to play '16 with The Dead Daisies when we were recording the *Make Some Noise* record. It was all advertised, then at the last minute, the Daisies camp didn't want to take the weekend off from the studio, so we canceled.

Other than the guys in Faster Pussycat and the London Quireboys, most of the bands that go on the cruise do not really hang out with anybody on the boat. They don't fucking mingle. I would get on the boat with my wife, we'd throw our luggage in our fucking cabin, then head up to one of the bars and sit there or at the pool the whole fucking time. I'd take photos if people wanted, sign shit, swim with people, drink with people, and then I'd go and do my gigs at the end of the day or at night. Then I'd walk around and watch the other bands, I would walk on stage with Tesla with a bottle of tequila and jam, or sit in and play a song or two with Stryper.

I was there, present, and just having fun. I was really one of the few musicians who walked around and mingled with people and since I had done so many of these cruises over the years, people started calling me the Mayor and Debbie the First Lady.

They held a charity event during the last couple of cruises, where they sold additional tickets for people to come in and have a nice steak dinner with me, along with wines and tequila. They sold-out the fifty or sixty seats and the ticket money was donated to charity.

Hopefully, the Mayor will be back on another Monsters of Rock Cruise in the years to come.

Even though I still call her Little Val, my stepdaughter is now a forty-year-old woman. She got married to a problem child who's been in and out of jail over the years. She was with him for a long time, and they'd break-up and then get back together again, then break-up again and get back together.

They're completely over and done now, but their relationship produced four great kids: Joe, Rudy, Nicholas, and Desiree. Joe's at (legal) drinking age, Rudy's a little bit younger, and Nick has just become a teenager, while Desiree is the youngest. They're all great kids, but they live in California, so I don't get to see them that much. When I'm in LA, I'll go see them or take them all out for dinner.

My son Ian met a woman, Carrie, who was a single mom raising two great kids. He started dating her and taking her kids under his wing to a degree. Carrie got pregnant around 2015, but unfortunately lost the baby. It was a sad time for her and Ian. Without being callous, I said to them, "Perhaps this is the Universe's way of saying to you both that you're not ready yet. Carrie, you've already got two kids, but you guys are struggling financially, barely making ends meet." I was just trying to put some positive fatherly spin on everything.

Ian called me at the start of 2017 and said, "Hey, Dad, I've got something to tell ya!"

As he said that, I replied, "You guys are pregnant again, aren't you?"

Ian said, "Yeah…with twins!"

"What the fuck? Are you fucking kidding me right now?" I said.

So now I always joke around with them by saying, "Well, the Universe tried to tell you the first time that you maybe weren't ready. Now this is the Universe saying, you didn't listen to me the first time, so now you can have two."

They named their identical twin girls Mary Jane and Lyla Mae. Mary Jane was a little small, and she had some heart issues due to blood going to her sister more when they were in the womb. They've worked through those complications now, and they're awesome. I still can't tell them apart, but they're adorable little girls who are funnier than shit. I don't get to see them that much as well though because I'm always gone. So, when I do see them, it's too quick.

On my last acoustic tour of Europe, I drove my tour manager Nicholas nuts because as we zipped through Europe, I kept seeing cute gifts for them. In Switzerland, I saw two little matching beanie hats, so I bought them and threw them in my suitcase. Then as we drove through France, I hit some store and saw two matching furry little coats and handed over the cash. Then I bought them some shoes, and more until Nick said, "Oh my God, dude. Between all the shit that you're buying for your granddaughters and the refrigerator magnets you're buying for your wife; your suitcase is going to weigh a hundred fucking pounds!"

We laughed about it, and when I got home from tour and gave it all to the girls, Ian and Carrie laughed, too. They asked, "How's that fucking Grandpop thing working out for you, Grandpop?"

I adore them though, they're awesome. Two little identical, mirror twin rug rats. They've got everybody wrapped around their fingers, and if my calculations are correct, they may have some money coming to them later in life, as I tend to do records that sell like shit when they come out but gain momentum many years later.

Being away from your family so often is honestly one of the things about the music industry that's a drag and most fans don't realize how fucking difficult it is. It's one of the hardest things about this business. I can't tell you how many milestones in my kids' lives I missed, like high school graduation.

Now my kids have given me grandkids, but here I am still playing shows around the world for fans—except when there's a fucking pandemic that shuts down the industry. As much as I love doing what I do, it's not very conducive to a strong family environment. It's a bittersweet, double-edged sword. It's hard being Grandpop when you just don't get to see anybody.

My ex-wife Valerie comes to Nashville sometimes to visit Ian and our granddaughters, so she'll stay with me and Debbie. Val's truly one of my best friends. We didn't talk for a while, but we have both realized and come to terms with our mistakes in our marriage.

Her father was a shithead, and her first fucking husband was an asshole and a cheat and a drug addict, so she always had jealousy and trust struggles. I think the final nail in our marriage's coffin was when I joined Mötley. If we could have got through that insanity, Val and I would probably still be married.

But we have kids and grandkids together, so we've learned to make the best of it for them. There's no point in holding onto animosity and anger like our parents did. And Debbie sees it the exact same way, which makes things really easy. Thank God!

I've been playing in clubs since I was a teenager, so it's really rare for me when I'm home to go out and hang at a club. When I'm on tour it's trains, planes, and automobiles, and clubs every night, so when I get home, I'll veg out for a couple days. I've been practicing and perfecting the art of enjoying life.

Debbie and I will go to a mall, go to dinner, maybe have a martini out somewhere, then come home and either chill and watch a movie inside the house, or outside on my RV. My driveway goes all the way along the side of our house through to the backyard, so I can pull my RV in far enough that I can open the side and watch the RV's outside TV. I have a fireplace out there, and Debbie and I will just sit outside with a martini and watch a movie or a football game on the RV in our own backyard.

Sometimes I'll invite friends over or maybe go to a barbecue at a friend's house, or perhaps an occasional concert. It's pretty fucking mellow when I'm at home; I'm just a homebody that likes to hang out with my wife and dogs. A treat for us is to pack the RV and drive to Nashville Shores RV Resort that's just twenty minutes from home. It's an RV resort in Nashville, situated on a peninsula overlooking Percy Priest Lake.

Summer or winter, we'll pull up, open the slides, get my grill out, sit around, and hang out. Debbie will get up in the morning, take a shower in the RV, drive her Jeep to work and cut hair all day, come back to the RV Resort, walk with the dogs, and just hang out. It's mellow, it's chilled, and the complete opposite of what I do when I'm on the road.

When my dad passed away in 2014, my brother Nicky got his truck and I got his two-door El Camino. I brought it from his New Jersey home to Nashville and decided to restore it in his honor. I put a new engine in it, new transmission, tires, a black paint job, new interior…I redid the whole car, except for the windows. It was a badass muscle car by the time I had it finished, with a lot of sentimental value.

Soon after I got home from tour as winter 2020 ended, I went out and started it up to give the engine a run, since it had been sitting there for a while. I turned it around in my street and backed it in all the way down my driveway to my yard. Then the battery died, so I jumpstarted it and sat in the car as I let it run for a while to recharge. After ten minutes, I went into my kitchen to grab something, and the El Camino exploded into a ball of flames. The entire car went up in fucking flames! Thank God I wasn't still sitting in it at the time; it was a close call. I could have been cooked and cremated at the same time.

The fire department came and put it out, before it was towed away as a complete write-off. I was devastated that the fire gutted my dad's car. I've since bought a 2019 silver Nissan 370Z sports car to drive instead, but it will never replace Dad's El Camino.

As each day goes by, I'm another day closer to my death, and so are you—we're mere mortals with an expiration date, of course. I've certainly had an eventful first sixty years on this planet, and it seems the older I get, the more the end tends to come to mind at times, which is normal.

These days, I'm like the patriarch of the family, since my youngest brother passed away a couple of years ago, my dad a few years before that, and my mom back in 1996. I question myself with what have I accomplished? What kind of a legacy am I leaving? Is my family going to be taken care of? Is everybody okay? You start thinking of things that you didn't normally think of when you were younger, like fucking life insurance and wills.

But I don't dwell on it all. I'll go to bed tonight, get a good seven or eight hours sleep and get up tomorrow, when the first thing I'll give a shit about will be my first coffee of the morning. And Lord knows, if I don't get my morning cup or two of coffee, we could be talking about YOUR departure from this world we live in.

I'd love to be like the actor Michael Douglas, working into the late years of life, although he's got something in his genes as his father Kirk passed at 103 years old (and his mother is over 100.) I would love to still be functioning and creating music or producing music to some degree for a very, very long time.

When my time finally comes and my number is up, though, I'm hoping that I just fall into a deep sleep at say ninety-six years of age after getting the most amazing blowjob ever and never wake up from the afterglow. (That's probably a visual you didn't need—sorry!)

Not knowing when or how you're going to die can be scary, but I think it'd be even scarier knowing. If someone said to me, "I don't know exactly when you're going to die, but it's going to be while playing tennis," I'd make damn sure I never fucking played tennis ever again!

As I sat around talking with my wife and some friends one night, conversation flowed to how Debbie had dated a bunch of different guys before she met me, and how I was married twice before. One of her girlfriends remarked, "Life is as it should be."

That stuck with me as a really powerful phrase, and the more I thought about it, I wanted it tattooed on my neck. Since I'm of Italian descent, I looked it up in Italian: *"La vita è come dovrebbe essere."*

I printed it out and gave it to my tattoo artist, who inked it on my chest around my neckline instead.

When I first looked at it finished in the studio's mirror, I thought it looked very cool, but a wave of anxiety rushed over me, as I hoped the translation was actually correct. I hoped it didn't read, "Punch me" or "I like cock in my ass." If everybody in Italy starts looking at me funny the next time I'm there, I'll know I got the wrong translation on my neckline. I had a couple of Italian buddies read it, and they said I was good, though.

The phrase rings so true to me. Going back to all the shit I experienced with Mötley, that really made me open my fucking eyes and realize the saying is true. Every decision I've ever made, there were consequences. There's been good times, bad times, good times, bad times, and more good times. You know I've had my share.

Every step you take in any direction leads you somewhere. Every girl I've ever married or dated, I thought they were the one. Every band I was in, I pictured myself walking up to a podium and accepting my Lifetime Achievement Award at the Rock and Roll Hall of Fame.

It didn't work out that way, but that's okay. It's been horseshoes and hand grenades, so I keep persevering and moving onto whatever comes next. Each step I've taken along my journey has led me to right here, right now, sharing my life's story with you, and you taking the time to read this—so, THANK YOU!

I had a very rough childhood. I made a ton of mistakes along the way. I married three times, had kids, ugly divorces, and been in way more bands than I ever wanted to be in...but that's been my path.

I can look at the glass half-empty and think, "Fuck, why am I not fucking driving around in a Testarossa, and why don't I have a 12,000-square-foot home? Why don't I have a Steven Tyler-size bank balance?" But I'm not hurting; I have my health, a great wife, two great kids, six awesome grandkids, and two great pups.

To me, one thing I can say, if I may be so bold for a second, is at the end of the day when people look at my entire body of work, I think they're going to say I was consistent. I may not have sold many millions of records or had countless awards bestowed upon me, but I think a lot of people would say my music creations were consistently pretty fucking good. I always want people to walk away from my shows and say, "That was good shit. They were great fucking tunes."

I think my biggest fear, though, is that it's gonna all go unnoticed and the regular, vanilla part of John Corabi is going to bury it all.

However, in the grand scheme of things, how many of the seven-billion-plus people on this planet can say they've recorded more than a dozen albums?

Not only have I performed so many rock tours with bands through all the usual regions like North America, South America, Europe, Japan, and Australia, but I've also been fortunate enough to play on stage before thousands in countries like fucking Cuba, India, South Korea, Belarus, and Israel at different points in my career.

The phrase horseshoes and hand grenades can mean coming close, but not succeeding is not good enough, but for me it is. I'm happy. My life is as it should be, and I'm good with it.

"La vita è come dovrebbe essere!"

30
New Day

I was doing a run of shows in March 2020. I'd been down to Georgia, South Carolina, and I was on my way to Ohio, driving in my motorhome, when I got a call from my booking agent. He said the Ohio show had just cancelled, and pretty much all the remaining shows were also cancelling because of this new disease that was spreading, and all the States subsequently starting to quarantine everybody.

Bypassing Ohio, I called the club in Michigan to check on the status of my next show and was told they were all good, so I drove there instead. As I parked my motorhome behind the venue, my agent called to say I needed to go on at 6:00 p.m. instead of 9:00 p.m. because the governor just announced that everything was shutting down at 10:00 p.m. Everyone had to be out of the club and on their way home before 10:00 p.m. After that show, I had a long drive back home to Nashville. I think I was in a state of denial, thinking it would blow over quickly and they'll have it all figured out in a week or two.

Well, a week went by, then a month, then three months. I watched my bank account shrink like my nutsack in a cold shower. Then I started getting worried, knowing I had to pay all the bills somehow, without my main source of income. It became a very stressful time over the next two and a half or three years that I was out of work.

Somehow, I managed to still be productive with a few new things though. First, it was working on creating this book. I also wrote a script for a TV series that may get off the ground and onto screens one of these years. Importantly, I also invested in myself by learning some new skills.

The first couple of months of the pandemic, I noticed lots of musicians were releasing music online. I was kicking myself, saying if only I was a little smarter in the earlier part of my career and paid more attention to the recording process, and learned how to record, then I could be writing music and making quality songs available on my website to download for a dollar. My phone must have heard everything because I started getting ads for *Learn How to Use Pro Tools*. With the pandemic in full force, I signed up for some Pro Tools music production software classes that were conducted via Zoom.

I bought everything I needed, rearranged our guest bedroom by getting rid of all the furniture, and set up a studio in it instead. I took the classes and learned how to record myself. I've still not mastered it to expert level though. My producer, Marti Frederiksen, laughs at me because it'll take me three days to do something that he'll do in an hour. But slow and steady wins the race, which is basically the story of my life.

The cool thing about having a motorhome during the pandemic was an ability to have different scenery, just for our own sanity. There's an RV park about twenty minutes' drive from home called Nashville Shores, situated by a lake. Although we weren't allowed to go visit anybody, we could get out of the house sometimes and go there. I called them to check if they were open, "Yeah, there's nobody here, though."

"Oh, that's even better. Perfect, I'm coming," I said. Debbie and I would load up the dogs, get in the RV, then head over there. Outside enjoying nature, we lit a fire at night, sat outside the motorhome watching the TV, watching movies for a different headspace as we tried to come to terms with what was going on. It was something a little different, and it helped. If I can find any sort of positive in the COVID era, we just kind of looked at our lives, did some self-reflection, while figuring out what's most important and a better way forward to become more self-sufficient.

Things eventually started opening again, and my wife and I got through the pandemic without loss. We count our blessings every day, because I know there are millions of people that lost homes, and lost family members. Still to this day, I can't believe we somehow weathered the storm.

Well, I did lose my motorhome for a while. Late in 2021, I decided to put it into a workshop to get some small repairs done. I just needed headlights and an awning replacement. The mechanic said it could take quite a while because they were backed up on the parts coming in from China, due to all the supply chain issues. Since I wasn't needing to tour with it, I left it with him and said, "Just let me know when it's done and I'll come pick it up."

My RV sat on his lot for seven months, then the day before I was supposed to pick it up, somebody broke in and tried to steal it, doing about $67,000 worth of damage in the process.

I then had to take it to another place to get all the damage repaired and didn't get it back until 2023. They called me and said, "Your coach is done." I got my coach back but there was still a bunch of things wrong with it, so I took it back in again.

About two months after finally having my coach back, my insurance company called and basically said, "You know what, we just gave you a check for like $70,000, so now we're going to have to change your monthly insurance premium payment from $250 to $950." Gee, thanks.

My first shows after the pandemic were in Australia during June 2022. I landed in Sydney and my co-author, Paul Miles, met me at the hotel and before long the first box of the first edition of this book was received via FedEx. It was amazing timing that we were able to unbox it together in person, see it and hold it at that moment after working on it over a couple of years.

With pre-orders built up, it was a number one new release on Amazon. We did a signing session for fans at the Sydney record store Utopia, and we sold out of all the books we had with every one in two people buying them at the acoustic shows around Australia. The response to the book globally was overwhelmingly positive and really appreciated. The only somewhat negative feedback was the number of times I apparently say *fuck!*

As 2023 came to be, the world was still fully getting back to work, and overseas travel was still a little janky. I had booked a tour in America of about thirty acoustic shows, opening for Tom Keifer and Winger.

Just prior to that, David Lowy reached out to me about rejoining The Dead Daisies. After a couple of records with them, their singer that replaced me, Glenn Hughes, apparently felt it was time to move on to other things he wanted to do.

David came to Nashville, so I joined him for dinner at Ruth's Chris Steak House, and he said they'd love to have me back. It sounded good, but I was sure to tell him, "I've got to be honest with you, bro, doing two shows in one day, or just the way we were touring before, it was over the top. Then we'd get done touring, and it was like, alright, right back in the studio to start working on an album. We're not twenty anymore, so I want to pace ourselves better."

He was in total agreement, saying, "Yes, me too. I don't want to burnout."

I then went out and did my acoustic shows with Tom Keifer and Winger, which was fun, squeezing in some rehearsals with The Daisies in New York City in between. I finished my tour at the Ryman Auditorium in Nashville on August 18, did my laundry the following day, then flew to Philadelphia on the twentieth.

The Dead Daisies released a Best Of album, and I made my return to the stage with them on August 22 at Mickey's Black Box in Lititz, Pennsylvania, which kicked off the Resurrected Tour of North America, before we toured Japan and Europe. It was boom, boom, boom, out the door, and I was gone again. It felt like I never left, and it was awesome to be back in the saddle again!

While touring Europe, it was decided we should start getting material together for a new studio album. We all started throwing ideas into the mix for the record that became *Light 'Em Up*. Writing commenced in Nashville before we went down to the historic Muscle Shoals Sound Studio in Sheffield, Alabama.

The studio is housed in a little building opposite a cemetery. We were shocked at how small it was, but once we walked into it, we could just smell the history, reinforced by pictures hanging on the walls of all these cats that have walked through the door before us—the likes of Duane Allman, Aretha Franklin, Etta James, Wilson Pickett, Rod Stewart, the Stones, Steven Tyler, and Bob Seger. It was pretty trippy.

While jamming some blues stuff there, we decided to actually *do* a blues record, as well. Perhaps it was the history of the joint that refocused us on recording a blues covers album instead, over the nine or ten days we were there, which we kept up our sleeve for a while, until we released *Lookin' for Trouble* in May 2025.

When it came to the song choices, we all threw ideas out there. Doug said he always wanted to do "The Thrill is Gone," and I suggested we do it like Zeppelin's "Since I've Been Loving You," so we played around with it a little more that way. "Black Betty" is probably my favorite track on the record, but I don't recall who suggested it.

John Lee Hooker's "Boom Boom" is just phenomenal. I heard Creedence does a little tip of the hat to that song on their version of "Susie Q." So, I started jamming a kind of seventh chord in a Creedence manner and singing "Boom Boom" over it. We recorded that song like how Creedence would do it. It just worked, and the whole album is just a bunch of knuckleheads drinking some wine, and just kind of fucking around in that famous little studio, having a good time.

We came back to Nashville after our Muscle Shoals experience and laid down all the tracks for *Light 'Em Up*. Once the rest of the guys split and went home, I worked with our producer, Marti Frederiksen, to put the finishing touches on everything. The title track was released as the first single.

The next single, "I'm Gonna Ride," clocked up almost three million views on YouTube in its first year. The song was an idea I started with Keith Nelson from Buckcherry, who has a studio in LA. I was there one day when I showed him the idea, and we laid it down. I played the guitars. He did some drums, then he played some guitars, but there were no vocals or even a vocal melody yet. We got a little overindulgent, adding some extra parts, before I filed it away.

Pulling it out again, Marti really liked the idea, and David Lowy loved it, so we took a closer look at it and Marti said, "Alright, let's cut this part out. You don't need it." He trims the fat off everything to get to the point. We jammed it and it had more of an AC/DC vibe, so we laid down the new version, and it kicked. That song gets a great response in concert.

I shot my motorcycle riding part for the video in Nashville on a day off, then more on another day off in Los Angeles when Doug and I got together and rode. With the video footage done, we went right back out on tour again. We went over to Japan and did Europe a couple times.

I had released a couple of solo singles, "Cosí Bella" and "Your Own Worst Enemy," as I tried to better understand how this new world of algorithms and streaming works. The intention was to keep releasing singles, then compile them all on an album. I was going to release a third single called "Love That'll Never Be," but then backed off on this whole computerized way of releasing music.

I wasn't sure what to do with the song, and when I played it to the guys in The Dead Daisies, they loved it, so I threw it into their pot of songs. We trimmed it by over a minute as I re-recorded it with them. It came out great, and was released on Valentine's Day as the third single from the *Light 'Em Up* album, but just thirteen days later, The Daisies released the first single, "Crossroads," from the blues album, so I was a little bummed that my song didn't have more time for promotion.

Thinking more about it later as attention turned to my next solo album again, particularly from a storytelling standpoint, I wanted to release the full song. I call it a reprise because it's the full original version with the entire lyrical story, acoustic guitars, and added strings. Marti was just sitting around his house one day watching TV, then all of a sudden went downstairs and started experimenting with strings because he heard something in his head that he wanted to try. That's how the strings came to be on that track. When I heard it, I said, "Dude, it's amazing. Absolutely awesome. Something about it reminds me of that song 'Bittersweet Symphony' by The Verve." That's Marti's brilliance shining through again.

I had a buddy named Chris that used to come out on my acoustic tours and sell my merch for me. On the last tour that we did, he was having some health issues and told me he had cancer. After we got home, I found out he took a turn for the worst, and then he sadly passed.

Shortly after, I got a call from my daughter, Little Val, who told me they found cancer in her during a recent medical checkup. She's been fighting and dealing with that for over a year now, and I admire her strength and positive attitude.

Then touring with The Dead Daisies in 2024, Doug told us he wouldn't be able to continue through Europe because he needed to have a procedure done after being diagnosed with throat cancer.

It was sobering that all these people in my world were getting cancer. I was really worried for Doug, but he was a trooper, just like my daughter. They've both been super positive and doing whatever it takes to heal themselves.

Winger's guitarist, Reb Beach, filled in on tour with us, until Doug was well enough to rejoin The Daisies again. *Fuck cancer!*

I love doing the stuff that I do with the Daisies. We were playing our song "Rise Up" on stage one night on our most recent tour and I was headbanging, when the thought hit me, what are you doing, dude? You're sixty-six and you're running around stage like you used to do when you were twenty-five!

I'd been listening to classic Creedence and Bob Seger's *Greatest Hits* a lot and the more I listened, the more I realized I wanted to put out an album like that. It's what I grew up listening to and it seems I've evolved to a somewhat reflective point in my life.

So, Marti Frederiksen and I sat down, and we wrote songs for a new record over a couple of weeks. We wrote about eight songs then recorded them—we were on a tear. I took a break because I had to go on tour with The Daisies, then I finished them with Marti once I came home. We sat with the songs for a little bit just to make sure they were exactly the way we wanted, then we mixed it, mastered it, and prepared *New Day* for release.

The guy that signed me to Frontiers Records, Tom, called my manager and asked to get me on the line with him. He then told us, "I've listened to the record a few times and I love it. There's not one bad song on this record. I can market it to rock radio. I can market it to Americana. I can even market a couple of the songs to country radio. This record is brilliant. You said you wanted to do a Bob Seger type record. Well, you nailed it!" They're excited about it. I'm excited about it. And I hope you are too.

I like that I was able to use different instruments like mandolin, guitars, piano, organ, strings, percussion, and pair that with lyrics that I'm really proud of. I'm super positive and I'm manifesting its success like a motherfucker because I really believe in this record. When I get together with friends that have heard the record, they ask, "Have you chosen your Grammy outfit yet?" So, we're all manifesting.

I watched a documentary on Netflix called *Echo in the Canyon* that was all about the popular music scene that came out of LA's Laurel Canyon neighborhood during the mid-Sixties and Seventies counterculture period, and the bohemian vagabond hippie community that used to live there, bands like the Byrds, Buffalo Springfield, The Beach Boys, and The Mamas and the Papas. Frank Zappa lived there, the guys in The Monkees, Crosby, Stills Nash and Young all lived up there, too—Jim Morrison, members of the Eagles, it goes on. Joni Mitchell. I got inspired by that era and I wrote the track "Laurel" about it, which is track seven on *New Day*.

Graham Nash and Joni Mitchell used to live together in Laurel Canyon. I saw an interview with Graham where he told a story about one night he went to sleep, then about two o'clock in the morning he was awakened because somebody was sitting on the end of his bed. He turned the light on, and George Harrison was sitting there rolling a joint, so they smoked it together. That was the community. You would go to sleep, and Jim Morrison would walk into your house and make himself a sandwich. It was just a really bohemian time and place as LA's folk musicians went electric.

Graham continued to tell the story of when he and Joni Mitchell got in their car one Sunday in autumn and drove up Laurel Canyon into the Valley. They had brunch and upon leaving the restaurant they went into a vintage shop next door. Joni bought a vase that she got excited about. When they got back home, he started a fire. He was looking out the window watching Joni cutting flowers and putting them in the vase. And he said, "I don't know why, but I was inspired. I walked over to the piano and sat down and I wrote the song 'Our House.'"

I recorded my own version of that song, which the record label loved and decided to use as the bonus track on the Japanese version of *New Day*. I did two acoustic guitar tracks, a piano track, then I sang it. My buddy, Daniel Karkos, did all the beautiful backing vocals, before Marti's son, Evan, re-did my drums.

The continuing inspiration didn't end there. I wrote the song "1969" about the summer of love and all these other things that happened during that momentous year. I had the riff and started to write some lyrics. I don't know why, but my first line came out as a reference to when I was a kid and you could buy weed in a nickel bag or a dime bag—it was five bucks for a nickel or ten bucks for a dime.

It also references actress Judy Garland and Brian Jones of the Stones, who both died in 1969. It welcomes the new president, Richard Nixon, who was inaugurated, talks about sending boys to the Vietnam War, John Lennon releasing "Give Peace a Chance," the first man on the moon, etc.

New Day ends with a cover of the song "Everyday People" that Sly and the Family Stone put out in 1969. I felt its lyrics are still just as relevant today as we've all got to live together while leaders try to divide us, instead of us being united. Lyrically and musically, I dare say *New Day* is the most retrospective and honest record I've ever released.

When it came time to put together the album artwork, I wanted a retro vibe like an old Haight-Ashbury poster, a Bill Graham Presents concert poster.

I was really trying to come up with something brilliant for the album's title, but the more I thought about it and listened to my song "New Day," I gravitated to that as the title. The lyric saying yesterday's gone and you cannot change it, today is the day to rearrange it, while tomorrow is just a day that may or may not come at all, kept playing on my mind. And with the chorus saying to just let the sun shine down on you, I started to look up sun images.

The first image that popped up was The Sun card from tarot decks. I looked into it and the card symbolizes positivity and represents a time of clarity and personal growth. It's associated with joy, success, and vitality. The sunflowers on the card symbolize growth and abundance while the imagery emphasizes happiness, clarity, and the triumph of light over darkness. That all resonated with me loudly and totally felt like the universe was giving me a sign.

I gave it to David Pear, our photographer and videographer for The Dead Daisies, and he worked it into the cover, adding a little smiling crab as he went. The sun has XIX on its forehead because The Sun card is the nineteenth trump card in the deck. What's crazy is that I then realized this is my nineteenth record I've played on! Another sign.

The songs for the album came together with such ease, like they just flowed out of me. The cover evolved with ease too and limited thought involved. On the one hand it seems it was all by fluke, but it also feels that for once in my life, I might just be in the right place at the right time. Perhaps the universe is orchestrating something special.

The team that I have around me is so excited. Marti Frederiksen has produced and worked on so many amazing albums, but even he said to me, "I've never had this much fun doing a record, dude. *I love this album!* I cannot stop listening to it." So, when I started booking my next solo tour, Marti said, "I want to play guitar for you live."

I talked to my friend Paul Taylor from Winger, who played some keyboards on the record, and he said, "Yeah, dude, count me in." With Jeremy Asbrock back on guitar with me, plus my current Dead Daisies bassist Michael Devin, and Tesla's former drummer, Troy Lucketta, I've got a killer band.

Everything has fallen into place. I've been late to every party I've ever showed up for, but it feels like this is my time now. I have never been this excited about a record in my life. I've weathered all the storms, now it's a new day and time to shine. *Here's to the future!*

Selected Discography

Various Artists
KNAC Pure Rock 105.5 - Son of Pure Rock
Rampage Records, 1988
Shake, Shake—Angora

The Scream
Let it Scream
Hollywood Records, 1991
Outlaw | I Believe In Me | Man In The Moon | Father, Mother, Son | Give It Up | Never Loved Her Anyway | Tell Me Why | Loves Got A Hold On Me | I Don't Care | Every Inch A Woman | You Are All I Need | Catch Me If You Can

Various Artists
Encino Man (Music from The Original Motion Picture Soundtrack)
Hollywood Records, 1992
Young and Dumb—The Scream

Mötley Crüe
Mötley Crüe
Elektra, 1994
Power to The Music | Uncle Jack | Hooligan's Holiday | Misunderstood | Loveshine | Poison Apples | Hammered | 'Til Death Do Us Part | Welcome to The Numb | Smoke the Sky | Droppin' Like Flies | Driftaway

Mötley Crüe
Quaternary
Elektra Records, 1994

Planet Boom | Bittersuite | Father | Friends | Babykills | 10,000 Miles Away | Hooligan's Holiday (Extended Holiday Version) | Hammered (Demo) | Livin' in the No (Demo)

Mötley Crüe
Generation Swine
Elektra Records, 1997

Find Myself | Afraid | Flush | Generation Swine | Confessions | Beauty | Glitter | Anybody Out There? | Let Us Prey | Rocketship | A Rat Like Me | Shout at the Devil '97 | Brandon

Union
Union
Mayhem Records, 1998

Old Man Wise | Around Again | Pain Behind Your Eyes | Love (I Don't Need It Anymore) | Heavy D… | Let It Flow | Empty Soul | October Morning Wind | Get Off My Cloud | Tangerine | Robin's Song | For You

ESP (Eric Singer Project)
Lost and Spaced
Rock Hard Records, 1998

Set Me Free | Four Day Creep | Free Ride | Still Alive & Well | Never Before | Goin' Blind | Teenage Nervous Breakdown | Changes | S.O.S (Too Bad) | Foxy Lady

Union
Live in The Galaxy
Deadline Music, 1999

Old Man Wise | Around Again | Heavy D… | Jungle | Love (I Don't Need It Anymore) | Man in The Moon | I Walk Alone | Surrender | Pain Behind Your Eyes | Power to The Music | Tangerine | October Morning Wind | You've Got to Hide Your Love Away

Union
The Blue Room
Spitfire, 1999

Do Your Own Thing | Dead | Everything's Alright | Shine | Who Do You Think You Are? | Dear Friend | Do You Know My Name | Hypnotized | I Wanna Be | No More

Twenty 4 Seven
Destination Everywhere
Melodic Mayhem Music, 2002

Due Time | Fall into Yourself | Dead Man's Shoes | Limelight | Something | Someone I Don't Want to Be | Good Times | Take Me to The Limit | It's All About You | No Matter What

Bruce Kulick
Transformer
Perris Records, 2003

It's Just My Life

Brides of Destruction
Here Come the Brides
Sanctuary Records, 2004

Shut the Fuck Up | I Don't Care | I Got a Gun | 2x Dead | Brace Yourself | Natural Born Killers | Life | Revolution | Only Get So Far

John Corabi
Unplugged
Rat Pak Records, 2012

Love (I Don't Need It Anymore) | If I Never Get To Say Goodbye | Are You Waiting | Crash | Everything's Alright | Father, Mother, Son | Hooligan's Holiday | If I Had A Dime | Loveshine | Man In The Moon | Open Your Eyes | I Never Loved Her Anyway

The Dead Daisies
Revolución
Spitfire Music, 2015

Mexico | Evil | Looking for the One | Empty Heart | Make the Best of It | Something I Said | Get Up, Get Ready | With You and I | Sleep | My Time | Midnight Moses | Devil Out of Time | Critical

The Dead Daisies
Make Some Noise
Spitfire Music, 2015

Long Way to Go | We All Fall Down | Song and a Prayer | Mainline | Make Some Noise | Fortunate Son | Last Time I Saw the Sun | Mine All Mine | How Does It Feel | Freedom | All the Same | Join Together

The Dead Daisies
Live & Louder
Spitfire Music, 2017

Long Way to Go | Mexico | Make Some Noise | Song and a Prayer | Fortunate Son | We All Fall Down | Lock 'N' Load | Something I Said | Last Time I Saw The Sun | Join Together | With You And I | Mainline | Helter Skelter | American Band | Midnight Moses

John Corabi
One Night in Nashville—Live '94
Rat Pak Records, 2017

Power to The Music | Uncle Jack | Hooligan's Holiday | Misunderstood | Loveshine | Poison Apples | Hammered | 'Til Death Do Us Part | Welcome to The Numb | Smoke the Sky | Droppin' Like Flies | Driftaway | 10,000 Miles Away

The Dead Daisies
Burn it Down
Spitfire Music, 2018

Resurrected | Rise Up | Burn It Down | Judgement Day | What Goes Around | Bitch | Set Me Free | Dead and Gone | Can't Take It with You | Leave Me Alone | Revolution

The Dead Daisies
Locked and Loaded (The Covers Album)
Spitfire Music, 2019

Midnight Moses | Evil | Fortunate Son | Join Together | Helter Skelter | Bitch | American Band | Revolution | Rockin' in the Free World | Highway Star

The Dead Daisies
Best Of
Spitfire Music, 2023

Miles In Front Of Me | Lock 'n' Load | Face I Love | Mexico | Midnight Moses | With You & I | Something I Said | Fortunate Son | Long Way to Go | Song and a Prayer | Make Some Noise | Resurrected | Rise Up | Holy Ground | Unspoken | Bustle and Flow | Hypnotize Yourself | Born to Fly | The Healer | Let It Set You Free

The Dead Daisies
Light 'Em Up
Spitfire Music, 2024

Light 'Em Up | Times Are Changing | I Wanna Be Your Bitch | I'm Gonna Ride | Back to Zero | Way Back Home | Take a Long Line | My Way and The Highway | Love That'll Never Be | Take My Soul

The Dead Daisies
Lookin' for Trouble
Spitfire Music, 2025

I'm Ready | Going Down | Boom Boom | Black Betty | The Thrill is Gone | Born Under a Bad Sign | Crossroads | Sweet Home Chicago | Walking the Dog | Little Red Rooster

John Corabi
New Day
Frontiers, 2026

New Day | That Memory | Faith, Hope and Love | When I Was Young | One More Shot | 1969 | Laurel | Good to be Back Here Again | Love That'll Never Be (Reprise) | Cosí Bella (So Beautiful) | Your Own Worst Enemy | Everyday People

Acknowledgments

Thanks to my small group of family members and friends who stuck by me through all of this and applauded my successes, but weren't afraid to tell me when I was being a fucking asshole.

Thanks to everyone who has been there to support me through my up times and my down times. To all my endorsement companies that stuck with me, I just want to say thank you.

I especially want to thank my fans, who continue to support me through thick and thin. You are the best and very much appreciated!

The authors would also like to shout out a huge thank you to:

Our managers John Greenberg at Shorebreak International, Kristen Mahar at Empire Talent, and Tammy Prock. We appreciate you being in the trenches with us the whole way and look forward to whatever comes next.

The awesome publishing team at Rare Bird for their belief, professionalism, and laughs along the journey—Tyson Cornell, Guy Intoci, Hailie Johnson, Ray Hartman, and Jennifer Psujek.

Those who contributed and assisted with photos—Lynn Preston, Brian Lockwood, Valerie Corabi, Angelika Morawska, Denise Truscello, Seraina Mars, Heather Warren, David Edwards, Cat Swinton, Ulf Zick, Katarina Benzova, and Oliver Halfin. So many great photos, such little space!

Thanks also to Doug Weber at New Ocean Media, Danny Bazzi at Silverback Touring in Australia, Adam "The Kid" Wakitsch at Kustom Thrills Tattoo, Matt Sorum and Seth Frank at Experience Vinyl, and Anthony Bozza.

And lastly, I truly hope that should life be dealing you fucking lemons right now, you too can persevere and push through it to enjoy better times ahead. Let the loveshine in.

About the Authors

John Corabi

American hard rock singer-guitarist-songwriter-raconteur John Corabi has entertained audiences with his powerful bluesy vocals over the course of his forty-year music career.

After emerging from his native Philadelphia rock scene, Corabi relocated to Hollywood's Sunset Strip and landed his first record deal with The Scream.

That soon led to him joining Mötley Crüe one weekend, at a time when they were one of the world's biggest rock bands, and he fronted them for the next five years. The 1994 self-titled album Corabi created with the band is now critically acclaimed, and even considered the best of their catalog by many, including guitarist Mick Mars.

He put together Union with ousted Kiss guitarist Bruce Kulick, before stepping into Ratt, where he was their rhythm guitarist for the better part of a decade.

In recent years, Corabi was lead singer for supergroup The Dead Daisies, performing on the planet's biggest festival stages—he's even played rock concerts in Cuba, India, South Korea, Belarus, and Israel.

From his home base in Nashville, Corabi continues to tour worldwide and perform his own solo acoustic and electric shows, thrilling crowds with songs that span his entire body of work, interspersed with his humorous storytelling.

John Corabi looks forward to playing for you soon—see you at the show!

Website: JohnCorabi.com
Instagram: @johncorabiofficial

Paul Miles

Australian Paul Miles is the historian of one of rock's most reckless and biggest-selling bands of all time: Mötley Crüe, having continuously documented the facts behind their sex, drugs, and rock-and-roll lifestyle for decades, and published it via his *Chronological Crue* website and book series.

Asked to contribute to the band's best-selling autobiography *The Dirt* (2001), you'll see that he gets "the biggest thanks of all" on the book's Acknowledgements page.

After writing the liner notes inside Mötley's first-ever live album *Live: Entertainment or Death* (1999), he later toured all-access with them across Australia (2005) and Japan (2008), experiencing life on the road and backstage firsthand. He also toured around Australia with John Corabi (2019), which sparked this book collaboration.

However, there's more to Miles than just the Crüe: his titillating confessional book *Sex Tips from Rock Stars* (2010) was released globally by the planet's biggest publisher of music books and documented the world's first extensive study of rock stars concerning sex.

Miles is also a Melbourne-based freelance rock music photographer. His hardcover photography book *Before I Hit the Stage: Backstage Rock 'n' Roll Moments in New York City* (2015) was the world's first to photographically document touring rock-and-roll bands backstage in one city during one year.

Furthermore, he fronts Aussie hard rock band SkinInc. as their singer, and wishes his voice was even half as good as John Corabi's.

Website: Paul-Miles.com
Instagram: @paulmilesphotography